Schelling's Late Philosophy
in Confrontation with Hegel

Schelling's Late Philosophy in Confrontation with Hegel

PETER DEWS

OXFORD
UNIVERSITY PRESS

Oxford University Press is a department of the University of Oxford. It furthers
the University's objective of excellence in research, scholarship, and education
by publishing worldwide. Oxford is a registered trade mark of Oxford University
Press in the UK and certain other countries.

Published in the United States of America by Oxford University Press
198 Madison Avenue, New York, NY 10016, United States of America.

© Oxford University Press 2023

All rights reserved. No part of this publication may be reproduced, stored in
a retrieval system, or transmitted, in any form or by any means, without the
prior permission in writing of Oxford University Press, or as expressly permitted
by law, by license, or under terms agreed with the appropriate reproduction
rights organization. Inquiries concerning reproduction outside the scope of the
above should be sent to the Rights Department, Oxford University Press, at the
address above.

You must not circulate this work in any other form
and you must impose this same condition on any acquirer.

Library of Congress Cataloging-in-Publication Data
Names: Dews, Peter, author.
Title: Schelling's late philosophy in confrontation with Hegel / Dews, Peter.
Description: New York, NY : Oxford University Press, [2023] |
Includes bibliographical references and index.
Identifiers: LCCN 2022026836 (print) | LCCN 2022026837 (ebook) |
ISBN 9780190069124 (hardback) | ISBN 9780190069155 (epub)
Subjects: LCSH: Schelling, Friedrich Wilhelm Joseph von, 1775–1854. |
Hegel, Georg Wilhelm Friedrich, 1770–1831. | Philosophy, German—19th century.
Classification: LCC B2898 .D49 2023 (print) | LCC B2898 (ebook) |
DDC 193—dc23/eng/20220728
LC record available at https://lccn.loc.gov/2022026836
LC ebook record available at https://lccn.loc.gov/2022026837

DOI: 10.1093/oso/9780190069124.001.0001

Printed by Integrated Books International, United States of America

For Harriet

> ... whene'er
> In our free Hall, where each philosophy
> And mood of faith may hold its own, they blurt
> Their furious formalisms, I but hear
> The clash of tides that meet in narrow seas,—
> Not the Great Voice, not the true Deep.
>
> Alfred Tennyson, "Akbar's Dream"

> ... whereby
>

Contents

Preface — xi
Notes on Translations and References — xv
Notes on Terminology — xvii
List of Abbreviations — xxi

Introduction — 1

1. Toward Nature — 19
2. Agency and Absolute Identity — 59
3. Freedom — 87
4. Thinking and Being — 117
5. Beyond the Idea — 140
6. Blind Existing-ness — 172
7. Mythological Consciousness — 206
8. Reason and Revelation — 227
9. History as Liberation — 253

Conclusion: Schelling's Affirmative Genealogy — 281

Figure 1. The Decompression of Contingently Necessary Existing-ness — 182

Figure 2. Schelling's Theory of the Mythological Process as Exemplified by Greek Mythology — 218

Figure 3. Schelling's Theory of the History of Consciousness — 272

Bibliography — 295

Index — 307

Preface

The origins of this book go back a long way. I first became aware of a distinctive late phase of Schelling's philosophy as a doctoral student concerned with affinities between post-Kantian Idealism and the French philosophy of the 1960s and 1970s. Intrigued, I studied the transcript of Schelling's first Berlin lecture course of 1841–1842, in the excellent paperback edition which Manfred Frank had recently produced for Suhrkamp Verlag. I came away from that reading with complex responses. On the one hand, with a sense of having encountered a philosophical intellect of immense power; on the other hand, with only the vaguest grasp of the enterprise on which Schelling was embarked, and of the arguments supporting it. Those conflicting impressions have proved to be the catalyst for repeated phases of thinking and writing about Schelling over the course of my professional life.

When I began my career, the current upsurge of interest in German Idealism in the English-speaking world was still in its infancy. Of course, ever since the Victorian era there has been an anglophone tradition of Hegel interpretation, even if often an emaciated one. But the last quarter of the twentieth century saw a new wave of interest not only in Hegel, but in the other major post-Kantian Idealists, in particular the earlier work of Fichte and—to a lesser extent—of Schelling, as well as in the thinking of related figures such as Jacobi and Reinhold, and of the Jena Romantics. However, Schelling's late philosophy—the systematic project which occupied him during the final third of his life—still remains almost entirely *terra incognita*, even for specialists in German Idealism. Such is the context in which the project of this book was conceived.

There does already exist a small body of literature written in English concerned with Schelling's late critique of Hegel (see, for example, the relevant items in the bibliography by Bowie, Houlgate, Lumsden, Rush and White). However, the focus of these discussions is often unsatisfactorily narrow. For example, it is almost impossible to understand the arguments—or even the terminology—employed by Schelling in the chapter on Hegel in his lectures *On the History of Modern Philosophy* from the 1830s without a broader knowledge of his late system, its structure, and its central themes. And it is this knowledge that is still, for the most part, lacking. This is not to suggest that Schelling's explicit comments on Hegel's philosophy do not reward the effort involved in understanding them. Far from it. However, I do not regard the direct critiques of Hegel which occur in some of Schelling's lectures after his former colleague's death, though not without interest, as the most productive focus for investigation. Rather, it is only by comparing Hegel's thought and Schelling's late philosophy along a broad front that the many significant differences in their systematic conceptions emerge. These differences point, in turn, to important and instructive disagreements concerning some of the most fundamental questions in philosophy.

I should add that this book could have contained many more endnotes referring to interpretive debates in the secondary literature on Schelling, which has flourished in German, French, and Italian. However, I did not wish the clutter the main lines of the argument between my two protagonists, given that the crucial issues are still so little understood, especially in the anglophone world. There is much to be learned from an exploration of the contrasting responses of these two major thinkers to the key philosophical concerns which emerged in the immediate post-Kantian context. Not least because it remains—to a large extent—our context. Studying the confrontation between Schelling and Hegel promises not only to promote a better comprehension of the inner life of German Idealism as a whole, but can throw light on many questions which continue to surge up for those who seek to grapple philosophically with the modern world, and the forms of human existence, agency, and self-understanding which it has fostered.

For support during the writing of this book I must thank first of all the University of Essex, which granted me two terms of study leave in 2015, and a further two terms in 2017. I am also grateful to the Humboldt Foundation for offering me a renewal of my Fellowship in the autumn of 2015. This enabled me to spend a whole calendar year in Berlin, where much of the spadework for the book was done. I must thank Rahel Jaeggi for acting as my host at the Humboldt University during my final months in Berlin; and also for welcoming me to her research colloquium throughout the year, and inviting me to present some of my preliminary conclusions there. Other friends and colleagues whom I must thank for helping to make my time in Berlin so productive and enjoyable include Georg Bertram, Estelle Ferrarese (who also invited me to address her seminar at the Centre Marc Bloch on Friedrichstraße), Antonia Hofstätter, Ulrike Kistner, Georg Lohmann, Iain Macdonald, and Martin Saar.

Other people I must thank for giving me opportunities to develop and try out some of the material in this book are as follows: Tom Whyman, for inviting me to participate in an Essex University workshop on Schelling and Adorno, supported by the British Society for the History of Philosophy, in September 2017; Vladimir Safatle, for inviting me to teach a course on Schelling in the summer school of the Faculdade de Filosofia, Letras e Ciências Humanas of the University of São Paulo in January 2018; Timo Jütten, for inviting me to give the Essex Lectures in Philosophy in the summer of the same year; Paul Davies, for inviting me as a visiting speaker to Sussex University the following November; Anne Clausen, for inviting me to address a conference on the "Life of Spirit" at the University of Göttingen in September 2019; John Callanan, for inviting me to give a paper to the King's History of Philosophy Seminar the following month; Joseph Schear, for inviting me to address the Oxford Post-Kantian Seminar in October 2021; and Dan Watts, for inviting me back to Essex for a seminar on Schelling and Sartre in the same month.

I am grateful to Charlotte Alderwick and Manfred Frank, pathfinder and friend, for sharing unpublished work on Schelling, and to David Batho, Sebastian Gardner, Thomas Khurana, Teresa Pedro, Robert Seymour, Wayne Martin, and OUP's anonymous reader for their helpful comments of various sections of the manuscript. Robert Seymour also kindly agreed to assist with the checking of the page proofs, which he did with extraordinary dedication, Jörg Schaub, ever ready to lend a hand, supplied some urgently needed texts electronically, John-Baptiste Oduor suggested improvements to the cover material, and my dear brother Robin Dews drew on his professional expertise to help me finalize the diagrams. Thanks must go to Lucy Randall, my editor at OUP in New York, for her prompt and encouraging replies to my queries during the difficult time of the pandemic, to Brent Matheny and Nirenjena Joseph for their helpfulness during the book's production, and to Jessie Coffey for her attentive copy-editing. I must give special thanks to my friends Barrie Selwyn and Joel Whitebook for their unflagging interest in and encouragement of the project. Finally, I owe my biggest debt of gratitude to Harriet Aston, for her love, care and support through good times and bad, and for spurring me on with a healthy dose of skepticism that I would ever make it to the final full stop. Her bravery, insight, and integrity as an artist are a recurrent source of joy and motivation, as is the rueful wit of her running commentary on the meaning of life. This book is dedicated to her.

Peter Dews
Clapton Pond
London E5
Autumn 2021

Notes on Translations and References

For any text which I have quoted more than a handful of times I have given parenthetical references using an abbreviation. For the principal philosophers discussed on this study, where a serviceable English translation is available, a reference to this is provided first, followed by a reference to the German or French original. For the works of Schelling, I have used the ongoing *Historisch-kritische Ausgabe* where possible, and otherwise the nineteenth-century *Sämmtliche Werke*, or single editions for writings and lecture transcripts in neither of these collections. For Hegel, I have quoted the *Werke in zwanzig Bänden*, edited for Suhrkamp by Eva Moldenhauer and Karl Markus Michel. This is a convenient and widely available edition which is now often used by scholars in referring to Hegel. For Fichte, I have quoted the *Gesamtausgabe* of the Bavarian Academy of Sciences, and for Kant the standard *Akademie-Ausgabe*.

I have long been aware of the frustration of reading references to collected editions which provide no indication of the specific text being quoted. Consequently, in references solely to German texts, an abbreviation for the specific work in question precedes the volume and page number in the relevant collected edition. In the case of dual references, where the German reference is to a collected edition, an abbreviated title of the original German text is not provided, to avoid the parentheses becoming too long and obtrusive. However, the German title can be found following the abbreviation for the English translation in the list of abbreviations. Throughout, I have very frequently amended published English translations, and in many cases the translation had to be my own.

References to Aristotle's *Metaphysics* use the standard Bekker numbering. Reference to Spinoza's *Ethics* is made using the following abbreviations: ax = axiom; c = corollary; d = demonstration; def = definition; le = lemma; p = proposition; pref = preface. The first number in the reference indicates which part of the *Ethics* (e.g., E: 2p13le3def = *Ethics*, part 2, proposition 13, lemma 3, definition). For references to Kant's *Critique of Pure Reason* I have employed the standard A/B edition pagination. In the case of the *Critique of Judgment* I cite the section numbers, as also for Hegel's

Encyclopaedia of the Philosophical Sciences (except in some rare instances where I quote prefatory material) and the *Philosophy of Right*. To indicate quotations from supplementary material drawn from Hegel's lectures and added to the relevant sections of his published texts by his editors, I have used the German term "*Zusatz.*" In the case of the *Encyclopaedia* and the *Philosophy of Right* I have supplied a page reference to the Suhrkamp edition of the *Werke* in addition to the section number, for convenience in checking the original. In the case of all these thinkers, details of the English translations I have used can be found in the bibliography.

Notes on Terminology

German philosophical terminology creates numerous headaches for the English translator, but even given this general expectation, the vocabulary of Schelling's late philosophy presents exceptional difficulties. Here I offer a brief commentary on a some of the most problematic cases.

Aufheben/Aufhebung

Schelling sometimes uses these terms, whose difficulties will be familiar to translators of Hegel. In the case of both thinkers, "suspend" or "suspension" captures much of what is required. For example, if an organization suspends one of its rules, the rule is not abolished, and its validity in principle is not negated, but rather it is neutralized by a higher authority, and it ceases straightforwardly to apply. However, "suspend" does not contain the implication of raising to a higher level through integration into a more comprehensive structure. Although Hegel's use of the term carries this suggestion more frequently than Schelling's, I have nonetheless decided for this reason to retain the rather antiquated English terms "sublate" and "sublation," which are widely used in this context, for both thinkers.

Das reine Daß

Schelling uses this term in some of his late texts to refer to the sheer fact *that* anything exists at all. Unfortunately, the English word "that" does service as a demonstrative pronoun as well as a conjunction. Consequently, to translate Schelling's expression as "the pure that" could give rise to serious misunderstandings. I have therefore followed the practice of some other anglophone interpreters of Schelling and retained the German word in the expressions "the pure *Daß*" or simply "the *Daß*."

Potenz

While, in general, I have tried to avoid carrying German terms over into English, there are special reasons for retaining *Potenz*. In German, it refers specifically to a mathematical power, and hence Schelling uses it in his early work as a quasi-metaphor to indicate a stage in a sequence which reflexively complicates or intensifies a preceding stage. For this general meaning the English equivalent most often used in the past in translating and writing about Schelling, namely "potency," has all the wrong connotations. "Power," of course, would be equally unsatisfactory because it is far too unspecific. In Schelling's later work, however, the term, while retaining some of its early connotations, acquires a meaning far closer to that of Aristotle's *"dunamis"*—now usually rendered as "potentiality." To mark this important shift in the significance of a key concept in Schelling's thought, I have simply taken over *"Potenz"* in most contexts when discussing Schelling's earlier work but have rendered the term as "potentiality" in the context of his late philosophy.

Das Seyende

I have chosen to use the term "being-ness" to translate *"das Seyende,"* which is a nominalized present participle. This is not a complete neologism. Étienne Gilson, for example, uses the term, without the hyphen, to translate Aristotle's *"ousia"* (see *Being and Some Philosophers* [Toronto: Pontifical Institute of Mediaeval Studies, 1952], 74). My use and rationale are different, however. Just as, in German, *"das Überzeugende an etwas"*—for example—is what is convincing about something, what endows it with convincingness, so *"das Seyende,"* in Schelling's thought, is *what endows any specific thing with being at all*. By contrast, *"das Seyn"* most frequently refers to being in a determinate form. Although Schelling is not entirely consistent, his use of *"das Seyende"* and *"das Seyn"* can therefore be regarded, very roughly, as reversing the polarity which these terms have in Heidegger. This is worth noting since the Heideggerian influence on recent European philosophy has led even some translators of Schelling into error. One should also bear in mind that Schelling no doubt intended to replicate the grammar of Aristotle's most general term for being, "τὸ ὄν" (*to on*), a nominalized present participle. Finally, it should also be noted that, in some of his last work, Schelling introduces a further refinement by distinguishing between *"das Seyende,"* as the noetic structure of the *a priori* possibilities of worldly being, and "*das, was das Seyende ist*": "that which is *das Seyende*," namely the "un-pre-thinkable" being *of* possibility itself.

Das Existirende

Schelling sometimes uses this as an alternative to *das Seyende* in the context of his positive philosophy. I have therefore translated it analogously as "existing-ness."

Das Existiren

Schelling sometimes replaces *das Existirende* with a nominalized infinitive. In this case the analogy with the nominalized infinitive "*das Seyn*" or "*das Sein*" can be misleading. It is tempting to render this term simply as "existing," taken as a verbal noun, but the complex relations between the use of the definite article in German and in English make this problematic, since "the existing" would normally be taken as referring to *something that exists*, rather than to the act or process of existing. I have therefore generally rendered *das Existiren* also as "existing-ness."

Das unvordenkliche Seyn

"*Unvordenklich*" in modern German suggests "immemorial." However, Schelling exploits the semantic components of the word to convey the notion of being in its momentary priority to thought, while avoiding the implication that absolute being is, in general, unthinkable. Like other Schelling scholars, I have therefore rendered the term as "un-pre-thinkable being." It is worth noting that, in this case, the word "*Seyn*" does suggest "being-ness" rather than determinate being. Schelling also sometimes uses "*unvordenklich*" as an adverb.

Das urständliche Seyn

In German "*Urstand*" means "primal state" or "original condition." However, in coining the expression "*das urständliche Seyn*," Schelling's exploits the morphological connection between "*Urstand*" and "*Gegenstand.*" The latter is the standard word for object, and suggests "standing over against." The Latin basis of the English word "object" uses the image of throwing rather than standing, but the etymology is comparable: the object is what is thrown in front of us, or in our way. Hence, I have coined the term "pre-jective" to preserve the morphological connection in English. "Pre-jective being" is being prior to any objectification—before undergoing any precipitation in front of thinking as its noetic correlate, which for Schelling occurs even when thinking is operating in pure or *a priori* mode.

Gendered Language

There are many historical, cultural, and political complexities to be negotiated here. One of these is that German has a word which simply means "human being," even though its grammatical gender is masculine, namely "*der Mensch.*" Traditionally, this term has been misleadingly rendered as "man" in many contexts, including philosophical ones. I experimented with referring back to the translation of "*Mensch*" as "human being" with the pronoun "she," in my English rendering of quotations from Schelling and other authors. But this, while providing a certain therapeutic shock, sounded fake and anachronistic. Presumably, when Schelling's predominantly male original readers and auditors encountered the word "*Mensch*" they thought in the first instance of a male human being. Sometimes I solved the problem by shifting "*der Mensch*" into the plural in English: "human beings." But this option did not always work, so I have often reluctantly left Schelling's prose, and that of other philosophers, with a masculine bias. This at least has the advantage of suggesting how far we still have to go to achieve that freedom from essentialized identity which Schelling's late philosophy, as we shall find, theorizes as a fundamental human aspiration.

Orthography

In this glossary I have employed Schelling's original spellings of key terms. However, in the course of the book I frequently use modernized spellings, depending on which edition of a text by Schelling I am quoting. No philosophical significance should be attached to these variations.

Abbreviations

For full publication details please see the bibliography.

Collected Editions

Kant: AA — *Akademie-Ausgabe*
Fichte: GA — *Gesamtausgabe*
Hegel: W20 — *Werke in zwanzig Bänden*
Schelling: SW — *Sämmtliche Werke*
Schelling: H-K — *Historisch-kritische Ausgabe*

Kant

CJ — *Critique of Judgment* (*Kritik der Urteilskraft*)
MM — *Metaphysics of Morals* (*Die Metaphysik der Sitten*)
R — *Religion within the Boundaries of Mere Reason* (*Die Religion innerhalb der Grenzen der bloßen Vernunft*)

Fichte

CCR — *A Crystal Clear Report to the General Public Concerning the Actual Essence of the Newest Philosophy* (*Sonnenklarer Bericht an das größere Publikum über das eigentliche Wesen der neuesten Philosophie*)
FNR — *Foundations of Natural Right* (*Grundlage des Naturrechts nach der Prinzipien der Wissenschaftslehre*)
FTP — *Foundations of Transcendental Philosophy* (*Wissenschaftslehre Nova Methodo*)
IWL1 — *First Introduction to the Science of Knowledge* (*Erste Einleitung in die Wissenschaftslehre*)
IWL2 — *Second Introduction to the Science of Knowledge* (*Zweite Einleitung in die Wissenschaftslehre*)
VM — *The Vocation of Man* (*Die Bestimmung des Menschen*)
WL94/5 — *The Science of Knowledge* (*Grundlage der gesammten Wissenschaftslehre*)

Hegel

Works in English Translation

Enc.1	*Encyclopaedia of the Philosophical Sciences. Part One. The Encyclopaedia Logic* (*Enzyklopädie der philosophischen Wissenschaften im Grundrisse [1830]. Erster Teil. Die Wissenschaft der Logik. Mit den mündlichen Zusätzen*)
Enc.3	*Encyclopaedia of the Philosophical Sciences. Part Three. The Philosophy of Spirit* (*Enzyklopädie der philosophischen Wissenschaften im Grundrisse [1830]. Dritter Teil. Die Philosophie des Geistes. Mit den mündlichen Zusätzen*)
EPR	*Elements of the Philosophy of Right* (*Grundlinien der Philosophie des Rechts*)
ILPH	*Lectures on the Philosophy of History. Introduction: Reason in History* (*Vorlesungen über die Philosophie der Geschichte. Einführung*)
LHP3	*Lectures on the History of Philosophy. Vol. 3: Medieval and Modern Philosophy* (*Vorlesungen über die Geschichte der Philosophie*) (individual volumes do not correspond)
LHP 1825-1826/3	*Lectures on the History of Philosophy. The Lectures of 1825–1826. Volume III: Medieval and Modern Philosophy* (*Vorlesungen über die Geschichte der Philosophie. Teil 4. Philosophie des Mittelalters und der neueren Zeit*)
LPR1	*Lectures on the Philosophy of Religion. Vol. 1. Introduction and the Concept of Religion* (*Vorlesungen über die Philosophie der Religion. Band 1*)
LPR2	*Lectures on the Philosophy of Religion. Vol. 2. Determinate Religion* (*Vorlesungen über die Philosophie der Religion. Band 2*)
LPR3	*Lectures on the Philosophy of Religion. Vol. 3. The Consummate Religion* (*Vorlesungen über die Philosophie der Religion. Band 3*)
PS	*Phenomenology of Spirit* (*Phänomenologie des Geistes*)
SL	*The Science of Logic* (*Die Wissenschaft der Logik*)

Works in German

VGP	*Vorlesungen über die Geschichte der Philosophie. Teil 4. Philosophie des Mittelalters und der neueren Zeit.*
VPG[H]	*Vorlesungen über die Philosophie der Geschichte* (Hoffmeister edition)
VPR (followed by volume number)	*Vorlesungen über die Philosophie der Religion*

Schelling

Works in English Translation

B	*Bruno, or on the Natural and Divine Principle of Things* (*Bruno, oder über das göttliche und das natürliche Prinzip der Dinge. Ein Gespräch.*)
CIWL	*Commentaries Explicatory of the Idealism in the Science of Knowledge* (*Abhandlungen zur Erläuterung des Idealismus der Wissenschaftslehre*)
FSC	*The Philosophical Rupture between Fichte and Schelling. Selected Texts and Correspondence 1800–1802* (*Fichte-Schelling Briefwechsel*)
FOS	*First Outline of a System of the Philosophy of Nature* (*Erster Entwurf eines Systems der Philosophie der Natur*)
FS	*Of Human Freedom* (*Philosophische Untersuchungen über das Wesen der menschlichen Freiheit*)
GPP	*The Grounding of Positive Philosophy* (*Einleitung in die Philosophie der Offenbarung oder Begründung der positiven Philosophie*)
HCI	*Historical-Critical Introduction to the Philosophy of Mythology* (*Historisch-kritische Einleitung in die Philosophie der Mythologie*)
HMP	*On the History of Modern Philosophy* (*Zur Geschichte der neueren Philosophie*)
IPN	*Ideas for a Philosophy of Nature* (*Ideen zu einer Philosophie der Natur*)
NPS	*On the Nature of Philosophy as Science* (*Über die Natur der Philosophie als Wissenschaft*)
OI	*Of the I as Principle of Philosophy* (*Vom Ich als Prinzip der Philosophie*)

OUS	*On University Studies* (*Vorlesungen über die Methode des akademischen Studiums*)
SET	*On the Source of the Eternal Truths* ("Über die Quelle der ewigen Wahrheiten")
STI	*System of Transcendental Idealism* (*System des transzendentalen Idealismus*)
WA3	*The Ages of the World* (*Die Weltalter. Bruchstück [Aus dem handschriftlichen Nachlaß]*)

Works in German

AD	*Andere Deduktion der Prinzipien der positive Philosophie*
DMS	*Darstellung meines Systems der Philosophie*
DN	*Darstellung des Naturprozesses*
DPE	*Darstellung des philosophischen Empirismus*
PM "Athen"/Eberz	*Philosophie der Mythologie 1836/37* (*Vorlesungsnachschriften* "Athen" und Anton Eberz)
PM Chováts	*Philosophie der Mythologie 1842* (*Vorlesungsmitschift* Andreas von Chováts)
PO	*Philosophie der Offenbarung*
PO41/42	*Philosophie der Offenbarung 1841/42*
PR	*Philosophie und Religion*
UPO	*Urfassung der Philosophie der Offenbarung*
UWB	"Über den wahren Begriff der Naturphilosophie und die richtige Art ihre Probleme aufzulösen"
VWS	*Von der Weltseele*
WA1	*Die Weltalter. Druck 1*
WS	*System der gesammten Philosophie und der Naturphilosophie insbesondere* ("Würzburg System")

Abbreviations for Works by Other Authors

AAG	Dieter Henrich, "Andersheit und Absolutheit des Geistes. Sieben Schritte auf dem Wege von Schelling zu Hegel"
AP	James Kreines, "Aristotelian Priority, Metaphysical Definitions of God, and Hegel on Pure Thought as Absolute"
BG	Gottlob Frege, "Über Begriff und Gegenstand"
BN	Jean-Paul Sartre, *Being and Nothingness*
E	Spinoza, *Ethics*
EBFW	Karl Leonhard Reinhold, "Einige Bemerkungen über die in der Einleitung zu den 'Metaphysischen Anfangsgründen der Rechtslehre' von I. Kant aufgestellten Begriffe von der Freiheit des Willens"

EN	Jean-Paul Sartre, *L'être et le néant*
HI	Robert Pippin, *Hegel's Idealism*
MF	Helen Steward, *A Metaphysics for Freedom*
OGH	Karl Jaspers, *On the Origin and Goal of History*
RW	James Kreines, *Reason in the World. Hegel's Metaphysics and its Philosophical Appeal*

Introduction

Since the final decades of the twentieth century, the English-speaking world has witnessed a major upsurge of interest in the development of German philosophy in the period directly after Kant. This new wave of research reflects the loosening of the once rigid boundaries between the analytical style, dominant in the anglophone and Scandinavian countries since the early twentieth century, and the various sub-traditions of philosophy which have emerged on the continent of Europe over the last two hundred years. Some of the most prominent analytically schooled thinkers of the present day now engage with major figures from the continental tradition, and a range of respected journals publish work from both sides of the previously sharp divide. In this context, is scarcely surprising that German Idealism—and its less systematic complement, Jena Romanticism—have received a good deal of attention. For there can be few phases in the history of European thought which can rival the half-century following the publication of Kant's *Critiques*, in terms of intellectual audacity, profundity and scope.

Naturally, the work of Hegel—by far the best-known thinker of this period—has been the focus of much discussion. Not the exclusive focus, however. Prior to the publication of Frederick Beiser's *The Fate of Reason* in 1987, there were probably few English-speaking philosophers who had even heard of the "Pantheism Dispute" of the 1780s, triggered by Friedrich Jacobi's disclosures concerning the elderly Lessing's purported Spinozism.[1] Yet the ensuing arguments, in which Kant himself became involved, and which addressed the existential consequences of the systematic use of reason in a manner that would energize the thinking of the entire subsequent period, have now become a familiar point of reference. Similarly, interest has burgeoned in the complex debates concerning the metaphysical implications of Kant's transcendental turn, and in the arguments centered on his theories of freedom and morality, which took off in Germany during the 1790s. Furthermore, there is now a widespread awareness that all the young thinkers of this generation, including the Jena Romantics, were engaged in a critical dialogue with Fichte, the first truly dominating thinker of the post-Kantian era. Indeed, a notable feature of the new engagement with this period is that the work of Fichte—a leading figure of German Idealism by any measure, although long dismissed in the English-speaking world as the exponent of an exorbitant idealism—has begun to receive, for the first time, a warranted level of scrutiny and assessment by anglophone scholars. Fichte's deep insight into the issues raised by Kant's new approach to the problem of the subject of experience, his theory of transcendental constitution, his innovative linking of self-consciousness and intersubjectivity, and his own challenging moral and political philosophy, have all become objects of inquiry.[2] It is notable, however, that the reception of the third major thinker of German Idealism besides Fichte and Hegel, Friedrich Wilhelm Joseph Schelling, has been far more patchy and tentative; it has not made much connection with more mainstream debates in English-language philosophy, and has tended to focus on his early philosophy of nature—replicating, in fact, the skewed profile of Schelling's renown during his own lifetime.

The Return of Hegel in the English-speaking World

To understand what lies behind this awkwardness in the reception of Schelling's thought, we need to consider the dominant orientation of the new wave of research on the German Idealist period, which began in the late twentieth century, with an initial focus on Hegel. In 1975 Charles Taylor, a Canadian philosopher with strong links to Oxford, but much influenced by European hermeneutics and phenomenology and hence critical of the scientific naturalism and reductionism of many of his peers, published a large-scale survey of Hegel's thought. This proved to be a turning point. Reflecting the social and political commitments of the New Left of the 1950s and early 1960s, in which he had been active, Taylor shifted away from the portrayal of Hegel as a systematic metaphysician in the tradition of Aristotle, the nineteenth-century view which a slender thread of tradition had preserved in Britain throughout the following century. Rather, he presented Hegel primarily as a critical diagnostician of modern society and its dominant frames of reference. In Taylor's account, Hegelian thought emerged as the most sophisticated and philosophically ambitious statement of what he called "expressivism": the view that the pervasive individualism and instrumentalism of the modern world function to inhibit the self-realization of human beings, as creatures in whom the natural, the cultural, and the spiritual are intimately intertwined.³

Taylor's interpretation played a pivotal role in removing the patina of antiquatedness from Hegel's thought and bringing home its contemporary relevance to a new generation of English-speaking philosophers (he was appointed to the chair of social and political theory at Oxford the year after the appearance of his monograph). However, as it turned out, his work functioned primarily as a transition between the dying echoes of Victorian Hegelianism and what was to become the dominant current of Anglo-American Hegel interpretation during the last decades of the twentieth century. For although Taylor portrayed Hegel as a deeply social and historical thinker, echoing a modest concurrent revival of interest in Hegel's work amongst political philosophers, he did not seek to conceal the speculative foundations of Hegel's thinking, or deny that, in some sense, these foundations could also be regarded as religious. In this respect, Taylor's image of Hegel was still out of kilter with the metaphysically deflationary and secularistic temper of the then-dominant trends in analytical philosophy. If Hegel's insights were to be made accessible to a contemporary audience, so it seemed, then his philosophy would have to be more thoroughly reworked and updated.

This task was undertaken in a new style of Hegel interpretation, advocated most prominently in the first instance by the North American philosophers Robert Pippin and Terry Pinkard. In his monograph, Taylor had argued unambiguously that, for Hegel, the inherently contradictory character of finite reality generates a dialectic which culminates in the notion of self-realizing spirit or *Geist* as metaphysically ultimate. As he put it, for Hegel "finite existence cannot be except as posited by cosmic spirit—a cosmic spirit whose nature is to posit its own essential embodiment."⁴ However, in his influential *Hegel's Idealism*, Pippin emphatically rejected Taylor's interpretation, and indeed any account attributing to Hegel a "pre-critical monism," which—he asserted—"is indefensible in itself and at odds with much of what Hegel actually says about his project" (HI: 177, 178). But if Hegel could not, on Pippin's view, be regarded as a monist (the intrinsically "pre-critical" status of monism was here taken for granted), interpreting every aspect of reality as a less or more self-conscious facet of *Geist*, this did not entail his being a dualist, or a substance pluralist. Rather, Pippin ventured, Hegel was not a metaphysical thinker at all.

Hegel's Idealism sought to establish this startling claim by portraying Hegel's philosophy as, in essence, an attempt to bring Kant's transcendental project to a satisfactory conclusion. In its general outline this was not a particularly original approach. However, Pippin's Kant was, in large part, the philosopher as reconfigured in the work of Henry Allison, a colleague during his time at the University of California. In his landmark study, *Kant's Transcendental Idealism*, Allison had defended Kant's sweeping claim that "until the critical philosophy all philosophies are not distinguished in their essentials."[5] It was Kant's distinction between "things as they appear and things as they are in themselves," Allison argued, which had definitively blocked the illusion of metaphysicians—of whatever stripe—that the human mind can access an absolute, "theocentric" view of the world, independent of the "epistemic conditions" whose constitutive role was established in the *Critique of Pure Reason*. These conditions, Allison insisted, should not in any way be regarded as limiting or constricting, but rather as simply enabling human knowledge; the Kantian distinction between "appearances" and "things in themselves" should not be confused with "the familiar contrast between 'how things seem to me' (given certain psychological and physiological conditions and so forth) and 'how they really are.'"[6]

Building on this interpretation of Kant's theoretical philosophy, hence endorsing the claim that transcendental idealism achieves a decisive "break with the metaphysical tradition" (HI: 16), Pippin suggested that Hegel's central concern was to remove the remaining constraints which—contrary to his own basic intention—Kant had built into his account of cognition: most notably the constraint implied by the opposition between a passive, sensory and an active, conceptualizing capacity of the human mind. Pippin summarized the resulting portrait of Hegel in the proposal that "by Absolute Knowledge Hegel is not referring to a knowledge of an absolute substance-Subject, a Divine Mind, or a Spirit-Monad." Rather, "Hegel's basic position preserve[s], even while greatly transforming, a Kantian project," one which is concerned with "the conceptual conditions required for there to be possibly determinate objects of cognition in the first place" (HI: 168, 176).

At around the same time—the late 1980s—Pippin's fellow Hegel interpreter, Terry Pinkard, was reaching similar conclusions from a different starting point: the work of the German neo-Kantian philosopher Klaus Hartmann. In an influential paper, Hartmann had proposed a "non-metaphysical" account of Hegel as a thinker essentially concerned with generating, through transcendental reflection, the system of concepts indispensable for our thinking about the world, in abstraction from all ontological issues.[7] In his first book—on Hegel's *Logic*—Pinkard, who had attended Hartmann's lectures in Tübingen, presented Hegel as developing precisely such "categorial theory." He argued that the immanent development of the *Logic* could best be understood as "a metaphorical movement of those conceptual unities produced by *describing* entities in a certain way."[8] On this account, then, Hegel was not concerned with the metaphysical structure of entities as such—which presumably was to be regarded as unproblematic. Finally, from the 1990s onwards, this approach to Hegel was reinforced by arguments drawn from the work of the mid-twentieth century American philosopher Wilfred Sellars, whose far-reaching critique of both classical empiricism and its twentieth-century successors, belatedly recognized as converging with the views of Quine and Davidson, was then contributing to a sea-change in analytical philosophy.[9] In the work of figures such as Richard Rorty, Robert Brandom, and John McDowell, Hegel—long *persona non grata* in analytical circles—began to emerge as having pioneered the critique of the "Myth of the Given," which Sellars, in *Empiricism and the Philosophy of Mind*, expresses in the well-known declaration:

> in characterizing an episode or a state as that of knowing, we are not giving an empirical description of that episode or state; we are placing it in the logical space of reasons, of justifying and being able to justify what one says.[10]

Sellars regarded himself as a scientific realist. He was opposed to mongrel philosophical explanations, which sought the base-level grounding of knowledge claims in something sheerly given—whether sensory or neurophysiological—to which reference could be made from *within* the "manifest image," or what phenomenologists term the human "lifeworld." But he also argued that the "scientific image" of the world—although still very much under construction—offered the possibility of an alternative holistic account of reality, superior—because more internally consistent—to the manifest image, despite the refinement and rationalization the latter had itself undergone in the course of human history. And he did not seek to conceal his belief that, ultimately, "the scientific image of man turns out to be that of a complex physical system."[11] However, the new wave of Hegel interpreters, who found powerful inspiration in Sellars' critique of the myth of the given, were happy to let the *Gestalt*-switch to scientific realism drop. What counted for them was the integrity of the space of reasons, regarded as an updated version of Hegel's vision of total conceptual mediation. For these thinkers, an emphasis on the pervasive conceptuality—and hence "normativity"—of the human lifeworld, and of all epistemic and ethical claims embedded within it, made possible the portrayal of Hegel as a "soft" naturalist, an orientation presumed to be within the bounds of acceptability, given the dominant outlook amongst anglophone philosophers. Because the "space of reasons"—viewed from within—appears as an "unbounded" *sui generis* arena which cannot run up against anything external to it,[12] Hegel's thought, on this interpretation, need not come into conflict with the picture of reality provided by the contemporary natural sciences, and requires no recourse to the notion of a unifying ultimate ground or absolute—a notion which, throughout the history of Western philosophy, has often coincided with the concept of God. In short, the "normative interpretation" of German Idealism, as Frederick Beiser has aptly termed it, in a persuasive highlighting of the parallels with historical neo-Kantianism's split between fact and value,[13] seemed efficiently to do away with Hegel's image as a purveyor of extravagant speculation.[14] It appeared to offer precisely the kind of naturalistic, secularistic, non-metaphysical account of his work that could render him *salonfähig* in the English-speaking philosophical world.

Delegitimizing Schelling

However, the view that German Idealism culminates in such a philosophical outlook, or—put less strongly—that such an outlook is the most plausible option for us now, and can draw support from a judicious interpretation Hegel, is hard to combine with due acknowledgement of Schelling's role, either in the initial development of post-Kantian Idealism, or in the transition to its mid-nineteenth century aftermath. For one abiding feature of Schelling's work, right from his first publications of the mid-1790s, is a conviction that one cannot ultimately separate normative—epistemological and moral-practical—questions from ontological and metaphysical ones. The young Schelling was convinced that there must be an original point at which the subjective and the objective—and at which "ought" and "is"—are fused, as only this can secure human knowledge, including transcendental knowledge, from the suspicion of being a mere construct, and prevent the natural world from seeming impervious to pure practical reason, without paying the unacceptable price of its reduction to a set of appearances. As we shall see, this insistence eventually led to an out-and-out conflict with Fichte. It is not surprising, therefore, that in *Hegel's Idealism*, perhaps *the* founding text of the "normative interpretation" of German Idealism, Robert Pippin devotes a whole chapter to an effort to airbrush Schelling out of the legitimate lineage of German Idealism, which he presents as running from Kant, via Fichte, to Hegel. Tellingly, chapter 3 of his book is entitled "Fichte's Contribution," while chapter 4 is devoted to the "Schelling problem" (HI: 61)—a formula which, in retrospect, can only be viewed as meaning: "problem for my interpretation of German Idealism."

Because of Fichte's strong emphasis on the "primacy of the practical" during his early period, it is not too difficult to acknowledge him as a precursor of Hegelianism in its normative interpretation. Long ago, in fact, in a respectful essay written for the centenary of the "Atheism Dispute," which culminated in Fichte's resignation from the University of Jena and move to Berlin, the neo-Kantian philosopher Heinrich Rickert portrayed him as an anti-metaphysical, even positivistic thinker, determined not to stray beyond the bounds of conscious experience, the ultimate basis of which should be regarded not as cognitive but volitional.[15] Pippin's "Schelling problem" was posed by the fact that, from very early in their philosophical careers, both Schelling and Hegel perceived the limitations of this strategy for moving beyond Kant. Indeed, in the first years of the nineteenth century, Schelling and Hegel, who had been friends since their schooldays a decade earlier in the Tübingen *Stift*, worked closely together at the University of Jena, jointly publishing a brief-lived journal. All the articles for the *Kritisches Journal der Philosophie* were written by the two colleagues, although the contributions were left unsigned, as if to proclaim their common philosophical front at the time. Both were convinced that the quest for a principle of ultimate subject–object unity, triggered by the pivotal role which Kant had assigned to the unity of apperception, could not terminate with the form of transcendental subjectivity as such, a proposal which Fichte had merely stated in the most radical manner. The explanation for this seemed more or less obvious to them: subjectivity—even transcendentally construed—could only function as one pole of the absolute unity being sought. Hegel's first major publication, *The Difference between Fichte's and Schelling's System of Philosophy* (the *Differenzschrift*), was, of course, a defense of Schelling's conception of absolute identity and a critique of Fichte's transcendentalism—regarded as an example of the "philosophy of reflection" in its replication of the damaging diremptions of post-Enlightenment culture.[16]

However, because of his insistence that the "problematic of German Idealism," as developed by Hegel, was the "*transcendental* problem of self-consciousness" (HI: 66), Pippin had no option but to dismiss the Schellingian tenor of Hegel's early writings as an unfortunate and misleading aberration. This he did partly by means of *ad hoc* historical and psychological suggestions to the effect that Hegel was somehow pressurized into adopting Schelling's position; partly by means of a perverse exegesis of Hegel's early publications, which tried to cast doubt on their commitment to a trans-subjective (and trans-objective) absolute that cannot be accessed through an abstraction from empirical consciousness in the Fichtean manner, since the result would then remain subjective and conditioned, but only through what Hegel himself terms "pure transcendental intuition";[17] partly by the simple expedient of rewriting Hegel, so that his ontological claims become epistemological ones. Pippin, for example, states: "The apprehension of any determinate cognitive object is dependent on (in Hegelian language 'is' a moment of) the 'free' self-articulations of reason" (HI: 61, 66–73, 68).

Here is not the place to engage in a detailed refutation of Pippin's highly prejudicial misrepresentation of the Schelling–Hegel relationship.[18] Suffice it to say that, in his lectures on the history of philosophy, delivered long after his years in Jena, Hegel did not at all condemn Schelling—as does Pippin—for swallowing up the differentiated empirical world in a philosophically cut-price, "romantic" intuition of the absolute. Nor did he accuse Schelling of transgressing the proper bounds of transcendental philosophy, or of venturing beyond epistemology into dubious claims about the ontological structure and dynamics of nature. On the contrary, he describes Schelling's identity system as the final "interesting, true shape of philosophy" prior to his own. In more detail:

> The main thing in Schelling's philosophy is that it deals with a content, with the true, and this is grasped as something concrete. Schelling's philosophy has a deep speculative content, which, as such, is the content with which philosophy was concerned throughout its entire history. Thinking is free and independent, though not abstract, but rather concrete in itself; it grasps itself as being—in itself—the world, not as an intellectual world, but rather as the intellectual-real world. The truth of nature, nature in itself, is the intellectual world. Schelling grasped this concrete content. (LHP3: 541–542/ W20, 20, 453–454)

The Return of Metaphysics

Since the 1980s, however, when the project of presenting an "analytically approachable" Hegel—to use an expression of Paul Redding[19]—began in earnest, the anglophone philosophical environment has been transformed. The analytical mainstream, partly in response to problems in the logical treatment of modality, has taken a turn toward forthright metaphysical inquiry, rejecting the view that such activity is inherently suspect or unviable. Alongside these developments, the weaknesses of the "normative interpretation" of German Idealism have come under scrutiny from younger commentators, who nonetheless know this sub-tradition from the inside, since they have been largely shaped by it. One central target here is the assumption that investigation of epistemological and practical norms, transcendental conditions, or categorial frameworks can be a primary, free-standing enterprise, innocent of metaphysical presuppositions or commitments. As James Kreines, probably the most influential of this new generation of Hegel interpreters, has often stressed, it is simply not possible to square this approach with the critique of the regress involved in "epistemology-first" conceptions of philosophy, which Hegel tirelessly repeats, and which can also be extended to more recent "semantics-first" and similar strategies (RW: 13-15). As Kreines puts it:

> The important point for understanding Hegel... is that there is no privilege of any epistemological domain over issues about reasons everywhere else—including issues about essences, forms, materialism, and so on. So the basic task is not to restrict ourselves to one case, but to face the issues in their full generality, learning how best to think about reason in the world. (RW: 15)

Mutatis mutandis, many recent developments in anglophone philosophy, breaking away from the mid-twentieth century preoccupation with language and meaning, echo this outlook. And indeed, some can be singled out as explicitly addressing issues which preoccupied the post-Kantian Idealists. One could take, for example, Galen Strawson's critique of the absolute metaphysical distinction between the physical and the experiential or subjective, and his advocacy of what he calls "Equal-Status Fundamental-Duality monism," which replicates in significant respects the position reached by Schelling during the phase of his "identity philosophy."[20] Or one could instance the revival of substantive debate around problems of free-will and determinism, with certain influential positions—such as that of Helen Steward—clearly echoing the concern of Idealist *Naturphilosophie* to develop a conception of nature able to accommodate the spontaneity and purposiveness of agency, both animal and human.[21] One could refer to contemporary arguments, centered on the interpretation of Spinoza, concerning the validation and scope of the principle of sufficient reason, with their clear renewal of the questions concerning rational systematicity and freedom raised by Jacobi in the 1790s.[22] Last but not least, one could mention Thomas Nagel's opposition both to scientific reductionism and to a complacent soft naturalism, his efforts to "find a way of understanding ourselves that is not radically self-undermining, and that does not require us to deny the obvious." Such a form of self-understanding, he suggests, would "reveal mind and reason as basic aspects of a nonmaterialistic natural order." Here the continuities with the project of German Idealism in its historical form—although not, of course, with the recent "normative," or neo-Kantian reworkings of German Idealism—are striking; indeed, the affinities with Hegel and Schelling are noted in passing by Nagel himself.[23]

Schelling's Late Philosophy and Hegel

The philosophical moment seems to have arrived, then, for a comparative examination of the thought of Hegel and Schelling which does not—at least implicitly—dismiss many of their central concerns as antiquated, or present such an implausibly deflationary image of Hegel's speculative thinking that no balanced or meaningful comparison with Schelling's work is possible. Once the essentially neo-Kantian discourse of a hypertrophied "normativity" is left behind, it becomes clear that both the mature Hegel and Schelling—during the final phase of his thinking, although building on advances achieved over the course of his career—seek to validate their deepest metaphysical insights through immensely ambitious, extended narratives of the emergence of human self-consciousness from nature, and its slow, painful, and hazardous evolution. Both believe that it is necessary to take such a long-term view to make sense of what it means to be human in our current historical situation. If we use the term "modernity" to describe this situation, we should be aware that modernity is not a state but a process, a transition—doubtless never fully achievable—away from deference to inherited authority and the power of tradition. Following Jürgen Habermas, it may be defined as a socio-cultural situation in which human beings cannot rely uncritically on the models of previous eras, but must develop the immanent logic of their practices to achieve normative orientation and the legitimation of their forms of life.[24] We should not jump to the conclusion, however, that the sole native resource of modernity is self-legislating reason—or, to be more precise, that there is no scope, within modernity, for a reasoned defense of sources of meaning and validation other than reason itself.

The issues in the interpretation of modern culture touched on here are ones which both Hegel and Schelling are deeply engaged. More concretely, they ask such questions as: how are human subjectivity and agency intertwined with the natural world, and how should we position ourselves in relation to the modern scientific image of that world as the domain exclusively of causal law? What explains the pervasiveness of religion, as a feature of human history and social life, and what should religious consciousness, if not dismissed merely as an illusion, an anachronism which should have been dislodged by the Enlightenment, be regarded as striving to apprehend and articulate? What is human freedom, according to our modern understanding, what are its ontological preconditions, and what role has it played—if any—as a driver of human history? How are philosophy and its truth-claims themselves positioned in relation to the historical process in which we stand—and what practical consequences, if any, follow from our conceptualization of this position? Finally, and relatedly, can philosophy, in seeking a comprehensive and integrated understanding of the world, regard the characteristic orientation of modernity toward the future, and in particular toward the moral-political horizon of general human emancipation, as being of no ultimate systematic importance?

The principal aim of the present work is to explore the divergences between the answers which Hegel's mature work and Schelling's late system—which is still so little known or understood in the English-speaking world—offer to these questions, in all their complex ramifications. In one sense, I regard this enterprise as returning to the path opened up by Charles Taylor's *Hegel*, which was cut off prematurely by the rise of soft-naturalist, "post-metaphysical" versions of Hegelianism. Taylor showed that one can emphasize the German Idealists' profound—and still pertinent—diagnoses of the existential, cultural, and socio-political dilemmas of the modern world, without needing to suppress the demandingly speculative character of their thinking. On the contrary, when correctly viewed, the focus on elemental questions and the self-reflexive audacity of the latter emerges as intimately linked with the concreteness and penetration of the former. Like Taylor, I perceive deep affinities—despite the two centuries now separating them—between modern-day traditions of social and cultural critique, as they emerged re-energized from the radical maelstrom of the 1960s, and the central concerns of German Romanticism and Idealism. The shaping of my own outlook by those traditions has sustained my enthusiasm for the thinkers of the Kantian aftermath over several decades. The present work, then, was written in the conviction that the divergences between Hegel and Schelling touch on some of the most enduring and pervasive problems in philosophy—yet can also throw light on some of our most pressing concerns as inhabitants of the contemporary world.

Outline of the Present Work

It would simply not be feasible, however, to plunge the uninitiated reader into the intricacies of Schelling's late thinking without some prior examination of the intellectual path which led to it—especially because, partly for reasons given above, Schelling's work as a whole is still so poorly known in the English-speaking world. I therefore begin with three chapters which follow some central threads in the evolution of Schelling's thought, from his youthful publications of the 1790s, through the phase of the "identity philosophy" and the writings of his middle period, up to the threshold of his late system in the 1820s. I hope that these chapters will also help to refute the widespread misconception that Schelling, in the earlier phases of his work, simply neglects the Kantian critique of metaphysics and plunges into inadequately justified "romantic" speculation. Schelling's move away from Kant, and his growing opposition to the radicalized transcendental approach forcefully advocated by Fichte, were motivated by deep philosophical considerations—and this is something which even those who, in the last analysis, disagree with his strategy should at least be able to acknowledge.

In chapter 1, I seek to show how these considerations drive Schelling's response to Kant's theory of the basic subject–object polarity of human experience and to his attempt, in the *Critique of Judgment*, to solve the conundrum of the appearance of purposiveness in a mechanistically interpreted natural world. In chapter 2, I explore Schelling's effort to resolve the tensions generated by view that human agency both must have a genuinely spontaneous dimension *and* emerges from nature, rather than being insulated from it by a noumenal/phenomenal—or, to use more recent terms, a normativity/factuality—distinction. It can hardly be claimed that the philosophical problems with which Schelling grapples here are superannuated. Finally, in chapter 3, I examine Schelling's slowly and arduously attained understanding, developed through the experimental texts of his middle period, that the conflict between freedom and necessity is not susceptible to philosophical resolution in any standard sense. It is this momentous advance in Schelling's thinking, combined with his realization that the appropriate response to this situation lies in a historical hermeneutics of the progressive *liberation* of human consciousness, a liberation re-enacted in the transition between what he terms "negative" and "positive" philosophy, which sets the stage for his late system.

Chapters 4, 5, and 6 cover what may appear to some readers to be rather abstract and arid terrain. It is here that my comparison with Hegel begins in earnest, however, for at their heart lies the problem of the relation between *a priori* thinking and being, which is necessarily of fundamental importance for both thinkers, insofar as they are objective idealists. I begin, in chapter 4, by outlining Schelling's historical perspective on the founding distinction between negative and positive philosophy, the hallmark of his late system. I then discuss Schelling's view of how to *begin* the process of *a priori* reflexive thinking, of what he terms "purely rational" (*reinrationale*) or "negative" philosophy, and compare this with opening of Hegel's *Logic*. The resulting considerations on the relation between the contrary and the contradictory negation of being (between "non-being" and "not being"—or "*mē on*" and "*ouk on*," in Aristotle's terminology) may seem unnecessarily abstruse. But here we find ourselves truly at the core of the metaphysical dispute between Schelling and Hegel, which concerns the status of potentiality (the—as yet—*non-being* of things, by contrast to their total *not being*). Schelling believes that human freedom cannot be authentically denied from an experiential, as opposed to a purely theoretical standpoint. But far from concluding that determinism can therefore be allowed to stand as an innocuous theoretical option, he argues that potentiality—in the Aristotelian sense of the status of that which *may* or *may not* be realized—must be a fundamental element in the fabric of the world. Hence a question begins to loom, one that will persist throughout the subsequent chapters of the book, concerning the meaning of freedom in Hegel's system, given that this has no ultimate place for potentiality. In other words, in view of Hegel's conviction that the proper concern of philosophy is with the rational necessity, which he regards as determining what it means to be actual, it is far from clear what becomes of freedom, understood as the individual agent's capacity to settle—in the sense of further specify—how the future will turn out, in a world which is not somehow fixed *ab initio*.[25] In the final part of chapter 4, I then examine how Schelling uses the concept of pure potentiality to generate the ontological structures of his negative or purely rational philosophy, as this is the key to his reconfiguration of the tension between the possible and the necessary.

Chapter 5 continues the concerns of chapter 4 by examining the complexities of the relation, in both thinkers, between the Idea—the complete system of *a priori* categories—and the realms of nature and spirit (together comprising the domain which Hegel's describes as that of "*Realphilosophie*"). At issue are divergences in the way in which the basic Idealist contention concerning the identity of thought and being is formulated and understood in the work of the two philosophers. By contrast, the first part of chapter 6 deals primarily with Schelling's manner of conceiving the priority of being over thinking. It seeks to bring his argument closer to more recent—and hopefully more familiar—points of reference through an extended comparison with Sartre's treatment of being "in-itself" and being "for-itself" in *Being and Nothingness*. It then takes up the topic from another angle, by comparing the ways in which Hegel and Schelling respond to and reformulate the pivotal argument of rationalist metaphysics in the modern era—the ontological argument. Following this, it considers how the two thinkers handle the intra-systemic transition from the realm of *a priori* thought to the domain of worldly being—from a sphere which is "still as yet logical" (*noch logisch*) to the sphere of the "externality of space and time" (*die Äußerlichkeit des Raums und der Zeit*), to use Hegel's terms. The chapter concludes by clarifying Schelling's position with the use of another modern frame of reference, assessing his account of the emergence of freedom in nature in the light of the "metaphysics for freedom" proposed by Helen Steward.

The final chapters of the book move onto rather different terrain. Both Schelling and Hegel regard a philosophical theory of the evolution of religion as the key to the comprehension of the history of human consciousness. Far from being antiquated, this approach is entirely understandable, if one accepts that religious thinking and practice are—historically speaking—the principal and most vital manner in which cultures have sought to make sense of the world, and the place of human existence within it, at the profoundest level. However, the basis of religious consciousness and the dynamic of its transformation over time differ dramatically in the work of the two thinkers. Schelling envisages a global rupture across human societies which commences in the first millennium BCE, and which concludes with a relatively abrupt transition from a static cosmos pervaded by mythological powers to a historical, forward-moving world, definitively disclosed in the Christian revelation. Hegel, by contrast, depicts a dialectical evolution of consciousness, with no single decisive break, although the process culminates in the Christian gospel of freedom, whose impact takes many centuries to work itself out. Chapters 7 and 8, then, conduct a comparison of Schelling's theories of mythology and revelation—the historical components of his "positive philosophy"—with the segment of Hegel's *Realphilosophie* which deals with religion. However, they also introduce the distinctive dialectic of alienation (or "*ecstasis*") and liberation which is fundamental to Schelling's late work. Advances in the consciousness of freedom, in his account, are fragile and vulnerable, liable to lapse back into the compulsion of one or another type of "mythology." In the modern, post-Cartesian world such regression takes the form of the dreamlike detachment and inexorability of what he terms "natural reason."

This dynamic is further explored in chapter 9, which deals with Hegel's attempt to resolve the "paradox of autonomy" bequeathed by Kant, by moving to a socio-historical conception of freedom. As mentioned earlier, during the arduous lead-up to his late system Schelling gradually concluded that the deep conflict between freedom and necessity or between liberation and alienation (of which the paradox of autonomy is an expression), is not susceptible to resolution in any standard philosophical sense. In contrast to Hegel's monumental attempt to construct a system ultimately unified by the concept of "absolute spirit," the bipartite structure of Schelling's late thinking—with its methodological opposition of a "positive" and a "negative" philosophy—now appears as his means of accommodating this insight without simply abandoning the systematic ambitions of German Idealism: without giving up on the project of showing how our diverse and apparently conflicting ways of encountering and making sense of reality—scientific, aesthetic, moral, religious, interpersonal—can be integrated in a coherent overall conception of the world.

My conclusion approaches this same constellation of issues from a somewhat different angle. Here the problem of freedom and necessity returns as the difficulty of incorporating the insights of the modern "hermeneutics of suspicion," whose founders were Marx, Nietzsche, and Freud, into our view of the obstacles confronting human freedom and its realization. How is it possible to do so, without undermining the possibility of the freedom we aimed to promote, though our very insistence on disclosing the concealed determinations of thought and action? I argue that Hegel avoids this problem only by adopting a rationalism so comprehensive that the very notion of unwarranted constraints on the agency of human beings or of the oppressive shaping of their consciousness has no place. Hegel's approach is grounded in his fundamental philosophical operation, namely self-negating negation. Schelling, however, gives a further twist to the definition of freedom which flows from Hegel's *Grundoperation*—"being with yourself in the other"— in arguing that, to be fully free, we must be free both to find ourselves and *not* to find ourselves in the other. His corresponding fundamental operation consists in a "decompression" of blind being-ness into the panoply of potentialities. This operation does not negate the priority of being-ness, and hence does not identify, from the absolute standpoint, possibility and actuality, self and other. At the same time, the operation also enables Schelling to think about the determination of human consciousness in a genealogical mode, as is shown by his analysis of mythological thinking, and the parallel he draws with the forms of illusion generated by a comprehensive, circular rationalism. Unlike Hegel, Schelling does not present his system as a closed circuit. Rather it consists in an ongoing verification and is structured by anticipation—oriented toward a future of expanding human freedom.

It should also be evident by this point that Schelling could develop his late conception of system only by anchoring his response to the dilemmas of modern consciousness in metaphysical investigation of the most subtle and far-reaching kind. At the same time, like the other major figures of the Idealist period, he did not forget that—after the Kantian revolution—metaphysical inquiry must be recast in an entirely new mold. If the present book can convey such a portrait of Schelling, and so contribute to establishing his standing in the English-speaking world as one of the great philosophical diagnosticians of modern world, I shall consider the years of research and reflection whose results are offered here as well rewarded.

Notes

1. See Frederick Beiser, *The Fate of Reason: German Philosophy from Kant to Fichte* (Cambridge, MA: Harvard University Press, 1987).

2. See, for example, Frederick Neuhouser, *Fichte's Theory of Subjectivity* (Cambridge: CUP, 1990); Wayne Martin, *Idealism and Objectivity: Understanding Fichte's Jena Project* (Stanford, CA: Stanford University Press, 1997); David James, *Fichte's Social and Political Philosophy: Property and Virtue* (Cambridge: CUP, 2011); Allen W. Wood, *Fichte's Ethical Thought* (Oxford: OUP, 2016); Michelle Kosch, *Fichte's Ethics* (Oxford: OUP, 2018).
3. See Charles Taylor, *Hegel* (Cambridge: CUP, 1975). Taylor summarized the social and political content of his reading of Hegel in a shorter subsequent book, *Hegel and Modern Society* (Cambridge: CUP, 1979).
4. *Hegel*, 99.
5. Henry Allison, *Kant's Transcendental Idealism: An Interpretation and Defense* (London: Yale University Press, 1983), 16. The quotation is from AA, XX, 335.
6. *Kant's Transcendental Idealism*, 25.
7. See Klaus Hartmann, "Hegel: A Non-Metaphysical View," in *Hegel: A Collection of Critical Essays*, ed. Alasdair MacIntyre (Notre Dame and London: University of Notre Dame Press, 1972).
8. Terry Pinkard, *Hegel's Dialectic: The Explanation of Possibility* (Philadelphia, PA: Temple University Press, 1988), 12. Emphasis added.
9. See Wilfrid Sellars, *Empiricism and the Philosophy of Mind* (Cambridge, MA: Harvard University Press, 1997).
10. *Empiricism and the Philosophy of Mind*, 76.
11. Wilfrid Sellars, "Philosophy and the Scientific Image of Man," in *In the Space of Reasons: Selected Essays of Wilfred Sellars*, ed. Kevin Scharp and Robert B. Brandom (Cambridge, MA: Harvard University Press, 2007), 393.
12. See John McDowell, *Mind and World* (Cambridge, MA: Harvard University Press, 1994), Lecture II, 24–45.
13. See Frederick Beiser, "Normativity in Neo-Kantianism: Its Rise and Fall," *International Journal of Philosophical Studies* 17, no. 1 (2009), 9–27.
14. Pinkard quite openly emphasized Hartmann's neo-Kantian orientation is his obituary tribute to him, proleptically substantiating Beiser's account. See Pinkard, "Klaus Hartmann: A Philosophical Appreciation," *Zeitschrift für Philosophische Forschung*, 46, no. 4 (October–December 1992).
15. Heinrich Rickert, "Fichtes Atheismusstreit und die Kantische Philosophie: Eine Sekulärbetrachtung," *Kant-Studien* 4 (1900), 156.
16. See Hegel, *The Difference between Fichte's and Schelling's System of Philosophy*, trans. H. S. Harris and Walter Cerf (Albany, NY: SUNY Press, 1977) (W20, 2: 9–138).
17. *The Difference between Fichte's and Schelling's System of Philosophy*, 173 (W20, 2: 115).
18. For suitably balanced accounts of Schelling and Hegel's time together in Jena, which stress the reciprocal influences, see Klaus Düsing, "Spekulation und Reflexion: Zur Zusammenarbeit Schellings und Hegels in Jena," *Hegel-Studien* 5 (1969), 95–128; and especially Hermann Krings, *Die Entfremdung zwischen Schelling und Hegel (1801–1807)* (Munich: Verlag der Bayerischen Akademie der Wissenschaften, 1977).

19. See "Robert Pippin's Hegel as an *Analytically Approachable* Philosopher," Paul Redding's introduction to a special issue of the *Australasian Philosophical Review* devoted to Pippin's interpretation of Hegel (vol. 2, no. 4 [2018]).
20. See, for example, Galen Strawson, "Panpsychism? A Reply to Commentators and a Celebration of Descartes," in *Consciousness and its Place in Nature*, ed. Anthony Freeman (Exeter: Imprint Academic, 2006), 184–280.
21. See Helen Steward, MF. A more extended comparison of Schelling's philosophy of nature and freedom with that of Steward will be found in chapter 6, 197–204.
22. See, for example, Michael Della Rocca, "A Rationalist Manifesto: Spinoza and the Principle of Sufficient Reason," *Philosophical Topics* 31, no. 1/2 (Spring and Fall 2003); Martin Lin, "Rationalism and Necessitarianism," *Noûs* 46, no. 3 (2012); Omri Boehm, *Kant's Critique of Spinoza* (New York: OUP, 2014).
23. Thomas Nagel, *Mind and Cosmos* (Oxford: OUP, 2012), 25, 32, 17.
24. See Jürgen Habermas, *The Philosophical Discourse of Modernity* (Cambridge MA: MIT Press, 1987), esp. 1–22.
25. For this concept of "settling," see MF, 39–42.

1
Toward Nature

Kant on Self-Consciousness and the Nexus of Experience

The new beginning in European philosophy marked by the appearance of the *Critique of Pure Reason* in 1781 can be summed up in the claim that Kant re-centered philosophical attention on the structure of the relation between the subject and the object of experience as such. The first *Critique* no longer asks how the mind can make cognitive contact with a reality assumed to subsist independently of it, or what it would mean to establish an accurate representation of such a reality. The very term "external world," as this is still employed by some philosophers, no longer makes sense within the Kantian framework because it confuses first-personal (transcendental) and third-personal (empirical) perspectives. Of course, Kant does not deny a fundamental distinction between the realm of material things in time and space and the mental domain. But this distinction is itself established as part of the *a priori* structure of experience, so that subjectivity and objectivity, when correctly understood, now appear as components of an integral nexus, in which neither can be prized apart from its interdependence with the other. As Kant states in the first version of the transcendental deduction:

> the original and necessary consciousness of the identity of oneself is at the same time a consciousness of an equally necessary unity of the synthesis of all appearances in accordance with concepts, i.e. in accordance with rules that not only make them necessarily reproducible, but also thereby determine an object for their intuition, i.e. the concept of something in which they are necessarily connected. (A108)

Clearly, this novel approach, in which the identity of the experiencing subject and that of the object mirror one another, has advantages in overcoming the kinds of skeptical problems which have plagued the prominent stream of modern philosophy that begins from the standpoint of the experiencing subject, and yet seeks to secure knowledge of a world taken to be ontologically independent of our experience of it. But at the same time, as with all major changes of paradigm, Kant's innovations generate their own set of perplexities.

No doubt one of the most irritating of these is the problem of the thing-in-itself. For Kant, synthesis is the fundamental process on which conscious experience depends. But synthesis cannot occur without a multiplicity of sensory data to be united. He is therefore obliged to argue that whatever accounts for the existence of the "manifold perceptions" (A112) which our receptive sensory capacity supplies to be forged into the experience of an objective world must itself lie beyond all possible experience. From very early on, this aspect of Kant's theory was regarded as glaringly inconsistent, with Friedrich Jacobi being among the most influential critics to register such an objection: "How is it possible to reconcile the presupposition of objects that produce impressions on our senses, and in this way arouse representations, with an hypothesis intent on abolishing all grounds by which the presupposition could be supported?"[1] This critique of the thing-in-itself was accepted in principle by all the German Idealists. However, the direction in which they sought an answer to the problem was precisely the opposite of that taken by Jacobi.

In his *Letters on the Doctrine of Spinoza* Jacobi put forward two arguments whose explosive combination was to have an immense influence on the development of post-Kantian thought: firstly, that the philosophical demand for complete explanation—in effect, the unlimited scope of the principle of sufficient reason—requires the construction of a system grounded in a single, self-grounding principle, Spinoza's monism of substance being the supreme example; and secondly, that such a system, as necessary as it may be in strictly philosophical terms, is incompatible both with our incontrovertible, spontaneous awareness of our freedom as self-conscious, self-determining agents, and our unshakeable belief that nature is revealed to us through its *impact* on our senses—that we are not locked in a world of ideas which merely runs parallel to the world of extended things. However, far from rejecting the need for an ultimate unitary principle in philosophy, the German Idealists believed that precisely such a principle was required to produce a fully cohesive account of the subject–object nexus of experience. Such an account would no longer be dependent on inconsistent supplements, such as the thing-in-itself, which simply fueled the skepticism which Kant's Copernican turn was intended to overcome. But given this project, one might at first be surprised by the direction in which this principle was initially sought, namely by looking toward the subject pole of the subject-object nexus. For if the two poles of the nexus are interdependent, how could one of them be regarded as suitable to function as a unitary ground?

With this question we are plunged into the thicket of some of the central problems confronting the German Idealists. On Kant's account, the subject and object poles of experience must be interdependent, as we only become aware of ourselves as an identical subject of our experience, persisting over time, through a contrast with the multifarious flow of that experience, while the content of that flow can only be *for* an experiencing subject. However, this interdependence does not entail that, in Kant's theory, subject and object are *co-constitutive*. Indeed, total co-constitution is an incoherent notion: if A is dependent on B for its determination as an existent, then B cannot in turn be dependent on A. Co-constitution, to the extent that the thought makes sense at all, would itself depend on a unitary ground of the related elements. And this entails that one pole of the nexus must in fact play a double role: somehow it must both be relative to its counterpart *within* the nexus and also be the constitutive basis of the nexus as a whole. Furthermore, it appears that the *subject* must play this role because, while the manifold of sensory input—of what Kant calls "intuitions" (*Anschauungen*)—requires unification through *a priori* concepts (the "categories") to take shape as an objective world, the subject of experience does not, in return, require pluralization. On the contrary, Kant emphasizes that if there were only a separate, punctual experiencer of each intuition or set of intuitions, there could be no coherent world of experience. Hence the subject *also* requires unification to bring about what Kant calls the "synthetic unity of apperception" (B132 ff.). However, it is fundamental to Kant's theory that sensory receptivity is passive, while thinking—the mobilization of the categories in judgments—is necessarily active. Hence it must be the subject, which alone is capable of thought, that plays the overall synthesizing role.

The same point can also be made in a more methodological vein. Transcendental inquiry does not analyze the interactions between an empirical, worldly subject and the objects which it encounters. Rather, it seeks to elucidate the structure of an experiential *perspective* on the world, isolating the features which are essential to *any* such perspective—and this means that it must be carried out by the philosopher from a standpoint which is *internally connected* with that of the subject whose perspective is in question. There is therefore an inherent directionality of transcendental elucidation, given that the philosopher *looks into* the perspective, as it were, rather than looking *at it*. In other words, the evidential basis for the transcendental clarification of the structure of the subject-object nexus depends on the subject being the agent of constitution of the nexus, an agent with whom the philosophizing subject both is and is not identical, in a form of participant observation.[2] It can be seen that the transcendental method thereby creates a complex situation in which the relation between the constituting and the constituted subject of experience is itself the focus of investigation of the philosopher, who must come to understand it by *re-enacting* it—because, for obvious reasons, it cannot be an *object* of inquiry. Evidently, we are pushing here at the limit of what philosophical discourse is capable of thematizing: seeking to experience the constitution of experience, to know the genesis of knowledge. It is not surprising, then, that Kant's various discussions of the transcendental and the empirical unity of apperception in the *Critique of Pure Reason* do not add up to a coherent theory—especially as his primary interest lay in the consequences which he could draw from his basic insight, and not in the perplexities attached to concept of the "I," of the subject of experience as such.

In fact, self-awareness seems to play two different roles in Kant's account. On the one hand, there is what he calls the "I think" which can accompany all my representations; this form of awareness delivers the sense of our own agency in all our mental activity, but without any determination of an agent, and entirely irrespective of the content of the activity. In his essay, "Die Identität des Subjekts in der transzendentalen Deduktion," Dieter Henrich calls this awareness simply "subjectivity."[3] On the other hand, there is what Henrich terms the "identity" of self-consciousness; in other words, our awareness of ourselves as a single enduring enjoyer of diverse experiences, which only emerges through a contrast with the synthetically constituted objective world. This duality clearly appears, for example, when Kant writes:

> it is only because I can combine a manifold of given representations **in one consciousness** that it is possible for me to represent the **identity of consciousness in these representations** itself, i.e., the **analytical** unity of apperception is only possible under the presupposition of some synthetic one. (B133/134)

Evidently, in this account, the I which carries out the combining cannot be equated with the identity of consciousness which results from the process, even though Kant insists that we could not formulate the thought "I think"—which is grounded in what he terms "pure apperception"—except as identical subjects of experience. The important point is that our status as subjects cannot consist simply in a formal unity which emerges through a contrast with what is constituted as the objective content of experience. There must also be an awareness of our spontaneity as thinkers, of which some explanation, or at least a plausible characterization, must be given.

It is clear that Kant is alert to this because he returns several times to the problem of my awareness of my spontaneous agency as a thinker, including in a revealing note to the "Paralogisms of Pure Reason" in the B edition of the first *Critique*. There he argues that the proposition "I think" is "an empirical proposition, and contains within itself the proposition 'I exist'" (B422n). Presumably, it is an "empirical proposition" not because it is ratified by experience in the usual sense, but because it is a contingent fact that I, as this particular subject of experience, exist. Because this awareness of contingent being is not made possible by any sensory or inner intuition, Kant proposes that the "I think," while an empirical proposition, is not an "empirical representation":

> On the contrary, it is purely intellectual, because belonging to thought in general. Without some empirical representation to supply the material for thought, "I think," would not, indeed, take place; but the empirical is only the condition of the application, or the employment, of the pure intellectual faculty. (B423n)

In other words, I have an intellectual or non-sensory awareness of my own existence as a thinker, albeit without any further awareness of *what* I am, as opposed to *that* I am. This Kantian argument will be vital for the further development of German Idealism, given that here Kant has effectively admitted the reality of "intellectual intuition"—of the thought of an existent which is simultaneously the direct awareness of its existence. In general, Kant denies the possibility of intellectual intuition for a finite, discursive intelligence, such as that of human beings. But this seems to be because he assumes that it could only take the form of a thinking which somehow generates its own not merely noetic object. However, none of the post-Kantians regard the primordial self as an object in this sense.

The Role of Fichte's *Wissenschaftslehre*

One cannot understand Schelling's distinctive response to the problems bequeathed by Kant without considering the role of Johann Gottlieb Fichte, the most important contemporary influence on his earliest published work. During the 1790s, Fichte aimed to develop a fully coherent transcendental philosophy, beginning from Kant but eliminating what he regarded as the gross inconsistencies of Kant's own version of the project. The most salient of these, of course, was the doctrine of the thing-in-itself. We can better understand Fichte's moves in this regard if we reflect that doing away with the thing-in-itself helps to resolve the skeptical problem of the "inference to reality" which many philosophers view as casting doubt on the viability of transcendental arguments. To close the gap between what such arguments show us having unavoidably to presuppose and what is actually the case, it seems that a shift toward idealism is required. But to prevent this from resulting in a form of subjectivism, a more radical deduction of the categories than the one Kant developed also becomes imperative. Rather than being extracted from a table of forms of judgment whose principles of classification can be traced back to Aristotle—the Kantian procedure—the categories must be derived from the basic structure of self-consciousness as such. Only then can we be sure that the categories do not suffer from arbitrariness, and so determine the necessary—that is to say, objective—structure of the world we encounter in experience.

For present purposes, what is most important about Fichte's innovations is the bringing of two aspects of Kant's theory of self-consciousness out into the open. Fichte insists that what Kant calls "pure apperception" is the precondition for the synthetic unity of apperception; otherwise, the acts of thinking which operate the synthesis would themselves have to be synthesized, and we would find ourselves in a regress which could never result in a unitary subject of experience. At the same time, pure apperception discloses a subject which—whatever else it may be—stands as the point of origin of an individualized perspective on the objective world. What is to be done about this seeming conflict between the absoluteness of what Fichte calls the "self-reverting activity" of the I of pure apperception and the awareness of the I as simply whatever remains formally identical in the manifold—as the locus of a *particular* "point of view"? Fichte's answer, in the first published version of his defining philosophical project, which he termed the "theory of systematic knowledge"—or *Wissenschaftslehre*—is that the conflict should not be downplayed or repressed. On the contrary, he argues, it can be shown that the developmental dynamic triggered by this conflict gives rise to all the fundamental structures of human consciousness, and furthermore even provides the basic moral-practical orientation which is inherent in the relation to the world of finite self-conscious beings such as ourselves. In other words, Fichte pioneers a dialectical theory of the constitution of the experienced objective world, profoundly influencing the subsequent development of German Idealism.

Fichte's dialectical procedure is apparent in the three principles which inaugurate his 1794/95 *Wissenschaftslehre*. The first of these is "A = A," which he treats as universally agreed to be indubitable. Because this principle does not assert the existence of A, but only its identity with itself, Fichte also construes it as the hypothetical judgment: "*If* A exists, *then* A exists" (WL94/5: 94/GA, I/2: 257). He argues that the apodictic status of this principle must rest upon that original unity of self-consciousness which we call the "I." There could be no positing of A as existing at all without an I which posits. But the I which is presupposed in any act of positing can be nothing other than its own self-positing, and it is this *self*-positing which guarantees that "A is A because the I *which has posited* A is the same as that *in which* it is posited" (WL94/95: 99–100/GA, I/2: 261 [emphasis added]). Hence A = A is not a Platonic logical truth to be passively registered; instead, it is performatively grounded in the assertion "I am," which posits the I absolutely and without need for any further ground (WL94/5: 97/GA, I/2: 258). Fichte's second principle is: "–A is not equal to A." In this case, Fichte asserts, we have a principle which is conditioned as to content (by which he means what we might call the "referent"), but unconditioned as to form (by which he means what is *asserted* about the content), because negation is a primordial act which cannot be derived from the positing of A = A in the first principle (WL94/5: 102–105/GA, I/2: 264–267).

However, we are now confronted with a fundamental problem. To put the matter in more concrete—and hopefully more accessible—terms: if we start philosophizing only with the principle of self-consciousness, then we can gain no epistemic access to anything other than modifications of consciousness. However, if we start from what *lacks* all consciousness—for example, from a world of the kind portrayed by modern scientific naturalism, consisting, at the base level, exclusively of physical processes—we will never arrive at consciousness; there is simply no place for it in such a world picture. As neither of these extreme views can account for the fact that we *subjectively* encounter an *objective* world, that there is a subject-object *nexus*, there must be a third principle, which will be conditioned as to form, because we know that it *must* assert the compatibility of the self and the not-self, but not as to content, as this compatibility must cashed out in terms of an entirely new notion, which turns out to be that of divisibility, as a basic feature of the I and the not-I: "*In the I, I oppose a divisible not-I to the divisible I*" (WL94/5: 105–110/GA, I/2: 267–272). We can regard this principle as expressing the first synthesis, as reconciling the original thesis (the I) and the original antithesis (the not-I). The subsequent course of Fichte's first presentation of the *Wissenschaftslehre* then seeks dialectically to unfold and resolve all the further contradictions which are contained within this synthesis. In other words, Fichte's goal is simply to stabilize the subject-object nexus. And this means rendering philosophically intelligible our basic grasp of ourselves as experiencing subjects enjoying a particular perspective on a world independent of our experience of it.

An obvious question raised by Fichte's procedure concerns the status of the absolute or self-positing "I," which functions as the basis of the validity of his first principle. On the one hand, Fichte regards it as a decisive advantage of his approach that this I is demonstrable within consciousness. The I is not a metaphysical entity about which we can only ratiocinate. Indeed, it is not an entity at all. It is not even something given in the manner of a fact but is rather what Fichte calls a *"Tathandlung"*—a "fact-deed," a self-reverting activity which establishes its existence as a function of its known identity with itself. But in view of the philosophically demanding—not to say, paradoxical—character of this notion, it is not surprising that Fichte finds it extraordinarily difficult to explain what our supposedly indubitable awareness of the spontaneously self-positing I consists in. At the very beginning of the 1794/95 *Wissenschaftslehre*, for example, he states that his first principle "is intended to express that *Act* [*Tathandlung*] which does not and cannot appear among the empirical states of our consciousness, but rather lies at the basis of all consciousness and alone makes it possible" (WL94/5: 93/GA, I/2: 255). However, in the "Second Introduction to the *Wissenschaftslehre*," written subsequently in 1797, he shifts away from this approach, which treats the existence of the I as a necessary presupposition, and appeals to the notion of intellectual intuition, defining this as:

> the immediate consciousness that I act and what I enact: it is that whereby I know something because I do it. We cannot prove from concepts that this power of intellectual intuition exists, nor evolve from them what it may be.

Everyone must discover it immediately in himself, or he will never make its acquaintance. (IWL2: 38/GA, I/4: 217)

At the same time, Fichte admits that intellectual intuition is never immediately accessed in its pure state, and that it requires "distinguishing what appears in combination in ordinary consciousness," as undertaken by the philosopher, to bring it into view (IWL2: 40/GA, I/4: 219). Yet intellectual intuition cannot be *merely* an abstraction, as then it could not play the fully foundational role which Fichte allots to it; at issue would be something closer to what Kant describes as the "formal unity of consciousness in the synthesis of the manifold of representations," which depends on "a function of synthesis in accordance with a rule" (A105). Because of this, Fichte sometimes states that it is the philosopher who brings intellectual intuition into existence, who animates, as it were, what would otherwise merely be "an inference from the obvious facts of consciousness" (IWL2: 39/GA, I, I/4: 218):

> This self-constructing self is none other than [the philosopher's] own. He can intuit the aforementioned act of the self in himself only, and in order that he may intuit it, he has to carry it out. Freely, and by his own act, he brings it about in himself. (IWL2: 35/GA, I/4: 214)

The Conflict of Life and Speculation in Fichte

The depth of Fichte's new insight into the nature of the self was transformative for a whole generation of German philosophers and creative writers, as Dieter Henrich has frequently underlined.[4] But these advances also raised an acute problem, which can be posed in both ontological and epistemological terms. If "being" is the most general category which we apply to what we encounter in experience, then it seems that being must be denied to the absolute I of Fichte's first principle, given that—as he puts it—the I is "the ground of explanation of all the facts of empirical consciousness" (WL94/5: 96/GA, I/2: 258). At the same time, being is declared to be secondary to transcendental agency, as a determination or limitation of it; as Fichte asserts, "*all existence signifies a restriction of free activity*" (IWL2: 66n/GA, I/4: 249). Accordingly, in the *Wissenschaftslehre nova methodo* of 1798/99, Fichte claims that "freedom"—in other words, the absolute spontaneity of the I— "is the ground of all philosophizing, of all being. Stand upon yourself, stand upon freedom, and you will stand firm" (FTP: 143/GA, IV/3: 362). But once Fichte has proposed this direction of dependency, why should the "freedom" or pure activity of the I not be accorded a *more fundamental* kind of being, on which the existence of natural or artificial entities—and indeed of theoretical constructs, and even moral realities—ultimately depends? After all, a strong case can be made that philosophical explanations must terminate in an ontological ground of some kind, and there are various places where Fichte himself asserts that the self-reverting activity of the I is precisely what establishes it as *being* (e.g., "*The I originally posits unconditionally its own being*" [WL94/5: 99/GA, I/2: 261]). On balance, however, it is fair to say that during the 1790s Fichte's basic tendency is to contrast empirical *being* and transcendental *activity*. He states, for example, that "Being is the character of the not-I, the character of the I is activity" (*Sein ist Charakter des Nicht Ich, der Charakter des Ich ist Thätigkeit* [FTP: 131/GA, IV/3: 356]). But given that the result of this activity is our necessarily individual and *perspectival* encountering of the world, a certain discomfort is produced by Fichte's unqualified prioritization of the having of a perspective as such over the reality which it is a perspective *on*. There seems—*prima facie*—to be considerable tension between Fichte's methodological insistence on the primacy of first-personal awareness, in all its philosophical elusiveness, and his equally strong foundationalism.[5]

It may be tempting to dismiss these somewhat abstruse ontological questions as largely a matter of semantics. Could we not simply regard Fichte's counterposing of "being" and "activity" as the result of a decision to use the term "being" in a restricted sense, even though—as we have seen—he is far from consistent in this respect? However, this issue has major consequences for the way in which we understand the relation between the processes described by transcendental theory and our everyday experience of the world. And here matters become more serious—even existential. We can summarize the problem with reference to Kant's famous claim that transcendental idealism is equivalent to empirical realism, or that—as he puts it—"the difference between the transcendental and the empirical ... belongs only to the critique of cognitions and does not concern their relation to their object" (A57). Fichte adopts this claim, while rejecting the Kantians' notion of the "thing-in-itself" as an *explanans* for which the only evidence is the *explanandum*: "Their earth reposes on a mighty elephant and the mighty elephant—reposes on their earth" (IWL2: 55/GA, I/4: 237). In consequence he is convinced, as we have just seen, that we must analyze the concept of objective reality entirely in terms of representations which are accompanied by what he calls a "feeling of necessity" (IWL1: 6/GA, I/4: 186). The metaphysical and epistemological difficulties involved in explaining how the human mind makes contact with an independent reality thus become the problem of explaining the mode of production of such necessary representations *within* the subject-object nexus made central by Kant. As Fichte explains: "Idealism has no not-I, for it the not-I is only another view of the I. In dogmatism, the I is a particular kind of thing, in idealism the not-I is a particular way of regarding the I" (FTP: 133/GA, IV/3: 356).

Typically, Fichte seems to think he is strengthening his Kantian credentials when he states that, if philosophers had correctly understood Kant's claim regarding the "I think," then "it would have been recognized that whatever we may think, we are that which thinks therein, and hence ... nothing could ever come to exist independently of us, for everything is necessarily related to our thinking" (IWL2: 71/GA, I/4: 253–254). The problem posed by this claim, of course, is that natural or everyday consciousness takes itself to be encountering objects which subsist independently of its awareness of them. Indeed, we could say that the duality which we discovered in Kant's conception of the subject of experience—the subject is portrayed as only a formal *abstraction* from the subject-object nexus, and yet cannot perform its synthetic functions unless it has some free-standing, originary status—is reproduced on the side of the object. For it seems to be intrinsic to the meaning of object-hood that to have experience of an object is to encounter something whose being is not fully reducible to what can be given in such experience, no matter how prolonged. To put this in another way, natural consciousness is spontaneously dogmatic in the special Fichtean sense that it assumes the existence of entities independent of consciousness; and this means that the transcendental philosopher is forced to swim against the tide of commonsense, as it were, to disclose the mechanisms generating what is in effect an illusion. As we noted, the burden of Jacobi's critique of Kant was that the latter could acknowledge the urgency of this issue only by allowing a basic inconsistency to blight his theory.

In his earlier writings of the 1790s Fichte seems to accept the implications of his basic strategy, and to claim that it is the task of philosophy to raise us to a higher viewpoint, from which the belief that the things we encounter in experience are "things in themselves" appears as a "deception," one which is "based upon stopping at the lowest level of reflection."[6] This task has a moral point, Fichte believes, as it is only if human beings cease to understand themselves as simply natural entities within a world of natural entities that they will adequately grasp their own freedom and the goals which it sets them. As the 1790s progress, however, Fichte becomes more cautious. He now places more emphasis on the need to *distinguish between* the transcendental viewpoint and the viewpoint of everyday life. Yet this move still raises the question of which standpoint is to be given ultimate priority, and it is therefore connected with the ontological problem.[7] The complexity of the situation in which Fichte then finds himself is brought out by a footnote in his *Second Introduction to the Wissenschaftslehre* of 1797:

> The philosopher says only in *his own* name: Everything that exists for the I, exists through the I. The I itself, however, itself says in its own philosophy: As surely as I am and live, something exists outside me, which is not there by my doing. How it arrives at such a claim, the philosopher explains by the principles of his philosophy. The first standpoint is the purely speculative one; the second, that of life and scientific knowledge . . . The second is only intelligible on the basis of the first; realism indeed has grounds apart from that, for we are constrained to it by our own nature, but it has no *known and comprehensible* grounds: yet the first standpoint, again, is only there for the purpose of making the second intelligible. Idealism can never be a *mode of thought*, rather it is merely *speculation*. (IWL2: 31n/GA, I/4: 210–211)

The difficulty of the position which Fichte attempts to outline here is that, on the one hand, he denies that there can be a consistent realist position in philosophy, yet, on the other hand, he seems to allow transcendental theory only an *instrumental* status in making everyday consciousness intelligible. This is not his predominant solution, however. For example, toward the end of his Jena period, in the second introduction to the *Wissenschaftslehre nova methodo* of 1798/99, he proposes that it is transcendental theory which discloses ultimate truth—but that this should not pose a problem as long as a strict separation is maintained between the transcendental and the natural or everyday standpoint. As he puts the matter, it is only the novice philosopher, failing to move with sufficient decisiveness from one standpoint to the other, who is "disturbed by REALISTIC doubts in speculation and also disturbed by idealistic doubts in action" (FTP: 107/GA, IV/3: 342).

However, there is surely something disquieting about a philosophical approach which requires such a compartmentalization in the first place. In the 1794/95 *Wissenschaftslehre* Fichte states that all pre-Kantian philosophy affronted common sense (WL94/5: 119/GA, I/2: 282). He presumably means that such thinking explains the status of the world as we naively and directly experience it by means of occult metaphysical entities. It follows from this view that the task of post-Kantian transcendental philosophy should be to render rationally transparent—and thereby vindicate—our everyday experience, by means of a reflexive, internal explication of its structure. We might summarize the anti-metaphysical thrust of Fichte's approach by saying that its aim is to present an alternative vision of our common reality rather than a vision of an alternative reality. However, this formula raises the question: at what point does an alternative vision of reality *become* a vision of an alternative reality? After all, there are many ways, apart from claiming that what is truly real occupies some metaphysical *arrière-monde*, in which things can be envisaged as other than they seem in everyday life. And, however hard he tries, Fichte does not seem able entirely to suppress his discomfort. For example, the *Sonnenklarer Bericht* (*Crystal Clear Report on the Essence of the Latest Philosophy*), a popular work published soon after his move to Berlin, was explicitly intended to debunk what it portrays as the widespread prejudice that the *Wissenschaftslehre* is contrary to commonsense. Here, Fichte goes very far in a fictionalist direction regarding the transcendental structures described by the *Wissenschaftslehre*, suggesting that everyday experience is the unshakeable basis from which philosophical reflection, at its various levels, must depart, and to which it must ultimately lead back. As he puts it:

> The whole difference between that first and the higher potentialities [*Potenzen*]—between the life which is given and gifted to us in advance, as it were, and which we need only accept to make it into our actual life, and the one which is not given, which can be produced solely through self-activity—should be only that one can gaze down from each of the higher potentialities [*Potenzen*], that one can let oneself down into a lower one; from the final one, however, nothing can be seen except itself and one cannot go further down, except into the realm of non-being . . . For this reason it is the authentic foundation and root of all other life. This is why I previously called it the first and fundamental determination of all life. (CCR: 56/GA, I/7: 204)[8]

At the same time, in the *Sonnenklarer Bericht* Fichte still tries to persuade his imagined reader and interlocutor that the meaning of statements regarding unobserved events—he gives the example of the movement of the hands of an unwatched clock, while the reader is sunk in reflection—should be given a strictly verificationist analysis (see CCR:53–55/GAI/7: 201–203). But why should this conception, in which the reality of objects and events must be cashed out in terms of counterfactuals confined to the subject-object nexus of *experience*, be any less an affront to common sense than the metaphysical conjectures which transcendental philosophy was supposed to have overthrown? And why should we be "constrained . . . by our own nature," as Fichte puts it, to be convinced of things which, on his own account, no philosophy can make coherent?

Schelling's Early Work

Fichte's difficulties in defining the relation of transcendental theory to our commonsense ontology provide an important context for understanding the thrust of Schelling's early work. His first published essay, *On the Possibility of a Form of Philosophy in General*, which appeared in 1794, when he was only nineteen, was much indebted to Fichte's programmatic text, *On the Concept of the Wissenschaftslehre*. The title of his second, more substantial publication of the following year, *Of the I as Principle of Philosophy*, sounds like a Fichtean clarion call. However, right from the very first sentences of this text, Schelling strikes non-Fichtean tones:

> Whoever wants to know something also wants his knowledge to have reality. A knowledge without reality is no knowledge. Either our knowledge must be purely without reality—an eternal circuit, a constant, reciprocal flowing of all individual propositions into one another, a chaos in which no element can crystallize—or there must be an ultimate point of reality on which everything hangs, from which all consistency and all form of our knowledge begin, which distinguishes the elements and describes for each the sphere of its ongoing effect in the universe of knowledge. (OI: 71/H-K, I/2: 85)

As we have seen, Fichte interprets the objectivity of our representations in terms of the transcendentally generated feeling of necessity which accompanies them. He fully admits that consciousness spontaneously attributes this necessity to the existence of things as external to itself. But, having described the role of this *process* of attribution, we have the basis of what—for the transcendental philosopher—should count as a satisfactory theory of the encounter between the self and the empirical world. Admittedly one awkwardness remains, namely that Fichte is obliged to posit a "check" (*Anstoss*) that cannot be immanent to consciousness, as it is what occasions the turning-back-on-itself that enables the originally boundless centrifugal impetus of I-hood to become self-consciousness in the first place (WL94/5: 190–191/GA, I/2: 356). But from a Fichtean standpoint this seems a relatively small price to pay for avoiding unsalvageable assumptions regarding a cognitive process in which an "external" reality somehow gets "into" the mind.

Clearly, however, what Schelling means by knowledge having "reality" (*Realität*) is something different from this; he makes no reference to a *feeling* of the necessity of certain representations as experienced by a subject, because what he has in mind is the coincidence of knowing and being as such. Furthermore, as the concluding part of the passage just cited indicates, it is reality—whatever that may turn out to mean—which is more fundamental than knowledge. This approach contrasts sharply with Fichte's suggestion, in the second introduction to the *Wissenschaftslehre nova methodo*, that the pure I disclosed by the philosopher must be regarded "as something necessarily thinkable, as something ideal," and hence as "nothing real" (or nothing "actual"["*würklich*"]). For this entails that the empirical reality of what he terms the "person" turns out to be ultimately—and quite counter-intuitively—dependent on something non-real (FTP: 104/GA, IV/3: 340). By contrast, we might paraphrase Schelling's claim in his opening sentences in the following way: knowledge *articulates* reality; but the necessary structure of knowledge is grounded in the reality which it articulates. The young Schelling's stance on this matter, then, is in certain obvious respects closer to the standpoint of natural consciousness than Fichte's.

The continuing proximity to Fichte is apparent in Schelling's strategy for answering the question: what is that ultimate point on which the validity of all our knowledge depends? He argues that this must be something in which the "*principium essendi* and *cognoscendi*" (the principle of being and that of knowing) "coincide" (OI: 123n/H-K, I/2: 168n). As Kant had already discovered, in considering the nature of the transcendental unity of apperception, there *is* something the thought of which discloses its existence, namely the subject or the self—although he failed to recognize this as a case of intellectual intuition. As we have seen, during the 1790s Fichte pursued and developed this insight from a variety of angles. Inspired by his example, in the *Ichschrift* Schelling mobilizes two main arguments to establish the original identity of thought and being. The first is reminiscent of Descartes. But whereas, according to its surface grammar at least, Descartes' *cogito* suggests that my existence necessarily *follows from* the thought of my existence, Schelling proposes a performative analysis: my being is a precondition of my entertaining the very thought of it. As he points out, in the statement, "If I exist, then I exist," the truth of the consequent is presupposed by the thinking of the antecedent, even though the statement has the form of a hypothetical. Hence it is equivalent to an absolute assertion of existence: "I exist because I exist." Schelling concludes: "My I contains a being which precedes all thinking and representing. It is by being thought, and it is thought because it is; this for the reason that it only is, and is only thought, to the extent that it thinks *itself*" (OI: 75/H-K, I/2: 90).

Schelling's second argument reaches the same terminus, which he calls the "absolute I," along a different path, by considering the status of the subject-object nexus. He points out that, if the subject and object of experience are entirely co-dependent or co-constitutive, then there must be something which grounds the existence of both, for, as we noted earlier, nothing can be dependent for its existence on something which is similarly dependent on it. As he puts it:

> the concept "subject" must lead to the absolute I. For if there were no *absolute I*, then the concept "*subject*," that is, the concept of the I which is conditioned by an *object*, would be the highest. But since the concept "object" contains an antithesis, it must be originally determined purely in opposition to something else that its concept flatly *excludes*, and it cannot therefore be determined merely in opposition to a subject which can only be thought in *relation* to an *object*, and thus not on condition of the *exclusion* of the object. Hence the very concept of an object, and the concept of a subject which is conceivable only in relation to this concept, must lead to an absolute which is flatly opposed to any object, excludes any object. (OI: 76/H-K, I/2: 92)

Schelling summarizes: "Thus the very concepts of subject and object are guarantors of the absolute, unconditionable I" (OI: 77/H-K, I/2: 93).

Both trains of argument are fraught with consequences for the later development of Schelling's thought. It will be noticed, for example, that in the first case, Schelling both asserts an *identity* of thought and being, in line with the concept of intellectual intuition, *and* refers to "a being which precedes all thinking and representing." As we shall discover, this apparent inconsistency will re-emerge, consciously worked out on a grand scale, in the final stage of Schelling's thought. Similarly, Schelling's argument from the reciprocal relativity of subject and object will be central to the second major phase of his work—the so-called "identity philosophy." In the two cases, it is also unmistakable that the quasi-phenomenological character of Fichte's approach is downplayed in favor of straightforward considerations of ontological grounding.

By the later 1790s, Fichte was committed to the view that the absolute, self-reverting activity of the I can be disclosed in consciousness—or at least in the specially focused consciousness of the philosopher. This claim is not easy to make plausible, however, given that the philosopher, like any other human being, is a finite experiencing subject, occupying a determinate perspective on the world. Right from the beginning, then, Fichte's conception encountered much skepticism. Friedrich Niethammer, for example, a philosopher and theologian who was also a colleague of Fichte's in Jena, had no hesitation in rejecting the Fichtean absolute I as chimerical, on the basis that no concept of the unconditioned can have any intuitable content.[9] As we have seen, Fichte tries to turn the incompatibility between the pure I and the empirical I—between "subjectivity" and "identity," to use Dieter Henrich's terms—into an advantage, into the dialectical motor of the *Wissenschaftslehre*. He argues that the conflict between what is absolute and what is relative within human self-consciousness generates the categories which structure our experience of an objective world and is subsequently expressed in a striving to overcome the resistance of objectivity itself, as a constraint on our rational agency. Ultimately, however, Fichte fails to resolve the problems posed by the dualism of condition and conditioned which is central to his mode of explanation. Unable entirely to dissociate explanatory and ontological primacy, he oscillates between the priority of the natural standpoint and that of transcendental determination—an instability which might be described as the revenge of the thing-in-itself.

By contrast, Schelling argues in a purely conceptual manner that there must be an absolute I (a non-objectifiable, entirely reflexive source of all reality) for there to be any genuine cognition, any synthesis between the subject and object of experience at all. Concomitantly, he also stresses, throughout the *Ichschrift*, the relativity and dependency of the Kantian "synthetic unity of apperception"—the unity of self-consciousness—and its epistemic separation from the absolute I. After declaring that "*The essence of the I is freedom*," in the sense of an absolute power of self-positing, Schelling goes on to ask:

> You insist that you should be conscious of this freedom? But are you considering that all your consciousness is possible only through this freedom, and that the condition cannot be contained in the conditioned? Are you considering at all that the I is no longer the pure, absolute I once it occurs in consciousness; that there can be no object anywhere for the absolute I; and that therefore even less is it able to become an object itself? (OI: 84/H-K, I/2: 104)

Schelling concedes that the "I cannot be given through a mere *concept*," because otherwise it could not function as the absolute ground of the unity of concept and intuition, and that therefore "*the I is determined for itself as pure I in intellectual intuition*" (OI: 85/H-K, I/2: 106). However, he then asserts that this intellectual intuition "can occur in consciousness just as little as can absolute freedom" (OI: 85/H-K, I/2: 106). This makes Schelling's position problematic in the opposite sense to that of Fichte. While Fichte struggles to explain how it is possible for the I to have unconditional, self-positing status if we do indeed have experiential access to it, Schelling struggles to establish the link to empirical self-consciousness of an intellectual intuition characterized in ontological terms that seem disconnected from human experience altogether. As he states, we cannot be helped by an intuition which, "insofar as our knowledge is tied to objects, is as alien to us as the I which can never become an object" (OI: 76/H-K, I/2: 91).

In the present context, one consequence of this divergence of views should be highlighted. Fichte's aim in this period is to provide an explanation of the basic structure of our experience, both cognitive and moral—something which cannot be delivered by transcendental realism, or what he calls "dogmatism." He is therefore not directly confronted with the question of *why* there should be an experienced world at all—it is the bare fact of such experience from which the philosopher works back to find its conditions, in a process which Fichte describes as carrying out an "experiment" with consciousness (IWL2: 30/GA, I/4: 209). Those conditions must be strictly immanent. As he states, "No reality other than that of necessary thought falls, therefore, within the compass of philosophy" (IWL1: 28/GA I/4: 207). By contrast, Schelling rises swiftly to the level of an absolute I which "*contains all being, all reality*" (OI: 89/H-K, I/2: 111). But this means that he is faced with the problem—which the *Ichschrift* fails adequately to confront—of accounting for the very fact of the differentiated world of finite experience.

The *Commentaries on the Idealism of the Wissenschaftslehre*

The long essay which Schelling published in installments in the *Philosophisches Journal* in 1797, and which was later republished as *Abhandlungen zur Erläuterung des Idealismus der Wissenschaftslehre* (*Commentaries on the Idealism of the Wissenschaftslehre*), represents a step forward in answering this question. Right from the start of the *Commentaries*, which begin by discussing the correct way to interpret the theory of experience of the *Critique of Pure Reason*, Schelling sounds his distinctive notes. Specifically, he endorses the implicit epistemology of the natural standpoint, rather than—like Fichte—reinterpreting the validity of that standpoint in terms which it would spontaneously resist:

> The sound understanding has never discriminated between representation and thing, let alone opposed them to one another. The consciousness proper to human beings has always consisted in the convergence of intuition and concept, of object and representation, and so too has the solid and incontrovertible conviction of a real world. (CIWL: 75/H-K, I/4: 80)

Schelling goes on to claim that it is "idealism"—by which he means what Kant terms "empirical idealism"—that first discriminated "between the object and the intuition and between the entity and the representation" (CIWL: 75/H-K, I/4: 80). It is clear, then, that Schelling intends to mobilize transcendental idealism against mentalistic idealism, precisely as a vindication of the common-sense conception of experience. For this reason, throughout the *Commentaries* he is critical of the interpretation placed by conventional Kantians on the notion of the "thing-in-itself." The suggestion that an inaccessible, unknowable reality gives rise to the sensory component of our experience is, he suggests, entirely incompatible with the natural attitude. Insofar as any philosophical role *can* be allotted to this clumsy notion, it simply points to the need for a supersensible ground of our experience (see CIWL: 118n/H-K, I/4: 150n). But supersensible, here, does not mean transcendent. Indeed, in the *Commentaries* Schelling does not present himself as dissenting in any fundamental way from Fichte's theory of the supersensible ground. But this immediately raises an exegetical question, because his robust defense of common sense seems incompatible with the two-tier theory—with its hermetic barrier against cross-contamination between life and transcendental philosophy—toward which Fichte was moving at this time. Schelling asks: "How can we retain our composure . . . when the belief in a real world—the foundation of our life and activity—is supposed to have originated not from immediate certainty, but from . . . shadow-images of real objects, not even accessible to the imagination but only to a deadened and uninspired speculation, and hence *our nature* (originally so rich and vital) is supposed to be corrupted and enervated to its very foundations?" (CIWL: 72–73/H-K, I/4: 76). Here Schelling's target is clearly Fichte's claim that our "nature" inclines us toward a realism which has no "known and comprehensible grounds," and that only a transcendental idealism so radical it pushes toward fictionalism offers a coherent theory of experience. But in view of this, how does Schelling interpret Fichte's *Wissenschaftslehre* so as to prevent it from becoming "deadened and uninspired speculation"?

The first point to note in this regard is that the pivotal concept of Schelling's *Commentaries* is that of "mind" or "spirit" (*Geist*) —not the concept of the "I." Naturally, there are strong affinities between the two notions, as both are used to refer to what Fichte calls "self-reverting activity." But there are also significant differences. The most basic of these is that in relating to itself—so Schelling argues—spirit inevitably objectifies itself. As he states, "I designate as *spirit* that which is exclusively *its own* object. To the extent that spirit is to be an object *for itself* it is not *originally* an object but an absolute *subject* for which *everything* (including itself) is an *object*" (CIWL: 78/H-K, I/4: 85). A second important difference is that—in contrast to Fichte—Schelling does not understand the experienced object as a *limitation* or *restriction* of the activity of spirit, on the model of the "not-I." Rather, it is a *realization* of the activity of spirit or, to use another term which Schelling frequently employs in this text, it is a "product" of spirit. In a footnote to the *Commentaries*, Schelling does refer to the product as "*experience*" (*Erfahrung*) (CIWL: 121n/H-K, I/4: 155n), but this phenomenological retreat does not represent the general direction in which he is moving. He also states plainly: "It is only through these modes of activity of our spirit that the infinite world exists and continues to exist, for it is indeed nothing other than our creative spirit itself in its finite productions and reproductions"

(CIWL: 74/H-K, I/4: 78). In other words, Schelling considers the common-sense view of experience as a coincidence of the objective and the subjective, as the convergence of what is *simply there* irrespective of us and our *knowing* of it, to be precisely what is ratified by his basic claim that spirit is simultaneously active and passive, conditioning and conditioned, objectifying and objectified. As he puts it: "This primordial identity of the pure and empirical in us proves to be the proper principle of *transcendental idealism*. It is by means of this principle alone that we can explain why, primordially, there exists in us no distinction between the real and the ideal, between what is *sensed* and what is *enacted*" (CIWL: 120/H-K, I/4: 153–154). This may *look* Fichtean but the difference from Fichte lies in Schelling's claim that experience of an empirical world is not a result of the *splitting apart* and *opposition* of the ideal and real dimensions originally united in the self-producing act of spirit—or of the Fichtean absolute I—but is rather a complex of *manifestations* of that original unity.

Schelling's emphasis on the oppositional polarity constitutive of spirit has a further consequence, which will prove to be crucial for his subsequent philosophical development. If spirit is defined as a unity of contrary tendencies, and if spirit necessarily objectifies *itself*, then the opposing tendencies must themselves be actualized in the object. More specifically, nature, as we experience it, will disclose an inner life or inner dynamic which mirrors or expresses the internally conflictual life of spirit. As Schelling puts it, "In intuition spirit *puts an end* to the original struggle of opposed activities by presenting them in a common product. Spirit *comes to rest*—as it were—in intuition, and sensation holds it fettered to the object" (CIWL: 89/H-K, I/4: 109). We can glean from such formulations that any particular objectification will both express *and* constrain the activity of spirit (bearing in mind that "spirit" is *nothing other than* its own activity). And from this Schelling draws the conclusion that the striving for self-objectification of spirit will realize itself in a developmental sequence of types of natural entity, each successively more adequate to what spirit is, in the sense of more fully and explicitly determining its own concrete existence. The basic model here will be *organic*, because it is in the organism that self-relating activity, the unity of opposing tendencies, finds its highest expression. As Schelling puts it: "Hence, *life* necessarily exists in nature. Just as there exists a series of stages of organization, there will also be a series of stages of life. Only gradually does the spirit approximate to its own nature" (CIWL: 93/H-K, I/4: 115). Nature, therefore, can be understood as process—as a dialectical development toward mind: "The external world lies open like a book before us, so that we may rediscover in it the history of our spirit" (CIWL: 90/H-K, I/4: 110).

It was stated a moment ago that, given Schelling's conception of spirit, nature "as we experience it," will manifest the same internal dynamism of which we are aware within ourselves, as self-conscious and self-determining subjects. But Schelling is on the brink of grasping that the restriction "as we experience it" is unnecessary. If spirit is understood simply as the oppositional unity of the objective and the subjective, of multiplicity and oneness, then there is no reason to consider this oppositional unity as actualized only in the structure of conscious experience. It could be embodied in the dynamic polarities of nature, independently of our specific cognitions of nature, no less than in human consciousness. The *Commentaries on the Wissenschaftslehre* stand at this tipping point, recording a dawning realization that one can turn transcendental consciousness inside out like a glove, as it were. So, it is no surprise that in the same year, 1797, Schelling published his first foray into the philosophy of nature, *Ideas for a Philosophy of Nature*, opening the door onto a new field of investigation, which he rapidly developed in the closing years of the eighteenth century.

Schelling's Philosophy of Nature

In one respect, turning transcendental consciousness inside out might seem like a fairly straightforward operation. It simply makes use of the mirroring relation between subject and object, which Kant has already emphasized, and which we have observed Schelling redoubling. His point is that if this relation is *intrinsic* to the subject, then it must itself be reflected in the internal structure of the object. However, in another sense, the operation is clearly problematic, when regarded from the standpoint of transcendental philosophy. Making knowledge claims about the *absolute inner constitution* of nature appears to conflict with the basic epistemological principle of the transcendental approach—namely that our certainty regarding the existence of worldly entities is derived from our apodictic awareness of the actuality of our own self-consciousness (which itself entails our standing as rational, self-determining beings). Objectivity, on this account, is a transcendental dimension of such self-consciousness, not a status abstracted from empirical encounters with obdurately independent things. As Fichte asserts, at the beginning of the *Foundations of Natural Right*:

> What emerges in the I's *necessary* acting ... itself appears as necessary, i.e. the I feels constrained in its presentation [*Darstellung*] of what emerges. Then one says that the object has *reality*. The criterion of all reality is the feeling of having to present something *just as* it is presented. We have seen the ground of this necessity; the rational being must act in this way if it is to exist as a rational being at all. Hence, we express our conviction concerning the reality of a thing as: "this or that exists, as sure as I live," or "as sure as I am." (FNR: 5/GA, I/3: 314–315)

Fichte does not seek to disguise the fact that his theory makes all existence immanent to consciousness. As he states a couple of paragraphs earlier in the *Foundations of Natural Right*:

> All *being*, that of the I as well as of the not-I, is a determinate modification of consciousness; and without a consciousness there is no being. Whoever claims the opposite assumes a substratum of the I (something that is supposed to be an I without being one) and therefore contradicts himself. (FNR: 4/GA I/3: 314)

Of course, to state that Fichte makes being immanent to consciousness is misleading to the extent that the meaning of the term "immanent" depends on a contrast with the term "transcendent." Because, for Fichte, the notion of a mode of being transcending consciousness is unintelligible, the notion of immanence to consciousness falls away also: what is irreducible is simply the subject-object nexus of experience, of which the transcendental philosopher is a participant observer, liberated from the need to posit occult metaphysical entities. A first question arises, then: what philosophical pressures induced Schelling to abandon the attractions of this approach and to develop a theory of nature as having absolute being in its own right?

This question is best answered with reference to the concept of an organism. In the introduction to his first foray into the philosophy of nature, *Ideas for a Philosophy of Nature* (1797), Schelling argues that certain objects which we encounter in experience compel us to understand them in terms of an inner, constitutive teleology. As he puts it:

> But when you think of each plant as an individual, in which everything concurs together for one purpose, you must seek the reason for that in the *thing outside you*: you feel yourself constrained in your judgement; you

must therefore confess that the unity with which you think it is not merely *logical* (in your thoughts), but *real* (actually outside side you). (IPN: 32/ H-K, I/5: 96)

Of course, Schelling is fully aware of the argument made by Kant, in his immensely influential discussion of organisms as "natural ends" in the *Critique of Judgment*: that judgments regarding the teleological structure of the organism are "reflective" and not determinate. In Kant's own words, we consider something to be an organism on the principle that it should be "*an organized natural product ... in which every part is reciprocally both end and means*" (CJ: §66). However, for Kant, this principle is only a "*maxim* for judging," as the only kind of causality we can comprehend is the temporal antecedent-and-consequent form legitimated transcendentally by its role in the synthesis of intuitions. As "regulative," the principle can foster and guide research into the processes which occur within living things, and in their interchange with their environment, but it cannot claim the objective status belonging to the processes thereby discovered. However, Schelling does not find this position satisfactory. As he puts it:

I have long desired to know just how you could be acquainted with what things are, without the form which you first impose on them, or what the form is without the things on which you impose it. You would have to concede that, *here* at least, the form is absolutely inseparable from the matter, and the concept from the object. (IPN: 33/H-K, I/5: 96)

Schelling's objection to the Kantian approach, then, is that making judgments of teleological structure non-objective deprives us of the means to explain why we feel compelled to regard some entities as organized in this way, but not others. In the *Critique of Judgement*, Kant offers no comment about this, apart from saying that "the concept of a thing as a natural end is, however, certainly one that is empirically conditioned, that is, one only possible under certain conditions given in experience" (CJ: §74). He provides no more precise account of what these "certain conditions" are. But this is not surprising. After all, what could these conditions be other than the fact that the entity in question is *objectively structured* by the reciprocity of means and ends in the interrelation of its parts which features in Kant's principle? As Schelling puts it:

if it rests on your choice whether or not to impose the idea of purposiveness on things outside you, how does it come about that you impose this idea only on *certain* things, and not on *all*, that furthermore, in this representing of purposeful products, you feel yourself in no way *free*, but absolutely constrained. You could give no other reason for either than that this purposive form just belongs to certain *things* outside you, originally and without assistance from your choice. (IPN: 33/H-K, I/5: 96–97)

Why is Kant resistant to this line of argument? Because his deduction of the concept of causality in the first *Critique*, which he derives from the structure of hypothetical judgments, rules out the possibility of an effect which could bring about its own preconditions. Hence, he asserts:

the organization of nature has nothing analogous to any causality known to us . . . *intrinsic natural perfection*, as possessed by things that are only possible as *natural ends*, and that are therefore called organisms, is unthinkable and inexplicable on any analogy to any known physical, or natural, agency, not even excepting—since we ourselves are part of nature in the widest sense—the suggestion of any strictly apt analogy to human art. (CJ: §65)

From these considerations he draws the conclusion that, "The concept of a thing as intrinsically a natural end is, therefore, not a constitutive concept either of understanding or of reason" (CJ: §65).

From Schelling's perspective, Kant's assertion that organic nature defies comprehension in terms of any notion of causality available to us can be connected with his difficulties in accounting for the kind of knowledge produced by transcendental investigation itself. The problem is that transcendental philosophy does not employ the schematized categories which, according to the first *Critique*, are necessary for cognition. But if transcendental philosophy does *not* provide a special form of *knowledge*, capable of assuring us that our everyday and scientific understanding of the world is immune to generalized forms of skepticism, what is the point of it? Once we have started down this path of inquiry, it becomes apparent that Kant's theory of experience—of the subject-object nexus—relies on precisely the notion of causality which he says is unavailable to us. This fact emerges if we examine the central argument of the first *Critique*'s "Transcendental Deduction."

Students of the *Critique of Pure Reason* are familiar with Kant's claim that the analytic unity of apperception is dependent on the synthetic unity of apperception. By this Kant means that it is only the forging of our sensory intuitions into an objective unity that enables to become aware of ourselves as the self-identical subject of experience. As he puts it:

> it is only because I can combine a manifold of given representations in one consciousness that it is possible for me to represent the identity of consciousness in these representations itself, i.e., the analytical unity of apperception is only possible under the presupposition of some synthetic one. (B133–134)

This claim may make it seem as though there is a one-way dependence of the unity of self-consciousness on the process of synthesis. But, of course, this cannot be Kant's meaning. For we can ask: what compels the synthesis in the first place? A question to which the answer seems to be: the pre-existing fact of my self-consciousness, which *requires* the unity of the manifold. Hence, we have here a case of the result occasioning its own preconditions. This point was brought out clearly by Norman Kemp Smith in his classic commentary on the *Critique of Pure Reason*. As he puts it:

> The unity of apperception is analytic or self-identical. It expresses itself through the proposition, I am. But being thus pure identity without content of its own, it cannot be conscious of itself in and by itself. Its unity and constancy can have meaning only through contrast to the variety and changeableness of its specific experiences; and yet, at the same time, it is also true that such manifoldness will destroy all possibility of unity unless it be reconcilable with it. The variety can contribute to the conditioning of apperception only in so far as it is capable of being combined into a single consciousness. Through synthetic unifying of the manifold the self comes to consciousness both of itself and of the manifold.[10]

It should be noted that Kemp Smith states that it is through the process of synthesis that the self "comes to consciousness" of itself. He does *not* suggest that the self—in the sense of the "analytical unity of apperception"—could be originally generated or brought into being by synthesis. As he writes, "the representation of unity conditions *consciousness* of synthesis, and therefore cannot be the outcome or product of it."[11] But this means that Kant, with his orientation toward Newtonian natural science, mistakenly denies that we can comprehend the kind of causality which characterizes organisms: for precisely this retroactive relation of cause and effect obtains between the analytic and synthetic unity of self-consciousness. The question which Schelling's critique of Kant raises, therefore, is whether it is possible to abstract this model from the manner in which it manifests itself in the awareness of the transcendental investigator. First, let us look at how Schelling articulates the model in its objective form—and then at how he justifies the process of abstraction involved.

At the very beginning of his *First Outline of a System of the Philosophy of Nature*, Schelling asserts that anything which is to be an object of philosophy must be regarded as unconditional. Although he does not fully spell out the reasoning behind this claim, it is not hard to supply. Philosophy seeks the rational comprehension of the world, and—as Kant had emphasized—the complete satisfaction of theoretical reason, were it possible, would require us to arrive at the unconditioned. Schelling then develops a series of reflections concerning the unconditioned which he derives from the tradition of transcendental philosophy. No *thing*, he states, can be the unconditioned, because, according to transcendental philosophy, thing-hood or object-hood is always a product:

> although only transcendental philosophy raises itself to the absolute-unconditioned in human knowledge, it nevertheless cannot help demonstrating that every science that is *science* at all has its unconditioned. The above principle thus obtains also for the philosophy of nature: "the unconditioned of nature *as such* cannot be sought in any individual natural object"; rather a *principle* of being, that *itself is not*, manifests itself in each natural object. (FOS: 13/H-K, I/7: 77)

Schelling then explains what this principle must be:

> Now, what is this *being itself* for transcendental philosophy, of which every individual being is only a particular form? If, according to the principles of transcendental philosophy, everything that exists is a construction of the spirit, then *being itself* is nothing other than *the constructing itself*, or since construction is thinkable at all only as activity, *being itself* is nothing other than the *highest constructing activity*, which, although never itself an object, is yet the principle of everything objective. (FOS: 13–14/H-K, I/7: 78)

He concludes that "*the concept of being as an originary substratum should be absolutely eliminated from the philosophy of nature* (just as it has been from transcendental philosophy)." In other words, "Nature should be viewed as unconditioned" (FOS: 14/H-K, I/7: 78).

Schelling's modelling of the philosophy of nature on transcendental philosophy is therefore completely overt, although—as he emphasizes at the very start of the *First Outline*—the philosophy of nature does not operate by seeking the transcendental *conditions* of our experience of the natural world, but rather seeks to construct or "create" (FOS: 5/H-K, I/7: 67) nature out of a recursive interplay of basic opposed forces. The dialectic between a tendentially indefinitely expanding and a constraining force is tracked, as it produces the phenomena of nature in their increasing complexity—a tracking which, if conceptually consistent, should converge with the results of scientific observation and experiment. But it is not simply that Schelling's theory of nature, in a reflective equilibrium, is confirmed—although not determined—by the results of scientific inquiry. In his "Introduction" to the *Outline* Schelling stresses that the notion of nature as abundant self-productivity conforms much better to our everyday experience than any mechanistic conception of it. The difference between common experience and philosophical investigation, then, concerns only the relative weight of emphasis placed on productive *activity*, as opposed to the product. As he puts it:

> Insofar as we posit the totality of objects not merely as a product, but necessarily also as productive, it rises for us to the level of *nature*. And this *identity of the product and productivity*, and nothing other than this, is indeed designated by the concept of nature in common parlance . . . Since the object is never unconditioned, something out-and-out non-objective must be posited in nature, and this absolutely non-objective is precisely that original productivity of nature. In the common view, this disappears in favor of the product; in the philosophical one, by contrast, the product disappears in favor of productivity. The identity of productivity and the product in the *original* concept of nature is expressed through the usual views of nature as a totality that is simultaneously cause and effect of itself, and which, in its duality (which pervades all appearances), is once more identical. (FOS: 202/H-K, I/8: 41)

With this conception of nature Schelling proposes a solution to a fundamental difficulty encountered by Kant's approach in the third *Critique*. We have noted some of the problems that arise for Kant because of his claim that the teleology at work in organisms can be captured only in reflective, and not in determining, judgments. However, Kant also holds that judgments concerning teleological causality will never be fully replaceable by mechanistic explanations. And this raises the further problem: how is the *interaction* between the mechanistically and teleologically structured domains of nature to be theorized? If this interaction is understood as teleological, then mechanisms can be inflected by purpose, and so cease to display the rigidity of standard physical causality. If the interaction is mechanistic, then the organism effectively ceases to be such: we would consider a presumed organism which reacted to physical stimulation or impact in the same way as a pebble or a wristwatch to be not in fact—or no longer—a living thing. In §77 of the *Critique of Judgment* Kant responds to this difficulty by arguing that, for an "archetypal" or "intuitive" understanding (a mind for which the thought of things and their being are indistinguishable) mechanical and teleological causality would not contradict each other. For such a mind, a synthetic grasp of the whole of nature coterminous with an understanding of the mechanical interaction of its parts would be possible. Our discursive intellects are not like this, however, and so we can never fully eliminate the incompatibility between teleology and mechanism. By contrast, Schelling's argues that his conception of nature as a self-producing, self-relating whole resolves the problem by revealing that mechanism can only function in patches *within* such a whole. "Unlimited mechanism," he states, "would destroy itself" (VWS, H-K, I/6: 69). We can understand why this is so by considering that mechanistic explanation accounts for the existence of wholes in terms of the causal interaction of their parts. But the internal configuration of the parts, taken as the ground of the kinds of interactions they produce, would in turn require mechanistic explanation, thereby generating a regress. Consequently, on Schelling's account, cause-and-effect sequences can only operate when *"enclosed within specific limits"* (VWS, H-K, I/6: 69), defined by self-related and self-determining totalities, and ultimately by the self-producing whole which is nature. As he puts it:

> Viewed from *this* height, the individual sequences of causes and effects (which deceive us with an appearance of mechanism) disappear, since they are infinitely small straight lines within the universal circular path of organism along which the world itself proceeds. (VWS, H-K, I/6: 69)

In other words, Schelling's solution to Kant's problem of the interface between mechanism and teleology is that *"One and the same principle binds together inorganic and organic nature*" (VWS, H-K, I/6: 69): the principle of self-organization.

But still, perhaps, one might have methodological worries about Schelling's approach. For by what right can he claim to have attained the panoramic "height" from which he presents his solution, by abstracting the principle of self-construction in transcendental philosophy from the unique, first-personal mode of access of the transcendental philosopher to the constructive activity? This question is directly tackled by Schelling in his important essay of 1801, "On the True Concept of the Philosophy of Nature and the Correct Way of Solving its Problems" ("Über den wahren Begriff der Naturphilosophie und die richtige Art ihre Probleme aufzulösen"). Here he points out that transcendental philosophy in the Fichtean mode simply presupposes the existence of—and focuses on—the self-consciousness of the investigator. Schelling therefore invokes, with explicit reference to the *Wissenschaftslehre*, the notion of philosophy *about* philosophizing (UWB, H-K, I/10: 89). And he goes on to state:

> There is no question that this philosophy concerning philosophizing is subjectively the *first* (in relation to the philosophizing subject). And it is just as little to be doubted that, in posing the question "how is philosophy possible?" I already take *myself* in the highest *Potenz*, and thus only answer the question for this *Potenz*. To derive this *Potenz* itself cannot be demanded of the process of responding, since the *question* itself already presupposes it. (UWB, H-K, I/10: 89)

How, then, is it possible to rise to the level of the highest—in other words: the most fully self-transparent—*Potenz*, that of a philosophical thinking which comprehends even its own preconditions, if self-consciousness circumscribes the domain which this thinking can legitimately explore? In "On the True Concept" Schelling insists: "I have not presupposed anything at all except what shows itself as a first principle immediately from the conditions of knowing" (UWB, H-K, I/10: 95). In other words, we are directly aware that self-consciousness consists in the unity of subject and object, or—in Fichte's language—that the self is that which posits itself *as* self-positing. Nothing *external* to this self-positing structure could bring it into existence: this is Fichte's fundamental point against "dogmatism," a term that he applies to any attempt to derive the I from the not-I, or to posit a ground of experience external to experiencing consciousness. However, according to Schelling, this does not entail that the self-positing structure could not first exist at a level below self-consciousness, and progressively rise to the self-conscious level, through a series of stages. And he proposes to arrive at this original structure by abstracting from the *subjective* aspect of intellectual intuition, through a process in which the I is "depotentiated" (*depotenziert*) (see UWB, H-K, I/10: 89). In other words, we need not assume that the structure under investigation is accessible uniquely from a participant-observer perspective—especially given our sense of its pervasive outer manifestations in nature. This does not, of course, mean that one can abstract from the *subjectivity of the philosopher* who reconstructs the unfolding of subject-object identity in its advance from its unconscious to its fully self-conscious form, with which transcendental philosophy usually begins. To the ensuing question whether transcendental philosophy or *Naturphilosophie* is to be considered primary, Schelling's answer is now unequivocal: "Without doubt, the philosophy of nature, since it is this which first allows the *standpoint* of idealism to arise, and thereby creates for it a more secure, *purely* theoretical foundation" (UWB, H-K, I/10: 96). This claim does not represent a lapse into dogmatism in the Fichtean sense, as far as Schelling is concerned, because "There is an idealism of nature, and an idealism of the I. On my reckoning, the former is the original, the *latter* is derived" (UWB, H-K, I/10: 88). Clearly, however, this new distinction between an objective and a subjective idealism is not one which Fichte could find acceptable.

The Debate between Fichte and Schelling

In the summer of 1799, the two philosophers began a sustained correspondence on friendly terms, seemingly in the conviction of being embarked on what was, in its fundamentals, a shared enterprise. There was even talk of launching a journal. Fichte was aware, of course, of Schelling's first publications on the philosophy of nature, but he avoided sending him any detailed assessment of them. This was not simply a matter of diplomacy. As we have seen, the methodology of Schelling's philosophy of nature is closely modelled on that of transcendental philosophy—so closely, indeed, that it would be quite easy to assume that Schelling is engaged in a transcendental deduction of the various levels of phenomena in nature. It is true that Schelling refers—for example, in the introduction of the *Ideas for a Philosophy of* Nature—to "the absolute identity of mind *in* us and nature *outside us*" (IPN: 42/H-K, I/5: 107). But the "us" in this formula *could* be taken to refer to human beings as empirical beings, and not to the subjective points of origin of perspectives on an objective world, whose transcendental structure can only be elucidated from within. However, once Fichte had read the *System of Transcendental Idealism*, which Schelling sent to him on publication in 1800, it was no longer possible to sustain the ambiguity, given that the preface to this work refers repeatedly to two opposed but complementary "fundamental philosophical sciences." The unmistakable divergence between the two philosophers which this formulation laid bare led to an ever more acrimonious exchange of views, and eventually to the breaking-off of their correspondence early in 1802.

In his letter to Schelling of November 15, 1800, Fichte clearly expresses for the first time his objections to the twin-track approach of the preface to the *System of Transcendental Idealism*, whose innovations still reverberate in Schelling's slightly later essay on the true concept of the philosophy of nature. Fichte refuses to accept the dualism of the philosophy of nature and transcendental philosophy, insisting that nature is constructed not according to its own laws but according to the necessary laws of our consciousness. It is only as a result of the abstraction carried out by empirical science, which takes nature alone as its object, that the natural world comes to appear as self-constituting. As Fichte puts it:

> However, I still do not agree with *your opposition between transcendental philosophy* and philosophy of nature. Everything seems to be based on a confusion between *ideal* and *real* activity, which we have *both* occasionally made; and which I hope completely to remove in my new presentation. In my opinion, *the thing* is not *added* to *consciousness*, nor *consciousness to the thing*, but both are immediately united in the I, the *ideal-real, real-ideal*.— The *reality of nature* is something else again. The latter appears in transcendental philosophy as something thoroughly *found*. Indeed, as something *finished* and *completed*; and the former, to be sure (namely, found), not according to its *own* laws, but according to the *immanent laws of intelligence* (as ideal-real). Science only makes nature into its object through a subtle abstraction, and obviously has to posit nature as something *absolute* (precisely because it abstracts from intelligence), and lets nature *construct itself* by means of a *fiction*; just as transcendental philosophy lets consciousness construct itself by means of an *equivalent fiction*. (FSC: 42/H-K, III/2,1: 276)

Fichte's endorsement of a fictionalist reading of transcendental idealism at this point is striking.[12] It highlights an important—and confusing—feature of the epistolary debate with Schelling. Both philosophers' views, but especially those of Fichte, are rapidly evolving during the period, so that criticisms made by their interlocutor are often directed at a moving target and are already outdated by the time they are formulated, frequently through no fault of the critic. In the present case, Schelling does not pick up on Fichte's fictionalism, but rather replies with a clear summary of the conception of the relation of *Naturphilosophie* and transcendental philosophy which he had reached by this point. He states that he finds in the I two opposed activities. Nature is the "ideal-real, *merely* objective, and for precisely this reason also producing I." The I of self-consciousness is the "higher *Potenz*" of this self-producing I, which is the activity which lies at the basis of nature. Reality is only *found* according to the "immanent laws of intelligence" by the philosopher—not, however, by the "object of philosophy" which is "not the finder, but rather that which itself produces" (FSC: 44/H-K, III/2,1: 279). Schelling goes on to state that, although Fichte's *Wissenschaftslehre* may bring the "formal proof of idealism" and therefore be the "supreme science," it is not what he now calls "philosophy," which constitutes the "*material* proof of idealism":

> In this discipline, the task is to deduce nature with all its determinations, indeed in its objectivity, its independence not from the I which is itself objective, but from the I that is subjective and does the philosophizing. This occurs in the theoretical part of philosophy. The discipline arises through an abstraction from the general *Wissenschaftslehre*. Specifically, one abstracts from the subjective (*intuiting*) activity that posits the subject-object as identical with *itself* in consciousness, and through that identical positing first becomes = I (the *Wissenschaftslehre* fails to suspend this subjective identity and is for that very reason ideal-realistic). (FSC: 44/H-K, III/2,1: 280)

Fichte's mistake, then, from Schelling's point of view, is to insist on interpreting the I exclusively in terms of his version of the unity of apperception, rather than grasping that, if the I is indeed the "ideal-real, real-ideal" unity, as Fichte claims, then it can also be understood *objectively*, as that activity of self-constitution which is *natura naturans*. Self-consciousness, according to Schelling, only emerges when this real-ideal activity itself becomes, through a further reflexive turn, explicitly the focus of consciousness.

Fichte's response to Schelling—in the draft of a letter, which he decided not to send—is predictable. In describing the self-conscious I as a higher potentiality of nature, and therefore as having arisen from nature, Schelling is simply revolving in a circle:

> The matter is as follows: in line with everything that has so far been clearly presented, the subjective—in its subjective-objective nature—cannot be anything other than the *analogue of our self-determination* (nature as *noumenon*) that *we*, through thinking, have *imported* into what is the creation (incontestably ours) of our imagination. The I cannot in its turn be explained *conversely* from something that elsewhere had been completely explained *by it*. (FSC: 48/H-K, III/2,1: 289–290)

However, a paragraph of Fichte's unposted letter (the gist of which is repeated in the response which he did finally send) makes a remarkable concession to Schelling's basic argument that the perspective on the world of finite intelligence cannot be regarded as the *absolute* philosophical point of departure. Fichte writes:

> transcendental idealism as the system that moves within the circumscribed area of the subject-objectivity of the I, as finite intelligence, and of its original limitation through *material feeling* and *conscience*, is able completely to deduce the sense world within this circumscribed area, but absolutely does not embark on any explanation of the original limitation itself. There still remains the question, were the right to go *beyond the I* first established, whether one might be able also to explain those original limitations; [to explain] conscience from the intelligible as noumenon (or God), and [to explain] feelings, which are only the lower pole of the former, from the manifestation of the intelligible in the sensible. This yields two new, completely opposed parts of philosophy, which are united in transcendental idealism as their midpoint. Finite intelligence as spirit is the *lower Potenz* of the intelligible as noumenon; and this intelligence, as *natural being*, is the highest *Potenz* of the intelligible as nature. Now, if you have taken the subjective in nature to be the intelligible, which consequently cannot in any way be derived from finite intelligence, then you are entirely right. (FSC: 48–49/H-K, III/2,1: 290)

Fichte's willingness to speak of going "beyond the I," even if only tentatively, makes clear that the relation between his thinking and that of Schelling is moving into a new phase. The two philosophers are now agreed that "finite intelligence," even in its maximally reflective mode, cannot be regarded as the ultimate basis of explanation, even though it may function as a provisional starting point. This convergence even seems to allow a temporary *détente* in the conflict between them. Thus, in one letter Schelling remarks that it appears

> that we both acknowledge only One and the same absolute cognition which is identical and ever-recurring in all acts of cognition, and which both of us endeavor to present and make evident in all domains of knowledge. (FSC: 52/H-K, III/2,1: 349)

The issue is now the method of gaining access to this absolute knowing and how it is to be characterized.

Fichte's first significant published move in this direction can be found in *The Vocation of Man* (*Die Bestimmung des Menschen*). This work, intended for the general educated public, was published in 1800, after Fichte's resignation from the University of Jena and move to Berlin, following the furore provoked by an article on religion he had published two years earlier in the *Philosophisches Journal*.[13] The text, written primarily in the form of a first-person meditation, is divided into three books. In the first, the meditator finds himself compelled by reflection on his place within nature to concede the irrefutability of a deterministic view of the world, a conclusion which leads to doubt and despair. In the second book, he is guided, through conversation with a visiting "spirit," toward adopting the standpoint of a radical transcendental idealism, in which the objective world is constructed by and for the experiencing self. At the start of the final book, however, it becomes clear that this conception cannot account for the plurality of experiencing subjects, nor for the fact that these subjects interact freely within a shared world, about which they are able to communicate. In fact, the meditator realizes that no theoretical demonstration can establish these truths, which impose themselves via an unconditional moral demand:

> I am aware of appearances in space to which I transfer the concept of myself; I think of them as beings like myself. Speculative philosophy, taken to its conclusion, has taught me or will teach me that these supposed rational beings outside of me are nothing but products of my own mind... But the voice of conscience calls to me: whatever these beings may be in and for

themselves, you ought to treat them as free autonomous beings completely independent of you . . . From this standpoint I will not be able to see them any other way, and that speculation will disappear before my eyes like an empty dream. (VM: 76/GA, I/6, 262)

From these reflections, the meditating self draws the general conclusion:

No knowledge can be its own foundation and proof. Every knowledge presupposes something still higher as its foundation, and this ascent has no end. It is faith, this voluntary acquiescence in the view which naturally presents itself to us because only on this view can we fulfill our vocation—it is this which first gives approval to knowledge and raises to certainty and conviction what, without it, could be mere deception. Faith is no knowledge, but a decision of the will to recognize the validity of knowledge. (VM: 71/GA, I/6, 257)

Fichte sent a copy of *The Vocation of Man* to Schelling, and in one of his letters he describes it as containing the first indications of a *"transcendental system of the intelligible world"* (FSC: 49/H-K, III/2,1: 288). It does so because faith (*Glaube*) now takes priority over knowledge and does the work of grounding self-conscious existence in something profounder than itself. Faith becomes the assumption of a law of the spiritual world, "which is not given by my will nor by the will of any finite being nor by the will of all finite beings taken together, but to which my will and the will of all finite beings are themselves subject" (VM: 104/GA, I/6: 290). "This will," Fichte continues, "unites me with itself; it unites me with all finite beings like me and is the general mediator between all of us. That is the great secret of the invisible world and its fundamental law" (VM: 107–108/GA, I/6: 293) Schelling, however, is entirely dissatisfied with this solution:

The necessity to start from seeing confines you and your philosophy in a thoroughly conditioned series, in which no trace of the absolute is to be encountered. The consciousness or the feeling of the absolute which this philosophy must itself have had, compels you, in the *Vocation of Man*, to transfer what is speculative into the sphere of faith, since you simply cannot find it in your *knowing*; in my opinion there can as little be discussion of faith in philosophy as in geometry. (FSC: 61/H-K, III/2,1: 374)

Schelling's dissatisfaction is not simply with the notion that faith could play a fundamental methodological role. As his first sentence indicates, he does not believe it possible to ascend via a series of syntheses from a "seeing"—from the self-transparency of transcendental reflection—to the absolute for which both he and Fichte are striving. As he puts it:

> Either you must never move away from *seeing*, as you express yourself, and that means precisely from subjectivity, and then *every single I*, as you say at one point in the *Wissenschaftslehre*, must be the absolute substance and remain so, or if you move away from it to an equally incomprehensible real ground, this whole reference to subjectivity is merely *preliminary*, something prior to finding the true principle ... *in order to maintain your system*, one must first *decide* to start from seeing and end with the absolute (the genuinely speculative), more or less in the way that, in the Kantian philosophy, the moral law must come first and God last, if the system is to hold up. (FSC: 61/H-K, III/2,1: 374)

We have already noted that these philosophical exchanges are made more tangled by the fact the views of both thinkers are constantly shifting. Schelling moves from a position which emphasizes the dualism of *Naturphilosophie* and transcendental philosophy, to a theory of absolute identity, of which nature and self-consciousness are the two relative facets. Similarly, a couple of months prior to Schelling's criticism of *The Vocation of Man*, in his letter of October 3, 1801, Fichte had already sent a letter which contained an extremely compressed, not to say obscure, presentation of the new philosophical position recorded in the 1801/2 version of the *Wissenschaftslehre*, which remained unpublished during his lifetime. Fichte now realizes that the status of certain objective truths—his example: the truth that there exists only one straight line between any two points—requires an expansion of the ground of truth beyond individual consciousness, in two respects. Firstly, it is apodictically clear to us *a priori* that this truth applies to *any* straight line. Such truths are universal in the dimension of what Fichte, in his letter to Schelling, calls the "*Von*"—the dimension of what they are *of* or about. But we also cannot doubt that that this truth must be valid *for* any possible consciousness, in the dimension which Fichte calls the "*Für*." Hence the self-consciousness of the individual is now located at the crossroads of these two dimensions of universality, and it is our knowledge of this very status of knowledge, which abstracts from everything perspectival, that Fichte now calls "absolute knowing" (see FSC: 54–59/H-K, III/2,1: 363–370). This development can in fact be seen as resulting from a new, destabilizing awareness on Fichte's part of the gap between what we implicitly *know* knowledge itself to be, and what can be demonstrated through transcendental argumentation. This gap has been the focus of two critiques that have recurred throughout the subsequent literature on the topic, right up to the present day: firstly, transcendental arguments are *parochial* (they can, at best, only demonstrate what is valid for "me" or for "us"); secondly, they are *subjective* (they show what I or we cannot avoid thinking or believing, but do not license any inference to what is objectively the case).[14]

However, even with his revised conception of the tasks of the *Wissenschaftslehre*, Fichte does not abandon the basic method of successive syntheses, intended to resolve the contradictions immanent in self-consciousness. Thus, the concept of our participation in an intelligible "world of spirits" or *Geisterwelt* resolves the conflict between particularity and universality within knowing; but the simultaneous union and disjunction (or plurality) of the world of spirits must itself be grounded in something more ultimate which Fichte calls the "absolute" or "God." From this new standpoint, Fichte feels empowered to accuse Schelling of "jumping over" the *epistemic* question regarding access to the absolute and its effects. As he puts it:

> The absolute would not be the absolute if it existed under some kind of form. But where does this form . . . come from under which the absolute *appears* . . . ? Or again, how does the *one* become an *infinity*, and then a totality of the manifold?—That is the question that a conclusive speculation has to solve, and which you necessarily have to ignore because you find this form straightaway in and with the absolute." (FSC: 66/H-K, III/2,1: 381–382)

Fichte now avoids the accusation that he has made the absolute, which should be the starting point, a product of synthesis (and hence had made the infinite dependent on the finite) by arguing that the absolute lies beyond what can be determined—beyond the last synthesis. All differentiation is introduced by knowing. As he puts it:

> it is entirely clear to me that the absolute can only have one absolute *expression*, i.e. in relation to manifoldness, it can only be an expression that is thoroughly *one*, simple, and eternally equal to itself; and this is precisely *absolute knowledge*. The absolute *itself*, however, is neither being nor knowing,

nor identity, nor the indifference of the two; but it is precisely—*the absolute*—and to say anything further is a waste of time. (FSC: 73/H-K, III/2,1: 403)

Even such a noted partisan of Fichte as Martial Guéroult, in his matchless account of the shifting relations between the two thinkers, concedes that Fichte was motivated to move beyond the standpoint of self-consciousness by Schelling.[15] However, the elder philosopher did not shift in the direction of Schelling's conception of the emergence of self-conscious subjectivity *from* material nature. In the correspondence, Fichte acknowledges that nature must be seen as a manifestation of the "intelligible," of which self-consciousness is a higher power. But he has great difficulty in accommodating philosophically the independent, self-moving power of organic life, as Schelling relentlessly pointed out in his later polemic of 1806.[16] At the same time, Fichte's warning to his rival regarding the inaccessibility of the absolute *per se* contains an insight which will only come to astonishing fruition much later in Schelling's own work. Schelling will eventually come to see that the "identity system," his theory of reality as self-differentiating reason, is—as Fichte presciently puts it— "in relation to the absolute only *negative*" (FSC: 72/H-K, III/2,1: 402).

Notes

1. Friedrich Heinrich Jacobi, "David Hume on Faith, or Idealism and Realism, A Dialogue," in *The Main Philosophical Writings and the Novel Allwill*, trans. and ed. George di Giovanni (Montreal and Kingston: McGill-Queen's University Press, 1994), 337.
2. For further helpful discussion of this point, see Sebastian Gardner, "Transcendental Philosophy and the Possibility of the Given," in *Mind, Reason and Being-in-the-World. The McDowell-Dreyfus Debate*, ed. Joseph K. Schear (London: Routledge, 2013), 112–118.
3. Dieter Henrich, "Die Identität des Subjekts in der transzendentalen Deduktion," in *Kant. Analyse-Probleme-Kritik*, ed. H. Oberer and G. Seel (Würzburg: Konigshausen & Neumann, 1988), 44.
4. See, for example, Dieter Henrich, *Between Kant and Hegel. Lectures on German Idealism* (Cambridge, MA: Harvard University Press, 2008), 216–230.
5. For an excellent discussion of these issues, to which I am indebted, see Sebastian Gardner, "The Status of the *Wissenschaftslehre*: Transcendental and Ontological Grounds in Fichte," in *Internationales Jahrbuch des Deutschen Idealismus/International Yearbook of German Idealism*, vol. 7 (Berlin: de Gruyter, 2009).

6. Fichte, "Concerning the Difference between the Spirit and the Letter in Philosophy," in *Early Philosophical Writings*, trans. and ed. Daniel Breazeale (Ithaca, NY: Cornell University Press, 1988), 206 ("Ueber Geist, u. Buchstaben in der Philosophie", GA, II/3: 331).
7. For an informative account of the oscillations in Fichte's position on this issue during his early period, to which I am indebted, see Daniel Breazeale, "The Standpoint of Life and the Standpoint of Philosophy," in *Thinking Through the Wissenschaftslehre: Themes from Fichte's Early Philosophy* (Oxford: OUP, 2013). Breazeale, however, does not draw any negative conclusions from his discussion with regard to the viability of Fichte's project.
8. Fichte's adoption of Schelling's term *"Potenz"* is a feature of a brief phase of his work in the early 1800s, confirming a certain influence of the younger thinker. Despite the increasingly hostile tone, theirs was not entirely a *dialogue des sourds*.
9. See Friedrich Immanuel Niethammer, "Von den Ansprüchen des gemeinen Verstandes an die Philosophie," in *Philosophisches Journal einer Gesellschaft Teutscher Gelehrten* (Hildesheim: Georg Olms Verlagsbuchhandlung, 1969). For a helpful discussion, see Richard Fincham, "Refuting Fichte with 'Common Sense': Friedrich Immanuel Niethammer's Reception of the Wissenschaftslehre 1794/5," *Journal of the History of Philosophy* 43, no. 3 (July 2005).
10. Norman Kemp Smith, *A Commentary to Kant's Critique of Pure Reason* (with a new introduction by Sebastian Gardner), (Basingstoke: Palgrave MacMillan, 2003), 285.
11. *A Commentary to Kant's Critique of Pure Reason*, 284.
12. For further discussion of this fictionalist shift, and an insightful treatment of the issues at stake in the Fichte–Schelling debate in general, see Robert Seymour, *Negative and Positive Philosophy in the Late Work of Fichte and Schelling* (PhD Thesis, University of Essex, 2019), chapter 2.
13. See J. G. Fichte, "On the Ground of our Belief in a Divine World-Governance," in *J. G. Fichte and the Atheism Dispute*, ed. Curtis Bowman and Yolanda Estes (London: Routledge, 2010). ("Über den Grund unseres Glaubens an eine göttliche Weltregierung," in GA, I/5.)
14. See David Bell, "Transcendental Arguments and Non-Naturalistic Anti-Realism", in *Transcendental Arguments: Problems and Prospects*, ed. Robert Stern (Oxford: Clarendon Press, 2003), 189–193.
15. See Martial Guéroult, *L'évolution et la structure de la doctrine de la science chez Fichte* (Paris: Les Belles Lettres, 1930), vol. 2, 6–39.
16. See Schelling, *Statement on the True Relationship of the Philosophy of Nature to the Revised Fichtean Doctrine*, trans. Dale E. Snow (Albany NY: SUNY Press, 2018) (*Darlegung des wahren Verhältnisses der Naturphilosophie zur verbesserten Fichteschen Lehre*, in H-K, I/16, 1).

2
Agency and Absolute Identity

Schelling's Response to Kant and Reinhold

In the previous chapter we found Schelling deeply preoccupied with the tension between common-sense realism and transcendental idealism. Fichte, the main contemporary influence on Schelling's early work, considers himself to be defending the full-blooded equation of empirical realism and transcendental idealism against the skepticism engendered by Kant's own distinction between appearances and things-in-themselves. Indeed, some commentators regard this anti-skepticism as one of the most important drivers of his early philosophy. But to achieve a watertight epistemological anti-skepticism, Fichte must deny the intelligibility of the notion of existence independent of transcendental consciousness. As noted in the previous chapter, in the introduction to the *Foundations of Natural Right*, he states: "All *being*, that of the I as well as of the not-I, is a determinate modification of consciousness; and without some consciousness, there is no being" (FNR: 4/GA I/3: 314). However, as far as Schelling is concerned, we emphatically do not—in everyday life—regard the objects which we encounter merely as "determinate modifications" of consciousness, or as radically dependent upon it. And Schelling is not satisfied with Fichte's expedient of partitioning natural from transcendental consciousness, with all the problems of priority that this maneuver engenders. We observed that, in his *Commentaries on the Idealism of the Wissenschaftslehre*, Schelling's resistance to the Fichtean interpretation of transcendental idealism leads to his move toward an innovative conception of the self-objectification of spirit, an advance which was to play a fundamental role in the subsequent development of German Idealism. But in the *Commentaries* Schelling also makes a significant intervention into the post-Kantian debates concerning human freedom.

In the second volume of his *Letters on the Kantian Philosophy* (1792), Karl Leonhard Reinhold had raised an influential objection to Kant's equation of freedom with the self-activation of practical reason, that is to say: with adherence to the moral law purely for the sake of its formal universality. He argued that Kant's view made it impossible to hold human beings responsible for their immoral actions because it entailed that we are *not* free when we transgress the moral law—and we cannot be held accountable for actions we do not freely perform. In a later text, the comments on Kant's introduction to his *Metaphysical Foundations of the Doctrine of Right*, Reinhold also points out that, if our immoral actions are unfree, in the sense of being compelled uncontrollably by our impulses or desires, then our moral actions cannot be free either, as they can then only occur *on condition that* a countervailing force is lacking.

In the *Critique of Practical Reason*, and—at greater length—in the first book of *Religion within the Boundaries of Mere Reason*, Kant tried to address this problem by introducing a distinction between "*Wille*" (rational will) and "*Willkür*" (power of choice). He argued that human beings must be regarded as making a defining noumenal choice of their intelligible character, which can only be morally good or morally bad. Which of these a person's basic moral disposition (*Gesinnung*) turns out to be will depend, in Kant's rigorist conception, on whether she does or does not accept the moral law as supreme in all circumstances. But this attempted solution to the problem of moral responsibility produced at least as many difficulties as it resolved. Most fundamentally, Kant has accepted the notion of a power of choice which appears to operate *prior to* moral obligation, given that it first sets a person *under* the moral law—in which case, how is it possible to argue that one *ought to choose* to place oneself under this law? Kant's argument also appears to make the inaugural option for moral evil inexplicable—for why would the will choose *not* to be free, in the sense of self-determining, thereby negating itself as will? These difficulties come into focus in a passage from the *Metaphysics of Morals*, where Kant states:

> Although experience shows us that man as a sensible being has the capacity to choose in opposition to as well as in conformity with the law, his freedom as an intelligible being cannot be defined by this, since appearances cannot make any supersensible object (such as free choice) understandable. We can also see that freedom can never be located in a rational subject's being able to make a choice in opposition to his (lawgiving) reason, even though experience proves often enough that this happens (though we still cannot conceive how this is possible). (MM: 52/AA, VI: 226)

In short, as Kant himself concedes, his theory makes the choice of moral evil philosophically unintelligible.

In opposition to Kant, Reinhold denies that practical reason as such is to be equated with the free will. Rather, in his account, reason determines the moral law but it is the will as a "capacity of the person" (EBFW: 217) which determines us to act either in accordance with this law, or—in pursuit of the satisfaction of our "selfish drive"—regardless of it. Kant's conception of practical reason is not irrelevant to Reinhold's account, as without an awareness of what it prescribes we would not understand the difference between moral and immoral behavior. But Reinhold not only insists that reason as such cannot bring about action; he argues that, if pure reason *could* be practical, the result would not be freedom but necessity, because it would be inflexible, universal rationality as such, and not the particular human subject, which would determine all genuine agency. He concludes:

> *Pure* will cannot therefore mean a particular *kind* of will, but only one of the two possible expressions of the *free will*, namely that which is in conformity with the practical law, the process of *willing morally* . . . The will ceases to be free if one regards it one-sidedly, and makes its nature consist either solely in its relation to the unselfish drive, or solely in its relation to the selfish drive, if one considers oneself *subjugated* by the law of nature. Through each of these two laws the will becomes independent of the other, but it is through the capacity for self-determination that it is dependent on itself alone. (EBFW: 256–258)

In the *Commentaries* Schelling expresses points of agreement and disagreement with both Kant *and* Reinhold:

> *Both* therefore (Kant and Reinhold) are correct; the *will gives* laws (according to Kant) which *reason announces* (Reinhold). However, when the former states that the will is nothing other than practical reason itself, it is more natural, rather, to say the reverse: practical reason (what is lawgiving in us) is the will itself; for everyone is immediately aware of a practical reason which commands us through the law, but not of the original will, whose voice only reaches us through the medium of reason. When Reinhold, on the contrary, states that the laws in general *stem* only *from reason*, that the moral law is the demand which *pure* reason places on the will, this is fundamentally false, and an assertion that cancels all autonomy

of the will. *For reason* (originally a merely theoretical capacity) only becomes *practical* reason by virtue of expressing the material of a higher will. It has no authority in itself, and no moral power over us; what it announces as law is valid only insofar as it is endorsed by the absolute will. (CIWL: 124–125/H-K, I/4: 159–160)

Clearly, Schelling thinks that Reinhold's approach cannot explain why reason's procedure of universalization should exercise any obligatory force over us. (Reinhold in fact invokes an "unselfish drive," in an attempt to fill this gap in his theory with a psychological mechanism.) This is because he lacks the notion of an "absolute will." For Schelling, Kant's conception of legislating reason must be understood as the expression of such an absolute will, if we are to comprehend how reason can be genuinely practical. But what exactly does Schelling mean by the "absolute will"? In essence, he treats the term as a synonym for the self-constituting activity of "spirit," which, as we learned in the previous chapter, takes the form of a repeated process of self-objectification, and overcoming of the resulting opposition. Schelling's argument, then, is that the obligatory force of the moral law is in fact the pressure exerted by spirit in its pure activity, seeking to bring the partly passive finite self into line with itself. Viewed from this angle, Reinhold's correction of Kant represents an advance—but only if rescued from Reinhold's own empiricist understanding of it.

Schelling emphasizes a point which Kant also makes: that the rational necessity of the absolute will places it beyond the dichotomy of freedom and unfreedom. As he puts it: "The law originates in the absolute will. The will, to the extent that it is legislating [and] absolute, can be called neither free nor unfree, for it expresses itself only in the law" (CIWL: 130/H-K, I/4: 166). We have seen that Kant introduces the concept of *Willkür* in an attempt to forestall the unacceptable consequences of this conception. The primordial exercise of *Willkür* is the noumenal process which determines our intelligible moral character, in a choice for or against the rational structure of *Wille*. However, to avoid the problems of Kant's out-and-out dualism of *Wille* and *Willkür*, Schelling proposes that what he calls "transcendental freedom"—namely our free agency vis-à-vis the empirical world, our ability to opt for action that is morally right or morally wrong—is the *way in which* the absolute will manifests itself under finite conditions. As he puts it:

> Without an absolute, legislating will, freedom would be a chimera. However, we do not become *conscious* of freedom in any other way than through power of choice, i.e. through the free selection between opposing maxims that are mutually exclusive and cannot coexist in the same will. (CIWL: 130/H-K, I/4: 167)

And he continues:

> Power of choice, as the appearance of the absolute will, differs from the latter not in *principle* but only according to its *limits*, by virtue of the fact that a positively opposing will counteracts it. Power of choice can thus be explained as *the absolute will within the limits of finitude*. (CIWL: 130/H-K, I/4: 167)

Schelling's fundamental thought, then, is that:

> If the *absolute* (pure) will was not *limited* by an opposing one, it could never become *conscious* of itself, i.e. of its freedom; conversely, if the *empirical* will (of which we become conscious) were to differ from the absolute will not only with regard to its *limits* but also with regard to its *principle*, there would once again be no consciousness of freedom in our empirical will. (CIWL: 130/H-K, I/4: 167)

It is important to note Schelling's emphasis that the empirical experience of choice is not simply an illusion, of which the absolute or rational will would be the underlying reality. As he puts it:

> Just as it is necessary that we become finite for ourselves, so it is equally necessary that the absolute freedom in us becomes power of choice. The fact that this appertains to our finitude and, to that extent, is an *appearance* [*Erscheinung*], does not immediately make it a mere *semblance* [*Schein*]; for it appertains to the necessary limits of our nature, beyond which we strive outward into infinity without, however, being able to suspend them entirely. (CIWL: 129/H-K, I/4: 165–166)

However, one can detect in this formulation—and in Schelling's general theory of the relation between *Wille* and *Willkür*—many of the tensions which will preoccupy him throughout the forthcoming phase of his work, and indeed far beyond. Firstly, what is the source of the impulse toward taking the "opposing principle" to that of the moral law as the basis for our maxims? Whence the force which pulls me in the wrong direction and makes my moral choice an effective opting between genuine alternatives? Secondly, if we cannot suspend the limits of our nature entirely—and the notion of "striving into infinity" is, for Schelling, simply another way of expressing this fact—then it seems that the finite reality we inhabit must have an ontologically self-standing character of some kind. These two points belong together, of course. It seems plausible to argue that it is only because our finite, natural existence has ontological heft that it *can* set us in opposition to the rational or absolute will. But, thirdly, if this is the case, how can Schelling also assert that "finitude is not our *original* state, and this whole finitude is nothing which could ever exist *through itself*"? (CIWL: 129/H-K, I/4: 166) How can our finite state both only be sustained by an infinite reality describable, in a practical mode, as the rational will, and yet also be in some sense independent of it? In part four of his *System of Transcendental Idealism*, published in 1800, Schelling retains the basic account of the relation between *Wille* and *Willkür* which he had developed in the *Commentaries*, while seeking to provide a more adequate and comprehensive answer to these questions.

Agency in the *System of Transcendental Idealism*

At the beginning of the section of the *System of Transcendental Idealism* which deals with the problem of freedom, Schelling makes a striking claim. The beginning of consciousness, he argues, presupposes "an act whereby the intelligence raises itself absolutely above the objective" (STI: 155/H-K, I/9,1: 230). However, because what is required is an "*absolute abstraction*" (in other words, consciousness must grasp itself as something ontologically distinct from the objective world with which it is confronted), this act cannot be a result of the series of unconscious acts which preceded it, which effect the transcendental constitution of the objective world. As Schelling puts it, "the concatenation of acts . . . is as it were broken off, and a new sequence begins" (STI: 155/H-K, I/9,1: 230). Naturally, the question arises: how is this possible? Following Fichte, Schelling considers self-consciousness to consist in a free act of self-positing. And, in the *System*, his explanation of how self-consciousness is initially attained by the individual also follows a Fichtean precedent: specifically, the theory of the eliciting of self-consciousness through a summons (*Aufforderung*) of the human other, which Fichte pioneered in his *Foundations of Natural Right*. By definition, a free act cannot be necessitated. But it can be *called forth* by a demand to respect the freedom of another rational being, when the demand is issued by that being. As Schelling puts it:

> The concept which mediates this contradiction is that of a demand, since by means of the demand the action *is explained if it takes place*, without it *having* to take place on this account. It may ensue as soon as the concept of willing arises for the self, or as soon as it sees itself reflected, catches sight of itself in the mirror of another intelligence; but it does not have to ensue. (STI: 163/H-K, I/9,1: 240)

As soon as the individual achieves self-awareness, a distinction is established between unconscious and conscious production. The "first world" of nature, as Schelling terms it, "now falls, as it were, behind consciousness, together with its origin" (STI: 159/H-K, I/9, 1: 235). We are simply confronted with nature in its objectivity, unaware of our transcendental authorship of it. However, Schelling stresses that there is no fundamental distinction between unconscious production and conscious production (in other words, purposeful agency), as far as their result—a certain configuration of the natural world—is concerned. What, then, accounts for the fact that some events but not others are experienced as our own actions? What structure of subjectivity is involved? Schelling argues that

> in practical philosophy the I as ideal is opposed, not to the real, but to the simultaneously ideal and real, and for that very reason, however, is no longer ideal, but *idealizing*. But for the same reason, since the simultaneously ideal and real, that is, the producing I, is opposed to an idealizing one, the former, in practical philosophy, is no longer intuiting, that is, *devoid of consciousness*, but is consciously productive or *realizing*. (STI: 157/H-K, I/9,1: 233)

Put in slightly less abstract terms, Schelling's thought is that agency involves what he calls a "concept of the concept." The original concept is an expression of the active dimension of the self, which fuses unconsciously with intuition, the passive dimension of the self, in the transcendental constitution—or "production," as Schelling prefers to say—of objective reality. The "concept of the concept" can therefore be understood as the way in which the object that arises in this manner is consciously grasped or interpreted in the light of a determinate practical project, in which the object features as a means. This is why the practical self can be described as "realizing" and "idealizing" at the same time. If we then further ask: what is the ultimate ideal toward which action is directed, the project of all projects, so to speak, Schelling's answer converges with that of Fichte, on the one hand, and that proposed by certain existential phenomenologists a century and a half later, on the other. It is the radical autonomy or total self-determination of the self as such. The ideal observing self, then, and the ideal-real acting self are engaged in a striving to overcome their separation, even though its final achievement is, of course, only an asymptotically approached endpoint.

It should be stressed that Schelling does not consider what he has said so far to provide an adequate explanation of the consciousness of freedom. This is because what might, in one respect, be regarded as an advantage of transcendental idealism, can also be seen as posing a serious problem. We can indeed take a step toward solving the mystery of how subjectively formed intentions are able to bring about happenings in an objective world structured by natural causality by adopting the standpoint of transcendental idealism. Schelling explains that:

> It is . . . one and the same reality which we perceive in the objective world, and in our action upon the world of the senses. This co-existence, indeed, reciprocal conditioning of objective action and the reality of the world, from outside and through each other, is an outcome wholly peculiar to transcendental idealism, and unattainable through any other system. (STI: 185/H-K, I/9,1: 269)

However, this integration of my agency into the objective world can only take place through what Schelling calls "the organic body, which must therefore appear as capable of free and apparently voluntary movements" (STI: 185/H-K, I/9,1: 269). Furthermore, "that drive which has causality in my action must appear objectively as a *natural inclination*, which even without any freedom would operate and bring forth on its own what it appears to bring forth through freedom." In short, "all action must be connected, no matter how many the links, with a physical compulsion, which itself is necessary as a condition of the appearance of freedom" (STI: 185–186/H-K, I/9,1: 269–270). But if this is the case, "if freedom, in order to be objective, becomes exactly like intuition, and is wholly subjected to its laws, the very conditions under which freedom is able to appear do away again with freedom itself" (STI: 186/H-K, I/9,1: 270).

It is at this point that Schelling's theory of opposing incentives, outlined in his commentaries on the *Wissenschaftslehre*, reappears. He argues that the activity of pure self-determination can only emerge in consciousness in the form of a *demand* opposed to natural inclination. This demand is what Kant calls the "categorical imperative," which expresses the structure of the moral will. And, by virtue of its contrast with this demand, self-interest, or the natural "inclination to happiness," itself becomes a countervailing direction of the will. As Schelling puts it:

> As necessarily, therefore, as there is a consciousness of willing, a contrast must exist between what is demanded by the activity which becomes an object for itself through the moral law, and which is directed solely to self-determination as such, and what is demanded by natural inclination. This opposition must be real, that is, both actions ... must present themselves in consciousness as equally possible ... This *opposition* is precisely what turns the absolute will into *power of choice*, so that *power of choice* is the appearance of the absolute will we were seeking—not the original willing itself, but the absolute act of freedom become an object, with which all consciousness begins. (STI: 189– 90/H-K, I/9,1: 274–275)

As this quotation makes clear, Schelling now thinks of self-consciousness as essentially practical. We become aware of ourselves through the exercise of our power of choice—as we constantly remake ourselves through what we decide, from moment to moment, to do.

The Problem of Purpose in History

However, the fact that human existence involves a continual series of choices now throws up a new set of problems. For if the individuals within a human community each decided on their own course of action without constraint, sometimes in conformity with, sometimes against the moral law, the result would be social chaos. In Schelling's account, law is the form of "second nature" which emerges to solve this problem. Its role is to provide an "instantaneous counter to the self-interested drive" (STI: 195/H-K, I/9,1: 282), a counter which is effective precisely because the threat of punishment for law-breaking does not rely on an appeal to moral reasoning but bears directly on our self-interest. However, a legal system could not have been first established through the concerted effort of individuals because this would presuppose precisely the co-ordination which law is required to bring about. Hence Schelling suggests that, "It is to be supposed that even the first emergence of a legal order was not left to chance, but rather to a natural compulsion which, occasioned by the general resort to force, drove men to bring such an order into being without their knowledge of the fact" (STI: 196/H-K, I/9,1: 283). The first forms of legal order, then, will have been crude and oppressive, but nonetheless preferable to anarchy. In the course of history such forms of order are refined, coming closer to an ideal of justice based on the separation of legislative, judicial, and executive power. However, Schelling contends, executive power will tend to acquire a dangerous preponderance within the individual state because of the need to protect society from external threats. Even a properly constitutional order will remain subject to the contingencies of its relation to other states, especially through its vulnerability to conquest. And an internal agency strong enough to rein in executive power would itself tend to become the supreme executive power. This means that the realization of freedom will ultimately require a peaceful federation of states under a common jurisdiction. However:

> Such general reciprocal guarantees are ... impossible until *firstly*, the principles of a true legal system are generally diffused, so that individual states have but one interest, namely to preserve the constitution of all; and until, *secondly*, these states have again submitted to a single communal law ... By doing so, the individual states can in turn belong to a state of states, and the quarrels between peoples be referred to an international tribunal, composed of members of all civilized nations, and having at its command against each rebellious state-as-an-individual the power of all the rest. (STI: 198/H-K, I/9,1: 285)

As is the case with national legal systems, however, this process cannot be imagined as occurring purely through freely coordinated initiatives: the temptation to break ranks and seek individual advantage is simply too strong. Hence, Schelling argues:

> How such a universal constitution, extending even over individual states ... is to be realized through freedom, which plays its boldest and least

inhibited game in this mutual relation between states, is a thing entirely beyond comprehension, unless this play of freedom, whose entire course is the history of humankind, is again governed by a blind necessity, which objectively adds to freedom what would never have been possible through the latter alone. (STI: 198/H-K, I/9,1: 285)

The Kantian resonances of this conception will be evident. In his philosophy of history, Kant invokes "nature" as a teleological force which works implicitly through the apparent disorder and conflict of human agency toward the full, harmonious development of the capacities of the human race. As he writes:

> The only option for the philosopher here, since he cannot presuppose that human beings pursue any rational end of their own in their endeavors, is that he attempt to discover an end of nature behind this absurd course of human activity, an end on the basis of which one could give a history of beings that proceed without a plan of their own, but nevertheless according to a definite plan of nature.[1]

Similarly, Schelling invokes a "necessity" which somehow directs the turbulence of human freedom toward emancipatory goals. But there is a crucial difference between the two philosophers in this regard, because Schelling—as we observed in the case of his philosophy of nature—does not regard the limitation of teleological reason to a merely heuristic function as a viable option. If it were taken that way, teleology would be no more than the projection of an already secured moral standpoint, as it were, rather than providing us with that assurance of the objectivity of a purposive order which is required to bolster moral action. Schelling concludes:

> Such an intervention of a hidden necessity into human freedom is presupposed, not only, say, in tragic art, whose whole existence rests on that presupposition, but even in normal doing and acting. Without such a presupposition one can will nothing aright; without it, the disposition to act quite regardless of consequences, as duty enjoins, could never inspire a person's mind ... Duty itself cannot bid me, once my decision is made, to be wholly at ease regarding the consequences of my actions, unless, though my acting surely depends on me, that is, upon my freedom, the consequences of my actions, or what will emerge out of them for my entire species, depends

not at all on my freedom, but rather upon something quite different and of a higher sort. (STI: 204–205/H-K, I/9,1: 293–294)

It is the apparently paradoxical demand for what Schelling terms an "absolute synthesis of all actions" (STI: 207/H-K, I/9,1: 297)—for the objective necessity of a process which must be brought about through freedom and is therefore subject to the contingencies of human choice—which prompts the celebrated conclusion of the *System of Transcendental Idealism*. Here Schelling theorizes the work of art as the locus of an unmistakable *experience* of the objective unity of freedom and necessity. The artist creates consciously and intentionally. But through that purposive activity an object is brought forth which displays the unity of deliberate and unconsciously determined activity, in a manner which the artist could not achieve simply through calculation and design, and which testifies to what Schelling, following Kant, calls "genius." Our vertiginous sense of the inexhaustible semantic depth of the artwork, counterbalanced by the feeling of tranquility which its contemplation induces, is, according to Schelling, the mark of the fact that the apparently irresoluble conflict of freedom and necessity—which he designates as *the* central problem confronting transcendental philosophy—has *de facto* been resolved. It is in this sense that, for the Schelling of the *System of Transcendental Idealism*, art takes up a supreme position as the "only true and eternal organ and document of philosophy" (STI: 231/H-K, I/9,1: 328). As he puts the matter in his concluding peroration:

> If aesthetic intuition is merely intellectual intuition become objective it is self-evident that art . . . ever and again continues to document what philosophy cannot depict in external form, namely what is unconscious in acting and producing and its original identity with the conscious. Art is supreme for the philosopher, precisely because it opens up to him, as it were, the holy of holies, where burns in eternal and original unitedness, as if in a single flame, that which in nature and history is rent asunder, and in life and in action, no less than in thought, must forever fly apart. (STI: 231/H-K, I/9,1: 328)

In aesthetic experience, transcendental philosophy, which has proceeded through a complex and protracted sequence of stages, each representing a higher and more comprehensive level of self-reflection, achieves systematic closure. It folds back on itself and re-establishes in a mediated form the original oneness of consciousness, prior to all reflection, with whose diremption it began.

The Instability of the *System of Transcendental Idealism*

Schelling's *System of Transcendental Idealism* has a consistency and completeness which are rare amongst Schelling's major works. Perhaps the only serious rival—unpublished during his lifetime—is the 1804 *Würzburg System*, the most complete expression of the next phase of his thinking, the *Identitätsphilosophie*. Yet whatever its status as a "progressive history of self-consciousness, for which what is laid down in experience serves merely . . . as a memorial and a document" (STI: 2/H-K, I/9,1: 25), and hence as an ambitious experiment paving the way for achievements such as Hegel's *Phenomenology of Spirit*, and however influential its metaphysics of aesthetic experience, the *System* was a transitional work. It formed part of a "twin-track" conception of the philosophical enterprise which was inherently unstable. At the same time, the sense that reality is ultimately one, yet riven by dualisms so fundamental that philosophy, in seeking to make sense of them, must divide into two distinct endeavors, and the ensuing problem of spelling out the interconnection of these tasks, are such enduring traits of Schelling's thinking that the *System* foreshadows many aspects of his later work. This becomes especially clear in reading the foreword to the *System*, which directly addresses the meta-systematic issues, whereas the body of the work develops only one track—a transcendental theory of nature, human agency, history, and the artwork—in counterbalance to the *Naturphilosophie* on which Schelling had concentrated over the preceding few years.

In the foreword and in the opening pages of the *System*, Schelling focuses on the unavoidable question of the relation between transcendental philosophy and his philosophy of nature. The awkwardness of the account which he proposes stems from the fact that he employs two different models of this relation which are not obviously compatible: parallelism or—better—mirroring, on the one hand, and complementarity or reciprocal completion on the other. At the start of the main text, Schelling lays out a conception of the mirror relation between philosophy of nature and transcendental philosophy:

> To make the *objective* what comes first, and to derive the subjective from it, is . . . the problem of *philosophy of nature*. If, then, there is a *transcendental philosophy*, its only option is the opposite direction, that of *proceeding from the subjective, as primary and absolute, and having the objective arise from this*. Thus philosophy of nature and transcendental philosophy have divided into the two directions possible for philosophy, and if *all* philosophy must set about *either* making an intelligence out of nature, *or* a nature out of intelligence, then transcendental philosophy, which has the latter task, is thus *the other necessary basic science of philosophy*. (STI: 7/H-K, I/9,1: 32)

The question which this and similar formulations highlight is the following: if we can fulfill the philosophical task *either* by proceeding from nature to intelligence, *or* from intelligence to nature, why are *both* sciences necessary? If these are simply two alternative approaches, each of which achieves a valid and comprehensive account of reality, why cannot we rest content with pursuing one of them? Such a conception would echo in some respects the earliest document of Schelling's inclination toward a deep methodological dualism, the *Philosophical Letters on Dogmatism and Criticism* of 1795, where he argued that Kant's critique of metaphysics had shown only that comprehensive metaphysical views, *however oriented*, are not *theoretically* justifiable. On this account, Kant opens up a *existential* choice between two fundamentally opposed attitudes to our existence in the world: an ethic of surrender to the world-process, inspired by a deterministic monism of Spinozist coloration, or an ethic of infinite striving for the realization of freedom as radical self-determination.[2] However, in the preface to the *System of Transcendental Idealism*, such a conception of *alternative* paths is contradicted by a more prominent strand of Schelling's discussion, which portrays *Naturphilosophie* and *Transzendentalphilosophie* as the two basic philosophical sciences which "reciprocally seek and complete one other" (*sich wechselseitig suchen und ergänzen*), together forming what he calls "the system of philosophy" (STI: 7/H-K, I/9,1: 32).

In the second paragraph of the foreword to the *System of Transcendental Idealism* Schelling seeks to elucidate more precisely the sense in which the philosophy of nature and transcendental philosophy are both distinct and complementary. He states:

> The conclusive proof of the perfectly equal reality of the two sciences from a theoretical standpoint, which the author has hitherto merely asserted,

is . . . to be sought in transcendental philosophy, and especially in that presentation of it which is contained in the present work; and the latter must therefore be considered as a necessary counterpart to his writings on the philosophy of nature. For in this work it will become apparent, that the same powers of intuition [*Anschauung*] which reside in the self can also be exhibited up to a certain point in nature; and, since the boundary in question is itself that between theoretical and practical philosophy, it is also apparent that it is therefore a matter of indifference, from a purely theoretical standpoint, whether the objective or the subjective be made primary, since only practical philosophy (though it has no voice at all in this connection) is alone able to decide in favour of the latter. From this it will also be clear that even idealism has no purely theoretical basis, and to that extent, if theoretical evidence alone be accepted, can never have the evidential cogency of which natural science is capable, whose basis and proof alike are theoretical through and through. Readers acquainted with the *philosophy of nature* will, indeed, conclude from these observations that there is a reason, lying fairly deep in the subject matter itself, why the author has opposed this science to transcendental philosophy, and completely separated it from it, since, to be sure, if our whole enterprise were merely that of explaining nature, we should never have been driven into idealism. (STI: 2–3/H-K, I/9,1: 25–26)

A number of points in this complex statement require elucidation. Firstly, why does Schelling attribute superior "evidential cogency" (*Evidenz*) to the philosophy of nature? The answer, presumably, is that he regards his speculative construction of nature, which tracks the dialectic of opposing fundamental forces and the recursive operation of these forces on their own outcomes, as confirmed by the results of scientific experiment and inquiry, even if the sometimes inadequate or inconsistent concepts with which scientists themselves seek to interpret those results may require philosophical rectification. Secondly, why does Schelling suggest that *Naturphilosophie* reaches its limit when we move into the domain of the practical? And why does he think, relatedly, that the basis of transcendental philosophy's treatment of action and agency cannot be purely theoretical—that commitment to the transcendental approach involves a decision? Finally, why does he use the expression "driven into idealism" (*auf den Idealismus . . . getrieben*), which seems to imply a certain reluctance to adopt the methodological standpoint in question, even while acknowledging that there is a compelling need to do so?

The fundamental insight around which Schelling is circling here is that freedom, as the essential concern of practical philosophy, can only come into view from the first-person standpoint of transcendental philosophy. Indeed, the self-consciousness which transcendental inquiry takes as its starting point is itself best understood as free self-relating *activity*. That adopting this standpoint involves a choice reflects the fact that the explicit, theoretical conception of ourselves as spontaneously active is not one which argument alone can compel us to adopt. There is a sense in which it *becomes* true through the process of adopting it. This need for conscious commitment is underlined by Schelling's emphasis on transcendental philosophy's *reversal* of the perspective of common sense. He states:

> If only the subjective has initial reality for the transcendental philosopher, he will also make only the subjective the immediate object of his cognition: the objective will become an object for him only indirectly; and whereas in ordinary cognition *the knowing itself* (the act of cognition) vanishes via the object, in transcendental cognition, on the contrary, the object *as* such vanishes via the act of knowing. (STI: 9/H-K, I/9,1: 35)

Schelling does not attempt to disguise what he calls the "artificiality" of this procedure, which, as he puts it, separates the statements "*I exist*" and "*There are things outside me*" so as to make the latter dependent on the former (STI: 9/H-K, I/9,1: 34). But ultimately, this is not a satisfactory situation. The philosophical comprehension of nature, it seems, can be achieved by a robust objective idealism. But then, in the second phase of Schelling's overall enterprise, the very objectivity of this idealism must be suspended *in toto* to allow for human freedom, in a manner which he nonetheless concedes to be artificial—which means, presumably, in contradiction with the commonsense realism whose deep metaphysical basis he had sought to elucidate throughout the later 1790s. Clearly, something had to give.

Identitätsphilosophie

It is not uncommon to characterize the "philosophy of identity" which resolved the dualism of the previous phase of Schelling's thinking as nourished by a "romantic," pantheistic feeling of the oneness of all reality. In view of this, it is worth emphasizing that the *Identitätsphilosophie* is based on the claim that what is absolute is "reason." Schelling briefly lays out the basis for this claim in the opening paragraphs of the *Darstellung meines Systems der Philosophie* (*Presentation of my System of Philosophy*) of 1801, the first statement of his new philosophical position. When we think rigorously, we think in a way which is in principle detached from the vagaries our subjective experience and our individual point of view on the world. But, as Schelling points out, if the functioning of reason as such cannot be characterized as *subjective*, it cannot be considered as objective either, given that the meaning of the two concepts is contrastive. Reason emerges, therefore, as that point of indifference (*Indifferenzpunkt*) between the subjective and the objective around which Schelling's philosophy had been circling, without his being quite bold enough to grasp the nettle. Furthermore, reason is not simply *posited* or *discovered* as this absolute point, as the "true *in-itself*" (DMS, H-K, I/10: 116–117), because nothing—not even reason—is sheerly given. Once we accept that only further reasoning can justify a given chain of reasoning—in effect, establish its status *as* an exemplification of reason—it makes sense to propose that what is ultimate or absolute must be reason's self-relation as such.

What is the form of this absolute? Schelling argues that it is expressed in the formula A = A, which does not express the *existence* of A, as subject, as predicate, or in general, but simply the validity the principle of identity as such. This validity is unconditional, since without it there could be no coherent thinking at all. As Leibniz puts it: "the principle of contradiction is the principle of all truths of reason, and if it is given up all reasoning is given up."[3] However, we can see from the structure of the formula, that absolute identity, or absolute indifference, can only *exist* as difference: it dwells in the opposition between subject and predicate—or, put more generally, between the ideal and the real—within the formula. Schelling then proceeds to argue that if we are to make sense of the relation between absolute identity and the multifarious world of entities we inhabit, we must assume that there can be *quantitative* variations in the mix of ideality and reality, of the subjective and the objective, which determine the character of particular entities, but not a *qualitative* difference, which would—of course—destroy identity. Schelling's complete formula for absolute identity, as presented in the *Darstellung*, is therefore the following:

$$\frac{\overset{+}{A}=B \quad A=\overset{+}{B}}{A=A}$$

When the preponderance is on the objective side, we are dealing with material nature; when it is on the subjective side, we are dealing with structures of consciousness. Hence "*Absolute identity IS only under the form of an identity of identity*"—that is to say, the identity of the two sub-forms of identity—"and this is the form of its being, which is inseparable from being itself" (DMS, H-K, I/10: 122). In other texts of the period, like the dialogue *Bruno* from 1802, Schelling expresses the same thought using formulae which, suggesting reciprocal influence, have a familiar Hegelian ring, such as "the absolute unity of opposition and unity" (B: 165/H-K, I/11,1: 387).

It is important to stress that, for the Schelling of this period, absolute identity only *is* under the form of non-identity (or, to put this is another way: being itself is understood as identity-as-difference), for this bears on the divergences which opened up between Schelling and Hegel. During their period of collaboration in Jena, from January 1801 to the middle of 1803, when Schelling left to take up a professorship in Würzburg, a back-and-forth between the two philosophers can be traced, although the basic model of an identity philosophy was shared between them. Soon after Schelling's departure, however, Hegel's conception of system, and of its method of construction, began to develop in a new and highly original direction. A few years later, in 1807, an exchange of letters which terminated friendly relations between the two thinkers was triggered by Hegel's notorious description of the concept of absolute identity, in the preface to the *Phenomenology of Spirit*, as the "night in which . . . all cows are black" (PS: 12/W20, 3: 22). Schelling wrote to Hegel regarding this comment, expressing confidence that, although the criticism might perhaps apply to some of his epigones, it clearly could not have been directed at him. Hegel never replied, however, and their relationship came to an end. But despite the widespread assumption that Hegel decisively dispatched Schelling's philosophy of identity with this one comment, on closer inspection, things are not so simple: there is in fact no role for blank identity in Schelling's identity system. The point was brought out well by Nicolai Hartmann, in his classic work on the history of German Idealism:

> But since this totality is nothing other than the complete universe—not just the cosmic universe, but also the universe of consciousness, and thus the redoubled epitome of everything subjective and everything objective—the principle which separates Schelling radically both from Spinozism and emanationism must be valid: "Absolute identity is not the cause of the

universe, but the universe itself; for everything which exists is absolute identity itself."[4]

The logic of the vision of reality summarized here by Hartmann has been analyzed by Dieter Henrich, with his characteristic penetration, in an essay comparing the basic conceptions of system in Schelling's *Identitätsphilosophie* and in Hegel's mature work. Given their critique of the dualisms of Kant's thinking, the problem for the post-Kantian system-builders, as Henrich emphasizes, was to develop the thought of a unitary ground of all reality, without thereby completely undermining the multifarious and evanescent reality of the finite. The difficulty, of course, is that if the universe of finite entities is conceptualized as entirely dependent on a unitary absolute ground, then the distinct ontological standing of the finite seems to be cancelled—the result is acosmism. This was the upshot of Schelling's system conception, according to Hegel's taunt concerning the night in which all cows are black. However, Schelling had some justification for countering that the criticism could not apply to him. For as we have seen, in the *Identitätsphilosophie* each individual thing is *also* absolute, in so far as it actualizes absolute identity—exists as an example of one quantitatively specified version of its structure (which Schelling terms an "idea"). As Henrich puts it:

> Because there is the infinite, and because the finite belongs entirely to it, for this very reason the finite is free-standing. And so Schelling can say that the finite is something which only participates in its idea within the absolute because it must also express the form of absoluteness in itself, namely through its free-standing existence. (AAG: 150)

As Henrich points out, the consequence of this conception is that:

> The absolute is thus from the very beginning to be thought in a double relation to the finite: by virtue of one and the same principle it endows the finite with a free-standing status which—with equal radicality—must be cancelled. (AAG: 151).

Correspondingly, the relation of the absolute to the finite consists in *both* constituting and cancelling, *both* positing and negating. As Schelling himself puts it, the finite leads a "double life" (*gedoppeltes Leben*) in the absolute (e.g.: B: 131/H-K, I/11,1: 353; see also WS, H-K, II/7, 1: 143).

It should be clear from the foregoing how Schelling's philosophy of identity could provide *one* starting point for Hegel's theory of absolute spirit, which provides an alternative solution to the problem of the relation between the infinite and the finite. From their very different perspectives, both Nicolai Hartmann and Dieter Henrich agree that to portray Schelling's metaphysics during this period as a form of "acosmism"—as dissolving the empirical world into a monistic substance—would be seriously misleading. At the same time, Henrich is surely right to suggest that, although Schelling's identity philosophy does trace the developmental stages of the world of finite things, beginning with basic physical processes and advancing through the forms of organic life to their culmination in self-conscious human existence, there is something "timeless and lacking resistance" (AAG: 150) about the overall conception. By contrast, during his time in Jena after Schelling's departure, Hegel began to work out a dialectical theory of the evolution of the categories of nature and spirit, based on a logic of contradiction. The criticism implied was that Schelling had opposed the ideal and the real as the two metaphysically basic attributes or qualities, without realizing that the concept of quality, if taken as foundational, is self-negating, because qualities are determined contrastively.[5] This dialectical approach pointed toward a conception of the internally *contradictory* character of finite things, when regarded as self-sufficient entities, in contrast to their Schellingian status as syntheses of merely *opposed* elements—a conception which began to define Hegel's distinct vision. Finite entities now lead a "double life" in the new sense that their self-negation *replicates* the self-negation undergone by the absolute itself through its entry into finitude: they are absolute, as it were, in their very non-absoluteness. Whether this enabled Hegel to evade an inherent limitation in the scope of the formula "identity of identity and non-identity," a limitation which Schelling later came to perceive in his own earlier work, is an issue to which we will return.

Freedom in the Identity Philosophy

As we have seen, a central element of Schelling's early practical philosophy is the notion that the exercise of the power of choice (*Willkür*) actualizes the absolute or rational will under finite conditions. In Schelling's identity philosophy this thought is completely abandoned, as is clear from his discussion of freedom, agency, and ethics in the unpublished 1804 *Würzburg System*, the most comprehensive statement of the identity philosophy. Schelling now argues that the supposed exercise of an individual power of choice in fact results in submission to what he calls "empirical necessity." Actions which we take to be freely determined are simply links in the chains of causality by which, in our status as finite entities, we are determined. As he writes: "The freedom which the individual attributes to himself as an individual is no freedom, but merely the tendency to be absolute in oneself, which in itself is null, and which is immediately followed by the fate of entanglement in necessity" (WS, H-K, II/7, 1: 423). In opposition to this erroneous conception of freedom, Schelling now states that "[w]e can only consider as a free cause that which, by virtue of the necessity of its essence, and without any other determination, acts according to the law of identity" (WS, H-K, II/7, 1: 413). He no longer considers the notion of "self-determination"—no matter how rational—as appropriate to describe freedom in this sense because it implies that action does not simply follow from the "necessity" of our "essence," but requires a kind of contrivance—an operation which is destructive of freedom because it divides us from ourselves. As he puts it: "Free self-determination is therefore a contradiction, because in absolutely free acting the determined and the determining are not two different things, but only one and the same" (WS, H-K, II/7, 1: 414).

It is easy to see that this argument entails the redundancy of the very notion of the "will," as Schelling had employed it up till this point, to refer to a capacity freely to choose between courses of action. Just as the essence of the soul is rational knowledge, which perceives the "infinity"—the absolute identity—expressed in finite things, so free action is an "affirmation of the infinite as something finite, of the ideal as something real." Indeed, these two ways of endorsing the identity of the finite and the infinite are ultimately the same: "The notion that there is something in us which knows and something different which acts is what first led to the idea that there could be a freedom independent of necessity" (WS, H-K, II/7, 1: 415). It follows from this conception that the individual as a locus of agency is dissolved, that "*we* do not act, but rather a divine necessity acts in us" (WS, H-K, II/7, 1: 425). The Spinozist tenor of this whole train of argument is evident. Schelling now asserts that true freedom consists not in striving to bring the world into line with a moral ideal, but in rational insight into the necessity which governs the world, and our role within it. As he puts it, true patience consists in:

thinking of all things as comprehended within the totality and respecting them in their own location; not, by contrast, in wanting to subject everything to a law and to force the multiplicity of the divine creation, which is disclosed pre-eminently in the human race, under a formula called the moral law. This is the greatest possible delusion, out of which not joyfulness and peace, but only listlessness and vain labour arise, as in the case of those among us who imagine themselves educators and improvers of the world. (WS, H-K, II/7, 1: 421)

However, there is an aspect of the Würzburg system which does not fit comfortably with the overall Spinozism of Schelling's conception. He becomes aware, in a new way, of the difficulties confronting any explanation of why, from our standpoint as finite beings, we do not comprehend and accept the absolute necessity of the world process, and in particular imagine that we have the freedom to make interventions which can shape the future course of things. Of course, the problem of the relation between a finite, perspectival and an infinite or absolute view of reality had been a central preoccupation of Schelling's right since the beginning. But in some of the most prominent texts of the identity-philosophy period he argued that the finite view and the absolute view were simply two alternative ways of grasping the same ultimate reality. In the *Bruno*, for example, he uses the term "the form of eternity" to refer to this reality, in which the finite and the infinite view—one understanding the world in terms of being and the other in terms of activity—converge, from opposite directions (see B: 200/H-K, I/11,1: 423). In the *Würzburg System*, however, Schelling no longer argues that the finite perspective can be metaphysically *explained* as one of two possible windows onto the absolute or the eternal. Rather, this perspective arises through a falling away (*Abfall*) from the absolute view of things. At first sight, this proposal may seem to be an abdication of Schelling's responsibility as a philosopher—or at least, as a post-Kantian Idealist—to strive for the full satisfaction of reason. What it registers, however, is a dawning realization that the indexicalized perspectives on the world of individual experiencing subjects cannot be derived seamlessly from universal rational structures. There is an explanatory gap which, it seems, cannot be bridged. In this context, Schelling writes:

> In our view, the basis of finitude lies exclusively in a *not*-being-in-God of things in their particularity, a *not*-being which can also be expressed as a

falling away [*Abfall*]—a *defectio*—from God or from the All, since, nonetheless, they are only in God, according to their essence or in themselves. Freedom, in its renunciation of necessity, in other words the particularity of one's own life as severed from the All, is nothing, and can contemplate only images of its own nothingness. To seize on what is immediately posited in things, through the idea of the All itself, as what is nothing, as a nullity, as though it were reality—this is sin. The life of the senses is nothing but the ongoing expression our not-being-in-God on account of our particularity; philosophy, however, is our rebirth into the All, through which we are able to participate in the contemplation of the All, and of the eternal archetypes of things. (WS, H-K, II/7, 1: 424)

According to the basic conception of Schelling's identity philosophy, however, the notion of "*not*-being-in-God" cannot make any sense—*everything* is an actualization of the divine absolute identity. One might think of repairing this discrepancy by pointing out Schelling's emphasis on the fact that finite reality, as it appears from this standpoint, is in fact "nothing." But such a response is undermined by Schelling's talk of a "break with necessity"—a notion which is underscored earlier in the paragraph, where he writes of the "fate of the freedom of power-of-choice [*Willkür*] as being-in-oneself [*in-sich-selbst-Seyn*]" (WS, H-K, II/7, 1: 424).

Within a properly Spinozist system, of course, there is no room for such an exercise of "power-of-choice"; Spinoza famously denies that human beings are situated within nature as "a dominion within a dominion" (E: 3pref). And this consideration seems to highlight once again the inconsistency which forces Schelling to distinguish between *two* kinds of necessity: the rational necessity which structures the universe, absolutely regarded, and the "empirical necessity" in which we become entangled in our attempt to enjoy a purely individual freedom of choice. On a sympathetic reading, the underlying problem here is ultimately not Schelling's, but Spinoza's. It is widely accepted that the Dutch philosopher encounters difficulties in explaining the existence of individual human minds, or of particular subjects of experience, given the basic metaphysical commitments of his monistic rationalism—although opinions vary, of course, on whether he has the means to overcome these hurdles. Spinoza's equally problematic view that, because of the inherently embodied character of the human mind, our perceptual experience cannot help but distort and misrepresent the true nature of things, has also given rise to much discussion. A brief examination of these contentious aspects of Spinoza's thinking may therefore help to explain why fissures began to appear in the edifice of Schelling's *Identitätsphilosophie*, culminating in the dramatic change of approach of his most renowned text, the *Philosophical Investigations into the Essence of Human Freedom* of 1809.

Proposition 13 of Part II of the *Ethics* states that "*the object of the idea constituting the human mind is the body, or a certain mode of extension which actually exists, and nothing else.*" It is clear from this that Spinoza wishes to explain the unity of the human mind in terms of its cognition of a particular body. (How and why the human mind has a *proprioceptive* relation to a specific organism—Spinoza employs the verb "*sentimus*"—is not something he tries to explain; this is simply stated as an axiom—number 4—at the beginning of Part II.) The problem, however, lies in elucidating what, in turn, constitutes the unity of the body. In the Definition supporting Proposition 13, Spinoza describes the distinct existence of a complex organism, such as the human body, in terms of the interaction of hard, soft, and fluid bodies which, he says, "communicate their motions to each another in a certain fixed manner [*certa quadam ratione*])." He then stresses, in the Demonstration of the next Lemma, that, even though the subsidiary bodies may undergo continuous change or substitution, "what constitutes the form of the individual consists in the union of the bodies." However, the "form," the "union," or the "certain fixed manner" is evidently not something which can arise out the interactions of the bodies, because it is what establishes the stable, systematic character of the interactions in the first place. In other words, Spinoza has no explanation for the unity of the body, and hence of the individual mind which is the idea of a human body.

In his theory of perception, Spinoza tries to understand our awareness of objects in terms of our ideas of their causal impact on our sensory apparatus. Because these must be ideas of the *interaction* between our physical constitution and the constitution of the object, so he argues, they will not clearly represent the object as such. But here Spinoza mixes up features of the physical process of perception with the phenomenological characterization of the perceived object. It is not the case, for example, that in being conscious of a multicolored child's building block in front of me, I have ideas of the physiological events, including brain processes, involved in the perception of the block. These processes, although undoubtedly conditions of perception, are the object of scientific hypotheses—they are not aspects of the perceptual experience, like the cubic thing in front of me. Hence, there is no reason derived simply from the physiology of perception for proposing that: "so long as the human mind perceives things from the common order of Nature, it does not have an adequate, but only a confused and mutilated knowledge of itself, of its own body, and of external bodies" (E: 2p29c).

But even setting aside Spinoza's muddling of the physiology and phenomenology of perception, there are basic elements of his theory of truth which make the very notion of *necessarily* confused and mutilated perceptual knowledge problematic; most obviously Part II, Proposition 32, which states: "*All ideas, insofar as they are related to God, are true.*" If we apply this proposition to the current example, we can ask: why should my idea, arising in perception, of the color one side of the multicolored block lead me, for example, to think mistakenly that I have a true idea of the overall coloration of the block? Given that for Spinoza an idea *intrinsically* involves an affirmative or negative judgment (see E: 2p49), why should my act of perception not consist simply in the judgment that *one side* of the block, the one I am seeing, is yellow? This judgment must presumably be described as a true idea in the mind of God. Hence, to defend his view that human beings only have a limited and distorted view of things, Spinoza has to argue that, "No ideas, therefore, are inadequate or confused unless in so far as they are related to the individual human mind" (E: 2p36). But as have seen, his explanation for the existence of an individual mind (as the formal reality of the idea of a human body) is not convincing. And, even if it were, reference simply to the limits of the perspective on the world available to a finite mind (to put the matter in non-Spinozist language) would not be enough *per se* to brand perceptual awareness as inadequate and confused. We normally take the partial character of our perception into account, so that this cannot be an inherent source of error, as some defenders of Spinoza have proposed. As we have seen, Spinoza tries to make good this defect in his argumentation by means of a detour through the physiology and neurology of perception—but this is not relevant one way or the other.

If we are trying to make sense of Schelling's theory of the *Abfall*, the failure of Spinoza's strategy brings two important points into view. Firstly, the existence of the individual human mind or locus of self-consciousness cannot be explained genetically starting from an absolute view of the world. Rather, we are forced to consider that, like Spinoza's substance, it is *causa sui*, that it brings itself into being. Secondly, if errors and misjudgments occur, such as the assumption, for example, that the building block is yellow all over, a large part of the explanation lies in our tendency to "forget" that there are perspectives on the world other than our own. But this forgetting is not entirely automatic. It involves an act of judgment, separate from the idea itself, for which we bear responsibility—a conception which Spinoza explicitly rejects in the Cartesian form in which it was familiar to him: "*Inadequate and confused ideas follow with the same necessity as adequate, or clear and distinct ideas*" (E: 2p36).

In a text, *Philosophie und Religion*, written in the same year as the *Würzburg System*, but treating the question of the *Abfall* in far more detail, Schelling brings these considerations together in a surprising move. He suggests that Fichte's theory of the *Tathandlung*, of the "deed-fact" through which the transcendental subject circularly constitutes itself, can be read as an account of the *Abfall*—of the loss of reality viewed *sub specie aeternitatis* and the emergence of the perspectival world of finite things, a world which lacks any ultimate metaphysical basis. As he writes:

> Fichte states: I-hood is only *your own deed*, your own activity, it is *nothing* apart from this activity, and it is only *for itself*, not in itself. The ground of all finitude in something which does not stand in the absolute, but only on itself, could not be expressed more precisely. How purely the ancient doctrine of genuine philosophy is expressed in this *nothing* of I-hood which is transformed into the principle of the world. (PR, H-K, I/14: 301)

In the same passage, Schelling makes clear that the ancient doctrine he has in mind is the theological theory of the Fall and its consequences. He offers a kind of inverted eulogy to Fichte for having conceptualized—*malgré lui*—the basic process of the Fall with unmatched rigor:

> The significance of a philosophy which formulates the principle of the Fall in the highest generality and makes it, albeit unwittingly, into its own principle, cannot be valued too highly, in comparison with the preceding dogmatism, with its miscegenation of Ideas with concepts of finitude. (PR, H-K, I/14: 301)

With the *topos* of the Fall, articulated in terms of transcendental philosophy, Schelling puts in place an important element of what will eventually become his final system. He now has the conception of two alternative visions of reality, both of which require to be given their due. But furthermore, as we found in examining Spinoza's struggle to explain the existence of finite individuated minds, these two conceptions are necessarily disjunct. There is no unbroken train of philosophical argument which leads from the *a priori* rationalism of the *Identitätsphilosophie* to the world as experienced by the individual human subject. As Schelling forthrightly states in *Philosophie und Religion*, "The *Abfall* cannot indeed be *explained* (as one puts it), for it is absolute and emerges from absoluteness" (PR, H-K, I/14: 300). However, this is not the only disjunction in play. Transcendental philosophy must also confront the conflict between what could be termed its "methodological solipsism," on the one hand, and the fact that the transcendental investigator knows herself to be one amongst many human subjects, on the other. For Schelling, this incoherence is summarized in Fichte's statement, in the 1794/95 *Wissenschaftslehre*, that "the I of each [human individual] is itself the unique highest substance" (*eines Jeden Ich ist selbst die einzige höchste Substanz*) (WL94/5:119/GA, I/2: 282). The result is a world which cannot be knitted together by reason—a world of competing absolutes, rival centers of I-hood. It is not too difficult, then, to understand why Schelling begins to interpret the Fichtean *Tathandlung* in terms of the theology of the Fall. While self-consciousness need not result inevitably in self-centeredness, there is a fateful slippery slope—as Schopenhauer was to emphasize a few years later in *The World as Will and Representation*. We each have a mode of access to our own mental states and doings which others do not, and the immediacy of this access gives rise to a deep temptation to prioritize our view of the world over that of others, or even to discount those alternative views entirely. But while the contrast between a rational—or rather rationalistic—theory of reality, and a view of the world as consisting in competing centers of selfhood will, from now on, remain a constant element of Schelling's thinking, his way of making sense of that distinction will undergo repeated changes. The deeply motivated dualistic dimension of Schelling's thought keeps coming into conflict with the equally legitimate philosophical demand for a unified system, giving rise to a series of ever more ambitious experiments. Clearly, there is something unsatisfactory about a bare assertion that the *Abfall* which separates the two conceptions of the world is inexplicable. And the next major milestone on Schelling's itinerary will reveal him struggling to reconcile the need of reason for a comprehensive system with his new sense of the central and irreducible role of individual human freedom. There is indeed a dominion within the dominion, giving rise to disruptions of the order that Spinoza regarded both as absolutely determined and as the realization of the divine. But how is this possible?

Notes

1. Kant, "Idea for a Universal History from a Cosmopolitan Perspective," in *Toward Perpetual Peace and other Writings on Politics, Peace and History*, ed. Pauline Kleingeld (New Haven and London: Yale University Press, 2006), 4.
2. See Schelling, "Philosophical Letters on Dogmatism and Criticism," in *The Unconditional in Human Knowledge: Four Early Essays (1794–1796)*, trans. Fritz Marti (Cranbury, NJ: Associated University Presses, 1980) (*Philosophische Briefe über Dogmatismus und Kriticismus*, in H-K, I/3).
3. Leibniz, *Die philosophischen Schriften*, ed. C. I. Gerhardt (Berlin: Weidmann, 1875–1890), vol. IV, 237.
4. Nicolai Hartmann, *Die Philosophie des Deutschen Idealismus: Teil 1: Fichte, Schelling und die Romantik* (Berlin: de Gruyter, 1960), 137; quoting Schelling, *Darstellung meines Systems der Philosophie*, H-K, I/10: 130.
5. For an excellent discussion, see Eckhart Förster, *The Twenty-Five Years of Philosophy: A Systematic Reconstruction*, trans. Brady Bowman (Cambridge, MA: Harvard University Press, 2012), 277–297.

3
Freedom

The *Philosophical Investigations into the Essence of Human Freedom*

Schelling's 1809 treatise on freedom—the *Freiheitsschrift*—is a complex, many-layered text, which even distinguished Schelling scholars such as Jean-François Marquet have dismissed as a rushed and inferior product, marred by "extraneous elements which the author has obviously not yet had time to assimilate."[1] More benevolently, the enterprise of the *Freiheitsschrift* has been compared to the attempt to solve a set of simultaneous equations.[2] What, then, are the problems Schelling is addressing in this famous work, and can any be described as the most prominent? In the preface he declares that, after the tearing up of the "root of the opposition" between nature and mind, an opposition made rigid by Kant's philosophy, "it is time for the higher, or rather the genuine opposition to emerge, that of necessity and freedom, along with which the inner mid-point of philosophy first comes into view" (FS: 3/H-K, I/17: 26). Two important points can be extracted from this statement. Firstly, it seems to imply a retrospective self-criticism: Schelling's *Identitätsphilosophie* had overcome the metaphysical dualism of nature and mind—indeed, this was one of its primary aims—but it had not, it seems, resolved the "genuine opposition." Secondly, the description of this opposition as the "inner mid-point of philosophy" seems to suggest that it may, in some sense, be *vital* to philosophy—and therefore, perhaps, is not to be eliminated, torn up by the root like its predecessor, in any straightforward sense. This implication is indeed confirmed, a few pages later in the main text of the *Freiheitsschrift*, when Schelling states that:

> Without the contradiction of necessity and freedom not only philosophy, but every higher willing of the spirit would sink down into the death which is characteristic of every science in which it finds no application. (FS: 9/H-K, I/17: 112)

Startlingly, this seems to suggest that the conflict between freedom and necessity demands both to be resolved—because it is a contradiction—and not be resolved, since to do so would be deadening. At this point, it might seem that the German Idealist project of a "system of freedom" has foundered on the rock of the irreducible opposition between the rational ideal of system as a "closed system of grounding" (*geschlossener Begründungszusammenhang*) and the notion of freedom as a "beginning without need of a ground" (*grundunbedürtiger Anfang*), to use Heidegger's formulations in his excellent lecture course on the *Freiheitsschrift*. However, as Heidegger goes on to argue in a resonant passage, Schelling has, in fact, concluded that:

> The question concerning the system of freedom is not simply an "object" [*Gegenstand*] of philosophy, it is also not merely its authentic and encompassing object, but it is firstly and fundamentally and finally the *condition* [*Zustand*] of philosophy, the open contradiction *in* which it stands, and which it brings about [*zustand bringt*] again and again.[3]

In a certain sense, Schelling's statements and Heidegger's insightful gloss on them offer the essential key to the subsequent development of Schelling's thinking. The issues raised will of course furnish the topics of subsequent chapters and cannot be fully explored here. What can be taken away, however, is the idea that Schelling is asserting a new equilibrium between necessity and freedom. The latter, as power of choice, no longer stands—as in *Philosophie und Religion* and the *Würzburg System*—at the center of a flimsy world of nothingness, to be contrasted with the universe of divine necessity. This is made clear right at the start of the main text, where Schelling describes the philosophical task before him as one of integrating the undeniable phenomenology of freedom—he refers to the "fact of freedom," the feeling of which is "immediately stamped into everyone"—into the "totality of a scientific world view" (FS: 7/H-K, I/17: 111). Such an undertaking implies, of course, that the emergence of human freedom can no longer be treated simply as an inexplicable *Abfall*—a self-exclusion from the true freedom of divine necessity, which nonetheless remains in force just as before. At the same time, in line with his insistence on the stubbornness of the contradiction, Schelling also intends fully to confront the fact that human freedom produces pervasive moral evil, is a source of disruption that stands as a major obstacle to our efforts to interpret the world as capable—in the last instance—of being a "system," a harmoniously integrated whole, as both reason (for the sake of intelligibility) and morality (with its built-in demand for ultimate justice) require.

For reasons which should by now be clear, the knot of problems with which the *Freiheitschrift* deals can be approached from multiple angles. But one entryway which can throw more light on the text than many others, by virtue of using a familiar reference point, takes Schelling to be addressing a severe problem which arises in Kant's later moral philosophy—where evil *must not be made* into a transcendental necessity, thereby removing human responsibility for it, without its being denied in its pervasive reality. It is difficult to overestimate how serious the problem of the human "inclination to evil" (*der Hang zum Bösen*) is for Kant, given his equation of genuine freedom with the exercise of pure practical reason. And it is worth considering again, in this context, the passage in the *Metaphysics of Morals* where Kant frankly confesses that it is not possible to explain philosophically why human beings choose so consistently to negate their own freedom-as-autonomy:

> Although experience shows us that man as a sensible being has the capacity to choose in opposition to as well as in conformity with the law, his freedom as an intelligible being cannot be defined by this, since appearances cannot make any supersensible object (such as free choice) understandable. We can also see that freedom can never be located in a rational subject's being able to make a choice in opposition to his (lawgiving) reason, even though experience proves often enough that this happens (though we still cannot conceive how this is possible). (MM: 52/AA, VI: 226)

Kant's problem is that it makes no sense to think—not even in an "as if" manner, to account for the appearances—of a *rational* subject choosing to flout the law prescribed by reason; but if the choosing subject is not conceived as rational, then not only does the choice become unmotivated and arbitrary, but the subject, who follows no principle, cannot be held responsible for it, indeed cannot be performing any genuine action at all. In short, specifically *moral* evil becomes inexplicable. This problem has persisted in Kantian practical philosophy right up to the present day, causing difficulties, in particular, for the influential "constructivist" school in the interpretation of Kant's moral thinking stemming from John Rawls. Writers in this tradition either frankly admit that Kantian moral theory renders "a free but evil will" both "unintelligible *from the standpoint of pure practical reason*" and theoretically inexplicable,[4] or they tend to ignore the problem of moral evil altogether, content to expound Kant's theory of the tight interconnection between reason, morality, and freedom, while avoiding the implications of the persistent human failure to achieve freedom, so understood. Relatively few recent Kantians have focused on what John E. Hare has termed the "moral gap" between the rigorous standard of selflessness set by the categorical imperative and the human capacity to respond adequately to it.[5] This problem provides a useful prism through which to view the structure of the *Freiheitsschrift* as a whole.

In this text Schelling introduces a new polarity, no longer between the ideal and the real, or between the subjective and the objective, but between what he calls "existence" (*die Existenz*) and the "ground" (*der Grund*) of existence. A crucial aspect of this innovation is a new emphasis on the dialectically *conflictual* or *contradictory*—and not simply *oppositional*—character of the relation between the two principles. As the principle of sufficient reason asserts, nothing can exist without a ground of its existence; but whereas existence itself is now conceived by Schelling as open, outflowing, expansive, self-communicating, the term "ground" evokes a tendency toward particularistic involution. The hostile interdependence of what are best conceptualized as two fundamental ontological drives or vectors arises from the fact that—so Schelling now contends—the ideal or universal requires a real basis which both supports it and threatens to drag it down into particularity, while the basis can only *be* at all, can only avoid the nullity of featureless particularity, by playing its role as foundation of the ideality which at the same time threatens to absorb it. This apparently irresolvable tension applies even to God or the absolute itself, although here the basis is fully internal to the all-encompassing existent which it ontologically sustains. As Schelling puts it:

> God has within himself an inner ground of his existence, which to this extent precedes him as an existent: but equally, God is in turn the *prius* of the ground, since the ground, even as such, could not be if God did not actually [*actu*] exist. (FS: 33/H-K, I/17: 130).

In effect, Schelling has pulled apart the two terms composing the notion of God as *causa sui*: God is no longer *identical* with his own ground, his essence is no longer the explanation of his existence. This means, of course, that God cannot be thought of as sovereign creator. Rather, the result is a pantheistic dialectic of attraction and repulsion, echoing Schelling's *Naturphilosophie*, which gives rise to the increasingly complex structures of the natural world, and culminates in the existence of human beings. In the case of humanity, basis and existence have become fully distinct, while also being antagonistically interrelated. In more concrete phenomenological terms: we are aware of our own awareness, in its limitless reflexivity, as something radically distinct from, yet also inseparably bound up with, the particularity of our natural, corporeal existence. This precarious structure Schelling terms "spirit."

Significantly, Schelling sometimes refers to his two principles as "*Universalwille*" and "*Partikularwille*," making clear that he has in effect transposed the Kantian notions of "*Wille*" and "*Willkür*" into an ontological register. Indeed, the theory of moral evil which Schelling develops in the *Freiheitsschrift* is in many respects Kantian. He argues that evil consists in an inversion of the proper relation between the universal and the particular will—just as Kant speaks of the prioritization of our natural impulses over the moral law—with the upshot that the particular comes to dominate, and thereby distorts, the universal. Correspondingly, the philosophy of history which Schelling sketches in the *Freiheitsschrift* and which, given the distinctive status of human beings, is also a moral history of the cosmos, consists not in a straightforward battle between particularity and universality, but rather one between the *dominance* of particularity *over* universality, and the reverse. The perspective is comparable to that of the philosophical ecclesiology outlined by Kant in his book on religion, which anticipates that the mutual encouragement of moral improvement within the form of human association we call a "church" will gradually—and no doubt never entirely—be able to dispense with the support of superstition, ritual, and dogma.[6] Readers of a secular cast of mind may prefer to think rather of the pre-figurative role of modern emancipatory social movements, which equally have need of their own ceremonies and utopian symbols. The vital difference between the two thinkers, however, consists in the fact that Schelling now has an *explanation* for the pervasive human gravitation toward moral evil: namely, the anxiety and vertigo induced in human beings by the openness of freedom, the anonymity of the purely universal—the terror of losing the particularistic anchor of their existence. As Schelling writes in a famous passage, the will of the ground:

> necessarily reacts against freedom as against what is supra-creaturely [*das Überkreatürliche*] and awakens in it the desire for the creaturely, just as he who is seized by dizziness on a high and precipitous summit seems to hear a secret voice urging him leap down. (FS: 59/H-K, I/17: 149)

It should be noted that Schelling does not assert that this reaction is inevitable—for to do so would remove responsibility for moral evil. But correspondingly he also denies that morality consists in the operation of pure practical reason, for this *would* result in an erasure of our particularity, justifying our anxiety concerning loss of self. A balance can be struck, however. In accord with the ontological presuppositions of the *Freiheitsschrift*, Schelling argues that there can be no moral goodness—which does indeed express itself in an inclusive, universalistic impulse—without a sublimation of the energy of the particular. As he puts it:

> A good without effective selfhood is itself an ineffective good. What becomes evil through the will of the creature (when it tears itself away entirely, in order to be just for itself) is in itself the good, as long as it is engulfed by the good and remains within the ground. Only selfhood which has been overcome, in other words brought back from activity to potentiality, is the good, and as a potential overpowered by the good, it continues to exist unceasingly within the good. (FS: 80/H-K, I/17: 165)

It is impressive that Schelling's last major published text manages to provide a metaphysical grounding for—to clarify in ontological terms—what had Kant left inadequately explained, when he referred to a "inclination towards evil" (*Hang zum Bösen*) and a "disposition toward the good" (*Anlage zum Guten*) as the basic conflicting features of our moral nature. The *Hang zum Bösen* stems from our fear of the dissolution of selfhood, while our disposition toward the good expresses our awareness that we can only *realize* our particularity by opening it out toward the universal. It should be obvious that this account establishes an asymmetry between the principle of good and the principle of evil, while giving each due weight. And Schelling emphasizes this in purely logical terms when, toward the end of the *Freiheitsschrift*, he wards off the accusation that his philosophy must erase the distinction between good and evil, given that being, on his account, consists in the essential interdependence of ground and existence. As he puts it, evil "in the root of its identity" is the good, and the good "regarded in its diremption or non-identity" is evil (FS: 80/H-K, I/17: 165). To put this in another way: the particular will, if it surrendered entirely to the spiral of its own involution, could not even sustain its identity *as* the non-identical: as the non-identity of non-identity it would sink into vacancy, becoming an "eternal hunger and thirst for actuality," as Schelling puts it (FS: 85/H-K, I/17: 169). The good, by contrast, as the identity of non-identity, that is to say, the identity of itself and its opposite, embodies an impulse toward the integration of contraries. However, this formal asymmetry as such, although implying the self-destructive character of evil, does not offer any *guarantee* that moral evil will not continue to erupt in ever new forms, on into the indefinite future.

It is far from clear, then, that Schelling has solved the central problem of the *Freiheitsschrift*, which he sets out with exemplary clarity right at the start of the work. There, as we saw earlier, he states that there are two sharply differing ways in which the nature of freedom can be approached philosophically, which we could roughly distinguish, in modern parlance, as phenomenological and conceptual:

> Philosophical investigations into the essence of human freedom can, in part, concern the correct concept of freedom, given that the fact of freedom—regardless of how immediately the feeling of it is stamped into every individual—is far from lying so much on the surface that, in order merely to express it in words, an uncommon purity and depth of receptiveness would not be required; in part, they can deal with the connection of this concept with the whole of a scientific worldview. (FS: 7/H-K, I/17: 111)

The difficulty is that it is not clear how these two approaches, each legitimate in its own way, can be rendered compatible. As Schelling puts it, "According to an old but in no way faded legend, the concept of freedom is supposed to be completely incompatible with system, and every philosophy making a claim to unity and wholeness is supposed to result in the denial of freedom" (FS: 7/H-K, I/17: 111).

Schelling goes on to argue that, despite its plausibility, this argument cannot be valid because the term "system"—etymologically, a "standing together"—does not refer primarily to a philosophical construction, but rather to the way in which the world itself coheres, "in the divine understanding," as he puts it. If we take the notion of system in this sense, freedom, the first-personal experience of which cannot be doubted, must in reality be compatible with systematic requirements, and the philosophical task can only be to make this integration intelligible. Such a framing of the problem suggests that Schelling has still not distanced himself adequately from Spinoza, whose influence was pervasive during the phase of the *Identitätsphilosophie*. Early in the *Freiheitsschrift* he vigorously defends Spinoza against the accusation that his system dissolves everything into God, allowing finite entities no independent being. It is not the pantheistic aspects of Spinoza's thinking which result in his inability to accommodate human freedom:

> The error of his system by no means lies in his placing of things *in God* but in the fact that they are *things*—in the abstract concept of worldly beings, indeed of infinite substance itself, which for him is precisely also a thing. Hence his arguments against freedom are entirely deterministic, in no way pantheistic. He even treats the will as a thing and then proves very naturally that the will, in all its activity, would have to be determined through another thing that is in turn determined by another, and so on *ad infinitum*. Hence the lifelessness of his system. (FS: 22/H-K, I/17: 122)

It appears that, on this view, life could be injected into a monist system if it acknowledged indeterminacy by avoiding reducing the will to a "thing." But this simply returns us to the original problem, as a passage toward the end of the text makes clear, where Schelling remarks that "Spinozism does not at all fail because it asserts an . . . unswerving necessity in God, but rather because it regards this necessity as lifeless and impersonal" (FS: 77/H-K, I/17: 162–163). As we have just seen, Schelling also equates the livingness of a system with its avoidance of a deterministic view of the will, and hence the fundamental difficulty remains. The notion, hinted at here, that only a *mechanistic* determinism is objectionable, cannot be taken seriously as a solution, in view of the *Freiheitsschrift*'s opening remarks on the pervasiveness of the conflict between necessity and freedom.

But perhaps the problem lies in the founding dualism of "ground" and "existence," which suggests that they can never be definitively reconciled? This is the thought that Schelling develops in the surprising turn which the *Freiheitsschrift* takes toward its end. Here he struggles to evoke a unitary principle *prior* to the distinction of the ground and the existent, which could be expected to exert some metaphysical pressure toward the eventual overcoming of their antagonism. This principle could not be described as a common *ground* of ground and existence because, even setting aside the regress, we would then, as Schelling puts it, have "one being for all oppositions, an absolute identity of light and darkness, good and evil, and all the inconsistent consequences which must befall any rationalistic system" (FS: 87/H-K, I/17: 170). He therefore uses the term "un-ground" (*Ungrund*) to refer to what he describes as the "absolute *indifference*" prior to the distinction between "being in so far as it is basis and being in so far as it exists," proposing that "*without* indifference, in other words, *without* an un-ground, there could be no duality of the principles" (*ohne* Indifferenz, d.h. *ohne* einen Ungrund, gäbe es keine Zweiheit der Prinzipien) (FS: 88/H-K, I/17: 171). We should be careful, however, not to interpret this statement as if the un-ground were comparable to Spinoza's substance. The ground and the existent are not two attributes, and the un-ground is not, Schelling stresses, the "absolute identity of both" (FS: 88/H-K, I/17: 171). It can only be considered the absolute "insofar as it separates into two equally eternal beginnings" *(indem er in zwey gleich ewige Anfänge auseinandergeht)* (FS: 89/H-K, I/17: 172), and these eternal beginnings are each "the whole or a mode of being all its own" *(das Ganze oder ein eigenes Wesen)*. In other words, unlike Spinoza's attributes, which simply run parallel, ground and existence are in *rivalry*, each claiming the status of the principle of being *tout court*. Perhaps the un-ground is best understood, then, as the common logical space in which both ground and existence must be located, if they are to enter into their relations of conflictual complementarity at all.

However, such a characterization, which Schelling has no choice but to apply to the un-ground, poses serious problems for the project of the *Freiheitsschrift*. Firstly: why should there be any exit from the abyss of its ultimate quasi-monism at all? Why is it the case that "duality breaks forth immediately from the neither-nor or from indifference"? (FS: 88/H-K, I/17: 171) Secondly, if the original indifference of the un-ground has simply a logical function, if actual being arises only from the interconnection of the two principles, how can it exert any metaphysical pressure toward an eventual resolution of their conflict, as Schelling claims it does, in the final move of his strategy for reconciling freedom and necessity? The pertinence of this second question is underscored when one considers that, in the *Freiheitsschrift*, the status of the absolute has been downgraded, as it were, in relation to the principles of being. The counterpart of the logical role proposed for the un-ground is the fact that, as Schelling emphasizes, the distinction between the ground and the existent is *not* merely formal or logical. As he puts it:

> Far from it being the case that the distinction between the ground and the existing might be merely logical, or only invoked as a makeshift to be dismissed in the end as spurious, it revealed itself to be a very real distinction, which was only properly validated and completely grasped from the highest standpoint. (FS: 88/H-K, I/17: 171)

This recalibration of the balance between the absolute and the dynamics of finite, temporal existence will be central to the intense experimental searching which dominates the next phase of Schelling's work.

The Ages of the World (1811–1815)

The key to Schelling's project, *The Ages of the World* (*Die Weltalter*), with which he struggled during the second decade of the nineteenth century, but which remained unpublished during his lifetime, is undoubtedly the motto which he placed at the head of all three drafts of the text:

> What is past is known, what is present is discerned, what is future is divined.
>
> What is known is narrated, what is discerned is portrayed, what is divined is foretold.
>
> [Das Vergangene wird gewußt, das Gegenwärtige wird erkannt, das Zukünftige wird geahndet.
>
> Das Gewußte wird erzählt, das Erkannte wird dargestellt, das Geahndete wird geweissagt.] (WA3: 83/ SW, I/8: 199)

However much in need of interpretation these gnomic statements may be, it is clear that they pose a challenge to the Idealist conception of system, one which pushes much further in the direction opened up by the *Freiheitsschrift*. There Schelling began by raising again, in a context shaped by the post-Kantian debates, the problem of the compatibility of our first-personal experience of freedom and the philosophical demand for complete application of the principle of sufficient reason. However, he did not put in question the need for a system, or what he terms a "scientific view of the world" (*wissenschaftliche Weltansicht*), as the only way to satisfy this demand. The opening motto of *The Ages of the World*, by contrast, implies that there cannot be a single way of knowing which applies to all three dimensions of time; to each belongs a distinctive mode of cognition, and to each of these modes there corresponds a different form of expression. It seems, then, that the very possibility of system, of an all-inclusive philosophical science based on a unified method, has been undermined by Schelling's conception of temporality—whatever that may turn out to be. This shift is highlighted most clearly by Schelling's inclusion of a distinct dimension of the future, which—almost by definition—prohibits closure. Of the future we can have an intimation or presentiment, but—by implication—no determinate knowledge.

However, Schelling's project in *The Ages of the World* is even more complex than this initial surmise might suggest. Contrary to appearances, it is precisely his new way of distinguishing the three dimensions of time which is intended to *resolve* a systematic inconsistency which occurs at the level of the principles of being. It is not simply that the "absolute"—which features in the *Freiheitsschrift* as the "un-ground"—has been reduced to a shadowy, logical existence, when compared with a world process shaped by the "very real distinction" between the ground and the existent. Rather, Schelling now portrays the absolute as *internally inconsistent*—an audacious move, but one which has several advantages. Firstly, it helps to explain *why* the qualitatively distinct, conflicting principles which underlie the empirical reality of nature and history break forth from the absolute. In other words, it offers a new solution to the age-old problem of the relation between the timeless and the temporal, the one and the many, the ideal and the real, which re-emerged in the wake of Kant, and had been central to Schelling's concerns right from the beginning. Secondly, it enables Schelling to develop an innovative, non-linear theory of time which anticipates the accounts of "ecstatic temporality" proposed by twentieth-century phenomenology, and provides the basis for his mature conception of freedom. And thirdly, it advances Schelling's new effort to break the grip of transcendental logic over the theory of history, as this had become consolidated the post-Kantian Idealist tradition, without lapsing into mere empiricism.

At one point in the *Freiheitsschrift* Schelling identifies the primordial form of being with "willing" ("*Wollen ist Urseyn*") and asserts that all the predicates of willing apply to it: "groundlessness, eternity, independence of time, self-affirmation" (FS: 24/H-K, I/17: 123). Clearly, Kant's treatment of the Third Antinomy in the *Critique of Pure Reason* is an important source for this characterization. Kant had argued that the assumption of a spontaneous or uncaused causality at the origin of, or underlying, the causal sequences of the empirical world is compatible with the exception-less necessity of those sequences, as long as we respect the distinction between appearances and things in themselves. He insists that the distinction is rigid. As he puts it, "the thoroughgoing connection of all appearances in one context of nature is an inexorable law" (A537/B565), while freedom, as "the faculty of beginning a state from itself" is "a pure transcendental idea" (A533/B561). Kant seems to overlook at this point that, as he argues elsewhere in the first *Critique*, we *do* have an experience of freedom, in the sense of an awareness of the spontaneity of our own thinking; even the firmest commitment to psychological determinism as an aspect of natural causality could not do away with, but only muffle this awareness (as Fichte puts it, the dogmatist "defends himself with passion and animosity" because there is "something within him that sides with the attacker" [IWL1: 16/GA, I/4: 195]). The most Kant concedes during the discussion of the Third Antinomy is that we cannot think of our reason and understanding as determined by sensibility; these faculties belong to our status as an "intelligible object"—in other words, their operation has no phenomenological correlate (A547/B575). But once we allow that we are aware of the spontaneity our own mental activity (which need not entail any knowledge of a *subject* who thereby acts), once the barrier between the empirical and the transcendental has been ruptured in this away, there seems no reason why the breach should not be extended. Kemp Smith, for example, in his commentary on the first *Critique*, suggests that "for ordinary consciousness the concept of causality has a very indefinite meaning and a very wide application. Causation may be spontaneous as well as mechanical, spiritual as well as material. All possibilities lie open, and no mere reference to the concept of causal dependence suffices to decide between them."[7] Schelling would no doubt agree. The *Freiheitsschrift* opens with the claim that we have a profound, if hard-to-articulate, sense of our own freedom, not just in thinking but in acting more generally, one which is not to be gainsaid by abstract metaphysical considerations. The statement that willing is primordial being, then, suggests that spontaneous process is pervasive in the world, although it can of course congeal into large patches of causal patterning. This metaphysical claim is supported, Schelling thinks, by our awareness of our own status as self-determining agents.

In the methodological and epistemological introduction, which Schelling places after the opening motto in all three versions of the *Weltalter*, this line of thought is further developed. It is far from easy to put into words our sense of our own freedom, as Schelling had stressed at the beginning of the *Freiheitsschrift*. However, if we do succeed in turning our attention toward our own subjectivity as such, what Schelling terms a "co-science of creation"—*Mitwissenschaft der Schöpfung*—may emerge (WA3: 84/SW, I/8: 200). Put in more prosaic terms, this expression suggests that the spontaneity of the subject is a *version* or a *manifestation* of the uncaused causality that grounds the empirical world. Kant himself also implies this, of course, since, given its noumenal status, there is no way of distinguishing between transcendental freedom as unitary or as a series of distinct acts. However, Schelling is not proposing, with his literal German rendering of the Latin "*conscientia*," that we can *obtain* or *possess* knowledge of the absolute—of what lies at the origin of things. Rather, as he puts it, the "human soul" is "not so much knowing [*wissend*] as it is itself this science [*Wissenschaft*]" (WA3: 84/SW, I/8: 200). Furthermore, human beings are not capable of directly accessing the "supraworldly" principle in its "primordial purity," but only as bound to a "lesser principle," by which Schelling means discursive, dialectical thinking. It is out of a weaving back and forth between discursivity and *Mitwissenschaft* that philosophical knowledge arises. Consequently, such knowledge cannot be conveyed by purely conceptual or argumentative means. Rather, Schelling suggests, it requires the form of a narrative, or what he describes as an "epic poem" (*Heldengedicht*) (WA3: 91/SW, I/8: 206). His three drafts of *The Ages of the World*, none of which were published in his lifetime, are attempts to construct the first part of that philosophical epic.

The Rotary Movement

One of the major innovations of the *Weltalter* is Schelling's designation of the absolute, in its initial form, as the "will which wills nothing." This puzzling formula may begin to make sense if we consider that, on the one hand, the absolute cannot be anything determinate (for this would raise the nonsensical question of what determines it), but that, on the other hand, it cannot be simply nothing either. The formula of the "will which wills nothing" circumvents this dilemma because an inactive will does not exist *as* will, but cannot be denied any existential status whatsoever. As Schelling says in a related passage elsewhere, it is "*not* nothing, but *as* nothing" (HMP: 115/SW, I/10: 99). In the first draft of the *Weltalter* he portrays the will which wills nothing as a state of blissful, boundless unselfconsciousness (WA1: 16), comparable to the mode of awareness one might attribute to a newborn infant. However, within this inaugural will there germinates a "will to existence" (*Wille zur Existenz*) or a "determinate will which wills something" (*der bestimmte Wille, der etwas will*) (WA1: 18). In Schelling's middle-period and late philosophy, willing always has this double aspect: it is both the absolute capacity to will or not will *and* the process of willing something. The double aspect is required because an activity that is strictly necessitated cannot be an expression of willing. In other words, Schelling belongs to the long philosophical tradition that regards the capacity to *forbear* or *refrain* as essential to willing, or—more generally—to agency; one can only will to do A if one can also will to do not-A (which is not equivalent to *not willing* to do A). In the present case, however, at the absolute beginning of things, there can be no object for the active will other than its own existence *as* willing. And for Schelling—playing on the homophony of the neuter possessive adjective and the verb "to be" in German—"being is its-ness, ownness; is separation" (*Seyn ist Seinheit, Eigenheit; ist Absonderung*) (WA3: 96/SW, I/8, 210): it consists in an insistence on—or a persistence in—particularity or selfhood, comparable in some respects to Spinoza's *conatus*. As a result, the determinate will, which is a condensation or contraction of the original boundless and quiescent will, enters into contradiction with it. The non-willing will is now forced to take on the explicit, determinate form of an outflowing, expansive will, as the only way to resist absorption by the limiting, negating force of its emergent counterpart. In Schelling's account, an ontological struggle ensues, which forces the precipitation of a third mode of willing, termed the "effective will" (*der wirkende Wille*). This third version of the will expresses a redoubled identity: it is the original will in a new guise, now seeking to overcome the difference—to quell the conflict—between its identity with the first will (which Schelling abbreviates as "B") and its identity with the second will (abbreviated as "A"). As he puts it:

> But it remains the case that one and the same = x is both principles (A and B). Not just in a conceptual sense, however, but rather in actual fact. Hence the same = x, which is both unities, must in turn be the unity of both unities; and along with the intensified opposition one finds intensified unity. (WA3: 102/SW, I/8: 592)

In *Prädikation und Genesis*, his pathbreaking interpretation of the *Weltalter*, Wolfram Hogrebe develops the idea that Schelling's three "wills" can be regarded as the ontological dimensions presupposed by predication. In fact, Schelling himself gestures toward such an approach in the *Weltalter* (e.g., WA1: 26-28), although without using his modern interpreter's helpfully explicit terminology, which distinguishes "pronominal being," "predicative being" and "propositional being."[8] Following these cues, we can appreciate that, despite its often quasi-mythical vocabulary, Schelling's *Weltalter* project is concerned with certain fundamental logical-ontological issues. What precisely is a subject or a predicate? And what is it that holds the two together within the structure of a proposition? Schelling's basic concern—one common to all the post-Kantian Idealists—is that propositional structure seems to imply difference and identity simultaneously, raising the question of how these two implications can be rendered compatible. In the distinctive language of the *Weltalter*, Schelling argues that a proposition *should be* the free integration of subject and predicate, the particular and the universal—or that this is what it purports to be. However, "propositional being" is unable to achieve this aim because it is *forced* into its unifying function by the conflictual incommensurability between subject and predicate. Therefore, rather than acting simply as a reconciler, it becomes a separate third dimension, a kind of ontological yoke which *imposes* identity, suppressing rather than resolving the difference of the first two dimensions. The result is a return to the starting point, in which the particularity of being asserts itself, only to be countered once more by the ontological drive toward the universality of the predicative. As Schelling writes:

> Thus, since the third is to the second what the second is to the first, there finally arises the most complete harmony, and it is only through the third that the whole is animated, as if by one breath. But even this third is not capable of subsisting self-sufficiently. For as long as blind necessity reigned, because there was no separation of the forces, that pure opposition-less essence (A^3) could only exist in conflict with the other forms of being-ness. It could not avoid turning back against them as a consuming fire; just as the opposition excluded unity, so the unity excluded opposition; but this was precisely the reason for that alternating movement—the constant reviving of the opposition, the constant return to the beginning—since there should have been neither unity nor opposition alone, but rather both unity and opposition. (WA3: 139/SW, I/8: 251)

The incessant alternation produces what Schelling calls a "cyclical drive" (*Umtrieb*) (WA3: 129/SW, I/8: 241) or a pulsating "rotary movement" (*rotatorische Bewegung*) (WA3: 211/SW, I/8: 322), driven by the inconsistency between the basic principles or vectors of being.

It should not be imagined that the problems with which Schelling is dealing here, and his apparently bizarre response to them, can be explained by the supposedly primitive, pre-Fregean theory of propositional structure which he employs—or that modern quantificational logic can easily release us from these perplexities. On the contrary, a case can be made that Frege's famous text, "Über Begriff und Gegenstand" ("On Concept and Object"), is itself, albeit unwittingly, an essay on the *rotatorische Bewegung*—the difference being that Frege's prime concern is to *prevent* the rotary movement from being triggered, rather than to show its inevitability. Frege's effort is naturally focused on denying that concepts can be objects, for the rotary movement begins when the inaugural "will that wills nothing" comes to feel its own uneasy indeterminacy (or "unsaturatedness" [BG: 197n]), to use the metaphorical expression Frege applies to concepts (*Begriffe*)—his standard term for what he also sometimes calls "properties". In response, the "will that wills nothing" contracts into the particularity of what Frege terms an "object" (*Gegenstand*), that is: the singular referent of any word or phrase which functions, in a broad sense, as a "proper name" (BG: 193, and *passim*). Now, Frege's notorious—and much debated—claim is that concepts cannot be objects, for if they could, this would leave no way of locking object and concept together in a stabilized propositional structure: one would be faced simply with a juxtaposition of two singularities. But in order to forestall this danger, Frege is forced to pay an exorbitant, not to say nonsensical price. Namely, he has to insist that, as Adrian Moore has put it, "there is something fundamentally awry with all talk of properties and with all talk of the *Bedeutungen* [i.e. references] of predicates."[9] Frege, then, is forced to concede that it is impossible for him to say what he *needs* to say in order to *prevent* the rotary movement, and is driven to appeal to the sympathy and co-operation of his readers, their willingness to grasp his perplexed hints (BG: 204). For, to state that a concept is not an object is already to place it in the role within a proposition which *makes* it one, and therefore Frege's only recourse is to employ negative formulae which insist that the change of status to objecthood eliminates all trace of conceptuality, such as: "the concept *horse* is not a concept" (BG: 196). But, to paraphrase Moore, if it is not a concept, what business do we have in calling it one?[10]

As if to complete his unintended survey of the rotary movement, Frege, at the very end of his essay, also considers the role of what he calls the "relation" (*Beziehung*), which—like Schelling's *wirkender Wille*—binds subject and predicate together. He argues that one cannot rely on the *relation* to dig one out of a hole—to connect object and concept—when one has allowed the concept also to have the status of an object and consequently ended up not with a proposition, but simply with the adjacency of two proper names. This is because the relation must in turn be "unsaturated" if it is to lock what Frege here terms 'subject" (*Subjekt*) and "accusative" (*Accusativ*) together by virtue of its own porosity to both (BG: 205). *Some* element must remain unsaturated in the propositional structure, Frege claims, and he takes this to be a decisive argument for his view that it is counterproductive to assert that concepts can be objects (see BG: 205). But surely it shows the opposite? Since talk about the relation, just like talk about the concept, cannot be declared improper or even impossible by self-stultifying *fiat*, one cannot prevent the unsaturated elements from becoming self-enclosed, resistant to connection, but also *needing* linkage to each other if they are truly to come to be; or, in Frege's parlance, to feature in the universe of judgments, whose referent is "the true" (*das Wahre*) or "the false" (*das Falsche*).[11] In other words, the *rotatorische Bewegung* describes an unavoidable dynamic engendered by the simultaneous affinity and repulsion between the dimensions of being. It cannot be stopped by preventive measures such as the contrivances with which Frege—who knows perfectly well that he is not concerned merely with language— seeks to establish a strict division of labour between them.

To put this in another way, Schelling rightly attributes the compulsive, repetitive movement to the lack of "separation" between the "forces," each of which at the same time seeks to monopolize being-ness. As an analogy, one can think of trying to superimpose different geometrical figures exactly on top of one another *as if* they were congruent, rather than laying them side by side in a pattern. The upshot is that the rotatory movement *can* be overcome, but only through a process of differentiation or dispersal. In Schelling's account, this consists in the emergence of a temporal world—in the transformation of the modes of willing into the three dimensions of time. His ingenious thought is that the dimensions of past, present, and future are *both* successive *and* para-temporally "simultaneous": in this way they can be separated, each assigned to its own distinct sphere, and yet fully integrated in the experience of time. In such a conception past, present, and future are not, of course, points on a temporal line, along which we travel metaphorically, the point at which we are located being the present. Rather, past, present, and future are dimensions whose intersection constitutes the happening of time as such. The pole of the past pulls us back toward particularity; the present is the locus of the struggle of the expansive, universalizing will to *overcome* this regression; and the pole of the future harbors a reconciliation of the conflict between particular and universal, whose anticipation energizes the universalizing will. Of course, the identification of each of the temporal dimensions with a mode of the primordial will does not mean that *only* that mode is active in the relevant dimension. Rather, it is the dominance of one expression of the will which determines the character of each. In the dimension of the past, particularity prevails; this means that the involution of the rotary movement, the repeated drag of the obscurely singular, characterizes the past as such. Correspondingly, a drive toward universality characterizes the present. But this drive raises a problem familiar in many philosophical domains, from epistemology to political theory to jurisprudence, and indeed just from living a human life: formal universality cannot do justice to the demands arising from unique situations. In the theory of time of the *Weltalter*, the future—of which we can have only a presentiment—holds out the promise of a progressive attenuation of this deep tension within human existence.

It should be clear by now why the distinction of temporal dimensions and forms of knowing which opens *The Ages of the World* should not be regarded simply as abandonment of the ideal of system. In the German Idealist conception, the point of *system* in philosophy is to resolve what appear to be profound incompatibilities between the different ways in which human beings experience and seek to comprehend themselves and their world: scientific, ethical, legal, political, religious, aesthetic, and indeed philosophical. The system should reveal the underlying structure which shows how these different ways of encountering reality can cohere, reassuring us that we need not suffer incurable "diremption" (*Entzweiung*). In *The Ages of the World*, however, this project seems, in a sense, to be *inverted*. It is the fundamental *principles* which are in conflict with one another. "Eternal time," as Schelling calls it (WA3: 123/SW, I/8: 235)—in other words the logical time of the rotary movement—is driven in an ceaseless circle by the "blind necessity of mutual inexistence" (WA3: 120/SW, I/8: 233), and it is the finite, temporal world, oriented from the past toward the future, that makes possible a certain pacification of the conflict: "Now for the first time there arises a before and after, a real articulation, and therefore composure" (WA3: 135/SW, I/8: 247). However, it would be a simplification to say that the conflict arising from the incompatibility of the principles is thereby resolved. In Schelling's theory of time, the present consists in a struggle to overcome the past, in an anticipatory thrust toward the future. Exertion is always required because the past does not cease to exercise the contractive pressure, the "force of negation" (*Verneinungskraft*) which is its essence, even after "simultaneity" has given way to "succession" (WA1: 25): "Pain is something necessary and universal, the unavoidable point of transition to freedom" (WA1: 40). This thought marks a decisive advance in Schelling's conception of freedom. Up until this point, Schelling has been torn between—has oscillated between—the two principal conceptions of freedom in modern philosophy: freedom as the entirely determined expression of one's rational nature, and freedom as the capacity to settle a course of events through one's choice of action. Toward the end of the first draft of *The Ages of the World*, however, Schelling proposes what can be regarded as a third conception: freedom as *liberation* (*Befreyung*) (WA1: 35)—as the overcoming of a pre-existing nature which has become a form of compulsion, as a tearing apart of the "darkness" (WA1: 10).

Freedom as Liberation

In this passage from the initial version of *The Ages of the World* Schelling directly attacks the notion of freedom as *liberum arbitrium*. He points out that, according to such a conception, the will would have to play two roles simultaneously. On the one hand it is suspended between alternatives, neither of which is irresistibly compelling; but, on the other hand, it must also act as the force which breaks the stasis, coming down on one side or the other. The problem is that:

> Something would have to be overcome by that very same something, the will in question would have to be in equilibrium and not in equilibrium simultaneously; hence to get out of this situation a power-of-choice [*Willkühr*] devoid of understanding is devised, which is independent of all motives and abolishes the equilibrium in a mechanical manner, but, on closer inspection, is nothing other than absolute contingency itself. (WA1: 96)

Typically, however, Schelling does not simply discard the notion of such an equilibrium. Rather, he *re-interprets* it as the stasis or fixity of the individual's character, from which a new impulse, which he terms "force and personality" seeks to break away (WA1: 96). The important point is that the inertia of "character" is both the blockage of freedom *and* the precondition for the emancipatory thrust of separation (*Scheidung*), which therefore occurs through a "doubling of the self" (*Selbstverdoppelung*). Schelling, in fact, refers to a "second I" or even a "better I," which realizes its freedom in this way; not through the exercise of choice, as he stresses, but through the "inner necessity of its nature" (WA1: 98), which is expansiveness or "love," rather than the self-centeredness of character.

It is easy to see that this foray into practical philosophy is based on the dynamic of ontological principles laid out at the beginning of the *Weltalter*. Indeed, Schelling himself emphasizes the connection. What he calls "character" can be regarded as the equivalent, at the level of the individual, of the "will to existence" which first lends genuine being to the indeterminate purity—suspended between being and not-being—of the "will which wills nothing." In fact, viewed as what Kant terms "intelligible character," a noumenon for whose basic disposition we are nonetheless responsible, it is not merely an equivalent, but a version of this will, sprung from the "bottomless abyss of eternity" as Schelling puts it (WA1, 76). Yet this account immediately raises a problem. For, as we have seen, the first will or vector of being gives rise to the rotary movement—"a wild, self-dismembering madness which is still the innermost trait of all things" (WA1: 43). What, then, prevents the "self-doubling," the key to Schelling's conception of freedom as liberation, from collapsing back into the rigid particularity of character, as a result of the compulsiveness to which the very conflict between the inertia of character and the effort to overcome it gives rise? Schelling himself stresses this possibility:

> That power of procreation and self-doubling [can] become so constricted that it only serves as a means to an ever greater intensification of selfhood, and no longer works as a liberation from it; indeed, there can come a moment when a human being loses that power of procreation entirely. (WA1: 97)

Schelling tries to downplay the inevitability of this process by suggesting that the doubling opens up the possibility for the self either to accept and endorse the expansive, emancipatory movement, or to capture and exploit it for purely particular ends. But if things *can* truly go either way, he has reintroduced the notion of choice which it was the whole aim of the theory to overcome. Or, to put this in another way, it is hard to see how the notion of choice could be operative here—yet not also in the original dialectic of the avatars of being-ness. And, if we follow this dialectic, the collapse back into particularity appears inevitable. After all, does not Schelling himself emphasize that the rotary movement is "the innermost trait of all things"?

Leading interpreters of Schelling, such as Jean-François Marquet, regard this problem as the explanation for the eventual failure and abandonment of the *Weltalter* project.[12] The difficulty is that the primordial "will which wills nothing" cannot avoid contracting into particularity in order to *be*, but then there is nothing further it can do to escape its own imprisonment. The problem is closely analogous, of course, to that posed by the inaugural choice of an evil moral disposition (*Gesinnung*) in Kant, who is himself following the Augustinian tradition in Christian theology. Once the will is corrupt, it no longer has the power to lift itself out of corruption, and this is the point at which even Kant is obliged to appeal to a notion of divine grace (see R: 65–73/AA, 6: 644–653). Schelling applies himself intensively to the solution of this problem in the third draft of the *Weltalter*, where the role of grace is played by what he terms *"das Überseyende"*—that which is "sublimely above being and not being." This difficult notion is rendered by Hogrebe as "*Propositionsraum*" or "*Propositionsdimension*"; in other words, as the logical space which makes possible the dialectic of pronominal, predicative, and propositional being.[13] He does his best to defend Schelling's claim that *das Überseyende*, despite its complete serenity and lack of force, can somehow exercise a polarizing effect on the rotary movement because of its affinity with the third, conjoining mode of being. However, the proposal is not convincing, either in Schelling's figurative presentation, or in Hogrebe's updated version of it. For one thing, Schelling stresses that *das Überseyende* is "nowhere existing in itself, but only relatively, over against something other" (*überall nicht in sich, sondern nur beziehungsweise gegen ein anderes seyend*) (WA3:144–145/ SW, I/8: 256). Given this *relativity*, it is difficult to see how *das Überseyende* could also have the *priority* it would require to induce a steady and reliable emancipatory polarization of the movement of temporality as a whole. But, even more fundamentally, Schelling cannot in the end distinguish between *das Überseyende* and the will that wills nothing—for both are described as prior to the polarity between being and not-being. This is simply another way of saying that the claim for the ultimate supremacy of *das Überseyende*, its immunity to the regressive drag of a constantly resurgent particularity, cannot really be sustained. Undoubtedly, during the period of *The Ages of the World* Schelling forged many of the elements which he would require to assemble his final system. But despite his immense intellectual struggle, at the end of this phase—as the failure to shape the material into publishable form suggests—the components still lay around the workshop in a considerable state of disorder. It would take another decade or more before the outlines of his mature system would start to become clear.

The Erlangen Lectures on the Nature of Philosophy as Science

In 1820, Schelling moved from Munich, where—since 1808—he had been General Secretary of the Academy of Fine Arts, to the University of Erlangen, to take up an honorary professorship without fixed teaching duties. Although he remained in Erlangen for seven years, he taught only during a few academic semesters. Shortly after his arrival, however, in the winter semester 1820–1821, he gave a lecture course that marked a significant step in his philosophical development, entitled "*Initia Philosophiae Universae*" (the German heading of one of the surviving transcripts suggests that this should be rendered as "Outline of General Philosophy"). The central line of argument which Schelling developed in this course is set out in the third to eleventh lectures, which were delivered in January 1821, and which Schelling's son—drawing on his father's manuscript, plus two auditor transcripts—published in an edited form in the *Sämmtliche Werke*, under the title "Über die Natur der Philosophie als Wissenschaft" ("On the Nature of Philosophy as Science"). In these lectures, Schelling takes up again a central question of German Idealism: how to think the "true system," one which is a "unity of unity and opposition, in other words, which shows how unity can coexist with opposition and opposition with unity, indeed how each is necessary for the existence of the other" (NPS: 210/H-K, II/10, 2: 613). Schelling here applies this conception to the history of philosophy itself which, as he presents it, consists of a chain of one-sided conceptions, each of which is fated to be displaced by an equally one-sided alternative, thereby forcing an advance toward new oppositions at higher, more complex levels of integration. He concludes that a philosophical system which genuinely solved the problem of the unity of unity and opposition would have to include all of these viewpoints as facets of itself for, "as long as the materialist denies the rights of the intellectualist or the idealist those of the realist, there can be no thought of the system κατ' ἐξοχήν" (NPS: 212/H-K, II/10, 2: 614). A presupposition of this approach of course—and this thought is traceable right back to Schelling's *Philosophical Letters on Dogmatism and Criticism* of 1795—is that the "primal strife" (*Urzwist*) between different philosophical outlooks is far from being arbitrary or contingent. Rather, Schelling contends, one must concede that it has an "objective ground, that it is founded in the nature of the subject-matter itself, in the first roots of all being" (NPS: 210–211/H-K, II/10, 2: 613).

The Hegelian influence on this overall conception is evident. Schelling had clearly been studying the *Encyclopaedia* and the *Science of Logic*. However, Schelling's divergence from Hegel emerges in the manner in which he theorizes the "subject" of this process, which is required if it is to have an overall unity. This subject, he argues, would unite the partial, mutually contradictory conceptualizations by actualizing itself in each of them in turn, and yet also passing through them all, not being identified definitively with any one of them. Drawing on the metaphor of the living body, Schelling suggests that freedom is achieved when each of the organs of the body correctly plays its vital but subordinate role, so that we are not even aware of the overall functioning. The unity of unity and opposition, then, is in this case not simply the unity between the various corporeal subsystems; it is also the unity of the unity and difference between the subject *and* its own body. The subject as such, Schelling argues, is a capacity—a *Können*, a "being-able-to"—and cannot be entirely equated with the functioning of the system of cooperating and mutually supporting organs.[14]

The question now arises: how is this subject to be known, made philosophically accessible? Here Schelling introduces a significant innovation. Clearly, what he terms in this text the "subject"—sometimes the "absolute subject"—is closely related to the "pure freedom" with which *The Ages of the World* begins. There, as we noted, human consciousness could be equated with "pure freedom," the "will that wills nothing," not insofar as it is the knowledge *of* anything—but only as *Mitwissenschaft* or awareness of the spontaneity of pure subjectivity as such. Schelling's step forward consists in dropping the suggestion that pure freedom can be accessed by a reflexive exploration of consciousness, of the kind pioneered by transcendental philosophy. In Fichte, and in earlier works of Schelling such as the *System of Transcendental Idealism*, the results of such exploration are presented in the form of a dialectical process—albeit one which, according to the view reached in the "Introduction" to the *Weltalter*, inevitably reifies what it seeks to articulate if its logic is severed completely from intuition. In the lectures on philosophy as science, however, Schelling argues that the subject of knowing must be dislocated or displaced, in order for the absolute subject to appear, while the absolute subject is blotted out by objectification when the subject of knowing steps onto the scene. In the final stage of this sequence, in which the absolute subject returns into itself at the end of the series of objectifications, the cognizing subject returns to a state of unknowing—but this is now a knowing unknowing, a *docta ignorantia*, since the lessons of the process that the subject has passed through are implicitly retained. We can envisage this trajectory with the help of a diagram which Schelling provides, in which the odyssey of the absolute subject (represented above the line) is reflected in *inverted form* in the phases which the philosophical subject (represented below the line) traverses:

$$\frac{A \quad B \quad A=B}{B \quad A \quad A=B}$$

Schelling refers to this schematic account as providing the "outline of a genuine theory of philosophy" (NPS: 232/H-K, II/10, 2: 632). However, the condition of unknowing knowing which the subject achieves at the end of this process is described as "wisdom" (*Weisheit*) rather than as philosophy.

The significant new term which Schelling employs to describe the dislocation of the subject of knowing in this process is "*ecstasis*." He emphasizes that the notion of ecstasy—etymologically: standing outside of oneself—has now replaced the concept of intellectual intuition, which, emerging from—though not endorsed by—Kant, played a central role in the development of German Idealism, including in some of Schelling's own early work. In fact, Schelling now quite explicitly connects the introspective movement of intellectual intuition with the notion of a futile "rotary movement," familiar from the *Weltalter* (NPS: 229/H-K, II/10, 2: 630). By turning inward on itself the subject fixes itself, and therefore loses precisely the pure subjectivity it was seeking; it then searches for it again in what was *not* determined by its seeking, namely the activity of seeking itself, thereby generating a cyclical process similar to that which lies at the heart of *The Ages of the World*. By contrast, *ecstasis*, Schelling proposes, involves a "crisis" (*Krisis*), in the sense of the turning point in the progress of a disease, a "separation" (*Scheidung*) from selfhood (NPS: 242/H-K, II/10, 2: 642), enabling consciousness to escape from the self-referential vortex. However, in language laden with religious overtones, Schelling emphasizes that this transcending of self, this achievement of wisdom, is achievable only by the few. The text on philosophy as science concludes with the pronouncement: "For only to the pure is the pure revealed" (NPS: 243/H-K, II/10, 2: 643).

Schelling as Theorist of the Axial Turn

The tone of haughty esotericism which pervades "On the Nature of Philosophy as Science" is admittedly unattractive. But in this text Schelling puts in place some of the final elements he will require to assemble his late philosophy. At this point, he needed to achieve just one more momentous advance in his understanding. This was the insight that the vision of the "will which wills nothing" ensnared in the rotary movement, which dominates the quasi-mythological narrative of the *Weltalter*, and the conception of a freedom so radical it is free to be free or unfree—of what Schelling calls the "absolutely primordial" (*das absolute Urständliche*) or the "genuinely transcendent" (*das eigentlich Transcendente*) (NPS: 224/H-K, II/10, 2: 626)—which is the focus of the *Initia Philosophiae Universae*, are themselves the signatures of two "ages of the world." They mark out two epochs of human history. In his influential *Lectures on the Method of Academic Studies* of 1803, Schelling had already outlined the distinction between the ancient Greek and the Christian world in terms of a contrast between a mythological worldview, in which "the infinite was perceived only in the finite and, in this way, even subordinated to the finite" (OUS: 84/H-K, I/14: 120), and an essentially historicized conception of reality. In the latter, the infinite cannot be adequately symbolized (or, more specifically, "symbols have no life of their own independent of their meanings, as do those of Greek mythology" [OUS: 90–91/H-K, I/14: 125]). In consequence, "the figures which represent the godhead are not abiding but transitory—not eternal beings of nature, but historical figures in which the divine is transitorily revealed" (OUS: 84/H-K, I/14: 120). What Schelling now realizes is that the stages of his own thinking have replicated this historical dichotomy. It is the development of human consciousness *as such* which is marked by a caesura, a shift in which the thinking of human beings—and not simply that of a handful of philosophical initiates—is opened up to a new awareness of transcendence. Correspondingly, the cyclical, immanent, compulsive character of mythological consciousness, in which Schelling became embroiled in the very process of seeking exploit the ontological resonance of mythical narrative during his *Weltalter* period, can in fact be seen as the general shape of human beings' world- and self-awareness during the immense tract of history preceding the first millennium BCE, when this transformation occurred.

Schelling begins to formulate the theory that, around the middle of this millennium, religious breakthroughs occurred on a global scale, which culminated in the coming of Christianity. Paradigmatically, these advances relativize everything finite and mundane through the contrast with a new conception of a transcendent, purely spiritual, and universal deity—the "God of all the earth," as the *Book of Isaiah* puts it (*Isaiah* 54:5). In some cases, they inaugurate a novel sense of temporality that abandons the cyclical in favor of an anticipatory forward movement of time toward an eschatological moment. Schelling presents the formal structure of such a relativization in "On the Nature of Philosophy as Science," where he goes out of his way to emphasize the radical transcendence of the "absolute subject," which stands even above our (inevitably reifying) conceptions of God: "Here everything finite, everything which is still an entity, must be abandoned, the last dependency must disappear; here *everything* must be left behind—not merely wife and child, as the saying goes, but what only *Is*, including *God*, for even God is, from this point of view, only an entity" (NPS: 217/H-K, II/10, 2: 619). What these developments suggest is that Schelling has begun to develop a theory of what is now referred to as the "Axial Age." (It is clear that he was aware of the novelty of his conception, since, in a letter to his son, he complained that Johann Sebastian Drey, the founder of the "Tübingen School" of Catholic theology, had plagiarized his views concerning the affinity of the Christian revelation with the preceding pagan religious consciousness, as harboring an obscure adumbration of its principles.[15])

The concept of an "axial age" was first formulated by Karl Jaspers in his book *The Origin and Goal of History* (1949), and has since been taken up widely by philosophers, historical sociologists, and theologians. Jaspers argued that around the middle of the first millennium BCE a decisive shift took place in human consciousness—the "most deepcut diving line in history" (OGH: 1)—on a global level: in China, with the teachings of Mozi, Laozi, Confucius, and other sages; in India, with the Upanishads and the appearance of the Buddha; in Persia, with Zoroastrianism; and—most significantly for the history of the West—with the Hebrew prophets and the flourishing of philosophy and tragedy in ancient Greece. The general character of this transformation was sketched by Jaspers in the following terms:

> What is new about this age, in all three areas of the world, is that man becomes conscious of Being as a whole, of himself and his limitations. He experiences the terror of the world and his own powerlessness. He asks radical questions. Face to face with the void he strives for liberation and redemption. By consciously recognizing his limits he sets himself

the highest goals. He experiences absoluteness in the depths of selfhood and in the lucidity of transcendence. All this took place in reflection. Consciousness became ... conscious of itself, thinking became its own object ... As a result of this process, hitherto unconsciously accepted ideas, customs and conditions were subjected to examination, questioned and liquidated. Everything was swept into the vortex. (OGH: 2)

Jaspers quite explicitly connects this shift with the decline of the "old mythical world" and the rise of the major religions which continue shape the world today (with the exception, of course, of the latecomer—Islam). Inevitably, Jaspers' sweeping thesis has been qualified and modified in many ways by subsequent generations of scholars. Nonetheless, it remains an important focus of research and debate.[16]

In the present context the important point is that Schelling had already formulated the fundamental idea, made influential by Jaspers in the second half of the twentieth century, of a break in the history of human consciousness, leading to a new reflexivity, and a new sense of freedom and agency, as well as an orientation toward humanity as such as the universalistic horizon of ethics. The socio-political world, when contrasted with the transcendent or the absolute, begins to appear in a new way, as questionable, mutable, and open to change. In fact, there is evidence of an indirect line of influence running from Schelling to Jaspers, who cites the nineteenth-century scholar Ernst von Lasaulx as having enunciated the basis for his thesis (OGH: 8). Lasaulx, who studied in Munich, and later became a professor of philology and aesthetics at the University there, arrived in the city in the autumn of 1828 to follow the lectures of Schelling, as well as Görres and Baader, and though he came a year too late to hear it, the published copy of the transcription of the lecture course of 1827–1828, *System der Weltalter*, is from Lasaulx's hand (see SdW: xxx–xxxiii). In Schelling's version of the axial turn, the process of revelation—the decline of a world ruled by cosmic powers and its replacement by awareness of a transcendent personal God—*culminates* in the coming of Christ, who overcomes the mythological process definitively through an ethically transformed repetition of it.[17] However, revelation only occurs as a gradual overcoming of obscurity and concealment and is therefore intrinsically tied to what is overcome. Accordingly, Schelling identifies the dawning of revelation, more than half a millennium before Christ, in the spiritual breakthrough of prophetic Judaism and in the Mysteries of Ancient Athens, which he explicitly sets in parallel (see PO, SW, II/4: 145). The high era of Athenian philosophy also forms part of this syndrome—Schelling emphasizes Plato's debt to Eleusinian cultic practice, as far as his doctrines concerning the soul and its destiny are concerned (see PR, H-K, I/14: 278).[18] But Schelling's sense of the scope of the axial turn is far from being restricted to the Mediterranean Basin. For example, he argues that the Jews only finally turned away from the idolatry which had tempted throughout their history after the Babylonian exile (c. 586–538 BCE), suggesting that this was the result of contact with the *more spiritual* monotheistic religion practiced amongst the ancient Persians (PO, SW, II/4: 144). He draws the general conclusion that:

> polytheism [was] nothing contingent, but rather a kind of universal sickness, like an epidemic, which ran its determinate course, and which gripped not merely a single people, or several peoples, but rather the whole human race. (PO, SW, II/4: 144)

Although it is not possible to examine all the details of Schelling's global account of the disintegration of mythological consciousness at this point, we should briefly consider his explanation for the fact that, in some major Eastern religious cultures, the end of mythology did not pave the way for a conception of a universal, personal God. His claim is that in these cases—Chinese religion, Buddhism—the reaction against the polytheism of mythology gave rise to forms of pantheism, in the sense of cosmic rather than personalized conceptions of the oneness of the world. For Schelling, these developments were expressions of an ontological pull towards de-differentiated unity which—for reasons that will receive detailed consideration later—he regards as essentially regressive. Unfortunately, in the few words he has to say about Islam, Schelling employs this contentious diagnosis again, arguing that the "blind and fanatical" features of Islamic monotheism, and its astonishing inaugural capacity for expansion, were the result of a resurgence of the "monstrous power of something past" (PM, SW, II/1, 167).

Hinduism represents a special case. Its heterogeneity is explained by the fact that mythological consciousness broke apart into its components, but without being dialectically reintegrated under the clear dominance of a unifying principle. Thus, while Shaivism is the religion of the many—for Schelling, Shiva embodies the destructive negation of an original undifferentiated unity (that of Brahma, a vestigial figure in Hindu practice)—the rival worship of Vishnu, the spiritual re-unifier, remains the preserve of the élite (see PO, II/2: 431–459). In this respect, Schelling's theory of Hinduism anticipates contemporary arguments that the diversity of belief and practice covered by the term suggests that "Hinduism" cannot be regarded as referring to a single religion at all.[19]

In summary, a clear anticipation of the idea of the axial turn stands right at center of one of the two enterprises constituting Schelling's late system, functioning as the hinge between its principal components: the "Philosophy of Mythology" and the "Philosophy of Revelation." Schelling's thinking, from the late 1820s onwards involved, on the one hand, the full working out of a hermeneutics of the history of human consciousness, a "positive philosophy," and, on the other hand, the development of what he terms his "negative" or "purely rational" philosophy. Negative philosophy is so called because the chain of determinations which it generates through a form of transcendental reflection progressively negates or removes what can be known about being *a priori*, until we reach the apogee of confrontation with an "un-pre-thinkable" absoluteness. Positive philosophy, employing different methodological principles, then constructs a hypothesis concerning the actual, not merely noetic process of re-descent. Schelling's basic contention, then, is that negative philosophy constitutes one of the two essential components of the required overall system of philosophy. However, when regarded as comprehensive and self-sufficient, negative philosophy becomes a form of entrancement and compulsion—in effect, it reverses the historical irruption of transcendence and relapses into a modern, conceptual version of mythology.

Notes

1. Jean-François Marquet, *Liberté et existence. Étude sur la formation de la philosophie de Schelling* (Paris: Gallimard, 1973), 414.
2. Sebastian Gardner, "The Metaphysics of Human Freedom: From Kant's Transcendental Idealism to Schelling's *Freiheitsschrift*," *British Journal for the History of Philosophy* 25, no. 1 (2017): 149.
3. Martin Heidegger, *Schellings Abhandlung über das Wesen der menschlichen Freiheit* (Tübingen: Max Niemeyer, 1971), 69; previously cited formulae, 75.
4. See Christine Korsgaard, "Morality as Freedom," in *Creating the Kingdom of Ends* (Cambridge: CUP, 1996), 173.
5. See John E. Hare, *The Moral Gap: Kantian Ethics, Human Limits and God's Assistance* (Oxford: Clarendon, 1996).
6. See Philip L. Quinn, "Kant's Philosophical Ecclesiology," *Faith and Philosophy* 17, no. 4 (2000).

7. Norman Kemp Smith, *A Commentary to Kant's Critique of Pure Reason* (London: Palgrave Macmillan, 2003), 494.
8. See Wolfram Hogrebe, *Prädikation und Genesis. Metaphysik als Fundamentalheuristik im Ausgang von Schellings "Die Weltalter"* (Frankfurt am Main: Suhrkamp, 1989), 79–105.
9. Adrian Moore, *The Evolution of Modern Metaphysics: Making Sense of Things* (Cambridge: CUP, 2014), 219.
10. *The Evolution of Modern Metaphysics*, 219n.
11. See Gottlob Frege, "Über Sinn und Bedeutung," *Zeitschrift für Philosophie und Kritik*, NF 100 (1892), 34.
12. See Marquet, *Liberté et existence*, 524; also Marquet, "La philosophie de Schelling," in *Chapitres* (Paris: Les Belles Lettres, 2017), 97–98.
13. *Prädikation und Genesis*, 102.
14. For a comparable argument that, in the case of higher organisms at least, and not only in the case of humans, we employ a self/body distinction, such that we refer to certain animals—a pet cat or dog for example—as "having" a body rather than "being" a body, see Helen Steward, MF: 113–114. Schelling's claim therefore needs to be specified as applying only to relatively sophisticated organisms.
15. See Grant Kaplan, "Did Schelling Live on in Catholic Theology? An Examination of his Influence on Catholic Tübingen," *International Journal of Philosophy and Theology* 80, nos 1–2 (2019): 58.
16. See, for example, the articles in the special issue of *Daedalus*, 104, no. 2 (1975), which launched the current wave of interest in the "Axial Age" hypothesis; more recently, Hans Joas and Robert N. Bellah, eds, *The Axial Age and Its Consequences* (Cambridge, MA: Belknap Press, 2012); Bellah, "What Is Axial about the Axial Age?," *Archives Européennes de Sociologie* 46, no. 1 (2005); Bellah, *Religion in Human Evolution: From the Paleolithic to the Axial Age* (Cambridge, MA: Belknap Press, 2011); Jürgen Habermas, *Auch eine Geschichte der Philosophie*, vol. 1 ("Die Okzidentale Konstellation von Glauben und Wissen") (Frankfurt: Suhrkamp 2019), 175–480.
17. This process will be explored in more detail in chapter 9.
18. For more on this issue, see Michael L. Morgan, "Plato and Greek Religion," in *The Cambridge Companion to Plato*, ed. Richard Kraut (Cambridge: CUP, 1992).
19. See, for example, Heinrich von Stietencron, "Der Hinduismus," in *Säkularisierung und Weltreligionen*, ed. Hans Joas and Klaus Wiegandt (Frankfurt: Fisher Taschenbuch Verlag, 2007).

4
Thinking and Being

Positive and Negative Philosophy in the History of Philosophy

The late phase of Schelling's thought begins at the point where he draws a clear distinction between two kinds of philosophical activity, which he will eventually term "positive" and "negative"—or "purely rational" (*reinrationale*)—philosophy. This first occurs in the lecture course of 1827/28, *System der Weltalter*, which marked his return from Erlangen to academic teaching at the recently founded University of Munich. In these lectures, Schelling refers to a distinction between "historical" and "logical" philosophy, rather than using the terms "positive" and "negative" (SdW: 12). However, it is evident that the fundamental contrast he had been groping toward for many years has now become clear in his mind. The theoretical shift is unmistakeable, despite the transcript of *System der Weltalter*, which was not published until 1990, being a somewhat disorderly text. It conveys the impression that Schelling was bursting with novel ideas, which he was still struggling to organize in a fully coherent manner. We will be concerned with examining Schelling's conception of the two modes of philosophizing, and with exploring the relation between them, for much of the rest of this book. However, by way of an initial orientation, it can be said that negative philosophy elaborates an *a priori* theory of the structures of being; whereas the task of positive philosophy is to confront the bare fact of the world's existence, and—operating abductively—to frame the most comprehensive explanation it can for the inner dynamic of nature and the evolving history of human consciousness.

Negative philosophy stands, in many respects, in the tradition of transcendental reflection inaugurated by Kant, but—in contrast to Kant—Schelling denies that there is any meaningful distinction to be drawn between supposedly subjective necessities of thought and the structure of being as such. Building on the theory of ontological vectors or "potentialities" (*Potenzen*) worked out in *The Ages of the World*, his negative philosophy develops a progressive, dialectical determination of the fundamental configurations of possible being, or of what Schelling terms the "inner organism of reason itself" (GPP: 142/SW, II/3: 76), by tracking the recursive interplay of the potentialities. In contrast to the indecision of his middle period thought, however, Schelling now stresses that such thinking cannot contribute to making sense of the sheer existence of the world. In negative philosophy, thought turns back on itself, reflecting on the manner in which it is logically compelled to think pure being. In positive philosophy, by contrast, it begins from one supreme fact—*that* the world exists—and seeks to frame an account of nature and the history of human consciousness, which, in a hermeneutic circle, is both guided by, and constitutes an ongoing confirmation of, its inaugural hypothesis concerning the intelligibility of the world's existence.

Schelling does not claim that the distinction between negative and positive philosophy is unprecedented. Rather, he contends, the opposition between two basic modes of philosophizing has been at work more or less obscurely in the history of European thought ever since ancient Greece: "The entire history of philosophy . . . reveals a struggle between negative and positive philosophy" (GPP: 191/SW, II/3: 145). However, he also argues that the distinction has never been adequately clarified, and that it is only by formulating it sharply that damaging confusion and conflict between the two kinds of thinking can be resolved (see GPP: 155–156/SW, II/3: 94–95). An initial clue to the character of the distinction can gained by considering the highpoints of ancient Greek philosophy—the legacy of Socrates, Plato, and Aristotle. Schelling's suggestion is that, in these thinkers, "dialectic" plays the role of negative philosophy, while the concerns central to positive philosophy are explored primarily through the medium of myth. In the thought of Socrates, as portrayed by Plato, dialectic plays a ground-clearing role, destroying the illusory knowledge of Sophists and Eleatics, but it does not culminate in any positive theory. It is in this context that Socrates' claim to uniqueness in knowing that he does not know acquires its significance. His lack of knowledge is a *docta ignorantia*, which refers both backwards and forwards. It points back toward the gap left by the demolition of false claims to knowledge of the essential natures of things; but it also highlights Socrates' awareness of the obscurity of those matters which are of paramount importance for human beings—questions, for example, concerning the origin and destiny of the soul, and the cosmological context of this destiny—of which philosophical knowledge is yet to be attained (see GPP: 157–159/SW, II/3: 97–100). Typically, Plato presents Socrates as dealing with these issues in a mythical mode, the break between dialectic and mythical discourse often being clearly signalled in the text, for example by making the myth the reported narrative of an unidentified speaker.[1] Schelling appears to have a strong case, then, that his dual conception of philosophy has Platonic antecedents.

Aristotle's thought presents a very different picture, however, since he purges Greek philosophy of its mythological dimension, and—in the *Metaphysics*—develops a style of thinking which Schelling regards as a precursor of his own negative philosophy. (He suggests that what can be classified as "positive" in Aristotle's thought—in other words, not purely constructible by reason—is only the empirical data, which are examined for the purpose of framing definitions that can then be used in syllogistic inference.) There are two fundamental features of Aristotle's thinking which are significant in this respect. The first is Aristotle's denial that the structure of the ideas, as understood by Plato, can play any role in explaining the *existence* of things. In this context, Schelling refers to Aristotle's criticism of "the confusion which arises . . . when the logical order is confused with the order of being," with the upshot that "inevitably the real causes of being are mistaken for the merely formal principles of science" (GPP: 160/SW, II/3: 101). At the same time, Schelling emphasizes that the explanation of existence as such is not Aristotle's fundamental concern. As he puts it, Aristotle:

> therefore has this whole world, which rational philosophy possesses in thought, as the existent, and yet the question is not that of existence; rather existence is, as it were, the contingent aspect, and only has value for him insofar as it is that from which he extracts the "what" of things. (GPP: 162/SW, II/3: 104)

This claim may appear to be contradicted by the fact that, on some modern interpretations at least, Aristotle regards essence or form as the prime *causal* factor in the existence even of material substances, and not simply as a defining set of properties.[2] However, Schelling's point concerns not the existence of individual things *within* the world, but rather the relation of the world as whole to Aristotle's God, the prime mover, who, as he reminds us, does not play any *explanatory* role in relation to the sheer being of the world:

> Aristotle also makes no use of the ultimate [*das Letzte*]—of God—as the actually existing, but expressly rejects this approach by only ever defining the ultimate as final cause (as αἴτιον τελικόν, not ποιητικόν); consequently, he

does not seek—for example—to make this ultimate into a real beginning, as he would do if he now had it as really existing. (GPP: 162/SW, II/3: 104–105)

In effect, on Schelling's reading, Aristotle "suppressed" the elements of a positive philosophy which were already present in Plato's dialogues in the form of a "mere anticipation" (GPP: 164/SW, II/3: 107); that is to say, in the form of the mythical or eschatological discourse to which Plato was unable to establish a strictly philosophical transition from the domain of dialectic.

In Schelling's narrative, the uptake of Aristotelian philosophy in the Christian thought of the Middle Ages produced an admixture of negative and positive philosophy, which he terms "rational dogmatism" or "positive rationalism" (GPP: 165/SW, II/3: 108). This is because Scholasticism tried to incorporate into the Aristotelian framework the notion of God as author of the world and source of revelation. Syllogistic reasoning and basic metaphysical principles (such as the principle of sufficient reason) were applied to experience and to common notions with the aim of demonstrating the existence of something beyond experience. But this "combination of elements" (GPP: 165/SW, II/3: 109) could only be held together by the institutional "force" (*Gewalt*) of the Catholic Church, and—after the Reformation, and as a result of it—the inconsistent thinking of the Scholastic period broke apart into rationalism on the one hand, and empiricism on the other. For Schelling, this represents an intellectual advance, insofar as the principles of two distinct modes of philosophical activity were beginning to emerge. At the same time, he stresses that empiricism and rationalism—despite their divergent methods—had convergent goals. Empiricists, after all, are not interested in the particularities of what is given in experience for their own sake, but rather for the purpose of extracting general principles from them, while a rationalism which found itself unable to account for the actual course of the world would rapidly lose its interest (see GPP: 165–167/SW, II/3: 109–112).

Schelling concludes his history of the implicit distinction between negative and positive philosophy by pointing out that empiricism, at its fundamental level, unjustifiably limits the scope of experience to the data provided by the senses, either denying that we have any cognitive access to the supersensible or contesting its very existence. A less myopic view is taken by what he terms "mystical empiricism," which is not committed to this denial, and which he subdivides into three forms. The first of these accepts the existence of the supersensible on the basis of a supposed divine revelation, which it treats as an "external fact." The second, which Schelling connects with the early philosophy of Jacobi, goes beyond all external facts, but relies on the inner fact of a supposedly undeniable feeling to provide knowledge of the existence of God. The third form is theosophy, which Schelling describes as "speculative or theoretical mysticism" (GPP: 173/SW, II/3: 119). He points out that theosophical currents existed throughout the Middle Ages, alongside Scholasticism, reaching their apogee in the post-Reformation period, in the thought of Jakob Boehme, who was himself—formally speaking—a Lutheran. Schelling does not defend the value of theosophy as cognition, but he regards the impulse behind it as the expression of a legitimate demand which will be central to his own positive philosophy. As he puts it, "What lies at the basis of Jakob Boehme's theosophy is the striving—in itself deserving of acknowledgement—to comprehend the emergence of things from God as a *real* sequence of events" (GPP: 175/SW, II/3: 121). However, Boehme fails in this attempt because for him God—in the end—becomes embroiled in the world process, becomes "the *immediate* substance of the world" (GPP: 177/SW, II/3: 125). In other words, theosophy is ultimately no less ahistorical than the Spinozist type of rationalism to which it is seemingly opposed. It fails to make the breakthrough to a positive philosophy whose essential content, for Schelling, will be the history of the emergence of freedom.

Schelling's effort, in lectures six and seven of his *Grounding of Positive Philosophy*, to demonstrate that the conflict between negative and positive philosophy runs through the history of the discipline concludes—as one might anticipate—with a discussion of Kant. Clearly, the Kantian distinction between the standpoints of theoretical and the practical reason points toward—and even provides a kind of template for—Schelling's distinction between the negative and the positive.[3] Transcendental philosophy provides knowledge of *how* the experienced world comes to be structured as it is; but, mindful of the limits of transcendental investigation, Kant assigns questions concerning the origin and purpose of the world to the non-epistemic domain of faith. Schelling does not object to this dualism as such, nor to Kant's emphasis on the limits of a purely transcendental enterprise, but only to his claim that the "positive" is inaccessible to *any* form of philosophical knowing. The problematic character of Kant's position, he argues, is revealed in his treatment of the antinomies of pure reason. For to assert that the world has no bounds and no ultimate components, that it has no beginning or ground, as the antitheses of Kant's antinomies do, is in fact to *fail* to assert the existence of a world at all, whereas the theses can be regarded as the basis for a positive conception of the world (GPP: 190–191/SW, II/3: 145–146).

This asymmetry emerges clearly in notebook entries written prior to the *Critique of Pure Reason*, where Kant described what were to become the antitheses of the antinomies as "principles of the exposition of appearances," whereas he characterized the theses as "principles of rationality or comprehension." These latter principles, Kant continued, were "propositions... subjectively necessary as principles of the use of reason in the whole of cognition: of the whole manifold of cognition of the understanding" (AA, 17, 709–710).[4] Schelling agrees with Kant that we require principles able to encompass the "whole manifold of cognition," and furthermore, that reason *as such* cannot make knowledge claims, and is limited to a form of subjective necessity (GPP: 191/SW, II/3: 146). However, the conclusion he draws is not the Kantian one: that attempts to determine the true world theoretically either as constituted by the pattern of appearances or as an underlying noumenal structure result in an irresoluble oscillation. Rather, he argues, to produce a determinate conception of the world, philosophy must pass beyond pure reason, without simply reverting to an exposition of the endless progress or regress of appearances:

> Reason, which by its nature is unable make assertions, also cannot posit a limit, and conversely philosophy which posits a limit must go beyond reason, and know more than can be *known* by means of pure reason. The so-called antinomy is not therefore, as Kant assumes, a conflict, a collision of reason with itself, but a contradiction between reason and what is more than reason, the authentic positive science. (GPP: 191/SW, II/3: 146)

At first sight, it may seem natural to assume that what Schelling understands by "negative philosophy" is a form of *a priori* reflection on the process of thinking itself, which, by virtue of its limitation to the subjectivity of the thinker, is unable to make contact with the actual world—the living, self-moving world of nature. Understood in this way, Schelling's conception of negative philosophy could be connected with his adamant sense of the one-sided character of Fichte's transcendental philosophy, which he had expressed in his correspondence with the older thinker, and which eventually led to the break between them. However, this would be to misunderstand the evolution of Schelling's thought. It is more accurate, in fact, to understand the negative philosophy as a *reinterpretation* of his own philosophy of identity. That is to say, in the course of Schelling's theoretical development, a philosophical strategy which—at first—he assumed had overcome the lopsided approach of transcendental philosophy, and thereby resolved certain seemingly intractable metaphysical oppositions, came itself to appear one-sided. Clearly, though, this second unilaterality had to be different from the first, and likewise the new aspect or dimension to which it was opposed. Similarly, there returns in a new guise a systematic conception, one which had haunted Schelling's philosophical development, in which two "fundamental sciences"—to use the terminology of the preface to the *System of Transcendental Idealism*—are required to collaborate. But again, there are also immense differences between the 1800 *System* and the *Spätphilosophie*. In the present context, the vital point is that the two basic sciences are no longer occasionally presented as *alternative ways* of articulating the same reality: they are unmistakeably complementary, although the nature of that complementarity is a complex—and contested—issue.

The Starting Point of Schelling's Negative Philosophy

Given the radicality of their ambitions, the problem of how to *begin* philosophizing is central to the work of all the German Idealists. How, then, does Schelling's negative philosophy start? In the chapter on Descartes of his lecture course *On the History of Modern Philosophy*, Schelling proposes the thought experiment of stripping away every determinate feature of an entity. If we do so, he argues, we are left with the notion that to be an entity entails, minimally, having some way of *being*, which he refers to as "*das Seyn*." As he puts it:

> Nothing is said anywhere and in any possible proposition but being [*das Seyn*]. If, e.g., I say: "Phaedon is healthy", then a kind of organic, further a kind of physical and finally a kind of general being is said; or I say: "Phaedon is a lover", and here I say a kind of mental being. But it is always being which is said. (HMP: 52/SW, I/10: 17)

However, Schelling then argues, there must be something ultimate to which a way of being can be attributed, and for this he uses a range of terms in his late work. Sometimes he speaks of the "subject of being" (*das Subjekt des Seyns*). However, in the lectures on the history of modern philosophy, he also uses the expression "*Was* Ist" ("*what* Is"), where the conventions of German orthography give the verb a quasi-nominal status, or alternatively—a common usage throughout his late work—"*das Seyende selbst*" ("being-ness itself"). But perhaps Schelling's most informative coinage occurs in the Munich lecture course of 1827/28, where he introduces the term "*das nicht Nichtsein-könnende*"— "that which is not able-not-to-be" (SdW: 28). Schelling is concerned, we might say, with what is helpless to *avoid* being—with necessary existing as "merely the opposite" of contingent existing. In *System der Weltalter* he then proceeds to give one of his most explicit accounts of how we reach this thought:

> To discover what the not able-not-to-be might be, we first have to ask what the able-to-be [*das Seynkönnende*] might be. The latter is obviously what I can also think away, and one can arrive at a concept of the former only along the path of abstraction, in other words at a concept of what cannot be thought away in general. Now in every proposition, only the predicate, not the subject, can be thought away; for if I think the latter away I have nothing left, and if I have nothing I cannot think anything away. The subject is therefore the primordial being [*Ursein*] that I cannot think away ... Primordial being belongs to this [subject], in other words—and in what follows we will call this the pre-jective [*das Urständliche*], the immanent, or being in itself, property-less, intransitive being; in German it could be well rendered as "*wesendes Sein*" [being-in-the-role-of-essence]. (SdW: 28)

As if this train of thought were not demanding enough, Schelling then suggests that primordial being undergoes an instantaneous transformation. As he puts it:

> We therefore have here a double being, one being as possibility of another being, and another being as being in itself. From this point on it makes sense that the subject of being is what-is-able-to-be [*das Seynkönnende*]. But if it has nothing else to do than to be, then it is the only-being-able-to-be, the *necessarily-being-able-to-be*. (SdW: 28–29)

Because the "subject" or possibility of *all* determinate ways of being *cannot not* itself *also* be (it is all that is currently available to be actualized, something which *must* occur to establish its status as possibility), it immediately becomes the *necessity* of being able to be (in some way or another). In short, it becomes the actualization of itself *as* possibility, and confronts the thinker as the principle of the objective or of the referent, of what stands opposed to the subjectivity of the thinking process as *that which is thought*, even if this subject-object structure as a whole still remains only noetic. As Schelling states in his lecture on Descartes:

> I *must* think [being-ness itself] in this nakedness, at least for a moment. But I cannot keep it in this abstraction; for it is impossible that *what Is*, of which I know no more than that it is the beginning, the entitlement to everything which follows, but is itself not yet anything—it is impossible that what is the entitlement, the precondition, the beginning for all being should not also be—this "be" taken in the sense of existence, i.e. of being also outside the *concept*. The concept now immediately turns itself around for us, into its opposite—we now find what we had determined as *being-ness itself* [*das Seyende selbst*] *also* again as being-ness [*das Seyende*] in a completely different—namely only in the predicative or, as we can also say, *objective* [*gegenständlich*]—sense, where formerly we thought it as being-ness [*das Seyende*] in the *pre-jective* [*urständlich*] sense. (HMP: 52–53/SW, I/10: 18)

This abrupt collapse of the subject of being into the sheer objectivity of being-ness is one of the key moments in Schelling's late thought. Schelling explains to his audience that:

> here, therefore, *you* now have the concept of what is necessarily in being, of the necessarily existing mode of being [*des nothwendig existirenden Wesens*] . . . and *you* grasp at the same time, via the genesis of the same, with what force it overwhelms consciousness, as it were, and deprives it of all freedom. It is the concept over against which thinking loses all its freedom. (HMP: 53–54/SW, I/10: 19; see also SdW: 8)

All freedom is lost because, with the subject of being—the primordial *possibility* of ways of being—now occluded, philosophy can only understand its *a priori* task as being to track the unfolding of the necessary consequences of unknowingly objectified being-ness. For Schelling, Spinoza is the thinker who expresses this situation in the most stark and unerring way:

> Spinoza calls God *causa sui*, but in the narrower sense that he Is through the sheer necessity of his essence [*Wesen*], thus *only* Is, and can no longer be held onto as being able to be (as *causa*); the cause has been completely absorbed

into the effect, and behaves only as *substance*, against which his thinking can do nothing. For surprised, as it were, by blind being [*dem blinden Seyn*], as the unexpected which no thought can forestall ... overtaken, I say, by being [*Seyn*], which blindly descends upon him, which swallows its own beginning, God even loses reflectiveness, all power of exertion, and all freedom of movement in relation to this being. (HMP: 65–66/SW, I/10: 35)

For Schelling, the "Spinozist concept ... has been until the present time the point around which everything moves, or rather the imprisonment of thinking, from which it has sought to emancipate itself through successive systems without yet being able to do so" (HMP: 65/SW, I/10: 34). And at the start of the lecture course *System der Weltalter*, Schelling vividly describes the lure of the occlusion of possibility, whose endpoint Spinoza reveals:

It is this necessity, this *natura necessaria*, that has brought hundreds and hundreds to grief, this Proteus lies like a sphinx at the entrance to philosophy. The inexperienced person is almost enraptured by his discovery and believes that in this necessity he has a jewel with which he can dismiss every reason [*Grund*]; but it is a magic spell which ensnares him. (SdW: 8)

Here we already gain a hint of how Schelling will conceive the historic responsibility of his late philosophy: its task will be to break the spell which has fallen on modern consciousness. A central challenge facing interpreters of late Schelling is to understand the precise nature of that spell, and to evaluate whether he is justified in viewing Hegel as its final necromancer.

Hegel and Schelling on Being, Nothing, and Non-Being

From a Hegelian perspective, it may seem obvious that Schelling's conception of "being-ness itself" (*das Seyende selbst*) or the "subject of being" (*das Subjekt des Seyns*) is illusory. After all, Hegel's *Science of Logic* begins with his much-discussed demonstration that the thought of "pure being," characterized as "indeterminate immediacy," is indistinguishable from the thought of nothing. Schelling, it seems, must be deceiving himself in imagining that, after the removal of all ways of being from the world, there would be anything left at all. Indeed, one *Zusatz* to the *Encyclopedia Logic*, clearly implies this:

One readily imagines being as absolute riches, and nothing, by contrast, as absolute poverty. But if we consider the whole world and say of it that everything *is*, and nothing more, we leave out everything determinate and then instead of absolute plenitude we have only absolute emptiness [*die absolute Leerheit*]. (Enc.1: §87, *Zusatz*/W20, 8: 188)

It would be a mistake, however, to think that Hegel has a fundamental objection to the *procedure* of abstraction. On the contrary, he does not conceal the fact that the thought of "*being, pure being*—without any further determination" (SL: 59/W20, 5: 82), which inaugurates his speculative logic (his genetic theory of categories or "determinations of thought" [*Denkbestimmungen*]), is itself the result of a process of abstraction. In fact, Hegel regards this process, which leads to the thought of pure being, as one of the founding achievements of Western philosophy. As he puts it:

This thinking or imagining which has before it only a determinate being, existence, must be referred back to the previously mentioned beginning of science which Parmenides made—the one who purified and elevated to *pure thought*, to being as such, his own otherwise pictorial representations and hence also those of posterity, thus ushering in the element of science. (SL: 65/WL, W20, 5: 90–91)

Hegel then goes on to state: "The move from *particular finite* being to being as such in its totally abstract universality is to be regarded not only as the very first theoretical demand but also as the very first practical one" (SL: 65/WL, W20, 5: 91). Correspondingly, in §78 of the *Encyclopaedia*, he compares the procedure which leads to the start of philosophical science with scepticism, in the sense of "doubting everything." However, he argues that such doubt is best conceptualized as "the decision to *will pure thinking*" made by "the freedom which abstracts from everything and grasps in its pure abstraction, the simplicity of thought" (Enc.1: §78/EL, W20, 8: 168). We will return shortly to the questions raised by the procedure of abstraction. For the moment, we should simply note that, for Hegel, what abstraction enables is the focusing of thinking entirely on itself.

From Schelling's point of view, Hegel's argument that the thought of pure being collapses into—has always already passed over into—the thought of nothing fails to distinguish between two distinct ways in which "mere being" (*das blose Sein*) can be regarded, which he distinguishes in the lecture course *System der Weltalter*: it can be thought as "negatively not-being" (*negativ nichtseiend*) or as "positively not-being" (*positiv nichtseiend*). The positively not-being is the "not-being which is posited *as such*, thus nothing at all." By contrast, the "negatively not-being" is the "not-being, which is only not-being where *actual* being is denied, but in which there is also the possibility to be some entity (*ein Seiendes zu Sein*)" (SdW: 113). Schelling frequently distinguishes these two negations of being by using the Greek expressions "μὴ ὄν" (*mē on*) and "οὐκ ὄν" (*ouk on*). Here he is drawing on Aristotle's theory of potentiality and actuality, as Aristotle uses the term "μὴ ὄντος" (*mē ontos*) rather than "οὐκ ὄντος" (*ouk ontos*) (that is to say, the expression for the contrary rather than contradictory negation of being) in order to describe the existing of properties potentially (δυνάμει—*dunamei*) as the negation of their existence in actuality (ἐνεργείᾳ—*energeiai*) (see, for example, *Metaphysics* XII.1.1069b18–20). In a later discussion of the same issue, Schelling uses an Aristotelian example: to describe a voice as "not white" one would use the negative "*ouk*," whereas to describe a sunburned face as "not white" one would use "*mē*" (see DRP, SW, II/1, 306–307). He further points out that, when Aristotle states the fundamental principle that the same thing cannot be and not be, he writes "εἶναι καὶ μὴ εἶναι᾽" (*einai kai mē einai*) rather than "εἶναι καὶ οὐκ εἶναι" (*einai kai ouk einai*), using "*mē*" rather than "*ouk*" to express negation. According to Schelling, modern philosophers *only* give this principle the "formal meaning" connected with contradictory negation, whereas Aristotle uses the expression that gives the principle a "wider extension" (see DRP, SW, II/1: 308–309). The reason for this broader scope, as Schelling explains in *System der Weltalter*, is that negative not-being can pass over into being or positive not-being (a potentiality can be actualized or fail to be actualized). In other words, negative not-being can result in positive not-being, but the reverse does not apply (see SdW: 114–115). The disagreement between Hegel and Schelling, therefore, hinges on whether the not-being of pure being should be understood as a distinctive negative mode of being, which cannot be accommodated by the Hegelian contrast between the thought of sheer being, on the one hand, and the thought—in intention absolutely opposed and yet, according to Hegel, logically indistinguishable—of its total absence or nullification, on the other. To register this important Schellingian distinction in a convenient form, I will from now on draw a contrast between *not-being* or *nothing* (*das Nichts*) and *non-being* (*das Nichtsein*). As Schelling himself points out, this opposition corresponds to the modern French distinction between "*le rien*" and "*le néant*" (e.g., DPE, SW, I/10: 285–286).

It is worth observing, in confirmation of Schelling's comment concerning the moderns, that well-known commentators on the opening of Hegel's *Logic* have characterized being and nothing in such a way that the thought of the negativity of pure being as the non-being characteristic of potential being is not ruled out, although it is not considered either. For example, in his classic exegetical work on the *Logic*, John McTaggart states: "to be completely free of any determination is just what we mean by Nothing."[5] Similarly, Stephen Houlgate writes: "There is being; it is all around us and is, minimally, pure and simple being, whatever else it may prove to be. Insofar as it is pure being, however, it is so utterly indeterminate that logically it vanishes into nothing."[6] Neither of these formulations rules out the option of considering "pure and simple being" as "non-being" rather than "not being,"—since pure non-being, understood as the *potentiality* of any determinate way of being, is equally as devoid of determinations as nothing. Theodor Adorno makes a similar argument when he describes how Hegel slides from equating being (*das Sein*) with *what is indeterminate* (*das Bestimmungslose*) to equating it with *indeterminacy* (*die Bestimmungslosigkeit*).[7] His point is that to be "completely free of any determination," to use McTaggart's phrase, does not *per se* transform what is indeterminate (*das Unbestimmte*) into what Hegel calls an "abstract negation," establishing the equivalency of being and nothing (see SL: 74/W20, 5: 104).

At this stage, one can imagine a further Hegelian objection: that the concept of "potentiality" is simply not available at the radical beginning of pure thinking. Hence it is important to note that, at the start of the discussion of being, Hegel does in fact consider the possibility that the contrary negation of being (which he refers to as "*das Nichtsein*"), rather than its contradictory negation (which he terms "*das Nichts*"), could be taken as following from the thought of pure being. He writes:

> If it is deemed more correct to oppose *non-being* to being, instead of nothing, there is no objection to this as regards the result, since in *non-being* there is contained the reference to *being*. Non-being is both, being and its negation as said in *one*: nothing as it is in becoming. (SL: 60/W20, 5: 84)

Hegel's concedes, then, that treating "non-being" as the next logical stage after "being" is not an inherently illegitimate move. He simply thinks the result would be a direct transition to one of the two moments of the subsequent category of becoming, which *combine* being and nothing—specifically, the moment of transition from nothing to being. It seems clear that Hegel must also have Aristotle's conception of the shift from potentiality to actuality— from *dunamis* to *energeia*—implicitly in mind here, and that he is using the expression "*das Nichtsein*" to render Aristotle's "μὴ ὄν." What is striking about this concession is that the phrase "nothing, as it is in becoming" renders rather precisely what Schelling describes as *das gegenständliche Seyn* (objective being), as opposed to *das urständliche Seyn* (pre-jective being). For *das gegenständliche Seyn* is pure, formless givenness—one might think here of unconceptualized Kantian intuitions which, as the first *Critique* says, would be "less than a dream" (A112), unless taken up into a process of categorial synthesis.

Despite all this, defenders of Hegel may still want to insist that his account is preferable to Schelling's because he does not help himself to the concept of possibility or potentiality to make his point regarding *das Nichtsein*. Furthermore, Hegel does not claim "nothing as it is in becoming" to be the *very first* thought of the *Logic*, whereas, for Schelling, *das gegenständliche Seyn* is noetically precipitated as soon as we try to think pure being. However, at this point, we find ourselves returning to the question of abstraction. It can be seen straightaway that Schelling's approach does not require us to "leave behind" the fact that we have reached the thought of *das Seyende selbst* through an abstractive process. This is because *das Seyende selbst* is the pure *potentiality* of any determinable being, and potentiality is intrinsically related to the actualization of which it is the possibility. So, thinking of pure being as "μὴ ὄν" rather than "οὐκ ὄν" does indeed involve thinking of it in mediated way. *Das Subjekt des Seyns* cannot entirely shake off its relation to the being of which it is the subject—as Schelling puts it at one point, potentialities "*exist* as waiting for" actuality (DRP, SW, II/1: 311). Yet, of course, this cannot be the whole story, else we would not find ourselves at any kind of radical beginning. It is fundamental to Schelling's conception, in fact, that pure being should be *double* in this way. On the one hand, we apprehend it as immediately identical with its concept; in his lectures *On the History of Modern Philosophy*, Schelling refers to this moment of thinking as the "concept of concepts" or the "pure concept"—an apprehension of existence which abstracts from any determinate grasping of something *as* something:

> I am also free to think *what Is* by itself or purely, *without* the being which I would first have to predicate of it—if I have thought it in this way, then I have thought the *pure concept*, that in which there is no trace of a proposition or a judgement, but precisely just the simple concept. (HMP: 52/SW, I/10: 17–18)

This is, Schelling asserts, "the point where thinking and being are one" (HMP: 52/SW, I/10: 18). However, as we have noted, no sooner do we glimpse thought and being in their oneness than they split apart, become non-identical. For the pure potentiality of being would not be such unless it actualized itself *as* potentiality, that is to say: confronted thinking not as something objective, but as what is capable of acquiring objective determinacy. Schelling's critique of modern philosophy, then, hinges on the claim that the primordial identity of thought and being (*"das urständliche Seyn"*), the most abstract expression of the freedom or spontaneity of thinking, is almost inevitably forgotten or obliterated, with the result that philosophy fatefully makes a beginning *not* with the pure possibility of being, but with some version or other of the notion of substance. As he states: "To begin philosophizing from being means nothing other than to stand philosophy on its head, means condemning oneself henceforth to never again being able to penetrate through to freedom" *(Die Philosophie vom Seyn anfangen, heißt sie geradezu auf den Kopf zu stellen, heißt sich verdammen, nun und nimmermehr zur Freiheit durchzudringen)* (PM, SW, II/2: 34).

In contrast to Schelling, Hegel writes:

> *pure being*, this absolute-immediate, is just as absolutely mediated. However, *just because* it is here as the beginning, it is just as essential that it should be taken in the one-sidedness of being purely immediate. If it were not this pure indeterminacy, if it were determined, it would be taken as something mediated, would already be carried further than itself: a determinate something has the character of an *other with respect to* a first. It thus lies in the *nature of a beginning itself* that it should be being and nothing else. (SL: 50/W20, 5: 72)

In this passage Hegel also appears to acknowledge the dual character of the beginning. But, in contrast to Schelling, he argues that the mediated status of pure being must be ignored, and it should be taken in the "one-sidedness" of immediacy, in order to make a radical beginning. However, this looks like special pleading, indeed circularity. Hegel uses a notion of the beginning of pure thinking to justify taking pure being in a one-sided way—yet it is only this one-sidedness which legitimates his conception of a radical beginning. What if one were to reply, in Schellingian style, that a genuinely radical beginning would need to acknowledge the duality, the double-sidedness? The difficult question for Hegel is whether it is in fact possible for the philosopher to "leave behind"—in a paradoxical act of deliberate forgetting—the process of abstraction which mediates the thought of pure being. The problem, as Kierkegaard—a thinker whose work stands in the shadow of late Schelling—points out in *Concluding Unscientific Postscript*, is that, to begin the *Logic*, Hegel requires us to *abstract from the reflective process of abstraction*—and this results in an endless regress, or an "infinite" activity of reflection and abstraction.[8]

The Dialectic of Schelling's Negative Philosophy

The issues raised by the contrast between Schelling's and Hegel's conceptions of what it means to think pure being are complex and profound. And a case can be made that there is no sense to try to resolve them definitively in a purely punctual manner, by comparing the apparent strengths or weaknesses of individual arguments. Deep philosophical disputes are not like that. Furthermore, such an approach would be inconsistent with the Idealist conception of system, which both Hegel and Schelling endorse. It would not fit with Hegel's well-known declaration that "the true is the whole" (PS: 13/ W20, 3: 24), nor with comparable assertions of Schelling, for example this statement from the *Initia Philosophiae Universae*: "There is no partial completion in philosophy. Just as one says of a human being that he cannot be blessed before his end, so philosophy only becomes true through its end."[9] It is, then, the overall shape and content of the philosophical systems in which the two philosophers' opposing conceptions of what it means to think being are embedded which should ultimately be decisive, reflecting back on our assessment of the detail. And this shape and content should in turn be evaluated in terms of the capacity to make sense of the world—of nature and human history—and of our experience of being located finitely within it. Subsequent chapters will proceed in this direction. But at this point we should take time to consider the extent to which Schelling's negative philosophy does indeed constitute a form of *a priori* reflection comparable to Hegel's *Logic*.

In his late thought, Schelling does not deny the possibility of—or indeed the absolute need for—a philosophical science of pure thinking. As he puts it:

> There comes a certain moment when human beings have to make themselves free not only of revelation, but of *everything* actual, in order to flee into an utter desert of all being, where nothing in any way actual is to be found, but only the infinite potentiality of all being, the sole immediate content of thinking, in relation to which thinking moves only within itself, in its own aether. In this content reason also has what is given to it by the totally *a priori* stance over against all being, so that starting from this content it is able to know not just pure being-ness in general, but the whole of being in all its gradations. (GPP: 142/SW, II/3: 76)

Schelling sometimes calls this enterprise "purely rational philosophy" (*reinrationale Philosophie*) or the "pure science of reason" (*reine Vernunftwissenschaft*). However, when it features as one of the two fundamental enterprises constituting his late system, he usually refers to it as "negative philosophy" (*negative Philosophie*), thereby linking up with a tradition of negative philosophy whose history, as he conceives it, we have already reviewed. In Schelling, the principles of this endeavor are what he calls "*Potenzen*." They are the fundamental possibilities, modalities, or vectors of being out of which particular kinds of entities are constituted. Etymologically, of course, the term "*Potenz*" is connected with notions of both power *and* possibility, and in Schelling's late work it conveys something close to Aristotle's concept of "potentiality" (*dunamis*)—one of his principal sources of inspiration.

It is clear from the passage just quoted that, for Schelling, when rational thinking explores its own *a priori* structure, it is thereby exploring the necessary structure of being. As he puts it:

> Reason, as soon as it directs itself onto itself, becomes an object for itself, finds within itself the *prius* or—what is the same thing—the subject of *all* being, and in this it also possesses the means for, or rather the principle of, an *a priori* knowledge of everything that is [*alles Seyenden*]. (GPP: 128/SW, II/3: 57)

Or, as Schelling frequently puts it, reason, as the "infinite potentiality of knowing" (*die unendliche Potenz des Erkennens*), has for its content the "infinite potentiality of being" (*die unendliche Potenz des Seyns*) (GPP: 142/SW, II/3: 75). This is the case because, for Schelling, concepts—in their universality—are configurations of what can be. The danger that transcendental reflection might find itself articulating merely subjective necessities of reason which do not correspond to being in its actuality has been eliminated because, as we saw, in the inaugural moment of the negative philosophy, being and thinking *are* indeed one: the "subject of being" and the subject of thinking are momentarily indistinguishable. It is only after thinking has passed through this point that the difference between Schelling's procedure and that of Hegel in the *Logic* begins to emerge. For Schelling, thought cannot think merely itself, since in this case the identity-in-difference between thought and its object required to think anything at all would be lacking. Rather what Schelling terms "*das urständliche Seyn*" ("pre-jective being," in its primordial state of identity with thought) is precipitated as "*das gegenständliche Seyn*" (being, regarded *as the possibility* of, the *dimension* of the objective) as soon as thinking is trained upon itself.

This transformation is the first move in Schelling's construction of the three potentialities—the ultimate avatars of being which have structured his thought almost since the beginning, although undergoing repeated modifications along the way. The first question which arises, then, is how and why being as the principle of objectivity—of what is opposed to the freedom of thinking—gives rise to a second potentiality. To understand this process, one should bear in mind that Schelling is not here concerned with the objectification or actualization of a *particular* potentiality or capacity. Rather he is concerned only with the actualization of potentiality *as* potentiality. This is the case because, at the very beginning, the pure potentiality of being has nothing to actualize except itself. And it *must* actualize itself because if it did not do so, it would not even qualify as potentiality (this is where the potentiality of *being as such* differs from determinate potentialities, which *can* remain perpetually in suspension). Schelling thinks of actualized pure potentiality as inchoate materiality, or what he terms "meaningless, boundless being" (PO41/42: 102), which cannot stabilize itself, as it lacks all form—any shaping ideal or universal dimension.

Again, there are obvious Aristotelian precedents for Schelling's conception (see *Metaphysics* IX.8.1050a15–17). Where Schelling differs from Aristotle, however, is in developing a generative dialectic of the different modalities of being. In his account, materiality—which need not, of course, consist in the principle of matter in any physical sense—"negates" pure being, understood as that which remained quiescent *as* potentiality. It threatens to eliminate it by occupying the entire space of being, as it were. Schelling's thought is that if the pure potentiality of being actualizes *itself* it ceases to be the potential for objectified potentiality, just as much as it does in the opposite case—if it never actualizes itself. This dilemma produces a split within being, which forces pure being to assert itself against materiality as a higher-level potentiality—the possibility of being as stasis, form, ideal determination, in opposition to being as the shapeless and restless. This potentiality is left no choice by the dilemma just outlined except to become actual at a second, higher level, striving to push "meaningless, boundless being" back into its appropriate status as an ontological substrate or support, compelling it to stop comporting itself *as if it could be actual by itself, in its formlessness*. As Schelling puts it:

> Because negation is unbearable to [the second potentiality], it is forced to restore its own state of tranquillity. It does not have the freedom to activate or not activate itself, but rather it *must* activate itself, in order to negate the first [potentiality], by which it was negated. However, this second negation can only consist in the fact that what has passed over *a potentia ad actum* is brought back *ex actu in potentiam* = is restored to itself from its *externalization*. (PO41/42: 104)

The ensuing struggle between these two potentialities gives rise to the concrete forms of being:

> Through the fact that the second potentiality posits *an inner and outer dimension* in the first [potentiality], the concrete arises. *The knitting together of matter with a potentiality or a concept forms the concrete*. The possibilities enclosed between these two possibilities are *possibilities of the concrete world*, which can in this way be conceptualized *a priori*, starting from the primordial potentiality [*Urpotenz*]. (PO41/42: 105–106)

However, the spatio-temporal world could not emerge unless relative stabilizations of the struggle between the first and the second potentialities can occur. And such superseding of the zero-sum game can only be brought about through a third potentiality, which constitutes the point of intersection of potentiality and being:

> This third cannot be pure being-able-to-be and also not pure being; for these sites are already taken. It can only be what is potentiality in being and being in potentiality, that in which the contradiction between potentiality and being is posited in its identity. (PO41/42: 106)

This collaboration of the three potentialities, which provides the ontological template for all natural kinds, constitutes what Schelling terms the "organism of objectively posited reason" (PO41/42: 103).

Because the dialectic of the potentialities, which he began to work out in *The Ages of the World,* is so central to Schelling's late thought, both to the negative and to the positive philosophy, and because the process is far from easy to understand, it may be worth recapitulating it straightaway from a slightly different angle. Reason, in abstracting from all determinacy of predication, understands primordial being as "the infinite potentiality of being." But how should we characterize the concept of that infinite potentiality? Given that the concept of something, on Schelling's account, just is the form of its possible existence, the concept of the infinite potentiality of being turns out to be the reflexive form of this potentiality itself. In this way the identity-in-difference of knowing and being in transcendental reflection is established. At the same time, the next thought which becomes unavoidable for the philosopher, that of the actualization of *being as potentiality*, should be carefully distinguished from the actualization of a *potentiality of being*. Of course, when Schelling compares the former actualization to Aristotle's πρώτη ὕλη (*protē hylē*—primordial matter), he is not just thinking of the unidentified, resistant stuff we bump into in the night, but to whatever must be formed to produce an entity of some kind, whether this be a bedframe, a poem or a geometrical figure. The problem which arises at this point is that, if beingness fully actualizes itself *as* objective potentiality, it is *no longer* potentiality in the sense of what may or may not actualize itself. Here again, Schelling is following Aristotle, who in *Metaphysics IX* distinguishes potentialities from causal powers, which are necessarily activated, given the relevant conditions. For Aristotle, causal powers can *themselves* exist potentially (*dunamei*) or actually (*energiai*).[10] Thus, the connotation of possibility strongly colors Aristotle's conception of potentiality: "That, then, which is potentially may either be or not be; the same thing, then, is capable of both being and not being" (*Metaphysics,* IX.8.1050b11–12). For being-ness itself (*das Seyende selbst*) to maintain its status as potentiality, therefore, it must resist its total actualization *as* potentiality, which would be self-negating; it must push back as "pure being" (*reines Sein*)—non-actualized being—*against* this actualization. This it can only do by becoming a second-order potentiality, which must realize itself as a counterforce. Such resistance seeks to hold the boundless substrate in check, to drive it back into its status as *mere* potentiality—to transform rampant materiality into the matter *of something*, as it were, through the imposition of form, which is essentially conceptual or ideal. However, the full victory of either mode of being-ness would destroy it *as* potentiality by eliminating the counterpart on which it dialectically depends for its actualization. This is why the conflict needs to be contained by the intervention of a third dimension of being in which actualization and potentialization intersect. In this respect, Schelling's reference to the "organism of objectively posited reason" makes use of an apt metaphor, since living organisms are pre-eminent examples of entities whose being is simultaneously actual and potential—whose existence consists precisely in an active, normative orientation toward the maintenance of their specific *form* of existence.

What has been said so far regarding the dialectic of Schelling's potentialities, both using Schelling's own words and in my commentary on them, has had the peculiarity of being on the one hand highly abstract, and on the other hand strikingly figurative. This not surprising, however, as the basic subject–predicate structure of human language is oriented toward attributing properties to entities, whereas Schelling is attempting to bring to light the interaction between the vectors of being which makes any kind of determinate existence possible in the first place. In this respect, it is instructive to compare Schelling's three potentialities with what Kant calls "sensibility," "understanding," and the "transcendental unity of apperception." The difference between Schelling and Kant consists primarily in the fact that Schelling "de-subjectivizes" Kantian theory; but making sense of the principles themselves and their interrelation is no more—or no less—difficult in Schelling's case than in Kant's. Jürgen Habermas once found a concise formulation for the contrast between the two thinkers: Schelling's negative philosophy is concerned "not so much with the conditions of possibility of all objects, as with the necessary conditions of their actuality as possible."[11] Clearly, Schelling also anticipates other more recent philosophers—one thinks, for instance, of Maurice Merleau-Ponty—in his use of metaphor to counteract the hypostatizing effect of talk about the pre-predicative dimensions of being. For example, he continues to use the anthropomorphic vocabulary of "will" and "willing" in his late philosophy to describe the dialectic of the potentialities. This is not simply so as to stress a conception of being as activity and process, but also because Schelling regards the phenomenology of willing as providing us with our most direct experience of possibility becoming actuality.

Certain obvious parallels between the enterprise of Schelling's negative philosophy and Hegel's *Science of Logic* have already been noted. However, crucial divergences have also become evident. Because, in Schelling's negative philosophy, the "immediate content of reason" (*der unmittelbare Inhalt der Vernunft*) *is* the "infinite potentiality of being" (*die unendliche Potenz des Seyns*) (GPP: 143/SW, II/3: 78), his form of pure transcendental reflection already gives us the structure of what he terms "the real" or "the actual" (*das Wirkliche*). As Schelling puts it, "the *a priori* science is... necessarily philosophy of nature and philosophy of spirit" (GPP: 137/SW, II/3: 71). This formulation could not make the contrast with Hegel clearer. When he arrives at the "absolute Idea" at the end of his *Science of Logic*, Hegel still has to confront the problem of the transition from the logical realm to the domain of what he calls "*Realphilosophie*"—of the philosophies of nature and spirit. Hence, although Schelling also reaches what he terms the "Idea" at the end of the unfolding of his negative philosophy, the significance of this terminus, and the problems raised by the transition, by the question of what—if anything—lies "beyond" the Idea, will find very different responses in the work of the two thinkers. It is to these issues that we now turn.

Notes

1. On Plato's use of myth in his Socratic dialogues, see Penelope Murray, "What is a Muthos for Plato?" and Christopher Rowe, "Myth, History and Dialectic in Plato's *Republic* and *Timaeus-Critias*," in *From Myth to Reason. Studies in the Development of Greek Thought*, ed. Richard Buxton (Oxford: OUP, 2002).
2. See Charlotte Witt, *Substance and Essence in Aristotle: An Interpretation of Metaphysics VII–IX* (Ithaca and London: Cornell University Press, 1989). Witt argues that "Aristotle's notion of form or essence is meant to explain why there is an individual substance there at all, not what features constitute the identity of a given individual substance within a domain of individual substances" (126).
3. This is the fundamental thesis of Axel Hutter's lucid study, *Geschichtliche Vernunft. Die Weiterführung der kantischen Vernunftkritik in der Spätphilosophie Schellings* (Frankfurt: Suhrkamp, 1996).
4. See the discussion of the development of Kant's distinction between the theses and antitheses of the antinomies in Paul Guyer and Allen W. Wood, "Introduction,"

in Kant, *Critique of Pure Reason*, trans. and ed. Paul Guyer and Allen W. Wood (Cambridge: CUP, 1998), 56–60.
5. John M. E. McTaggart, *A Commentary on Hegel's Logic* (Bristol: Thoemmes, 1990), 15.
6. Stephen Houlgate, *The Opening of Hegel's Logic: From Being to Infinity* (West Lafayette, IN: Purdue University Press, 2006), 264.
7. See Theodor Adorno, *Vorlesung über Negative Dialektik* (Frankfurt: Suhrkamp, 2007), 91–94 (Adorno is discussing Enc.1: §86, *Zusatz* 1/W20, 8: 184).
8. See Søren Kierkegaard, *Concluding Unscientific Postscript* (Princeton, NJ: Princeton University Press, 1968), 102–103.
9. Schelling, *Initia Philosophiae Universae* ("Grundzüge der gesammten Philosophie"), H-K, II/10, 2: 677.
10. See Charlotte Witt, *Ways of Being: Potentiality and Actuality in Aristotle's Metaphysics* (Ithaca and London: Cornell University Press, 2003), 37.
11. Jürgen Habermas, "Dialektischer Idealismus im Übergang zum Materialismus. Geschichtsphilosophische Folgerungen aus Schellings Idee einer Contraction Gottes," in *Theorie und Praxis* (Frankfurt am Main: Suhrkamp, 1971), 209.

5
Beyond the Idea

Schelling's Negative Philosophy

Schelling's negative philosophy is a large, complex structure, consisting of a philosophy of nature and a philosophy of spirit.[1] Its full details cannot be explored here, but the interaction of potentialities, which generates a system of natural kinds or fundamental forms, can be explained. Schelling often refers to the first potentiality of being, when regarded as part of a dialectical process, as "B." However, it should be borne in mind that this is really shorthand for "$A^1 \rightarrow B$." In other words, the negative philosophy begins with an instantaneous shift which occludes the non-being—the *néant*—of pure potentiality, which is "being-ness itself": "B" is always also the cipher for a certain opacity. The actualization of the first potentiality of being, which Schelling interprets modally as "*das Seynkönnende*" (that-which-*has-the-capacity*-to-be), activates the second potentiality, whose abbreviation is A^2, and whose modal interpretation is "*das Seynmüssende*" (that-which-*has*-to-be). Necessity emerges at this point because pure being-ness is *forced* to take on the form of form, as it were, to prevent its complete eversion into objectified potentiality. The resulting conflict between B and A^2 can only be mitigated by a third potentiality, which expresses what they have in common as possibilities of being, and which Schelling annotates as A^3 (modally interpreted, this is "*das Seynsollende*"—that-which-*ought*-to-be). It certainly makes sense, intuitively speaking, to regard normative force as expressing what is *necessary as a possibility*, or *possible as a necessity*. However, the structuring of matter and form in a determinate fundamental type of entity is itself something particular, and it therefore becomes the matter or basis for more complex, higher-level actualizations. In Schelling's own language, the potentialities are repeatedly "de-potentiated," the higher becomes the lower, in an advance along the spectrum between the particular and the universal, the material and the ideal, which is driven by the striving of the potentialities to re-unify themselves as the original being-ness from which they broke out. This process generates the successive forms of inorganic and organic nature, culminating in the emergence of human beings, who—in principle—are able fully integrate the first and second potentialities, in the mode which Schelling terms "*Geist*" (mind or spirit). In other words, human existence is the re-emergence, in a finite from, of pure being-ness. As such, it is inherently unstable.

In becoming explicitly *self*-conscious, human beings fall back under the particularizing sway of the first potentiality, and this sets them—as spirit—in opposition to the material world, thereby estranging spirit and nature, while paradoxically also reifying spirit, forcing it to play by nature's rules. The consequences of the human attainment of self-awareness had been a preoccupation of Schelling's ever since his student days, when he was influenced—like many of his contemporaries—by Kant's interpretation of the third chapter of Genesis;[2] in the form of the *Abfall* this topos played a pivotal role, foreshadowing his late thinking, in the text *Philosophy and Religion* of 1804. In Schelling's *negative* philosophy, these consequences are played out in the successive attempts of human beings to overcome their estrangement from the world. The most complete of these—following on from mystical religion and art—is negative philosophy itself, which seeks to achieve a rationally transparent comprehension of the forms of being, and thereby overcome their alien-ness. "Pure rational philosophy," then, itself appears at the end of Schelling's negative philosophy, which thereby theorizes its own emergence. It is via this path to the paradigmatic terminus of German Idealist inquiry, in which the object of investigation and the process of investigation merge, that we reach what Schelling terms the "Idea." He explains that the Idea:

> Is no longer the mere, indeterminately existing ὄν, also not merely the concept (potentiality = concept) of something other, but for this reason the concept of itself, which remains standing by itself, unique of its kind, the goal of the whole movement, and in this sense to be called **Idea**. (PO41/42: 108)

With the Idea—the completed system of rationally generated concepts—we reach the turning point in Schelling's late philosophy. The Idea sustains the whole panoply of the fundamental concepts or possibilities of being because—as in Hegel's *Logic*—none of the preceding categories (in Schelling's case, none of the constellations of potentialities) is stable without it. But we are now confronted with the question of the *ontological status* of the Idea itself. Schelling's engagement with this question in his late philosophy typically takes the form a dialogue with Kant because, in his view, the Kantian theory of the scope of pure reason represents the pioneering example of a *self-consciously negative* philosophy—a philosophy which limits itself to establishing the categorial structure of the experienced world through transcendental reflection, while prescinding from questions concerning the "why?" of the world's existence. At the same time, of course, Kant is far from being insensitive to the pressure of these questions. Hence his attempt to define the limit of what reason can achieve, not by dismissing such questions as meaningless, but by showing that they lie beyond the bounds of the rationally determinable, poses a crucial challenge for his successor. For, as we noted in the previous chapter, Schelling claims that, beyond negative philosophy, there lies *another mode* of philosophical knowing, one which does indeed address the "fact of the world" as such.

The Idea as Turning Point

In the "Transcendental Dialectic" of the first *Critique*, Kant presents what he terms the "Ideas"—concepts of the soul as the substantial unity of the person, of the world as a totality, and of God—as the coping stones of the systematic unity of knowledge to which reason aspires. Because the Ideas are the transcendent principles guiding the acquisition and organization of all empirical knowledge, and because for Kant all genuine knowledge has an empirical element, the Ideas themselves cannot be known. Not even bare existence can be attributed to them as something known. Clearly, Kant's conception has dramatic consequences for traditional metaphysical arguments intended to prove the existence of God. Nonetheless the *concept* of God—or what Kant refers to as the "Ideal of Pure Reason"—plays an important role in the architectonic of the first *Critique*.

Kant argues that our basic assumption that the reality of empirical objects implies their complete determinability (in other words, either a predicate or its negation must apply to any given object) "is grounded on a transcendental substratum, which contains as it were the entire storehouse of material from which all possible predicates of things can be taken . . . [and] . . . this substratum is nothing other than idea of an All of reality (*omnitudo realitatis*)" (A574/B603). When we think of this substratum as possessing all positive predicates, then we have produced the Idea of a being which is the source of all reality, and which Kant refers to as the "Ideal," to indicate that what is at issue is *not* a universal, but a unique entity. An ideal, Kant explains, is the concept of something singular which carries a certain attribute or set of attributes to a maximum which lies beyond empirical exemplification. Because the entity in question here contains the maximum of reality, it qualifies as an ideal. And because it is generated *a priori* by reflection on the conditions for the complete determinability of objects, which itself follows from the principle of non-contradiction, Kant terms it the Ideal of *pure reason*. Given the role of the Ideal, Kant argues, we can also call this entity the "original being," the "supreme being" or the "being of all beings" (*ens originarium, realissimum, ens entium*) (A631/B659). In other words, Kant takes himself to have shown how reason alone, rather than—for example—deep anxieties aroused by our finitude, vulnerability, and mortality, as suggested by more recent thinkers such as Feuerbach, Nietzsche, or Freud, intrinsically generates the concept of God.

Kant stresses that the thought of the "being of beings" "does not signify the objective relation of an actual object to other things, but only that of an **idea** to **concepts**, and as to the existence of a being of such preeminent excellence it leaves us in complete ignorance" (A579/B607). Indeed, Kant claims that "reason notices the ideal and merely fictive character of such a presupposition" (A583/B611) and is only pushed toward assuming the existence of a being corresponding to its Ideal because it is "urged from another source to seek somewhere for a resting place in the regress from the conditioned, which is given, to the unconditioned, which is in itself" (A584/B612). This source is found in common experience, and takes the form of the reflection that, "If something, no matter what, exists then it must be conceded that something exists **necessarily**... That is the argument in which reason grounds its progress to the original being" (A584/B612). Slightly later in the *Critique of Pure Reason*, in his discussion of the cosmological proof of the existence of God, Kant examines this train of thought in more detail. He argues that we may assume "the existence of a being of the highest sufficiency as the cause of all possible effects, in order to facilitate reason's search for the grounds of all explanation" (A612/B640). However, it would be theoretically presumptuous to state categorically that such a being exists. As he puts it:

> The entire problem of the transcendental Ideal comes to this: either to find a concept for the absolute necessity or to find the absolute necessity for the concept of some thing. If one can do the first, then one must be able to do the other too. For reason cognizes as absolutely necessary only what is necessary from its concept. (A612/B640)

But because the "impudent assumption of an apodictic certainty" which assertions concerning such a necessity would involve cannot satisfy the understanding, Kant concludes that "The unconditioned necessity, which we need so indispensably as the ultimate sustainer of all things, is for human reason the true abyss" (A613/B640).

In his Berlin lecture course of 1842/43, *Grounding of Positive Philosophy*, Schelling refers to this passage in Kant to show that his predecessor had reached the verge of the transition to what he terms "positive philosophy." Schelling's interpretation becomes plausible if one considers that, in referring to "unconditioned necessity" and "absolute necessity" in the passages just quoted, Kant—inconsistently—must be groping for a necessity *beyond* that needed by reason for the systematic completion of its tasks, since he has already shown that we *do* have a concept which performs that role: namely, the Ideal. Despite his attempt to show that reason can be satisfied simply by policing its own immanent aspiration, Kant seems to be haunted by a sense that reason demands *more* than it can generate from its own resources alone.[3] Hence Schelling suggests that:

> One would completely misunderstand Kant, if one were inclined to perceive in the passage in question a rejection of that idea (of groundlessly necessary existence); what he aims to express is rather merely its incomprehensibility; for he is imbued with a sense of the unavoidable necessity of reason to assume something groundlessly being. And incomprehensible—yes, this existence is indeed that, if one understands the incomprehensible as what cannot be conceptualized *a priori*. (GPP: 205/SW, II/3: 164–165)

Schelling's interpretation of this unusually dramatic passage from the first *Critique* looks even stronger if we consider what Kant says about the abyssal thought of unconditioned necessity. For he comments:

> One cannot resist the thought of it, but one also cannot bear it that a being which we represent to ourselves as the highest among all possible beings might, as it were, say to itself: "I am from eternity to eternity, outside me is nothing except what is something merely through my will; but whence then am I?" (A613/B641)

Kant states clearly here that the thought of necessary existence is irresistible, but we also find it intolerable that we are forced, as a result, to regard the necessary existence of the highest being—God himself—as groundless. However, this is the precisely point at which Schelling begins to push at the limits of onto-theology. For he *detaches* the concept of necessary existence from the concept of God. He writes:

> For the necessarily existing is not the necessarily existing because it is God; because then it would precisely not be the necessarily, the groundlessly existing, since in the concept of God, a ground of necessary existence would be found. For the necessarily existing is indeed not such as a result of a preceding concept, but what exists *from itself*, or as one used to say, *a se*, in other words, *sponte, ultra*, without a preceding ground. Here then lies the knot of previous metaphysics, which can only be unravelled by holding the two concepts of being apart. (GPP:207/SW, II/3: 168)

It is clear from this statement that, for Schelling, absolutely necessary existence must be regarded as what we first encountered in *System der Weltalter* as "*das nicht Nichtseynkönnende*"—that which is powerless not to be. Necessary existence conceived as dependent upon a ground simply raises the question of the necessity of the ground, and Schelling—for reasons which we will consider in more detail further on—does not accept, not even in the case of God, that a concept can contain the ground of its instantiation. But he does not rule out the possibility that (groundlessly) necessary existence may turn out to be the *basis* of the existence of God as the "necessarily necessarily-existing" (*das nothwendig Nothwendigexistirende*)—indeed, the notion of this connection performs a pivotal role in his positive philosophy. However, should this link be established, it will not be a purely conceptual one. It will be—as he puts it in this context—"not necessary, but *factical*" (nicht nothwendig, aber *faktisch*) (GPP: 208/SW, II/3: 169). The problem with Kant's position, then, is that:

> Kant thinks about . . . necessary existence in so far as it is already also God; but at the beginning of positive philosophy we must still disregard this, and take it as the sheerly existing, we drop the concept of *God*, precisely because it is a contradiction to posit the sheerly existing, and yet posit it as already *something*, by means of a *concept*. (GPP: 204–205/SW, II/3: 164)

It is important to note that this approach to the question of necessary existence does not transgress Kant's prohibition on purely rational inference to reason-transcendent existence. As Schelling puts it:

The transcendence of positive philosophy is absolute, and precisely for this reason *not* transcendence in the sense which Kant prohibits. If I have begun by making myself immanent, in other words enclosed myself in pure thinking, then a transcendence is scarcely possible; but if I start from the transcendent (as does the positive philosophy), then there is in fact nothing which I might have transgressed. Kant forbids transcendence to metaphysics, but he forbids it only to dogmatizing reason, that is, reason which, starting from *itself*, aims to reach existence by means of inferences. (GPP: 208/SW, II/3: 169–170)

We have acquired, then, a first inkling of what Schelling understands by "positive philosophy." We *begin* from the transcendent, which is groundless or without reason ("*grundlos*"), with the aim of inquiring if and—to what extent—reason can make sense of it, by searching for pattern, direction, or purpose in its consequences. As Schelling puts it: "The content of negative philosophy is being which can be comprehended *a priori, that of positive philosophy is being which is a priori incomprehensible*, with the intention that it should become comprehensible *a posteriori*" (PO41/42: 159–160).

The Transition to Positive Philosophy

The epistemological structure of the positive philosophy, Schelling's method of making the existence of the world intelligible, and the upshot of his hermeneutics of nature and history, will preoccupy us in the following chapters. But before moving on to these major topics, we need to explore Schelling's conception of the pivot from negative to positive philosophy. One obvious concern arises at this point: how does Schelling's description of reason's experience of the *end point* or limit of negative philosophy, a limit which forces Kant into his precarious balancing act (his theoretical agnosticism regarding the existence of the Ideal, which is nonetheless generated and required by reason), differ from Schelling's portrayal of the *starting point* of negative philosophy, which he finds in the thought of the "subject of being" (*das Subjekt des Seyns*), or of "being-ness itself" (*das Seyende selbst*)? This question is made especially pressing by the close parallels between the two accounts—by the fact, for example, that Schelling draws on Spinoza's concept of substance as "that whose nature cannot be conceived except as existing" (*id, cujus natura non potest concipi nisi existens*) (E: 1def1) to specify both the starting point and the end point of negative philosophy.

The reference to Spinoza provides a clue for answering the question. For, as we saw in the previous chapter, Schelling describes the Spinozist concept of substance as "up to the present time, the point around which everything moves, or rather the imprisonment of thought, from which thought has sought to emancipate itself through the successive systems without yet being able to do so" (HMP: 65/SW, I/10: 34). Schelling means by this that Spinoza's concept of substance as "*causa sui*," as cause of itself or self-grounding necessity—a necessity which is then transmitted to the theory of nature, and of human psychology as an integral part of nature—established the supremacy of the principle of sufficient reason in subsequent rationalist philosophy, and was even decisive for post-Kantian attempts to generate a comprehensive system through reflection on the necessary structure of reasoning itself. This includes Schelling's own negative philosophy, since the inaugural apprehension of "being-ness itself" launches the dialectical development of the potentialities of being which pure thinking is immanently compelled to run through. But, as Schelling's reference to the "imprisonment of thought" suggests, his attitude to this rational necessity reflects the profound ambiguity of the situation. While, on the one hand, negative philosophy unfolds the "content of reason" (*der Inhalt der Vernunft*), giving us insight into the way in which the world is essentially structured, it simultaneously occludes being-ness itself. Or, to be more precise, it occludes being-ness—which is precisely what it is seeking to think—in the very process of disclosing it in the form of the interplay of its potentialities. As Schelling states in theological mode in the *Urfassung*—the original draft—of the *Philosophy of Revelation*, "It is [God's] own shape which he continues to glimpse through the potentialities; the potentialities are, as it were, the disguise of the original shape of his being" (UPO: 89). This is the process which Michael Theunissen had in mind, when, in a classic essay, he described Schelling's late project as the exposure of the powerlessness internal to the very power of reason—the power reinstated in an even more ambitious mode by German Idealist philosophy, after its Kantian limitation, and brought to its apogee by Hegel.[4] We can perceive the dialectic evoked by Theunissen at work in a remark Schelling makes concerning the start of his pure rational philosophy: "The *potentia pura*, the beginning of negative philosophy, was even powerless to be a potentiality, and could not maintain itself as such" (*Die potentia pura, der Anfang der negativen Philosophie, war sogar impotent, Potenz zu sein, und konnte sich als solche nicht halten*) (PO41/42: 165).

Taking a lead from Theunissen, one can say that the limit of negative philosophy is reached when this powerlessness emerges *for* reason itself. In its confrontation with being-ness, reason—as Schelling asserts in his *Begründung der positiven Philosophie*—is "set outside itself, absolutely ecstatic" (GPP: 203/SW, II/3: 163); it is "motionless, as if frozen, *quasi attonita* [as if thunderstruck]" (GPP: 206/SW, II/3: 165). Similarly, in the inaugural Berlin lecture course, reason—at this moment—is described as "paralysed" (PO41/42: 110). Reason, having worked through all the dialectical moves of "negative philosophy," to the point of having reflexively retrieved the stages of its own itinerary, has exhausted *a priori* definable possibility. If we *still* cannot avoid presupposing existence at this point, therefore, the necessity involved cannot be that of reason's immanently determined movement. This is why, at the transition point from negative to positive philosophy, Schelling refers to "groundlessly necessary existence" (*grundlos notwendige Existenz*) (GPP: 205/SW, II/3: 164–165). Reason is now confronted with sheer existence, which it knows it cannot conceptually derive because it has already reflexively closed the circle of *a priori* content. Sheer existence is pre-modal. It appears as *contingent*, in comparison with the immanent necessity of reason's own self-unfolding, yet it also appears as *necessary* in the sense of being exempt from any grounds or conditions, including purely rational ones. This is why Schelling refers to it, in what might at first appear a deeply perplexing phrase, as the "merely contingently necessary [process of] existing" (*nur zufällig notwendig Existieren*) (PO41/42: 166). To put this in another way, Schelling's basic, anti-Hegelian contention is that the full *self-explication* of reason, which is a feasible and legitimate project, should not be inflated into the *self-grounding* of reason because *das Existieren*, as such, lies beyond reason's scope.[5] In Kant, the assumption of this equivalence is innocuous because reason is ontologically neutralized, as it were. But in Hegel, as we shall find in a moment, it becomes the claim that reason grounds the existence of the world as a whole, thereby eliminating what Schelling, in the context of the transition from negative to positive philosophy, often describes as "un-prethinkable being" (*das unvordenkliche Seyn*)—in other words, being which is neither identical with its concept nor derivable from it.

Schelling often refers to "un-pre-thinkable being" as "blind being-ness" (*das Blindseiende*) (e.g., PO41/42: 154, 155) or as "blind existing-ness" (*das Blindexistierende*) (PO41/42: 157). However, the status of raw being-ness has subtly changed since the starting point of his negative philosophy. There, it was the result of a process within *a priori* thinking: the precipitous self-objectification of being-ness *as* pure potentiality, in a mode which Schelling describes metaphorically as aimless, uncontrolled willing. But now the internal dilemma of being-ness in its primordial state cannot be evaded by plunging into the immanent dialectical movement of reason, because that movement has reached its terminus:

> But precisely with blind being-ness philosophy has come across that which needs no grounding. It cannot be reached from any starting point . . . *Blind existing-ness is that* which strikes down everything deriving from the concept, and *before which thought is struck dumb*. (PO41/42: 157)

It is important to stress that the pivot from negative to positive philosophy is in no sense a slide into irrationalism. The moment of muteness and paralysis of reason marks only a point of transition. The fact that "[t]he first science came across something, at its end, which could no longer be cognized using its method" (DRP, SW, II/1: 564) does not entail that reason must be abandoned, but rather that it must now be reactivated in a new form. At the start of the positive philosophy, Schelling argues, reason "submits to [un-pre-thinkable being] only so as to raise itself up immediately over against it, namely with the question, *what* the un-pre-thinkably existing is" (PO, SW, II/4: 345). He presents this methodological shift both as the appropriate consummation of negative philosophy, disclosing what it sought but was constitutionally unable to find, *and* as a liberation from it—an *emancipati*on of reason: "The negative [philosophy] triumphs in positive philosophy; for it is the science in which thinking posits itself in freedom from all necessary content" (PO41/42: 153). In other words, the repetitive "*how?*" question of negative or pure rational philosophy, the search for ever more fundamental conditions of possibility, is replaced by reason's "*why?*" question. This can no longer be answered simply through reason's own movement, but is addressed to existence as such, by which it is confronted. Reason must now seek to make sense of something other than itself—of what Schelling, in his late work, sometimes calls "*das reine Daß*" (the pure fact *that* anything exists at all). Hence, the new-found freedom which Schelling frequently attributes to positive philosophy can be concisely described as the freedom of hermeneutic *responsiveness*, as opposed to freedom conceptualized as an inward-turning process of logical self-determination. In his first Berlin lecture course Schelling describes the result of this emancipation with a term that could be rendered as "reason released from stress" (*die gelassene Vernunft*), or even—using colloquialism to highlight the point—as "laid-back reason"; this is reason which "liberates itself from itself" (*die Vernunft die sich von sich selbst befreit*) (PO41/42: 157).

Hegel's Theory of the Idea

Schelling's theory of the Idea, and of what lies "beyond" the Idea, deals with issues which were naturally also of profound concern to Hegel. For Hegel seeks to make the most compelling case that the process of thought's rational self-determination, culminating in the Idea, provides the template for all real-worldly or trans-logical existence. This raises the intriguing question of the sense in which any kind of empirical existence can be said to lie beyond the logical for Hegel. But whatever the answer to that question may be, if he is right, there will be no need for a transition from "pure rational" philosophy to a different style of philosophical activity, along the lines of Schelling's turning-inside-out of reason, his "inverted Idea" (GPP: 203/SW, II/3: 162). This is not to deny that Hegel's system is also characterized by a basic structural dualism. At the end of the *Logic* there occurs an obvious shift into new philosophical register—a move onto the terrain of what Hegel calls, by way of contrast, "*Realphilosophie*." However, we can know in advance that what we will find there will be the continuing process of reason's self-determination, albeit in another medium: not in pure thought, but in spatio-temporal reality, which Hegel refers to in the *Encyclopaedia* as "worldly existence, external objectivity" (*weltliches Dasein, äusserliche Objektivität*) (Enc.1: §54/W20, 8: 138). Of course, this conception raises the question of the character and *rationale* of the transition from the *Logic* to the *Realphilosophie* in Hegel. And this in turn raises the prior issue of what he understands by the term "Idea."

We should note, first of all, that there are major differences—as well as significant similarities—in the manner in which Schelling and Hegel envisage the character of pure rational science. Hegel's *Science of Logic* develops a system of categories which are intended to be independent of application to any specific aspect of worldly reality; it articulates the forms of intelligibility, the "determinations of thought" (*Denkbestimmungen*), which are presupposed by thought or talk about any subject matter. Categories whose application is limited to a specific "sphere"—Hegel's own term—are not developed in the *Science of Logic*, but rather in the various branches of the *Realphilosophie*. By contrast, Schelling's negative philosophy does not draw this distinction. Although it develops dialectically through a recursive action of the potentialities on the templates of being which they have already cooperated in constituting, it determines a sequence of *types* of entity, which advances from the natural, to the anthropological, socio-political, and cultural. In this respect, the negative philosophy takes the reader on a journey more closely comparable to Hegel's *Philosophy of Nature* and *Philosophy of Spirit* than to his *Science of Logic*, or its condensation in the first part of the *Encyclopaedia*. But conversely, the *Encyclopaedia*'s *Philosophy of Spirit*, for example, is not a theory of the stages of human consciousness whose ultimate validation is empirical. Hegel must be committed, for instance, to the view that, in any world in which there are rational self-conscious creatures, such beings will pass through an evolving series of forms of religious consciousness; furthermore, that the supreme form of religion will revolve around the conception of a purely spiritual but also uniquely incarnate God. Not only this: the final form of religion will eventually shed its symbolic guise and transform itself into a fully conceptualized theory of the basic structure of reality comparable to the *Science of Logic*. Hegel's *Realphilosophie*, then, like Schelling's negative philosophy, culminates necessarily in the thinking of the Idea.

We can summarize Hegel's conception of the Idea in the statement that it is the immanent structuring principle of whatever truly *is*. It is not a set of categories which subjects employ to systematize a reality which subsists independently of those categories, and neither is it a set of principles which determine the interactions between the entities which populate the world. It is clear, then, that Hegel's Idea is a descendent of Kant's Ideal of pure reason, as the totality of rational conditions for anything to be, which, for Kant, means: to be fully determinate. At the same time, Hegel emphasizes that—contrary to Kant's assumption—the Idea is not a transcendent "concept of reason" (*Vernunftbegriff*) which can never be realized in any finite entity (see SL: 670–672/W20, 6: 462–464). Rather, entities only have being at all in so far as they embody or exemplify the Idea. To the extent that they do *not* do so, Hegel asserts, they are "mere *appearance*, something subjective, accidental, arbitrary, which is not the truth" (bloße *Erscheinung*, das Subjektive, Zufällige, Willkürliche, das nicht die Wahrheit ist) (SL: 671/W20, 6: 464). This conception of the essential unity of true being and the

Idea first manifests itself in an *objective* form as the category of life. This is because living organisms have a self-sustaining, autotelic structure—their functioning is guided by the *kind* of entity which they are (in other words, by their concept). However, this self-relatedness is not self-conscious, but embedded in an objective process. Life is an inadequate or one-sided realization of conceptuality because it fails to express the concept's *explicit* or self-conscious reflexivity.

The Idea therefore next appears as "Cognition." But, because cognition presupposes a separation and opposition between knower and known, it takes two counterposed forms: the Idea of the True and the Idea of the Good. The Idea of the True expresses the thought of the Idea as the essential structure of reality—but as something standing over against self-consciousness, and to be discovered by it. By contrast, the Idea of the Good, incorporates self-consciousness into its understanding of the world, releases it from transcendental exile, as it were, by making it practical. But it does so at the cost of transforming the Idea from the target of the "drive for truth" (*Trieb der Wahrheit*) into the ultimate aim of the subject's drive to *realize itself* through world-transforming action. Although this represents an advance, because the Idea now "has not only the dignity of the universal, but of the straightforwardly actual and effective" (SL: 729/ W20, 6: 542), it still leaves the Idea as something subjectively projected, standing over against objective reality. This situation confronts consciousness with the dilemma of deciding which is more important: the abstract, unrealized Idea or the concretion of the existing world. According to Hegel, this dilemma can be overcome only by comprehending that the Idea—in the form of the Good—has *always already* realized itself in the world, through the very process that produces self-consciousness beings who necessarily think that they must strive for the Good. It is the history of those efforts—and the overall structure of reality which makes that history possible—which is truly the Good, not some projected goal separate from the actuality of the world. As Hegel puts the matter, from the subjective standpoint of agency:

> What still *limits* the objective concept is its own *view* of itself, which vanishes through reflection on what its actualization is *in itself*. This view means that it is simply standing in its own way, and what it has to do about this is to turn, not against an outer actuality, but against itself. (SL: 733/ W20, 6: 547)

The culmination of this logical movement, then, occurs in grasping that the fully unfolded meaning of the concept of pure being, with which the *Logic* began, is the always already completed self-realization of the Idea. Hegel terms this comprehension of the status of the Idea the "absolute Idea."

It is important to bear in mind that, by the end of the *Science of Logic*, we have still only reached the *concept* of the unity of "the concept"—that is to say, conceptuality—and being. We have realized that what Hegel—playing on the standard definition of truth as *adequatio rei et intellectus*—terms the "*adequate concept*" (SL: 670/W20, 6: 462) is not a subjective form imposed on extraneous material, but it rather the inner constitution of that material. But we have yet to consider how the Idea, as the system of "determinations of thought," is instantiated in the world of time and space. In the *Encyclopaedia Logic*, for example, Hegel draws a distinction between what he terms the "'ideal' content" of the Idea, which is "nothing but the concept in its detailed terms," and its "'real' content," or the presentation (*Darstellung*) which "the concept gives itself in the form of external existence" (Enc. 1: §213/W20, 8: 367). Correspondingly, the exposition of the Idea at the end of Hegel's *Logic* deals primarily with the method of speculative logic itself, which produces the sequence of categories constituting the Idea. Hegel terms this method "the absolute form" (SL: 737/W20, 6: 568), since it has no content to which it is relative: rather its form is the content. Accordingly, what Hegel understands by "being" at the end of the *Logic* is not worldly or external being—"*äusserliches Dasein*," as he sometimes calls it (e.g., Enc. 1: §24, Zusatz/W20, 8: 82; SL: 731/W20, 6: 544)—but the fully unfolded, and reflexively stabilized system of conceptual determinations:

> The method is the pure concept, which relates only to itself; it is therefore the *simple self-reference* that is *being*. But it is now also *fulfilled* being, the *self-conceptualizing concept*, being as the *concrete* and just as absolutely *intensive* totality. (SL: 752/W20, 6: 572)

The "fulfilled being" to which Hegel refers here, then, is the complete, interrelated system of *a priori* determinations: we are not yet engaging philosophically with spatio-temporal, or even merely temporal, entities. But we can anticipate that qualifying as an entity will involve expressing or exemplifying at least some of the features of this totality.

The point we have now reached in Hegel's *Logic* has long been recognized as a crux in the overall structure of his system. In a nutshell, the following problem arises: given that Hegel defines the absolute Idea as *"true being,"* the "unity of *concept* and *reality,"* the *"subject-object"* and so forth (SL: 673/ W20, 6: 466), how can it also be one-sided or incomplete, as its status as the culmination only of the first part of Hegel's system implies? Hegel's theory of the absolute Idea presents it as an accomplished totality of determinations, the last of which closes the circle because it is the reflexive grasp of the process of generation of that totality itself. It seems, therefore, that there is no further *logical* move which needs to be—or could be—made. But at the same time Hegel suggests unmistakably, at the end of his monumental enterprise, that the fact that the Idea has been constructed purely in thought is a limitation. He writes:

> This Idea is still logical [*noch logisch*], it is shut up in pure thought, and is the science only of the divine *concept*. Of course, the systematic exposition is itself a realization of the Idea, but confined within the same sphere. Because the pure Idea of cognition is to this extent shut up within subjectivity, it is the *drive* to suspend this [subjectivity], and pure truth as the final result becomes also the *beginning of another sphere and science*. (SL: 752/ W20, 6: 572–573)

One remarkable aspect of these comments is that the absolute Idea now appears to be *subsumed* under the *Idea of cognition*, which was supposed to be simply one of its moments. Accordingly, Hegel invokes a "drive" to overcome the confinement within pure thought of the absolute Idea, which is "shut up in subjectivity" (*in die Subjektivität eingeschlossen*)—"drive" (*Trieb*) being the term which he had employed earlier to describe the response of practical consciousness, guided by its Idea of the Good, to the split between subject and object set up by the Idea of the True.

It should be clear, then, that the projects of Hegel and Schelling cannot be distinguished simply by reference to the need for a philosophical move *beyond* the logical Idea. Just as Schelling's late thought is divided between his "negative" and his "positive" philosophy, so Hegel's system is divided between the *Logic* and the *Realphilosophie*, which embraces the concrete domains of nature and spirit. The difference between the two thinkers must therefore consist in *the way in which they conceptualize* the passage beyond the Idea—and not in the acknowledgement of the need for such a transition. We know already that Schelling evokes an "*ecstasis,"* in which reason is reversed or set outside itself, as it finds itself confronted with "contingently necessary existing-ness." However, another term which Schelling often employs in this context, "un-pre-thinkable being" (*das unvordenkliche Seyn*), provides the best clue to where the difference between his approach and Hegel's will lie. For although Hegel distinguishes between the "ideal content" of the Idea—which is "the concept in its determinations"—and its "real content," he claims that this "real content" is "only [the concept's] presentation, which it gives itself in the form of external existence (*in der Form äusserlichen Daseins*), and, as this shape is enclosed in its ideality, in its power, [the concept] thus maintains itself in it" (Enc.1: §213/W20, 8: 367). In other words, Hegel believes himself to have shown that "external existence" offers no fundamental resistance or opacity to the concept—reveals nothing "un-pre-thinkable," requiring an entirely novel *a posteriori* effort of conceptualization. Hence, whatever the debates over the relation between the *Logic* and the *Realphilosophie*, and over Hegel's own account of the transition between them, his commitment to what he terms the "omnipotence of the concept" (*die Allmacht des Begriffs*) (SL: 586/W20, 6: 350)—in the sense of its capacity to permeate being, to unify the subjective and the objective, without any remainder except the merely arbitrary and contingent—should not be at issue. As Hegel puts it: "the principle of philosophy is the *infinitely free concept*, and all its content rests on this alone." (SL: 728/W20, 6: 540).

The Transition from the Idea to "External Existence" in Hegel

Hegel emphasizes that the shift from the domain of logic to nature is *not* a "having become" (*Gewordensein*) or a "transition" (*Übergang*), that it is "free" (that is, not a logical consequence), and that it is the result of a "decision" (*Entschluβ*—arguably, this follows from its characterization as free, once we rule out—as Hegel must—the existence of the world as random) (SL: 752–753/W20, 6: 573). In light of this, the best sense to be made of the major scene-change within his system seems to be the following. The circular closure of the sphere of logic as a whole both confirms the internal self-sufficiency of the sphere *and* reveals it as determinate or limited—as the sphere of what is "still as yet logical" (*noch logisch*). This one-sidedness generates the philosophical drive to move into another sphere. To put the matter in rather intuitive terms: the *concept* of the unity of being and the concept (that is, the absolute Idea) comes to appear one-sided, requiring a counterpart in the *being* of the unity of being and the concept. This, in essence, is the interpretation proposed by Rolf-Peter Horstmann, in the thoughtful, refreshingly non-partisan chapter on Schelling's critique of Hegel in his survey of German Idealism, *Die Grenzen der Vernunft*.[6] According to Horstmann, Hegel does not need to assume that the logical movement of thought is capable, at its culminating point, of metaphysically producing nature. Rather, Horstmann reverses the direction of dependency, suggesting that the existence of "externality" (spatio-temporal reality) is a condition of possibility of Hegel's logical structures because—as we have just surmised—they would remain in some sense deficient, if not *also* instantiated in the worldly domain. Indeed, he goes to so far as to claim that what Hegel is proposing is a "naturalized logic."[7] If we ask *why* there exists a spatio-temporal reality, the other of the Idea and yet—as the "external Idea" (*äußerliche Idee*) (SL: 753/W20, 6: 573)—pervaded by it, Hegel's response would presumably be that the question does not make sense. For it to be intelligible, we would have to abstract in thought the being of the empirical world from every determinate feature of that world. Yet as he states, in a quotation from the *Encyclopaedia Logic* we have already noted: "But if we consider the whole world, and say of it only that everything *is*, and nothing more, we leave aside everything determinate, and, instead of absolute plenitude, we have absolute emptiness [*die absolute Leerheit*]" (Enc.I: §87, *Zusatz*/W20, 8: 188). According to Hegel, then, there is no coherent distinction to be made between the being or not being of the world as a whole. Hence there can be no meaningful question of the kind trailed by Leibniz concerning why anything at all exists.

Correlating Hegel's *Logic* and *Realphilosophie*

While there may be much disagreement about the metaphysical relation, in Hegel, between the domain of logic and the domain of the *Realphilosophie*, on any account we can be assured in advance that whatever has genuine being must express, at least to some minimal extent, a conceptual content which is expressive of the Idea. As Hegel puts it in the *Encyclopaedia Logic*:

> Everything actual, in so far as it is true, is the Idea, and has its truth by and in virtue of the Idea alone. Every individual being is some one aspect of the Idea: for which, therefore, yet other actualities are needed, which in their turn appear to have a self-subsistence of their own. It is only in them

altogether and in their relation that the concept is realized. (Enc.1: §213/ W20, 8: 368)

Hegel puts this claim in another way when he states, at the end of the *Science of Logic*:

> The method is therefore to be acknowledged as the universal, internal and external mode, free of restrictions, and as the absolutely infinite force to which no object, in so far as it presents itself as something external, removed from reason and independent of it, could offer resistance, or be of a particular nature opposed to it and incapable of being penetrated by it. (SL: 737/W20, 6: 551)

However, this general claim concerning what it means for something truly to be, leaves wide open the question of the *precise correlation* between the stages of Hegel's *Logic* and the various real-philosophical spheres, given that individual entities specifically embody only "one aspect of the Idea."

One way of answering this question would be to propose what Vittorio Hösle has described as a "cyclical" series of correspondences between the structures of the *Logic* and the domains of nature and spirit. According to this approach, the sequence from "Being" to "Essence" to "Concept," which marks out the three main stages of Hegel's *Logic*, would occur repeatedly in different sub-domains or spheres of the *Realphilosophie*. There is warrant for this conception at various points in Hegel's work. For example, in a lecture course based on the *Encyclopaedia*, Hegel correlates the domains of mechanical, non-organic, and organic nature with the logical spheres of being, essence, and the concept; he further asserts that "*Spirit* is as being the *soul*, 2) as essence the stage of reflection or *consciousness* 3) as concept the *spirit as such*" (Der *Geist* ist als Seyn die *Seele*, 2) als Wesen oder Stufe der Reflexion *Bewußtseyn* 3) als Begriff der *Geist als solcher*).[8] Connoisseurs of Hegel could readily proliferate such correspondences, obvious examples being the spheres of the family, civil society and the state in the *Philosophy of Right*, or the three realizations of absolute spirit—art, religion, and philosophy. But as Hösle points out, one problem with this approach, is that it fails to take account of the *increasing complexity* of the real-philosophical domains to which the logical categories apply and so tends to become an unilluminating formalism. (It should be noted that this criticism does not entail that Hegel lacks good reasons for regarding triadic dialectical structures as a pervasive feature of reality.) A connected difficulty with this mode of correlation is that it would deprive Hegel of the *logical* explanation he needs for the advance through the spheres of the *Realphilosophie* toward the summit of absolute spirit.[9]

It seems more promising, therefore, to establish a system of *linear*—rather than cyclical—correspondences, in which the increasing richness of Hegel's categories would be mirrored in the increasing intricacy of the real-philosophical structures which body them forth. However, if we take the *Logic* as a conceptual map of the Hegelian system as a whole in this way, we are still confronted with problematic choices. There seem to be two basic options: we can take the *Logic* as the cartography of a real-philosophical system consisting of *two parts*, the philosophies of nature and spirit; or we can adopt what could be termed a "reflexive" approach, which understands the *Logic* to include itself, as one of the *three parts* of the system which it charts. A straightforward version of this second approach, appears to have the advantage, from a dialectical perspective, of setting up a fundamentally triadic system, rather than a dyadic one accompanied by its *a priori* outline. It would give us the following global correspondences:

Logic of Being ------> Science of Logic
Logic of Essence ------> Philosophy of Nature
Logic of the Concept ------> Philosophy of Spirit

However, as Hösle has also pointed out, there are numerous difficulties with this schema. For instance, the most appropriate match for the "Doctrine of Being" would appear to be the philosophy of nature. After all, Hegel unmistakeably presents the concept of space, at the very beginning of the philosophy of nature, as corresponding to the category of being, in its indeterminacy and immediacy. In addition, the relation of transition (*Übergang*) that obtains between the categories of the "Doctrine of Being" seems to correspond most closely to the reciprocal externality of natural entities. Similarly, the "Doctrine of Essence," in which the concepts of reflection-into-self and reflection-into-other play a central role, would seem more apt as the foreshadowing of the structure of spirit or self-consciousness, with its inwardly related subjective and objective poles. Finally, the "Doctrine of the Concept" looks best matched with the field of logic itself, which elucidates the inner structure of reality as revealed in the forms of syllogistic reasoning.

Although there is no specific warrant for the move in Hegel's own rather rare meta-systematic reflections, we could attempt to resolve some of these problems by shifting the correspondences. This would then give:

Logic of Being	------->	Philosophy of Nature
Logic of Essence	------->	Philosophy of Spirit
Logic of the Concept	------->	Science of Logic

Again, however, there are problems with the schema. For example, on Hegel's account, the logic of essence is not able to supersede the oscillation of inner and outer, of the subjective and the objective. Hence, although it might pair well with subjective spirit, it cannot mirror the concrete unity of subjective and objective which occurs at the level of those socio-historical formations which Hegel terms "objective spirit," nor the increasingly self-conscious comprehension of such unity at the level of absolute spirit, in art, religion, and philosophy. In this respect, Hegel's account of the development of "the concept" in volume two of the *Science of Logic* (the "Subjective Logic"), culminating in the unity of subjectivity and objectivity in the Idea, seems to offer the best anticipation of the later stages of concrete spirit.

These difficulties suggest that a more viable approach to the question of the mapping function of speculative logic may require us to treat this function as *non*-self-inclusive. Such a strategy would have the advantage that the *Realphilosophie* could then be seen as developing in accordance with Hegel's basic (and undeniably powerful) tripartite dialectical schema—in which an immediate unity unfolds into conflictual opposition, which is resolved a more complex, more self-conscious unity—rather than being divided anomalously into the two spheres of nature and spirit. The correspondences could then be set up in the following way:

The Objective Logic and Subjective Logic up to the Category of Life	----->	Nature
The Idea of Cognition in the Subjective Logic	----->	Self-Consciousness
The Absolute Idea	----->	Spirit

However, as Hösle points out regarding this proposal, such a pattern raises serious problems of proportionality. For why would the section of the *Logic* correlated with spirit—which is, after all, the most important concept of Hegel's

Realphilosophie, and arguably the central concept of his philosophy as a whole—consist only of a short section at the end of both the *Science of Logic* and the *Encyclopaedia Logic*?[10] In the *Encyclopaedia*, the absolute Idea first emerges on the terrain of *Realphilosophie* in the second division of the "Philosophy of Spirit," dealing with "Objective Spirit," which begins with the declaration: "Objective spirit is the absolute Idea, but only existing *in itself*" (Enc.3: §483/W20, 10: 303). Hence the problem is not only one of proportionality, but also of vapidity. For the upshot is that the complex dialectical evolution of the socio-political domain of objective spirit, and of spirit's explicit self-relatedness, in the forms of art, religion, and philosophy, is covered by only *one* logical category. Given this solution to the problem of the *Logic–Realphilosophie* correlation, the advance through the final stages of Hegel's system, from the emergence of objective spirit onwards, appears to occur in what Hösle terms a "logical vacuum."[11]

By contrast, Schelling's negative philosophy does not encounter such correlation problems because it is a theory of ontological vectors whose interaction generates natural kinds, and not a theory of "determinations of *thought*" (*Denk*bestimmungen [emphasis added]) whose real-world instantiations—although guaranteed to exist—still remain to be identified. Of course, it is well known that, in the *Science of Logic*, Hegel criticizes the theory of "*Potenzen*"—understood as strictly analogical to mathematical powers—as a reversion to the "helplessness of childhood," and as no substitute for a theory of thought determinations (SL: 179/W20, 5: 246). But although Hegel's barbs may have had some validity when directed against Schelling's identity philosophy, they cannot be applied to his mature theory of potentialities. As we have seen, in his late philosophy Schelling develops a fully dialectical—not mathematical—theory of the emergence and interaction of the potentialities, starting from his inaugural conception of pure being-ness, and then uses this to elaborate an *a priori* theory of the basic forms of being. As a procedure, it is hard to see why this should be intrinsically more objectionable that Hegel's generation of his whole system of categories—including mechanism, chemism, teleology, and life—from no more than an initial oscillation between being and nothing.

Schelling's Direct Critique of Hegel

Hegel died in 1831, before he could take cognizance of Schelling's late thinking, whereas Schelling, who lived until 1854, had many years to consider and respond to Hegel's completed system. However, in examining

Schelling's explicit critical response to Hegel, it is important not to overlook how much the two philosophers have in common. They would agree that it makes no sense for reason to contest its own validity, or seek to overcome itself, as such a procedure would equally invalidate the challenge—all conceptualizing would cease (see DRP, SW, II/1: 267). For both, reason is its own presupposition—although Schelling would add: *logically*, but not ontologically speaking. Furthermore, they both believe it possible to elaborate an *a priori* science of the content of rational thinking. Schelling often makes the point that it is Fichte who deserves the credit for having advanced from the Kantian critique of reason to a science, a *Wissenschaft der Vernunft*, in which reason discovers "within its own original content the content of all being" (GPP: 132/SW, II/3, 62). In Fichte's case, however, this science is still elaborated in terms of the conditions of possibility of *experience*, and therefore records the subjective movement of thought rather than the inner life of things. But once this restriction is lifted, as Schelling makes clear, the view that a "pure rational science" can only be concerned with concepts, prescinding from all ontological considerations—the very view which interpreters such as Klaus Hartmann and his North American successors proposed so as to *defend* Hegel—becomes baseless. As Schelling puts it:

> Negative philosophy as an *a priori* philosophy is therefore not merely logical, in the sense that it would exclude being. It is true that being is the content of pure thinking only as potentiality. But whatever is potentiality is by its nature on the verge of passing over into being, so to speak. Thinking is drawn out of itself by the very nature of its content. For what has passed over into being is no longer the content of mere thinking—it has become the object of an (empirical) cognition which goes beyond mere thinking. (GPP: 160/SW, II/3: 102)

In other words, negative philosophy can spell out *a priori* the structures of being—specify the types of entities which we will encounter in experience—and in this sense there is no gap between thinking and being. At the same time, Schelling makes clear that there is a danger of illusion built into the very process whereby the content of *a priori* thinking is precipitated in the *form* of objective being. He comments:

> The infinite *potentiality* of being, or *infinite being-able-to-be*, which is the immediate content of reason, is not a mere capacity to exist, but the

immediate *prius*, the immediate *concept* of being itself . . . as soon as it is thought it is on the verge of passing over into being; thus it cannot be restrained from being, and is for thinking what immediately *passes over* into being. Indeed, because of this necessary transition thinking cannot remain at the stage of being-able-to-be [*das Seinkönnen*] (and here lies the justification of all progress in philosophy). However, inevitably many think first of an actual transition and imagine that the actual becoming of *things* is thereby explained. But this would be to miss the whole point . . . Precisely in the fact that the science of reason deduces the content of actual being, in other words has experience at its side, there lies for many the illusion that it has not merely grasped *the real* [*das Wirkliche*], but reality itself [*die Wirklichkeit*], or that reality *arose* in this way, that that merely logical process is also the process of real becoming. However, in this nothing external to thinking occurs, it is not a real but a merely logical process that unfolds here; the being into which potentiality passes over itself belongs to the concept, hence is only a being in the concept, and nothing external to it.
(GPP: 133–134/SW, II/3: 64–65)

This description of the dynamic of pure rational science lies at the heart of Schelling's critique of Hegel. Hegelian logic is a thinking of thinking itself, of the self-generation of "determinations of thought," rather than, like Schelling's negative philosophy, an *a priori* exploration of the dialectic of the modal vectors of being. These latter have more in common with the Aristotelian causes (specifically, material, formal, and final causality), as Schelling himself recognizes (see, e.g., PO41/42: 200), than with categories, understood as *genera* which are not species of a more fundamental *genus*. Hegel does indeed equate the "merely logical process" with "actual becoming," because—as we have seen—his speculative logic can only serve its grounding and elucidating function if "worldly being, external objectivity" is entirely permeable by the concept, and hence ultimately expresses its movement. Of course, the decisive issue here is what Schelling understands by "actual becoming," as opposed to a "merely logical process"—and answering this question will require detailed examination of Schelling's positive philosophy, a task reserved for subsequent chapters. However, it is clear that a Hegelian response to a critique based on a distinction between "logical process" and "actual becoming" would contend that it betrays a subjectivist misunderstanding of what Hegel means by "the concept." And a similar response would doubtless be made to the other principal way in which Schelling expresses his critique:

The *true* thought of a philosopher is precisely his fundamental thought, the one from which he starts out. Now, Hegel's fundamental thought is that reason is related to the in-itself, the essence of things, from which it follows immediately that philosophy, insofar as it is a rational science, is concerned only with the "what" of things, with their essence. This distinction has been interpreted to mean that philosophy or reason does not deal at all with what is; and it would indeed be a pitiful philosophy which had nothing to do with what exists [*mit dem Seyenden*], and hence presumably only with a chimera. But this was not the right way to express the distinction; rather, reason has to do with nothing except precisely what is, but with what is in so far as the *matter* or *content* is concerned (this, precisely, is what exists in its "in-itself"). But it is not reason's job to show *that* it is, since this is longer the concern of reason but of experience. (GPP: 130/SW, II/3: 60)

It is not easy, however, to pin onto Schelling the accusation of simply failing to grasp what Hegel means by the "concept" (*der Begriff*). On the contrary, as a former close friend and collaborator, he has an intimate understanding of Hegel's ambitions. For example, in the chapter on Hegel in his lectures on the history of modern philosophy, he states:

The proposition: the movement of the concept is the universal absolute activity leaves nothing else for God to be than the movement of the concept, in other words to be himself the concept. Here "concept" does not have the meaning of the mere concept (Hegel protests most keenly against this) but the meaning of the *thing itself*. And just as it is stated in the ancient Persian scriptures that time is the true Creator, one can definitely not accuse Hegel of holding the opinion that God is a mere concept. His opinion is rather that the *true* Creator is the concept; with the concept one has the Creator and needs no other besides this. (HMP: 135/SW, I/10: 127)

The definition of the movement of the concept as the "*universal absolute activity*" is taken *verbatim* from the *Science of Logic* (SL: 737/W20, 6: 551 [italicized in the original]). For corroboration of the religious construal one need look no further than Hegel's lectures on the philosophy of religion, where he states that God is "coincident with the logical Idea," but that God—in addition—gives himself "objectivity" (*Gegenständlichkeit*) (LPR1: 119/VPR1: 35).

That-Dependency and What-Dependency in Schelling and Hegel

The view that Schelling, far from failing to understand Hegel, has identified a troublesome point in his theory seems confirmed by the recent history of approaches to Hegel's *Logic*. As we noted, the "category theory" tradition stemming from Klaus Hartmann in effect deflects Schelling's criticism that Hegel attributes the wrong kind of ontological significance to his *Logic*, by denying that the *Logic* has any ontological implications at all: it is about how we think, not what there is. But, from a historical perspective, it strains credulity to attribute that position to any German Idealist. The real issue concerns what *kind* of knowing of being an *a priori* science makes possible—and here the category theory tradition is even more metaphysically abstemious than Schelling, who in turn thinks that Hegel over-reaches himself in trying to make negative philosophy do the work of its positive counterpart. Hence, although a significant commentary on Hegel's *Logic* in the tradition of Hartman is subtitled "*The Explanation of Possibility*," in apparent endorsement of Schelling's view that transcendental reflection is concerned with the "infinite potentiality of knowing" (*die unendliche Potenz des Erkennens*), its author, Terry Pinkard, would doubtless reject the thought that this can be equated with the "infinite potentiality of being" (*die unendliche Potenz des Seyns*). Hegel's categories, on Pinkard's view, merely "express basic conceptions in terms of which we describe and evaluate the world."[12] Allied thinkers, influenced by Wilfred Sellars' argument for the autonomy of the "space of reasons," for example Robert Brandom and Robert Pippin, are similarly keen to divorce justification and ontology in their interpretations of Hegel. Of course, there have also been recent defenders of a more traditional view of Hegel's *Logic*, such as Stephen Houlgate. But here the tendency is to suggest that the domain of the *Realphilosophie*, although metaphysically distinct from that of the *Logic*, is somehow reached by a *logical* move beyond the absolute Idea: a proposal which is both incoherent and at odds with what Hegel says.[13] The most promising solution, if we are looking for a proposal which respects Hegel's texts to the maximum while avoiding the connection of the absolute Idea with theological notions of creation, appears to be that—discussed earlier—of Rolf-Peter Horstmann.[14] In this interpretation, spatiotemporal being is understood as a *condition* of the logical domain because the Idea—as the *unity* of subjectivity and objectivity—would be inconsistent with itself if it remained merely the *thought* of that unity, and failed to be also instantiated in a material world. Horstmann does not deny that there is much that is murky about this solution. After all, the inconsistency in question, as we considered earlier, cannot be strictly logical, and we are therefore left wondering exactly what explanatory force it could have. But even after making allowances for this, Hortsmann's suggestion may not be plausible as it looks at first sight.

This becomes apparent if we consider the work of James Kreines, a leading figure of the effort to move beyond the categorial or "space of reasons" interpretation of Hegel. In Kreines' view, Hegel is not primarily concerned with the autonomous or self-sufficient generation of a set of conditions of possibility of experience or knowing, or with explaining how there can be normativity without a context-transcending foundation (as claimed by what he calls the "social pragmatist" reading [RW: 266]), but with a "metaphysics of reason," or with "reason in the world." This is to say, first of all, that Hegel takes Kant's account of reason's demand for the unconditioned or for complete satisfaction seriously, but that, contrary to Kant, he believes that it *can* be fulfilled theoretically. Reason seeks to explicate the inner determining principle of things, or what Hegel terms "the concept." However, we can have more or less adequate conceptions of the concept; those which are less adequate are marred by internal discrepancies which push forward the quest of reason for what Kreines calls a "complete explainer." If we follow the dialectical sequence generated by these inconsistencies, we will eventually reach the absolute Idea, which *is* the complete explainer because it fully resolves the contradictions that drive the movement of reason leading up to it (RW: 240).

Kreines realizes that the absolute Idea would not in fact *be* the complete explainer if Hegel had left a dualistic gulf between thought and reality, so that its truth would be simply a matter of internal coherence. As he puts it:

> The *Logic* also aims to demonstrate the metaphysical conclusion that there is a sense in which there must really be an absolute idea, and the epistemological conclusion that everything real can be understood in terms of its relation to the absolute idea in one system. (RW: 240)

At the same time, Kreines wishes to resist the suggestion that the Idea can be seen as the explanation for the sheer existence of the world. He therefore draws a distinction between "epistemological" and "metaphysical" monism. Hegelian monism is of the former kind, he argues, because Hegel does not claim that every aspect of spatio-temporal being can be explained by the

Idea. On the contrary, Hegel's absolute is *dependent* on a realizer—on the empirically contingent, on a morass of explanatory loose threads—constituting the element in which the rationality of the Idea can be actualized, in which its teleology can show up *against* a penumbra of the arbitrary and accidental. On this basis, Kreines perceives in the *Logic* a "*general* argument against *any* foundationalism," a view which he dubs "*realizer-required.*"[15]

It is not hard to detect a tension in Kreines' position, between his critique of "epistemology-first" and other analogous approaches to Hegel, on the one hand, and his distinction between metaphysical and epistemological monism on the other. After all, if the *Logic* aims to show that "there really must be an absolute idea," the claim that "everything real" can be understood in terms of its relation to it cannot be merely an "epistemological conclusion." That would not fit at all with Kreines' central contention that Hegel is interested in the objective "why" of things, with reason in the world, and not with structures of explanation taken as something distinct from what they seek to explain. Not surprisingly, then, he has sought to clarify what is involved in separating metaphysical and epistemological monism. And this endeavour has led him to move in an "inflationary metaphysical direction," as he puts it, conceding the proximity of the Hegelian absolute Idea to Aristotle's conception of God, or Spinoza's of substance, while still resisting the pull of metaphysical monism (see AP: 19, 36n).

Kreines new strategy involves distinguishing between relations of what he terms "that-dependency" and "what-dependency," relations which he defines in the following way:

> Y <u>that-depends</u> on X iff Y could not be if X were not.
> Y <u>what-depends</u> on X iff what it is to be Y depends on what it is to be X.

Accordingly:

> X is <u>that-prior</u> to Y iff Y that-depends on X, and not *vice versa*.
> X is <u>what-prior</u> to Y iff Y what-depends on X, and not *vice versa*. (AP: 25)

By making these distinctions, Kreines argues, it is possible to reconcile the claim that the absolute, according to Hegel, has total what-priority, so that everything non-absolute depends, for its being what it is, on the absolute and not *vice versa*, with the claim of "realizer required." More specifically, the metaphysically determining role of the absolute Idea can be affirmed without metaphysical monism, once we regard Hegel as accepting Aristotle's anti-Platonic argument that substantial form that-depends on individual actualizations of the form, even while those individuals cannot be what they are at all without their substantial form, in other words: they both what-depend *and* that-depend on it. Generalizing, we can then say that, for Hegel, the absolute Idea is metaphysically prior, as it is the condition for the existence of finite entities, but that, at the same time, "absolute thought is reciprocally that-dependent with its non-absolute realizations" (AP: 35).

Despite the ingenuity of this argument, one can still doubt the conclusion. After all, how can something absolute be dependent on something non-absolute? As Kreines himself puts it, anticipating the objection, "The absolute is dependent, in being that-dependent. Is that not some mitigation of its absoluteness?" (AP: 35) He answers this question negatively, on the basis that what the absolute depends on are "forms of itself." But this is misleading. The absolute Idea is not dependent on its own forms, if that means not the logical "thought determinations" as such, but their particular spatio-temporal instantiations. Indeed, it is doubtful whether Hegel would have conceded that a *Denkbestimmung* depends on having *any* instantiations. For example, to suppose that, were all living organisms to be erased from the universe by a cosmic accident, the category of life would itself disappear makes no sense within Hegel's metaphysics. For the erasure of one category from the absolute Idea would destroy its whole structure, thus making the "abstract basis of the logical," which—for Hegel—is the "absolutely true" (*das absolut-Wahre*) (SL: 37–38/W20, 5: 55–56), dependent on fluctuations in the empirical world. Hegel's famous description of the content of the *Logic* as "*the exposition of God as he is in his eternal essence before the creation of nature and of a finite spirit*" (SL: 29/W20, 5: 44) seems to suggest, in fact, that the validity of the *Logic* is independent of the real existence of any spatio-temporal world at all. Of course, even acknowledging such a form of *a priori* validity need not be equivalent to making the absolute Idea *responsible* for the existence of the world.

Kreines is inclined to run these two issues together, however: "neither thought nor anything else exists independently of nature, and should be held responsible for the fact *that* nature exists" (AP: 34). But this formulation, with its readiness—far from universal amongst philosophers—to regard the existence of nature as a fact, and its italicized "*that*" (the emphasis is Kreines'), poses a problem for his proposed solution. It ineluctably raises a "why" question—"What is the explanation for the *fact* that nature exists?"—which falls outside the scope of the absolute Idea, as the "complete explainer." It contravenes Kreines' endorsement of what he presents as Hegel's view: that there is no principle of sufficient reason "that would encompass distinct issues concerning that-dependence, or suggest the need (in this sense) of an explanation of why there is something, rather than nothing" (AP: 35).

It will come as no surprise to learn that Kreines indicates a debt to the discussion of Hegel in Schelling's *Spätphilosophie* for the distinction between "that-dependency" and "what-dependency" (AP: 25). However, he does not pause to investigate Schelling's own conception of the relation between conceptuality and being, which offers an alternative way of addressing the issues with which he is grappling. Schelling outlined his view in a compressed form in "Über die Quelle der ewigen Warheiten" ("On the Source of the Eternal Truths"), the text of the last lecture he gave to a plenary session of the *Berlin Academy of Sciences*, on January 17, 1850. In this address, Schelling begins by reviewing the philosophical problem of the status of essences—of eternal truths or truths of reason—from the Scholastics onwards. He homes in on the fundamental difficulty that, if the eternal truths are simply a matter of God's will, as argued by Descartes, they cannot also be *immutable* truths, as reason requires. We might try to resolve this problem, as did Leibniz, by locating the eternal truths in the divine understanding. But then we are once again faced with a dilemma: either the eternal truths are *determined* by God's understanding, and we are returned to a form of divine voluntarism, or there is a kind of absoluteness which is independent of God. We might try to solve this problem, Schelling suggests, by arguing that the rational or eternal truths simply *are* God—the allusion to Hegel is clear, although he is not named in the text. However, in Schelling's view, this reduction of God to reason provides no explanation for the existence of a world of finite entities, which are far from being simply embodiments of reason. Because Hegel's logical domain is entirely self-sufficient, we would be required to suppose that:

> The very idea which is first presented as the most perfect, and which *no* dialectic could have any further power over, that this idea, without having any inner reason, in actual fact, as the French say, *sans rime ni raison*, could break apart into this world of contingent things, opaque to reason and resistant to the concept. (SET: 63/SW, II/1: 584)

As we have seen, Kreines' own proposal is that the Idea is only what-self-determining; it is *that-interdependent*, we might say, with the "world of contingent things." But, as we also noted, even on Kreines' account the that-dependence of the absolute Idea can be only on the *fact* of the existence of nature, not on its contingent configuration. On reflection, we can see that this must be the case because talk of the absolute as "dependent" can only make sense at all if what it is dependent on—in the sense of being a *transformation* of—is *also* absolute. At the same time, the prior absoluteness in question would have to be of a different kind. It would have to be a matter of "not being-able-not-to-be," as Schelling puts it in *System der Weltalter*, rather than the fully self-determined "what-ness" of the Idea. By pursuing this line of thought, we reach the conception of a double absolute which Schelling develops in "Über die Quelle der ewigen Wahrheiten."

Schelling's answer to the problem of the eternal truths is to equate God—initially, at least—with what he terms the "*pure* [fact] *that*" (*das reine Daß*). This is only an initial equation, however, because his aim is to define an *asymmetrical interdependence* between conceptuality and being. God, he argues, is being-ness in its uniqueness or ipseity (*das Selbst-seyende*), and, as such, he enables the eternal truths to be—he is not their *cause* but their ontological "source" (*Quelle*). God therefore appears to have absolute "that-priority," to adopt Kreines' terminology. But, at the same time, being-ness itself would be a nothingness, a *néant*, not disclosed in any way, not truly being-ness, unless it were the being-ness *of* something. As Schelling puts it, the "being-one" of thought and being is "the highest law, and its meaning is this, that whatever *Is* must also have a relation to the *concept*, and what is *nothing*, in other words what has no relation to thinking, also *Is not in the true sense*" (SET: 65/SW, II/1: 587).

As universals—as Hegel's "thought determinations"—the eternal truths must *receive* their being; but in turn they alone make the being which they receive manifest *as* being. Without them, the *Daß* would be *as* nothing, although this does not mean of course that when we think about the ontological basis of the eternal truths, what we are really thinking about is no more than the eternal truths themselves. Schelling is quite forthright about the consequences:

> The unity I have in mind here reaches all the way to the highest opposition; so that [unity] is also the final limit, is that *beyond which one cannot pass*. However, in this unity, priority does not lie on the side of thought; being [*das Seyn*] is the first, thinking only the second or following. This opposition is likewise that of the universal and the sheerly individual [*das*

schlechthin Einzelne]. But the path does not go from the universal to the individual, as people generally seem to hold nowadays. (SET: 65/SW, II/1: 587)

This means that, for Schelling, we need not try to derive the *fact* of worldly being from pure reason, the eternal truths, or the absolute Idea, as occurs in interpretations of Hegel of the type which Kreines is keen to avoid. Rather, reason *transforms* raw being-ness, opening the way to a differentiated empirical world. As Schelling puts it, in the final paragraph of his lecture:

> The *Was* leads from itself into the open [*ins Weite*], into multiplicity [*Vielheit*], and thus also naturally to the dominance of the multiple [*Vielherrschaft*], for the *Was* is something other in each thing; whereas the *Daβ*, by its nature and hence in all things, is only one; in the great commonwealth [*Gemeinwesen*] that we call nature and world there reigns a single *Daβ*, excluding all multiplicity from *itself*. (SET: 67/SW, II/1: 590)

Arguably, if we wish to sustain an explanatory project of the Idealist kind, committed to the ultimate satisfaction of reason, yet also to separate epistemological from metaphysical monism, we cannot avoid a distinction comparable to that drawn by Schelling between negative and positive philosophy. Negative philosophy is the domain of the "eternal truths." Positive philosophy, as we shall explore in more detail in the next chapter, begins from the *Daβ*— which Schelling also terms the "un-pre-thinkable" (*das Unvordenkliche*), or, more disquietingly, "blind existing-ness" (*das Blindexistierende*).

Notes

1. The fullest and clearest account of Schelling's negative philosophy remains Karl Groos, *Die reine Vernunftwissenschaft: systematische Darstellung von Schellings rationaler oder negativer Philosophie* (Heidelberg: Georg Weiß, 1889). As well as being philosophically informative, Groos's prose has a *Belle Époque* charm all its own.
2. See Kant, "Conjectural Beginning of Human History," in *Toward Perpetual Peace and Other Writings on Politics, Peace and History*, ed. Pauline Kleingeld, (New Haven, CT: Yale University Press, 2006), 24–36.
3. I owe this important point to conversations with Sebastian Gardner.
4. See Michael Theunissen, "Die Aufhebung des Idealismus in der Spätphilosophie Schellings," *Philosophisches Jahrbuch* 83 (1976).

5. See Dietrich Korsch, *Der Grund der Freiheit. Untersuchungen zur Problemgeschichte der positiven Philosophie und zur Systemfunktion des Christentums im Spätwerk F.W.J. Schellings* (Munich: Kaiser Verlag, 1980), 260.
6. See Rolf-Peter Horstmann, *Die Grenzen der Vernunft. Untersuchungen zu Motiven und Zielen des Deutschen Idealismus* (Frankfurt: Vittorio Klostermann, 2004), ch. 6.
7. *Die Grenzen der Vernunft*, 260.
8. "Unveröffentlichte Diktate aus einer Enzyklopädie-Vorlesung Hegels," *Hegel-Studien* 5 (1969): 21–22.
9. See Vittorio Hösle, *Hegels System* (Hamburg: Felix Meiner, 1978), vol. 1, 101–104.
10. See *Hegels System*, vol. 1, 114–115.
11. *Hegels System*, vol. 1, 121.
12. Terry Pinkard, *Hegel's Dialectic: The Explanation of Possibility* (Philadelphia, PA: Temple University Press, 1988), 13.
13. See, for example, Stephen Houlgate, *An Introduction to Hegel: Freedom, Truth and History* (Oxford: Blackwell, 2005), 108: "nature is an absolute logical necessity"; "pure abstract being *determines itself* logically to be nothing but nature."
14. See *Die Grenzen der Vernunft*, 254–260.
15. James Kreines, "Fundamentality without Metaphysical Monism: Response to Critics of *Reason in the World*," *Hegel Bulletin* 39, no. 1 (2018), 149.

6

Blind Existing-ness

Schelling and Sartre on Being

In the previous chapter we encountered Schelling's expression "*das reine Daβ.*" In his late philosophy Schelling employs numerous terms to convey what this expression points toward, each with its own nuance of meaning. Among the most prominent are: "blind being-ness" (*das Blindseiende*), "contingently necessary existing-ness" (*das zufällig nothwendiges Existieren*), and "un-pre-thinkable being" (*das unvordenkliche Sein*) (see, e.g., PO41/42: 157, 166, 164). As the last of these formulas suggests most clearly, at issue is being of a type whose necessity cannot be inferred from anything logically or conceptually prior to it, or taken to be identical with it. Schelling's positive enterprise begins with the question that arises when we run up against the limit of negative philosophy. It asks "**what** un-pre-thinkable being-ness is" (AD, SW, II/4: 345).[1]

Some basic issues raised by this question should be clarified at the outset. Firstly, Schelling is not proposing the incoherent exercise of trying to conceptualize what he has indicated to be entirely unconceptualizable. The being which inaugurates the positive philosophy is un-*pre*-thinkable; in other words, there is no concept in which its actuality is contained, or from which it could be derived, as in standard versions of the ontological argument for the existence of God. But this does not preclude it from being *post*-thinkable; indeed, the entirety of Schelling's positive philosophy constitutes an attempt to accomplish this task. It approaches this endeavor, as it must, in an *a posteriori* manner, by interpreting the way in which un-pre-thinkable being, via many transformations, has manifested itself in the happening of the world: in nature, in the history of human consciousness, and in our anticipations of the future. Of course, this does not make the positive philosophy totally *a posteriori*: what Schelling terms its "*prius*"—namely un-pre-thinkable being—is initially disclosed *a priori*, but the meaning of the *prius* can only be revealed through a hermeneutics of the history of consciousness, and in particular of religion, regarded as the fundamental way in which human beings articulate their sense of what is transcendent or absolute. Secondly, un-pre-thinkable being is not to be equated with "*das Seyende selbst*" or "*das Subjekt des Seyns*"—the pure being-ness which is the starting point of *negative* philosophy. Being in this guise is the inaugural possibility of all that there is. It is what remains when we abstract from the determinacy of everything existing, and it therefore *can* be attained by means of a logical operation. Because, as we saw, being-ness in this sense must objectify itself *as* potentiality in order to *be* the potentiality of anything determinate, Schelling's version of transcendental reflection articulates *das Wirkliche*—the necessary structures of the actual—by tracking dialectically the isomorphism of being and thinking within thinking itself. Such reflection can be confident that this congruence—more precisely: this identity-in-difference—is not itself merely a transcendental illusion, since in negative or purely rational philosophy, we begin from a momentary apprehension of the original identity of thought and being as pure potentiality.

In order to bring Schelling's approach to un-pre-thinkable being, and the problems which it raises, into focus, it may help to draw a comparison with a historically more recent and—no doubt to many—more familiar philosophical project which proposes a similar conception of being: that of Jean-Paul Sartre in his 1943 masterpiece, *L'être et le néant* (*Being and Nothingness*). "Being," Sartre states in the Conclusion of this work, "is without reason, without cause, and without necessity" (BN: 619/EN: 683). Sartrian being, then, which he further specifies as "being-in-itself" (*l'être-en-soi*) or simply the "in-itself" (*l'en-soi*), in contrast to consciousness or the "for-itself" (*le pour-soi*), cannot be regarded as the cause of itself, or as the necessary realization of its own thought possibility. Indeed, in Sartre's view the notion of "*causa sui*" is viciously circular. Hence, as he puts it, "Being-in-itself is never possible or impossible, it *is*. This is what consciousness expresses . . . by saying that it is superfluous [*de trop*]; in other words, that it is absolutely unable to derive it either from nothing, or from another being, or from something possible, or from a necessary law" (BN: xlii/EN: 33). Any philosophical interrogation of being, including attempts to determine its basic modality, will always lag behind it: "All the "whys" in fact are subsequent to being and presuppose it" (BN: 619/EN: 683). Schelling seeks to capture this same situation by describing un-pre-thinkable being as "contingently necessary existing-ness" (*das zufällig nothwendiges Existieren*).

Although Sartre does not work out his line of thought with sufficient clarity, it would be a mistake to conclude that he is deploying a form of cosmological argument—an inference from his own contingent existence as a thinker to an absolutely necessary ultimate cause of his existence. Sartre's view, rather, is that we grasp directly that consciousness, which is no kind of entity but rather sheer negativity, must ride on something, must have a basis in what it negates—and at the most general level this can be termed "being." He sometimes expresses this insight in reversed form by using the verb "*être*" in a transitive sense, for which one could coin the English term "to being": the nothingness of consciousness, he states, "*is being-ed*" (*est été*) by the in-itself (e.g., BN: 620/EN: 684). However, this conception highlights a problem with which both Sartre and Schelling are confronted: an ontological basis cannot *per se* provide an *explanation* for the existence of consciousness, and the whole panoply of phenomena which go along with it: meaning, intentionality, purposive agency, and so forth. In Sartre's case this is because consciousness is a "nothingness" (*un néant*): it can be defined only privatively as *not being* that of which it is the consciousness. But nothingness cannot be caused or produced by being, or any interaction of entities. Although Schelling approaches the issue in more post-Kantian terms, he has the same fundamental thought. In the *Critique of Pure Reason*, Kant had argued that there cannot be thinking which lacks even an implicit awareness of its own spontaneous character: the "I think" is "an act of spontaneity, that is, it cannot be regarded as belonging to sensibility" (B132). How, then, does a capacity for conscious experience, which requires such spontaneity in the application of concepts, emerge from the blank necessity of un-pre-thinkable being?

Sartre, in fact, does not begin to tackle this question until the final chapter of *Being and Nothingness*, where he returns to the promissory note which had rounded off the book's introduction. There he had stated, "it is obvious that we cannot truly grasp the meaning of either [type of being] except when we are able to establish their true connections with the notion of being in general and the relations which unite them" (BN: xxxix/EN: 30–31). The problem, however, is that the relation of the in-itself and the for-itself to being in general cannot be explicated by means of phenomenology, the philosophical method to which Sartre is committed, because—on his account—all phenomenological analysis presupposes and is structured by an irreducible opposition between the two modes of being. To deal with this difficulty, he introduces a distinction between "ontology" and "metaphysics." Ontology, in Sartre's definition, describes the features of the two basic modes of being, and their interconnections, within a static framework. By contrast, metaphysics consists of speculation concerning how the difference between the two modes of being first came about. The relation of ontology and metaphysics, Sartre suggests, in a not entirely satisfactory analogy, can be compared to that between sociology and history (BN: 619/EN: 683).

Metaphysical speculation, as Sartre envisages it, has a number of distinctive features. Firstly, as the comparison with history suggests, it takes a quasi-narrative form, as describing the "event" through which negativity emerged within being, which in itself is "solid" (*massif*) or "full positivity" (BN: xlii/EN: 33). Negativity or nothingness, as we have just observed, is the key to the characterization of consciousness. However, metaphysical explanation must be qualified as merely *quasi*-narrative because genuine temporality appears only along with the for-itself. The process which it is the task of metaphysics to determine is therefore described by Sartre as "this ante-historical process, the source of all history" (BN: 621/EN: 685). Metaphysics connects being, which is an "individual adventure" (that is to say, *not* a universal or Platonic *eidos*), with what he calls the "absolute event" (or the upsurge of negativity as such) (BN: 621/EN, 685). This event must be "absolute" because, by definition, it can have no antecedent cause or occasion within the featurelessness of being. Sartre stresses, however, that speculations concerning this event prior to all experience cannot claim anything more than the status of a "hypothesis," and that the validity of hypotheses in this domain should be assessed in terms of "the possibility of unifying the givens of ontology which they offer us" (BN: 621/EN: 685).

Metaphysics as a Hypothesis

At first sight, the parallels between the situation faced by Sartre, in seeking to account for the emergence of the for-itself from sheer being, and hence for what he calls "*this* world as a concrete and singular totality" (BN: 619/EN: 683), and the situation confronting Schelling at the beginning of his positive philosophy are striking. As Schelling states, in his most philosophically compressed—but also most informative—treatment of these issues, the *Andere Deduktion der Prinzipien der Positive Philosophie*: "Our point of departure is the unconditionally existing, prior to all thought" (AD, SW, II/4: 337). However, Schelling then defines his task quite differently to Sartre:

Our task is to find the genuine *monas* precisely in what alone is given in advance, in other words what endures, the principle which stands above all things; for whether we have already found this in the being which precedes all thinking, which we term un-pre-thinkable being, whether the *monas* is already found with the un-pre-thinkable, *is* precisely the question. (AD, SW, II/4: 337)

What does Schelling mean by the "*monas*"—the "one"? And does it connect with any aspect of Sartre's metaphysical reflections at all?

As we have seen, Sartre focuses primarily on the question of the origin of negativity. He is struggling with the philosophical requirement to think the compossibility of the in-itself and the for-itself within an overall structure. But because, as far as he is concerned, the only form which this structure could take is that of an absolute self-grounding, in which the in-itself is transformed into the intentional correlate of the for-itself that initially emerged from it, one would end up with a version of the divine *causa sui*. As Sartre declares this metaphysically impossible, he allows the structure only the status of a fiction. He writes, for example:

> Everything happens as if the world, man, and man-in-the-world only succeeded in realizing a missing God. Everything happens therefore as if the in-itself and the for-itself were presented in a state of disintegration in relation to an ideal synthesis. Not that the integration has ever *taken place* but on the contrary precisely because it is always implied and always impossible. (BN: 623/EN: 687)

In this connection, Sartre also uses the expression "detotalized totality" to describe the relation between in the in-itself and the for-itself. But, as Sebastian Gardner has pointed out, in an illuminating comparison of Sartre and Schelling's *Ages of the World*, this formula cannot properly be used even as a heuristic fiction, if the concept of totality being invoked is—by Sartre's own lights—incoherent.[2] The difficulties in which Sartre becomes entangled through denying the coherence of an "ideal synthesis" which is nonetheless "always implied" emerge with particular clarity in a passage toward end of *Being and Nothingness* where he expands on the notion of a "de-totalized totality":

> the *ens causa sui* remains as what is lacking, the indication of an impossible upward surpassing, which by its very nonexistence conditions the level

movement of consciousness; in the same way, the vertical attraction which the moon exercises on the ocean has for its result that horizontal displacement which is the tide. (BN: 620/EN: 684)

It is hard to see how something which does not exist can condition a movement "by its very non-existence," and in this respect the comparison with the action of the moon on the ocean is revealing, since it shows Sartre struggling to avoid the implication of his own account—namely, that the ontological totality must be more than an incoherent fiction. These Sartrian perplexities are relevant to the interpretation of Schelling because the "*monas*" can be understood as the overarching oneness of being which haunts Sartre's thought, even though he declares it impossible. Schelling's question concerns the equation between the *monas* and the "being which precedes all thinking." The issue is whether what Sartre calls the "for-itself"—freedom understood as the capacity negatively to transcend all that is given, for which Schelling's corresponding notion is "primordial possibility" (*Urmöglichkeit*)—does not genuinely differ from the in-itself, but only *appears* to do so from its own perspective; or whether the *monas* somehow "unifies the givens of ontology" without suppressing their difference. The concepts of the for-itself and of potentiality can be legitimately treated as interchangeable in this context, given that Sartre's well-known definition of the ontological status of the "for-itself" or consciousness—"not to be what it is, and to be what it is not" (e.g., BN: 79/EN: 117; and *passim*)—applies also to potentiality: it *is* what it is not (yet), and *is not* (the actuality of) what it is. In fact, Sartre himself argues that the possible "is a structure of the *for-itself*" (BN: xlii/EN: 33).

But if the "being preceding all thinking" *were* the *monas*, what would that entail? It would mean that the human world, which is a world of *possibility*—one in which we experience ourselves as able to perform or not to perform specific actions, or to decide between practical alternatives—is, metaphysically speaking, an illusion. Everything, at bottom, would be an aspect of what Schelling calls "blind"—that is, intention-less and purposeless—existing-ness. However, at least since the time of the *Freiheitsschrift*, Schelling has been convinced that a theory cannot bring us genuinely to doubt the phenomenology of our own freedom, despite the philosophical tensions which are thereby generated. And in his late philosophy he argues that we need to address those tensions by engaging in an exercise which he terms "speculation," and which is comparable to what Sartre—in connection with the need to explain the origin of negativity—describes as "metaphysics." Schelling also contends, again anticipating Sartre, that speculation can at most seek abductively for optimal explanations: "To speculate means to look around for possibilities through which a certain goal in science can be achieved" (AD, SW, II/4: 345). Finally, both Schelling and Sartre refer to an explanation reached in this way a "hypothesis" (e.g., AD, SW, II/4: 346). However, we should not allow these remarkable parallels to obscure the considerable difference in the weight of these considerations within the work of the two thinkers.

In Sartre's *Being and Nothingness* "metaphysics" appears almost as an afterthought. At first sight, one might regard this as leaving a large explanatory gap because Sartre seems to treat the phenomenology of freedom as indubitable. In fact, these two features of Sartre's thinking—the reluctant metaphysics and the insistence on freedom—can be seen as evidence of a philosophical difficulty, which Sebastian Gardner has highlighted. For the stronger Sartre makes the claim for the validity of his phenomenology, the more ineluctably he is pulled toward a Copernican turn in the Kantian sense, toward treating the immanent description of experience as self-sufficient, and hence toward the *de*-legitimation of metaphysical speculation. At the same time, the structure of Sartre's account of human freedom pushes him toward providing speculative foundation for it.[3] By contrast, Schelling, as we have just seen, does not consider that the phenomenology of freedom, however compelling it may be, entitles us to dispense with ambitious metaphysical inquiry.[4] While the kind of determinism which, in contemporary philosophy, most frequently takes the form of scientific naturalism, cannot make us *experience* ourselves as mechanisms, it might persuade us to *believe* that this is what we are, with potentially disastrous moral and political consequences. It is therefore important to show that there is a plausible alternative account of nature and its ground. Furthermore, the fact that the history of Western thought has been deeply marked by the conflict between freedom and necessity—in many, many versions—itself requires an explanation, and suggests that, even though "blind existing-ness" may not be the whole ontological story, it must have an important role to play. However, an alternative metaphysics which takes all this into account will involve no return to pre-Kantian naiveté. Rather, the inaugural hypothesis of Schelling's positive philosophy expresses an existential commitment to the reality and the value of freedom, which he believes has been incubating throughout human history, and which is deeply embedded in modern life. Indeed, Schelling assumes that we cannot sustain that commitment without adhering—even if only in an implicit or semi-articulate manner—to a hypothesis of the kind he proposes. By contrast, Sartre seems to treat it almost as though it were a detachable extra, with no bearing on the validity of his phenomenology.

The Decompression of Un-pre-thinkable Being

Positive philosophy, then, begins with a conjecture which, for Schelling, both expresses our fundamental human interest in freedom, and seeks to explain how such freedom can be a reality. But what is Schelling's hypothesis, and how does it fare in comparison with that of Sartre? We should note first that for Sartre, "it is through the for-itself that the possibility of a foundation enters the world" (BN: 621/EN: 685). Sartre thinks this because—on his account—to be grounded is to be integrated into the self-relating structure of consciousness. As he puts it, "every process of self-grounding is a rupture of the being-identical of the in-itself, a withdrawal of being in relation to itself and the appearance of presence-to-self or consciousness" (BN: 620/EN: 684). We might therefore conjecture that the primordial "in-itself" gives rise to the "for-itself" to achieve complete self-grounding, to become "*causa sui*." But as Sartre is fully aware, no such intention can be attributed literally to the in-itself, as this would presuppose that it was *already* "for-itself." Hence, "Ontology will limit itself to declaring that *everything happens as if* the in-itself, in a project of grounding itself, were giving itself the modification of the for-itself" (BN: 621/EN: 685). The problem with this proposal, however, as with Sartre's notion of a "de-totalized totality," is the lack of coherence even in its own terms. Strangely, Sartre goes on to assert that this hypothesis regarding an intention of the "in-itself" to ground itself is the only acceptable one. However, if Sartre claims that the only way to make sense of the ontological structure of the experienced world is to proceed "as if" a certain absolute event has occurred, yet also denies intelligibility to this "as if," *even as a fiction*, he has effectively declared that there is *no explanation available*.

Furthermore, even if we could disregard this problem, there is a gap in Sartre's metaphysics between the upsurge of negativity as such, and the world as it appears in the consciousness of an individual human being or "for-itself." In evoking the absolute event, Sartre emphasizes that the nihilation introduced by the in-itself effects a radical change in the status of the in-itself: "it suffices for this nihilation that a total transformative upheaval *happens* to the in-itself. This upheaval is the world" (BN: 617–618/EN: 682). At the same time, Sartre also asserts that "The for-itself is not nothingness in general but a singular privation, it is constituted as the privation of *this being here* [*en privation de cet être-ci*]" (BN: 618/EN: 682). These claims are not consistent. Because there *is* no world prior to the upsurge of the for-itself, there can be no originating "singular . . . privation of *this being here*," an expression which presumably alludes to the unique relation of each human consciousness to its own specific, embodied existence in the world. Demonstratives cannot apply to bare being in-itself. Sartre simply jumps from the absolute event, which must indeed be the upsurge of "*le néant en général*," as he calls it, to "*une privation singulière.*" It is worth noting that, a few pages later in *Being and Nothingness*, Sartre refers to the original upsurge as a "nihilating [*néantisante* – i.e., not "annihilating"] decompression of being" (BN: 620/EN: 685), which captures more accurately the metaphysical process involved, and has nothing of a limited "privation" about it, as implied when he describes the original negative upsurge as "a *minimal* nihilation which finds its origin at the heart of being" (BN: 617/EN: 682 [emphasis added]). In short, Sartre fails to explain how the general "decompression" of the in-itself—admittedly, a useful and evocative metaphor—could pluralize and singularize itself as a multiplicity of embodied human consciousnesses confronting a differentiated world of entities.

This suggests that the route from the "absolute event" to the world of situated human experience must be much longer and more circuitous than Sartre imagines—or perhaps can afford to imagine, because to do so would contradict the "Copernican" commitment of his phenomenology. By contrast, Schelling, along with the other major thinkers of German Idealism, is centrally concerned with tracing this path—with understanding the relation between the absolute ground and the empirical world of finite entities. Nonetheless, however truncated Sartre's hypothesis of "a nihilating decompression" of the in-itself may be, it *can* provide an entryway into the complexities of Schelling's argumentation. This is because the metaphor of decompression contains resources which Sartre himself does not exploit. More specifically, as we have just seen, Sartre finds himself in the uncomfortable position of having to ascribe the spontaneous upsurge of an "intention" to the "in-itself," which does not make sense even as a hypothesis. While Schelling does not suggest that the decompression can be explained, as the conditions for the distinction of ground and consequent do not yet exist, there is no inconsistency involved in thinking of the decompression—retrospectively—as the emergence of the modalities of being out of the premodal blankness of blind existing-ness. We can imagine them as "contained" within it, as it were. For Schelling's purposes, all that is required is that there should be nothing to *prevent* the emergence of the modalities, each of which is one mode of potentiality in general, or of what he calls "infinite being-able-to-be" (*das unendliche Seinkönnen*) (PO41/42: 101). He describes this process in the following way:

> Thus pure being cannot be potentiality in advance, in other words, before it is; but it does not follow from the fact that being cannot be potentiality in advance, that subsequently, *post actum (in actual fact)*, *after it is*, therefore *a posteriori*, it should not *indeed* be *that-which-is-able-to-be*. It is simply that being, the *actus*, must precede. But nothing prevents it, and it is not contradictory to the nature of that which purely is for *a possibility of being something other than what it is un-pre-thinkably* to be subsequently presented to it. It finds itself in this possibility without any active contribution from itself. Let us assume that this occurred. (PO41/42: 162)

This statement helps to make clear that the opacity and solidity which Sartre attributes to primordial being-in-itself are in fact retrojected: they are characteristic of the way the in-itself appears to the for-itself, *once* the duality of modes of being has been established, and in those moments when the veneer of meaning which the projects of the for-itself impose on the in-itself dissolves—Roquentin's encounter with the tree-root in *Nausea* being the most famous example.[5] By contrast, for Schelling, the "decompression"—to use Sartre's term—is not "contradictory to the nature of that which purely is" because un-pre-thinkable being, as sheer *actus,* can also be regarded, from another angle, as pure potentiality. One could say that all that is involved is a switch from an objective to a subjective genitive: from the (quasi-transitive) *being* of possibility to the being *of* (the being which belongs to) *possibility*. Were the response to be made that Schelling does, though, describe un-pre-thinkable being as "blind," the defence would be that this is simply a synonym for radical pre-conceptuality and does not exclude the reconfiguration of being-ness *as* potentiality, which—for Schelling—is closely related to conceptuality. The intelligibility of *this* reconfiguration—regarded as a hypothesis—is underscored by Schelling's use in this context of the term "contingently necessary [process of] existing" (*das zufällig nothwendiges Existieren*) (PO41/42: 166). For the formula can be seen as expressing the originary fusion of the three potentialities which subsequently emerge in the process of decompression: primordially, contingency *is* necessity, and vice versa, and the copula—existing-ness—both unites and is the unity of both.

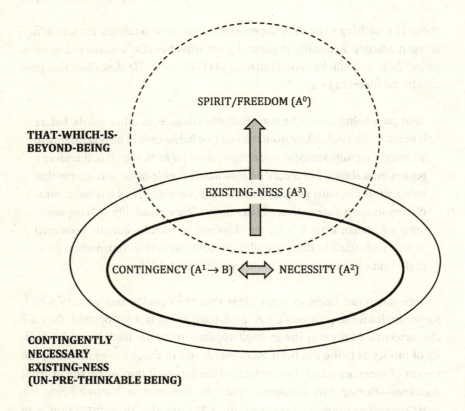

Figure 1 The Decompression of Contingently Necessary Existing-ness into the Modalities of Being (Potentialities)

The process of decompression can therefore be presented schematically as in Figure 1.

We can elucidate this diagram as follows. To mutate into primordial possibility (*Urmöglichkeit*) or infinite being-able-to-be (*das unendliche Seynkönnen*), blind being must become the possibility *of* something. Schelling specifies this as the only thing it could be at this stage: a mode of being *other than* un-pre-thinkable being—a being-otherwise, an *Anderssein* (PO41/42: 170). Furthermore, because nothing except possibility is currently available to be realized in this alternative mode, it must, in the first instance, take the form of self-actualized possibility as such. But a dialectic is thereby triggered which will be familiar from the treatment of "*das Seyende selbst*" in Schelling's negative philosophy. In the shape of *das Seynkönnende*, actualized pure possibility runs up against a negating countermovement. This *has to* occur because un-pre-thinkable being is *necessary* being; but it can now only assert its necessity, against its total actualization in the guise of *das Seynkönnende*—as the ontologically unstable, elusive basis of all possible entities—in a new "potentiated" form, as Schelling calls it: pure static being as a mode of possibility. This is the ideal dimension of being, which is *forced* to assert its necessity in a clash with actualized possibility (the dimension of pure materiality), and which Schelling therefore terms "*das Seynmüssende*." However, the incompatibility of *Anderssein* in these two modalities would result simply in an endless oscillation, there could be no progress along the path toward the empirical world as we know it, without the emergence of a third, unifying possibility. This potentiality cannot be either the *necessary* or the *possible* result of the conflict between *das Seynkönnende* and *das Seynmüssende*—for then it could not play a mediating role. It is *das Seynsollende*, which participates in both these modes of being. It is:

> what hovers freely between both as spirit, freely, because it would behave towards being-able as being, and towards being as being-able. For un-pre-thinkable being makes itself free with respect to being-able [*das Können*] and being-able makes itself free with respect to un-pre-thinkable being, so that it can be *and* not be both of them—pure being-ness, on the one hand, and what it can be by virtue of being-able-to-be, on the other. (AD, SW, II/4: 339)

It is fundamental to the structure of Schelling's late philosophy that, on the basis of this analysis, spirit be characterized as "free" and as "that which is beyond being" (*das Überseyende*)—beyond being in the sense that it is not constrained or determined by the modes of being which are united in it, either separately or in their conjunction. Of course, these characterizations go together because freedom is not any kind of entity, nor is it simply a process. However, Schelling's use of the term "*Überseyende*"—which implies that spirit is not simply a pocket of negation *within* being (of the kind envisaged by Sartre) but stands *above* being as a whole—points to a more demanding aspect of his train of argument. For he also characterizes *das Überseyende* as the "necessarily necessarily-existing" (*das nothwendig Nothwendigexistierende*), by contrast with the "contingently necessarily existing," or un-pre-thinkable being (PO41/42: 171). The "necessarily necessarily-existing," or the "*naturâ suâ Existierende*" (that which exists by virtue of its nature), is evidently a version of the God of the ontological argument. But how could this be the case? How could God both be that which exists by immanent necessity *and* have a precondition? The inaugural hypothesis of the positive philosophy seems to combine two incompatible viewpoints. On the one hand, Schelling states in his first Berlin lecture course that, "*Without the preceding blind being, God could not be God, not be that which is beyond being*" (PO41/42: 175). This seems to imply a *dependence* of God on blind or un-pre-thinkable being. Yet he also asserts in the same passage: "However, that being which precedes everything, which God has without any doing on his part, is *only a momentary thought*, not a temporal presupposition, but rather a presupposition in accord with the matter at hand. Just as he is in that un-pre-thinkable being, he knows *immediately* that he has no need of this act of existing, that he is what is necessary by nature; and it is precisely in this transcendence of original being that he is God" (PO41/42: 175–176).

It may help to make sense of Schelling's train of thought if we return once more to the parallels with Sartre, whose argument, in *Being and Nothingness*, seems to suffer from a similar inconsistency. On the one hand, he insists that the freedom of the for-itself remains *ontologically secondary* in relation to the in-itself. On the other hand, the for-itself is also characterized by Sartre as a "non-substantial absolute" (BN: xxxii/EN: 23). By this he means that, as the nothingness of consciousness cannot be caused or produced by something other than itself, consciousness must be its own reason for existing. Indeed Sartre, ignoring his own strictures on the notion, goes so far as to suggest that consciousness—*unlike* being-in-itself—can be characterized as "*causa sui*" (BN: xl/EN: 31). In the introduction to *Being and Nothingness* he develops further the implications of this insight: "consciousness is not produced as a singular instance of an abstract possibility, but . . . surging up at the heart of being it creates and sustains its essence, that is to say the synthetic organization of its possibilities" (BN: xxxi/EN: 21). He continues: "This also means that the type of being of consciousness is the opposite of that revealed by the ontological proof: since consciousness is not *possible* before it is, but rather its being is the source and condition of all possibility, it is its existence which implies its essence" (BN: xxxi/EN: 21). Here Sartre replicates Schelling's train of thought quite closely. After all, what Schelling calls "spirit" also posits and sustains its own essence, synthesizing or holding together contradictory potentialities. In other words, Schelling *also* reverses the ontological proof. Does this simply mean that Schelling and Sartre both fall into a similar incoherence? Such a conclusion would be a hasty because it would overlook the illicit jump that we have already detected in Sartre's thinking, between the original "nihilating decompression of being" and the "singular privation" of being in which finite human consciousness consists. Schelling's equivalent of the "nihilating decompression"—his account of the transformation of un-pre-thinkable into "primordial possibility" (*Urmöglichkeit*)—is not intended *directly* to explain the emergence of individual human consciousness, but rather to build freedom into the foundations of our systematic conception of the world. The parallel with Sartre is underlined by the fact that he occasionally describes the absolute event as the emergence of the mobility of "negation" within the stasis of blind being-ness.[6] However, as we have noted, Schelling proposes not simply a reversal of the ontological argument, but rather a *reversal* (*Umkehrung*) of the *reversed* ontological argument. This reversal of the reversal, possibility absorbing its ontological "precondition", is the founding "hypothesis" of Schelling's positive philosophy. But before examining this conjecture in more detail, it will be useful to compare more generally the reworking of the ontological argument in Hegel and Schelling.

The Ontological Argument in Hegel

It is an assumption common to all the German Idealists that freedom cannot be injected into a philosophical system at some point prior to its very beginning because the gapless explanatory coherence required by the system does not permit such a strategy. To return to Heidegger's summary of the problematic of the *Freiheitsschrift*: the "closed nexus of grounding" (*geschlossener Begründungszusammenhang*) to which philosophy—which can leave nothing unexplained in good conscience—aspires allows no internal space for a "beginning which requires no ground" (*grundunbedürftiger Anfang*).[7] Hence, if freedom is understood as an unconditional capacity to begin, it can itself only be the system's absolute ground. Correspondingly, given that the concept of God is the central concept inherited from the tradition by means of which the German Idealists approach the question of ultimate grounding, different understandings of the divine and of divine freedom will have crucial repercussions for the understanding of human freedom. The ontological argument for the existence of God, which claims to derive his being purely from his concept, and to which Hegel and Schelling respond in importantly different ways, can provide a thread to guide us through this labyrinth. Hegel staunchly defended the ontological argument against the Kantian critique, but only in a drastically reformulated version, which he expounded, amongst other places, in the last lecture course which he gave before his death (see LPR3: 351–358/VPR3: 271–276). In contrast, Schelling apparently rejects the validity of the ontological argument. Yet he also argues that it reveals a profound philosophical meaning, in its very failure to achieve its goal.

From Descartes and Malebranche, via Spinoza, to Leibniz and Wolff, the ontological proof was central to rationalist metaphysics, in its quest to establish an ultimate ground of reality, and to justify its claims concerning the deep structure of the world. Confidence in the success of the ontological proof had been on the wane in the decades prior to the publication of the *Critique of Pure Reason*, but it was Kant who dealt the argument a fatal blow, at least as far as conventional philosophical opinion was concerned. In fact, the immediate post-Kantian situation, as described by Dieter Henrich in his book on the topic, has endured, for the most part, up to the present day:

> Since there was unity with regard the assertion that the error of the ontological argument lay so open to view that it was hard to believe that it had remained hidden from significant thinkers for so long, it soon seemed scarcely worth the effort to refute it in detail.[8]

Of course, while this may have been the view of the conventional followers of Kant, it could hardly be the considered opinion of the leading thinkers of post-Kantian Idealism. For a central aim of the German Idealists was to restore the possibility of knowledge of reality in an absolute sense, a form of cognition which Kant had placed beyond human reach. At the same time, the Idealists were also aware that Kant had raised the theory of the relation between the knowing subject and the object of knowledge to an entirely new level of sophistication, and that this advance could not be reversed without lapsing into metaphysical naiveté. Indeed, one could argue that their aim was to extend rather than reverse the Kantian revolution in this regard, by overcoming the residual objectivism in Kant's treatment of what he characterized as the "noumenal" or "supersensible" realm. Hence, while the Idealists were necessarily concerned with the ontological argument, as the crucial hinge between *a priori* thought and the ground of all being, there could be no question of trying simply to revive the argument in one of its pre-Kantian forms. This complex attitude accounts, at least in part, for the difficulty of disentangling the various strands in the assessment and reconfiguration of the argument undertaken by the Idealists.

In the *Encyclopaedia*, Hegel states that the ontological argument expresses a vital truth, namely that "God is simply true being" (Enc.1: §50/W20, 8: 132). However, this does not mean that he denies the obvious, everyday opposition between thought and being. His objection to Kant's famous example of the hundred thalers, which do not vary in any characteristic, whether they are merely an object of thought or jingling in one's pocket (A599/B627), is not that Kant was wrong to argue that being is not a real predicate, one which contributes to the determination of a thing, but rather that the example is trivial. As he puts it:

> Nothing can be more obvious than that anything which I only think or represent to myself is not yet on that account *actual;* that thought, mental representation, or even the concept, do not reach as far as being. (Enc.1: §51/W20, 8: 135–136)

As if aware that this statement seems to contradict his usual account of the conceptual, Hegel continues:

> It could not unfairly be termed a barbarism to call something such as a hundred thalers a concept. Even putting this aside, those who repeat again and again, against the philosophical Idea, that being and thought are different, should concede, after all, that philosophers also are not unaware of this; what more trivial item of knowledge could there be? (Enc.1: §51/W20, 8: 136)

Accordingly, in the discussion of Anselm in his *Lectures on the History of Philosophy*, Hegel praises the thought of the scholastic period for having raised the "highest opposition," that of thinking and being, to clear consciousness. The problem with Anselm's version of the ontological argument, he argues, is that it attempts to overcome the gap between thought and being, starting from the assumption that *even the highest representation*, that of God, is fundamentally something subjective. As he puts it:

> The highest representation cannot simply be in the understanding, it must also pertain to it that it exists. This is quite right; but the transition is not demonstrated, the fact that subjective understanding suspends itself. (LHP3: 64/W20, 19: 556–557)

Hegel clarifies what he means by this self-suspension of the subjective understanding in a passage from the *Encyclopaedia*:

> The metaphysical proofs of the existence of God are therefore deficient interpretations and descriptions of the elevation of the spirit from the world to God, because they do not express the moment of *negation* which is contained in this elevation, or rather they do not emphasize it. For it is inherent in the fact that the world is *contingent* that it is merely something subject to decay, merely apparent, and, in its own terms, a nullity. The meaning of the elevation of the spirit is that the world does indeed have being, but being that is only appearance, not true being, not the absolute truth. This lies rather beyond appearance only in God, and God is simply true being. To the extent that this elevation is a *transition* and *mediation*, it is also a *suspension* of the *transition* and the mediation. For that through which God might appear to be mediated, the world, is rather declared to be null; only the *nullity* of the *being* of the world forms the bond of elevation, so that what exists as mediating disappears, and thereby the mediation is suspended in this process of mediation itself. (Enc.1: §50/W20, 8: 132)

In short, when human consciousness rises to God, it grasps the objectively rational process which culminates in the human capacity for religious and philosophical thinking, and which is therefore the precondition for the possibility of that very ascent:

The consciousness of finite spirit is the concrete being, the material in which the concept of God is realized. We are not here talking about any adding of being to the concept or about a simple unity of concept and being—expressions like that are misleading. The unity in question is to be grasped rather as an absolute process, as the living activity of God—but in such a way that both sides are also differentiated in it so that it is the absolute activity of eternally producing itself. We have here the concrete representation of God as *spirit*. (LPR3: 356/VPR3: 275)

Schelling's Response to the Ontological Argument

In the lectures *On the History of Modern Philosophy*, which Schelling gave in Erlangen in the 1820s and repeated in Munich in the following decade, he twice addresses the issue of the ontological argument—in the context of his discussion of Descartes and, later, in his account of Spinoza and Leibniz. In his response to Descartes, Schelling's strategy is to shift the center of gravity of the concept of God from the notion of the perfect being to the notion of necessary existence. He first suggests that Descartes' argument can be restated in the following way:

> It would contradict the nature of the perfect being to exist just *contingently* (as, e.g., my own existence is simply contingent, precarious and for this reason doubtful *in itself*), therefore the most perfect being can only exist necessarily. (HMP: 50/SW, I/10: 15)

However, Schelling contends, Descartes falls victim to a paralogism, moving from the fact that, by definition, God can only exist necessarily to the conclusion that God necessarily exists. One cannot advance from being *inside the scope* to being *outside the scope* of the modal operator:

> In the major premise (the perfect being can only exist *necessarily*), it is only a question of the *manner* of existence (it is only stated that the perfect being could not exist in a contingent *manner*); in the conclusion (in the *conclusio*), however, it is no longer a question of the *manner* of existence (in this case the conclusion would be correct) but of [any] existence at all, therefore there is *plus in conclusio quam fuerat in praemissis* [more in the conclusion

that there was in the premises], i.e. a logical law has been broken, or the conclusion has an incorrect form. (HMP: 50-51/SW, I/10: 15-16)

However, Schelling does not regard his own critique as depriving Descartes' argument of all interest or validity, for he states: "There would, I suggest, be no objection to [Descartes'] argument, particularly if one agrees that the concept of necessary existing should be understood to mean merely the opposite of contingent existing" (HMP: 50/SW, I/10: 15). What Schelling intends by this rather cryptic statement is spelled out in the following pages, where he argues that the "true meaning of the conclusion" of Descartes' ontological argument ("*either* God does not exist at all, or, if He exists, then He *always* exists necessarily") is that the concepts of "God" and of "necessary existence" have been pulled part—can no longer be considered as "simply *identical* concepts" (HMP: 51/SW, I/10: 16-17). Thus, when Schelling refers to a "necessary existing" which is "merely the opposite of contingent existing," he means a mode of existing which is not dependent on anything other than itself (and, in that sense, is not contingent), but at the same time is not necessary *by nature* in the sense of *causing* itself. As we noted in chapter 4, Schelling regards Spinoza as the thinker who brings the tradition of the ontological argument to its culmination, by equating God's necessity with this kind of necessity—allowing God to be swallowed by his own blind being-ness, as it were. The result is an elimination of freedom. Given that Hegel is a post-Spinozist thinker also committed to a version of the ontological argument, it is to be expected that Schelling will direct a similar critique against him. In the chapter on Hegel in his lectures *On the History of Philosophy* Schelling writes:

> If one were to ask a follower of this philosophy whether absolute spirit externalized itself at any particular moment in the world, he would have to answer: God *has* not thrown himself into nature, but rather he throws himself into it over and over, in order, similarly, to keep returning to the summit again; it is an eternal happening, that is to say, a perpetual happening, but precisely for that reason not a genuine, or a real [*wirklich*] happening. This God is certainly free, furthermore, to externalise himself in nature, that is to say, he is free to *sacrifice* his freedom . . . his life is a cycle of forms, in which he perpetually externalizes himself in order to return to himself again, and always returns to himself in order to externalize himself anew. (HMP: 159-160/SW, I/10: 160)

Hegel, of course, positively endorses this consequence in emphasizing the circular character of his system: "What is essential for science is not so much that something purely immediate should be the beginning, but that the whole of science should be a cycle in itself, in which the first also becomes the last and the last becomes the first" (SL: 49/W20, 5: 70). Such a cyclical process, however, can only be deterministic—as regards what is essential, everything has always already happened, and can only happen in the same way again and again. To summarize: the cost of an ontological argument which equates being and the concept is the absorption of the potentiality of the concept into the compulsion of blind being. By contrast, Schelling considers the oblique element of truth in the ontological argument to be that "*if* [God] exists, *necessary existence* is his prius, the *prius of divinity*" (PO41/42: 156). This statement, in distinguishing between God and his own necessary existence, which in a certain sense precedes him, clearly descends from the contrast between the ground and the existent which Schelling introduced in the *Freiheitsschrift*, and which played a reworked role in the *Weltalter* project. It returns us to the question of the "reversal of the reversal," which was touched on above, as the means by which Schelling seeks to avoid a conception of God—of the absolute—which entails determinism, indeed seeks to understand "*freedom*" as "what is highest for us and for divinity" ("*Freiheit* ist unser und der Gottheit Höchstes" [UPO: 79]).

Perhaps the most enlightening way to approach Schelling's argument is to regard it as a response to the *impasse* that resulted in his failure to complete the project of *The Ages of the World*. As we observed, the problem which arose from finding a radical beginning in the "will that wills nothing" was that, in order to *be*—rather than remain suspended in a state of non-being—this will had to contract into the particular "will which wills something," thereby giving rise to the incessant "rotary movement." Once this gyration is triggered, not even the separation and distribution of the modes of willing as the three existentially interlaced dimensions of time seemed able to prevent the contractive pull of the past from outweighing the future-oriented thrust of the happening of time. In other words, once the originary pure freedom (*lautere Freiheit*) has fallen into the grip of necessity it no longer has any means of escaping again: precisely the problem which Schelling diagnoses in Hegel's theory of the externalization of absolute spirit. In his *Spätphilosophie*, Schelling realizes that the only way to avoid this outcome is to make un-pre-thinkable being the absolute starting point. For this entails that the coercion of blind being-ness is *already overcome* in principle, in the very process through which such being-ness is transformed into potentiality. As Schelling puts it:

> Here we can only start from being, and arrive from this starting point at potentiality, which is thereby secured against all overthrow because it does *not* have being *ahead* of itself, but rather *behind itself as what it has overcome*; as past. *The beginning of positive philosophy is thus being which has never been* potentia, *but always* actu. (PO41/42: 161)

We could express Schelling's argument in another way by saying that the genuine absolute, the absolute which engenders the dialectic of potentialities which will come to structure the empirical world, is itself nothing other than the process of liberation from blind being-ness. As Schelling puts it:

> Thus being would be raised to the *potentia potentiae*, to a potentiality which has potentiality in its hand. It would see itself set free over against its un-pre-thinkable being, raised to what truly and actually is. (PO41/42: 162–163)

Contingently necessary being, we can say, has become the necessary or self-sustaining being *of* freedom, or pure potentiality itself. Consequently, "*Here the concepts are reversed*; blind being-ness now shows itself as the impotent, the negative, and the being-able-to-be, which blind being-ness preceded, as the positive" (PO41/42: 169).

It is hard to overlook one apparently paradoxical consequence of this conception, in which the reversal of the ontological argument involved in positing God's necessary being as *prior* to his essence or concept, is itself reversed. The result of Schelling's account is that the God of the ontological argument—or what he terms "*das naturâ suâ Existierende*"—plays a fundamental role, but *only* as dependent on a condition. Absolute freedom must be its own ground, nothing can cause it or bring it into being, and it therefore fulfils the conditions for existing by nature, yet it is also *not* what Schelling calls the "*prius*," or the absolutely first. As he puts it quite bluntly: "*Without the preceding blind being God could not be God, not be that which is beyond being*" (PO41/42: 175). This claim becomes less paradoxical, however, if we consider that here *one kind* of absoluteness (that of the inability not to be, or what James Kreines has termed a "*default* sense of absoluteness" [AP: 22]) simply becomes *another kind* of absoluteness (that of pure freedom). As Schelling puts it, "Nothing prevents it from being the case that what, *a priori*, was being-ness, should subsequently, *post actum* (as we can rightly say here), be the being-able-to be" (AD, SW, II/3: 338). As a result of this reversal, blind being *becomes the necessary being* of the divine essence, which is the unity of the potentialities, and therefore the ground of everything which could become actual. This process, as Schelling puts it, "*tore God (accusative) from his rigid eternity* and set him in freedom *against his blind being*" (PO41/42: 169). In his first Berlin lecture cycle Schelling shows himself to be fully aware of the perplexing and demanding character of his argument, remarking at one point, "We are wandering here—*along previously untrodden paths, trains of thought which are alien to our time*" (PO41/42: 165). In the Conclusion I will return to consider to the rationale of the process.

Creation

It is important to recall that, at the start of the positive philosophy, we are still dealing with a dialectic of pure potentialities and *not yet* with the spatio-temporal world. The first task of positive philosophy is to think the "*Umkehrung*"—the reversal of the reversed ontological proof—in order to reach the thought of what is "beyond being" (*das Überseyende*), namely self-sustaining freedom or the pure capacity to be or not be. However, the spatio-temporal world is already on the horizon, as it were, because to rise above contingently necessary existing-ness, primordial possibility must be the possibility *of* something—and this can only be the possibility of a mode of being *other than* un-pre-thinkable being. As Schelling puts it, the "essence and self" of the actual process of existing (*das actu Existieren*) "sees itself in the freedom to oppose *to un-pre-thinkable actuality another* being, which it makes possible, and which stands entirely in its power" (PO41/42: 171). Although Schelling uses the language of "creation" in this context, his concern is not with a supposed *causal origin* of the spatio-temporal world, but rather with the world interpreted as the actualization of an ontological structure. His basic idea is that God, who is "essentially freedom" (PO, SW, II/4: 112), seeks to *liberate himself* from his own un-pre-thinkable being. Of course, there is a sense in which God is already liberated because this being has become his own necessary being *as* freedom. But all the same, this necessary being was not willed or chosen: the necessity of absolute freedom was not originally in the gift of this freedom (the thought which makes Kant shudder, which he declares both irresistible and unbearable, that even God would have to look into the abyss of his own un-pre-thinkable being [A613/B641], is therefore openly embraced by his successor). Hence, Schelling suggests, God-as-freedom can only be fully realized through the actualization of a mode of being—worldly being—which is *other than* his own primordial being. A possible anthropomorphic image for this process is the relief obtained through the verbal expression of an obsessive thought—which nonetheless could not oppress me if it were not a product of my own thinking. Emancipation is only fully achieved, Schelling suggests, when primordial being is neutralized: "He can only decide to *suspend that* actu *eternal being* by virtue of something other external to him, of which those potentialities must be the means of realization. *Only as Lord of a being different from himself is God completely away from himself, absolutely free and blissful*" (PO41/42: 176). Schelling, therefore, is not envisaging a creation *ex nihilo*, but rather a series of transformations of un-pre-thinkable being, which result in the "suspension" of the eirenic constellation of the merely possible modes of being—the noetic unity of the potentialities—in the form of a spatio-temporal world.

In recent times some commentators, especially in the English-speaking world, have compared Schelling unfavorably with Hegel on the grounds that Schelling's thinking remains "theological," and therefore—by implication— antiquated and backward-looking, whereas Hegel's work is presented as more readily compatible with the secularistic and naturalistic outlook common in the contemporary West. This assessment and its presuppositions raise many issues, some of which will be explored in later chapters. For the moment, it will suffice to observe that *both* Schelling and Hegel are confronted with the problem of accounting for the transition from a foundational, but atemporal dialectic—in Schelling's case, that of the potentialities, in Hegel's case, that of the concept—to the concrete spatio-temporal world; and that Hegel also uses the theological term "creation" (*Schöpfung*) on some occasions to describe this transition, even outside the context of his philosophy of religion (e.g., SL: 49/W20, 5: 70). Some commentators have tried to manage this problem in Hegel's case, by arguing that the move from the *Logic* to the *Realphilosophie* is itself logically necessitated. But, as we noted in the previous chapter, this interpretation cannot be sustained. Hegel is quite clear that, when we reach the absolute Idea, by definition *all* the logical moves have been exhausted. Furthermore, it is important for Hegel's systematic conception that this should be so. For, as he emphasizes on the final page of the *Science of Logic*, unless the Idea "in this freedom," a freedom consisting in the fact that it is now fully self-determined, nonetheless "determines itself as simple being"

(SL: 752/WL, W20, 6: 573), then the empirical world will lack ontological independence, will be simply an emanation of the Idea. At the end of the *Science of Logic*, we can say, Hegel is interested in two forms of freedom. The spatiotemporal world can be said to be "free" in the sense of self-standing, more than a mere projection of the logical. But Hegel also stresses that this "*externality of space and time*," initially devoid of all subjectivity, is "for the sake of this *freedom* [of the Idea]" (*um dieser Freiheit willen*) (SL: 753/W20, 6: 573). In other words, Hegel shares with Schelling a sense that divine freedom (in his case, the freedom of the "divine Idea") would itself be compromised if nature were simply a prolongation of the original timeless structure. To emphasize the hiatus between the logical realm and nature, Hegel refers specifically to a "decision" (*Entschluß*) of the Idea, both in the *Science of Logic* and in the *Encyclopaedia Logic*, a fact which Schelling famously highlights as betraying a problem with Hegel's systematic conception: the decision is "already an approximation to *historical* philosophy"— "*geschichtliche Philosophie*" was Schelling's original term for positive philosophy—with which Hegel, *nolens volens*, is forced to supplement the negative theory presented in the *Logic* (PO41/42: 133).

As well as sharing the view that there cannot be a logically compelled transition *beyond* the logical domain, Hegel and Schelling both associate this transition with the thought that there is something cramping and confining about an exclusively *self*-thinking process. As Hegel puts it, the systematic development of the Idea in the *Logic* is indeed a "realization" of it—but only within "the same sphere" as that of which it is the realization. It is "shut up within subjectivity," and hence gives rise to a "drive" to suspend this one-sidedness (SL: 752/W20, 6: 572). Similarly, Schelling argues, with reference to the notion of God as subject-object (a definition which Hegel also provides for the Idea [SL: 673/WL, W20, 6: 466]), that "in this necessity eternally to think oneself there would lie a monstrous limitation" (PO41/42: 176). The difference between Hegel and Schelling consists in the fact that, for Hegel, "the simple being to which the Idea determines itself remains perfectly transparent to it and is the concept that, in its determination, abides with itself" (SL: 752–753/W20, 6: 573). In other words, dialectical necessity continues in the new medium of *äusserliches Dasein*, and can be fully articulated, as the process whereby the Idea struggles toward and finally achieves full self-consciousness in its passage through nature and history. By contrast, for Schelling, logic and ontology *only* coalesce in negative philosophy—but they do coalesce nonetheless. This means that Schelling does not need a

Realphilosophie in the Hegelian sense, which would involve the generation of further categories for conceptualizing nature and history, with all the ensuing problems of co-ordination between the *Logic* and the *Realphilosophie* which we examined in the preceding chapter. Rather, the transition from negative to positive philosophy can be regarded, schematically, as the move from a transcendental ontology, which generates a system of basic forms or natural kinds, to a hermeneutics of the event and its consequences. Because of this distinction, Schelling could never declare, as Hegel does, that the concept is "everything" (*Alles*) and that its movement is the "universal, absolute activity" (*allgemeine absolute Tätigkeit*) (SL: 737/W20, 6: 551). However, it may not be obvious straightaway how Schelling is able to avoid a similar conclusion: namely, that it is the *a priori* dialectic of the potentialities which determines how things will unfold in the empirical world.

The answer to this question lies in the different role which the potentialities play in the negative and in the positive philosophy. In the former they function as principles of being, and the results of their interactions, culminating in their stabilization in the Idea, can be worked out in advance, in a process which Schelling describes as the experimental activity of pure thinking (DRP, SW, II/1: 386). In the latter, they have become ontological tendencies or drives which stand in an ongoing relation of tension and conflict. Put in another way, the difference is one between the patterns made by the interacting *concepts* of potentialities, and the results of the interaction of those potentialities themselves, in the course of their actualization. Admittedly, at the lower levels of nature there will not be much of a formal distinction between these two processes. But, in Schelling's view, as we advance up the natural scale, we will find there is increasing scope for agency, in the sense of a variable actualization of tendencies or drives (which do not, after all, display the rigidity characteristic of modern scientific conceptions of natural causation). To give just one example, Schelling's philosophy of mythology, the first historical component of the positive philosophy, deals with a range of mythological systems, which are distinguished by their various stages of adequacy or completion. Although he believes that there was in fact one fully achieved system—that of the ancient Greeks—there is no *a priori* reason why this completion had to occur, despite there being a deep ontological dynamic pushing in this direction. Alternatively, several could have occurred. But before turning to examine Schelling's theory of the evolution of human consciousness in the next chapter, we must first consider in more detail his conception of the emergence of freedom within nature.

Freedom in the Natural World

We have followed how, according to Schelling's "hypothesis," un-pre-thinkable being "decompresses" into the constellation of potentialities. In this process, blind existing-ness becomes the dialectical unity of the potentialities, a unity which provides the ontological platform, as it were, for transcendent or absolute freedom. However, when the potentialities are pushed beyond their noetic status, and become the structuring principles of a spatio-temporal world, they enter into a new tension (*Spannung*) with one another because they embody monopolistic but incompatible ways of actualizing being. Their pre-worldly, atemporal integration has been suspended, though it has not been rendered completely inoperative, as nothing can destroy the fundamental oneness of being. To return to the comparison with the Sartre explored earlier, in Schelling's account, God—the "ideal synthesis"—cannot be dismissed as an inconsistent fiction but continues to function implicitly as the ultimate pole of ontological attraction. Without this horizon of oneness, now felt or anticipated—for example, in religious consciousness—as the locus of reconciliation, there would be no *Spannung*. As Schelling puts it:

> The same potentialities which emerge in the negative philosophy as *a priori*, emerge again here, but not as potentialities which precede being, rather as having being *prior* to them. And they are held together by *being that is posited as the essence, as a supra-material spiritual oneness*. They are held together by this oneness, even when they have become actual, and through this oneness they are put in a *state of tension* and difference. (PO41/42: 177)

Once the potentialities have been set in conflict with one another, a process unfolds in the self-constitution of nature which is mapped out in broad terms in the negative philosophy, and more concretely at the beginning of the positive. We need not enter into the details of this process, but we can note that the dialectic of the potentialities gives rise to a series of equilibria which are metastable, since the conflict between the first and second potentialities has not been fully resolved. Each outcome in turn is "de-potentiated," becoming the material for the actualization of higher-level potentialities, and this process gives rise to increasingly self-directing kinds of natural entity, in a trajectory from the objective toward the subjective, the real toward the ideal. The complexities of this development are laid out in the late lecture course, *Darstellung des Naturprocesses*—the most complete statement of Schelling's final philosophy of nature (SW, I/10: 301–390). However, most important for present purposes is Schelling's ultimate philosophical aim, which is to explain how beings who are free, in the sense of having a capacity to act or refrain from acting, or to fix certain possibilities which, up until the point of decision, had been part of the open texture of the world, can be produced by natural processes.

This aspect of Schelling's thinking should be of considerable interest to anglophone philosophy. After a period in which the majority of philosophers either adopted some form of compatibilism or—influenced by constructivist interpretations of Kant or the quietist legacy of the later Wittgenstein—appeared to assume that adopting a "soft" form of naturalism could defuse the conflict between determinism and freedom, defenses of a libertarian conception of freedom have re-emerged as a force to be reckoned with, in the context of a re-animated discussion of the metaphysical issues. The views put forward by the British philosopher Helen Steward are especially relevant in the present context, since—operating strictly within the parameters of contemporary analytical philosophy—she arrives at many positions strikingly reminiscent of those proposed by Schelling in his philosophy of nature and freedom. For example, one of Steward's main contentions is that philosophical discussions of freedom often begin at too elevated a level, where conscious decision-taking capacities and the exercise of the will are the focus of attention (see MF: 2–3). In a challenge to this ingrained tendency, she argues that, to avoid human beings appearing, in the libertarian portrayal of them, as a strange metaphysical anomaly, a view which understandably calls forth deterministic reactions, we should focus rather on the notion of agency. On Steward's account, agency cannot be a matter of consciousness intervening in a natural world separated from it by a metaphysical gulf, or of purely mental processes initiating physical ones; the applicability of the concept of agency extends quite far into the domain of non-human nature. As she writes:

> For me to be able to settle whether my body will move in a particular way is merely for me to be able, in the actual context in which I find myself, both to bring about that particular movement of my body and to be able not to bring it about. But nothing is said or implied by this conception of settling about any antecedent thinkings, wishings, plannings, or the like . . . The animal body, on this conception, is not merely the instructed instrument of that animal's will. On the contrary, the complex set of embodied systems that enliven it are constitutive themselves of the phenomenon of willing.

The "I" that settles things in my sense, is therefore not to be conceived of as a pure will ... It is to be conceived as a whole, functioning animal whose systems of agent control are various and only some of which involve the paradigmatically mental phenomena often said to be essential to the causation of action. (MF: 48–49)

Steward argues, further, that a philosophical conception of this kind is implicit in our everyday experience of the animal world:

Watching a bird pecking around for food or a cat stalking a mouse is just utterly unlike watching, say, trees blowing in the wind or a car drive down a road. To watch a creature engaged in such goal-directed activity is ... to think of it as a moment-to-moment controller of its own body, a centre of subjectivity ... This way of thinking is, moreover, a way of *seeing*. (MF: 93)

Such a description of our experience of the natural world as pervaded by agency, where this implies a capacity to *settle* how matters evolve, something that is prior to anything like explicitly reflective self-consciousness, shows deep affinities with Schelling. Both philosophers share the view that freedom, in this sense, must be integrated into our philosophical conception of nature, and that the more sophisticated, reflective forms of human decision-taking, and the notions of moral responsibility that go along with them, should be understood as emerging in this context.

In the final chapter of her book, *A Metaphysics for Freedom*, Steward tackles the larger issues concerning causality and the natural order which are raised by her theory of freedom. Her basic claim is that there are no good metaphysical or scientific reasons to think of causality in a reductionist, one-size-fits-all manner, as consisting in invariant connections between microphysical events. As she puts it:

Causation is best thought of as a *category*: a large and ontologically flexible umbrella concept under which we bring a wide diversity of ontologically various relations and relationships, unified only by their connections to our interest in the explanation, prediction, and control of phenomena. (MF: 210)

This approach involves rejecting the "supervenience thesis," the view that lower-level conditions are always constitutively sufficient to explain higher-level conditions that are supposed to be dependent on them. This thesis, Steward argues, involves "thinking of the world in a kind of instantaneous, freeze-frame, snapshot view" which is "deeply misleading" (MF: 241). Instead, we should accept the reality of "top-down" causality: it is a pervasive and entirely normal feature of our world that higher-level entities shape the behavior of their elements. A whirlpool provides a good an example taken from nature. Once the whirlpool is in existence, its configuration will affect the behavior of the water molecules which are caught up in it, rather than the behavior of the molecules constituting a series of momentary "supervenience bases"—microphysical constellations—each of which is presumed exhaustively to determine its successor. As Steward writes:

> So far as causality is concerned, the pertinent fact is that once a whirlpool has formed certain forces tend to sustain it in existence unless and until the delicate equilibrium that maintains the whirlpool is disturbed by the intervention of some further factor. The complex arrangement that constitutes each individual momentary supervenience base therefore has a cause only in so far as it is a whirlpool-instantiating phenomenon; further details of the nature of the base (such as which individual molecules it contains) may be accidents relative to antecedent circumstances. So it is more accurate to think of the causality here as a kind of causality in which the phenomenon of the whirlpool creates the subsequent supervenience bases that then contribute to sustaining it, rather than the other way around. (MF: 242)

In the case of an artefact such as a wheel, Steward argues, it is even clearer that bottom-up causality cannot do the job:

> From the point of view of low-level physics (say), it is just not possible to gain any understanding of how the co-occurrence of these different phenomena required for the production of a wheel have been provided for by the universe ... It is only when we raise our view to the higher level that we begin to find the resources to make sense of what has occurred, when we can speak, for example, of persons and their plans and designs ... In one sense of the word "emerge", indeed, it is more accurate to say that the basal conditions emerge from factors favouring the existence, in these circumstances, of the higher-level entity, rather than the other way around. (MF: 237)

But as plausible as Steward's view may in general terms, given its consonance with our non-estranged experience of nature and human activity, it raises a fundamental genetic question: how did the higher forms of organization emerge in the first place? In other words, what could the "factors favouring the existence" of beings capable of planning and designing be? For Schelling, as we already know, these factors are the basic ontological vectors which he calls "potentialities." However, it is important to note the reversal which occurs between the philosophy of nature of his early and middle-period writings, and the conception of nature in the *Spätphilosophie*. In Schelling's earlier work, the *real* dimension of absolute identity is associated with the *objective*, while the *ideal* dimension is connected with the *subjective*. One distinguishing feature of his late thought, however, is that this correlation is turned around. The concept of "subject" is now taken, in the first instance, in its meaning of "*subjectum*" or "*hypokeimonon*"—it is what underlies and supports the qualities which define a particular entity. Correspondingly, those qualities—universals predicated of the entity—are what lend it determinate, experienceable objectivity.[9] With these assumptions, Schelling will then describe the "process of nature" as the gradual forcing of the first potentiality (annotated as B), back into its proper role as basis by the second potentiality (annotated as A+). A+ functions as the principle of differentiation and stability, in contrast to the chaotic restlessness of B, its expansive drive to exclude any other mode of being. Of course, the integration of B and A+ at different levels of material existence, measured in terms of an increasing complexity and interiority, is only possible because A±, the subject-object, is already implicitly at work from the start.[10]

However, with this account Schelling has not yet told the whole story. The ingenuity of his theory stems from the idea that B is the objectified version of A− (the pure possibility to be or not to be), which is immanently compelled to actualize itself as contingent materiality. (We recall that, in Schelling's notation for the potentialities, B is in fact $A^1 \to B$. In his late philosophy of nature, he replaces superscript numbers with mathematical symbols to indicate that he is discussing the ontological vectors of nature itself, which find themselves in tension, not the noetic structure of the potentialities). As a result, what appears to be the *constraint* of B by A+, as it is forced back into the role of *hypokeimonon*, is implicitly the *liberation* of B, its return to the role of potentiality in its original form (A−). In this role, as the *possibility of becoming determinate*, it merges with A±, the principle of unity of a natural entity. In other words, for Schelling, freedom as the actualization of possibilities, the core of agency as Steward understands it, is built into the material process of nature from the very beginning. It is for this reason that he criticizes Aristotle's view of matter:

> The metaphysical concept of matter is ... perhaps the most difficult, because matter must be something real, in other words an *actus*, and yet behave again as a potentiality towards what it is to become. Therefore, matter cannot be classified as a principle, as Aristotle did; it is itself something which has become [*etwas Gewordenes*]. (DN, SW, I/10: 310)

Correspondingly, for Schelling the "top-down" causality at work in the sustaining of the ontological coherence of the familiar entities which populate the world can be seen as resulting from a *transformation* of their contingent materiality, and is not a bizarre exception to it, of the kind which provokes the reductionist backlash.

It is worth noting that this theory of nature also simultaneously addresses the problem of "how complex arrangements of things have arisen," as Steward puts it (MF: 237n). Design, as she concedes, cannot be the whole answer because designs can only be framed by already existing complex organisms. Regarding this issue, Steward offers only a few tentative references to Darwinian evolution (MF: 237n). However, the explanation of the historically increasing complexity of organisms, which brings with it possibilities of agency, is itself a highly contentious issue within Darwinian evolutionary theory. Adaptation to an environment can quite frequently be a matter of simplification rather than complexification (cave fish, for example, have lost their vulnerable and energy-consuming organs of sight). Darwin himself was aware of this, referring to a "retrogression of organization," and he also had to face the problem posed by the continuing pervasive existence of the simplest forms of life.[11] Hence, while arguing that increased complexity could, in many situations, give rise to competitive advantage, Darwin never went so far as to claim that increasing complexity is a *necessary* implication of his theory of natural selection. As Timothy Shanahan has summarized the matter: "while he rejected any notion of evolutionary progress as determined by a necessary law of progression, Darwin nonetheless accepted evolutionary progress as a contingent general consequence of natural selection."[12] The debates over the connections (if any) between evolution via natural selection and increasing complexity, and over the very validity of the notion of "progress" in evolutionary theory, have continued ever since.[13] Steward's position on this issue is unclear. But for many philosophers, up to and including contemporary thinkers such as Thomas Nagel, the claim that the domain of values—of rationality, truth, and moral goodness—which emerges along with self-conscious agency is simply a contingent upshot of material processes, including those of evolutionary biology, would undermine the whole axiological domain, in a kind of vast performative contradiction. For such thinkers, some deep directionality or purposiveness in nature, over and above what evolutionary theory can generate, must be assumed. Nagel, for example, calls for "an expanded but still naturalistic understanding" directed toward explaining:

> the appearance of life, consciousness, reason, and knowledge neither as accidental side effects of the physical laws of nature nor as the result of intentional intervention in nature from without but as an unsurprising if not inevitable consequence of the order that governs the natural world from within.[14]

Schelling's mature theory of nature seeks to describe exactly such an order.

There is one final point. Steward's concentration on the freedom implied by the agency which human beings share with the higher animals is a welcome corrective. The downside, of course, is her lack of exploration the distinctive form of freedom disclosed in human beings' moral and existential choices. How does this differ from animal agency—and indeed, in what sense can it be said to emerge from it? Schelling has an ingenious answer to this question. He argues that the dialectic of the potentialities results in a process which has a *necessary* directionality—but *only so long as they are in tension*. Once the potentialities reach their full reintegration in human consciousness, the tension is dissipated. The unity of B and A^1 in the third potentiality (A^3), permits an existence which is both and neither of the first two; it results in an equilibrium which is exempt from the unstably competing ideal and material forces operative in nature and in animal existence. But there could be no finite freedom of this kind if the world-process were the expression of a *unitary* principle. Only if the principle is *ab initio* double, divided against itself, can the balance which enables self-conscious freedom emerge. Schelling is convinced that there is no other way to account for the freedom of a being who is also fully part of nature:

> Accordingly, the ultimate, in which the *three causes* enter into unity, comes to stand between them as something free; it is free from the first cause by virtue of the second, and because it has B as its basis, it is free against A^2. It is like the pointer of the scales ... *This is the only way to explain how a freedom could be created.* (PO41/42: 200)

In its structure, therefore, human freedom is the restoration of the logical or atemporal equilibrium of the potentialities—it is the "realized Idea" (DN, SW, I/10: 388), the finite form of spirit. Viewing from a different angle, one can say that the human being is "not, like everything else a being, but rather once again *being-ness*" (nicht wie alles andere ein Seyendes, sondern wieder das Seyende) (DN, SW, I/10: 389). In the *Darstellung des Philosophischen Empirismus* (*Presentation of Philosophical Empiricism*), Schelling elaborates the same thought in terms of the concept of divinity:

> The human being is the bond of divine unity, and in *this* sense it is quite correct that God as such exists nowhere in the whole world—only in the human being, specifically in the true human beings who find themselves in their original condition. And when Lalande asserted that he had been unable to find any God in the whole edifice of the world, this is entirely understandable; for God as such is not in the separation and tension of the world forces, but only in that in which all tension is cancelled and the three causes find themselves in completely equal and shared splendour. (DPE, SW, I/10: 273)

It will noted that Schelling attributes this release of tension only to human beings in their "original state." That fact that divine freedom has emerged immanently from *within* the natural order renders it highly insecure and unstable. As we shall find, much of Schelling's positive philosophy is concerned with interpreting the far-reaching consequences of this precarity.

Notes

1. See Alexandra Roux, *Schelling—l'avenir de la raison. Rationalisme et empirisme dans sa dernière philosophie* (Paris: Éditions du Félin, 2016), 207–217. Roux's book provides an informative overview of the structure Schelling's late system in general.

2. See Sebastian Gardner, "Sartre, Schelling and Onto-Theology," *Religious Studies* 42, no. 3 (2006): 258–259. The present discussion is greatly indebted to this essay, although Gardner uses the *Weltalter* for his comparison between Schelling and Sartre, rather than the *Spätphilosophie*.
3. See "Sartre, Schelling and Onto-Theology," 249.
4. For further discussion of this issue see Peter Dews, "Theory Construction and Existential Description in Schelling's Treatise on Freedom," *Journal of the British Society for the History of Philosophy* 25, no. 1 (2017).
5. Jean-Paul Sartre, *Nausea* (London: Penguin, 2000), 185–188.
6. "Und *auf diese Weise kommt in das unbewegliche Sein eine Beweglichkeit*, es bekommt eine Negation in sich . . ." (PO41/42: 164).
7. Martin Heidegger, *Schellings Abhandlung über das Wesen der menschlichen Freiheit* (Tübingen: Max Niemeyer Verlag, 1971), 75.
8. Dieter Henrich, *Der ontologische Gottesbeweis* (Tübingen: Max Niemeyer, 1960), 189.
9. For a lucid discussion of this fundamental reversal occurring between Schelling's middle period and his late work, see Jean-François Marquet, "L'articulation sujet-objet dans la dernière philosophie de Schelling," in *Restitutions: Études d'histoire de la philosophie allemande* (Paris: Vrin, 2001).
10. For an account of Schelling's theory of nature as based in an ontology of powers, aimed at accommodating human freedom while maintaining continuity between human existence and the natural world, see Charlotte Alderwick, *Schelling's Ontology of Powers* (Edinburgh: Edinburgh University Press, 2021). Alderwick highlights significant similarities between Schelling's view and contemporary dispositionalism.
11. See Timothy Shanahan, *The Evolution of Darwinism: Selection, Adaptation and Progress in Evolutionary Biology* (Cambridge: CUP, 2004), 185.
12. *The Evolution of Darwinism*, 188.
13. Part III of *The Evolution of Darwinism* (173–282) provides an informative discussion of the issues, dealing with both the philosophical problems and the intellectual history.
14. Thomas Nagel, *Mind and Cosmos* (Oxford: OUP, 2012), 32–33. At one point, as noted in the Introduction, Nagel describes himself as "an objective idealist in the tradition of Plato, and perhaps also of certain post-Kantians, such as Schelling and Hegel" (17).

7
Mythological Consciousness

Primordial Consciousness

Schelling's late philosophy of nature culminates in the emergence of human consciousness, and in his attempts to characterize its uniqueness. In the philosophy of mythology, the first part of the positive philosophy to deal with the actual history of consciousness, Schelling continues this effort by frequently describing "primordial consciousness" (*das Urbewußtsein*) as "God-positing" (*Gott-setzend*) (e.g., HCI: 144–145/SW, II/1, 207–208). There is no denying that this is a puzzling term, and care must be taken in unpacking it. Certainly, it should not be interpreted to mean that the first humans knowingly believed, however vaguely, in the existence of an all-powerful being, understood as the creator and sustainer of the world. Rather, it is clear from Schelling's struggle to elucidate the notion of "*Urbewußtsein*" that what he is seeking to evoke is a mode of consciousness prior to the emergence of any reflective self-awareness, before ascription by consciousness to itself of a continuous "owner" or "possessor." In this context, Schelling often employs expressions such as: "consciousness in its pure substance, without actus . . . (substance is the opposite of actus)" (PM "Athen"/Eberz: 185). But why exactly does he describe this consciousness as "God-positing"?

The underlying thought is contained in statements such as the following:

> In accord with their first origin human beings are only consciousness, but not consciousness of self, since this would be an act. For the nature of this consciousness can indeed be the basis, but not an object; hence it can only be consciousness of God, for otherwise it would not be consciousness in its pure substance. (PM Chováts: 149)

We can begin our effort to interpret this statement by considering that Schelling stands in the tradition, stemming from Kant, which considers experience of a coherent world, as opposed to a "rhapsody of perceptions" (A156/B195), to require the formal unification of a multiplicity of elements.

When we limn the structure of such experience from within, we apprehend the subject-pole as the pole of unification, as Kant does in his theory of the transcendental unity of apperception, and as Fichte does in his theory of the self-positing "I." In the present case, however, there is no subject—no "I think"—to play the unifying role; therefore, Schelling concludes, the required unity is indistinguishable from the oneness of the being of the world as such, from which consciousness has not yet reflectively separated itself. Corroboration of Schelling's line of thought can once again be found in Sartre. In *The Transcendence of the Ego*, Sartre argues that the phenomenology of consciousness should begin from an impersonal transcendental field, and not from a "transcendental ego," as does Husserl. In Sartre's account the ego is merely a transcendent point of synthesis of the activity of consciousness, one which is constructed in reflection. However, this does not entail that, prior to reflection, the field of consciousness is not unified (although for Sartre it is clear that a transcendent object such as the ego *could not be* the unifier, despite its often being imagined as such). Rather, as he puts it, "If one were looking for an analogy, in the case of unreflected consciousness, for what the ego is for second-order consciousness . . . we should think rather of the *World*, conceived of as the infinite synthetic totality of all things."[1] Although Sartre does not state this, it seems clear that the only thing which could unite an *infinite* synthetic totality is being-ness as such. However, the non-numerical one of being-ness—the *Daß*—is, for Schelling, the initial core of what we mean by "God." This is why he states, in his 1837 lectures on the philosophy of mythology:

> Human beings are thus—in themselves and prior to themselves, as it were—consciousness of God. They do not possess this consciousness, but are it, and they do not have it, because they are not it for themselves. Human beings are thus precisely in the non-act and in non-movement truly God-positing. (PM "Athen"/Erberz: 86)

Another way to make sense of what Schelling is trying to say in such passages would be to move from phylogenesis to ontogenesis, and to compare the mode of consciousness he evokes with that of a newborn child. The comparison seems plausible, if we wish to get a grip on the notion of human experience without a self-consciously experiencing subject. However, it also seems open to an obvious objection. For how could we possibly attribute a sense of the oneness of being to a newborn infant, on the assumption that this is indeed the core meaning Schelling intends to convey here with the concept of "God"? This suggestion may become more plausible, however, if we bear in mind two considerations. Firstly, human beings are capable of an awareness of the existence of the world *as such*, and many thinkers regard this awareness as central to the understanding of religious experience. Wittgenstein, for example, refers to it as the "mystical" (*Tractatus*: 6.44). Secondly, such an awareness cannot be attained incrementally, by adding together the consciousness of the existence of particular entities, and expanding ever outward, as it were. If both these contentions are valid, then even small children must already have a sense—however inchoate and inexplicit—of *das reine Daß*, as this is not something which can be subsequently *acquired* through experience.

Support for this view can be found by considering the logic of existential judgments, as this was discussed intensively by nineteenth-century logicians. As Wayne Martin has recounted, the debate can be traced back to Kant's argument that being is not a "real predicate" because it does not contribute to the determination of the thing of which it is predicated. From this Kantian starting point logicians tried to devise an analysis of existential judgments that would avoid assigning the status of a predicate to sheer existence.[2] Taking a cue from Martin, we can illustrate such strategies of avoidance, and their consequence, in the following way. If I say, for example, "There is a rose bush in the park" (i.e., "A rose bush in the park *is*."), rather than attributing existence to the plant, I am saying something about the park, namely that a rose belongs to its range of flora. But this statement can only tell us that the rose exists insofar as I can also make an existential claim about the park itself, which would need to be cashed out using the same procedure—for example by asserting that the park is a feature of the city where I live. Through repetition of this process, we will end up referring to the totality of existent things, amongst which features our particular rose.[3] Clearly, however, the *existence* of this totality cannot be established by a further repetition of the process. Hence, there must be an *immediate* apprehension of the being of the totality, for us to make any existential judgment at all.

These considerations are reinforced if we consider the argument of Hermann Lotze, one of the protagonists of the nineteenth-century debate, that singular existential judgments refer to "the all-embracing thought of reality, which takes now one shape, now another."[4] Lotze suggests that, in the case of a German impersonal construction such as "*Es blitzt*" ("It lightens"), it would be a "scholastic artifice" to translate this into standard subject-predicate form as "Lightning is" (*Das Blitzen ist*), rather than as "Being is [now] lightning" (*Das Sein ist [jetzt] blitzend*). This is because, "By nature thought never grasps the individual happening as subject, being as predicate, but only universal being [*das allgemeine Sein*] as subject, the happening as its predicate."[5] However, there is an ambiguity in Lotze's exposition because it is not clear whether the "all-embracing thought of reality" includes the *existence* of reality as a whole (and similarly, whether "*das Sein*" should be understood as the *existence* of the totality of existents, or simply as the existents in their totality). Lotze's ambiguity is understandable, however, if one considers that, if existence as such needs to be attached to the "all-embracing thought of reality," it cannot be through the procedure which he uses to explain the meaning of existential judgments but must be a matter of a *sui generis* relation of consciousness to being as such. Schelling seems to be thinking of this when he writes: "To be sure, we must not proceed from an original *knowledge*, no matter how glorious, but rather from a *being* of man in the divine unity" (HCI: 143/SW, II/1: 206). He is writing here in a speculative historical mode—but, underpinning this speculation, as I have tried to show, are defensible arguments concerning the genesis and structure of human consciousness.

The *Katastrophe*—Schelling's Interpretation of the Fall

Schelling describes the "purely substantial consciousness of God" (HCI: 129/SW, II/1: 185) with which his narrative of human existence begins as "*suprahistorical*" (*übergeschichtlich*). (HCI: 128/SW, II/1: 184). As one might anticipate, therefore, history begins with the transition to explicit self-consciousness: at the point when human self-awareness is actualized, or—we might say—activated. This is the first major turning point in the narrative of the positive philosophy. Schelling, like other German thinkers of the late-eighteenth and early-nineteenth century, theorizes it within the general frame the biblical myth of the Fall. His basic thought is that, when human beings become self-conscious, they find themselves as entities in a world of entities. But, more than this, each individual's awareness becomes indexicalized, entailing a certain cut-offness or incommunicability. To use John Perry's terminology, a gap up opens between "belief states" and what can be captured in propositions, taken as the universally accessible objects of belief. Focused on ourselves, and where and when we are located, belief states have an ineffably singular element which no "conceptual ingredient" can replace. Indeed the existence of propositions with absolute truth-values may be, as Perry puts it, "merely an illusion engendered by the implicit nature of much indexicality."[6] In consequence, human consciousness ceases to function as the general medium holding the potentialities together; they split apart again into the condition of tension and conflict in which they found themselves at the beginning of the process of nature. As Schelling puts it:

> It was within the *power of human beings, to maintain the world in God. Since they put themselves in the place of God, they had the world for themselves, but outside God. This world* of human beings has been stripped of its splendour and *no longer has a point of unity within itself, which the human being should have been*. After that condition of inwardness, which the world should have attained, was bungled, the world was delivered over to an externality in which each individual thing has lost its standing as a moment, and each appears contingent, meaningless, external to the other. (PO41/42: 202)

Once again, although Schelling puts his point in historical terms, one can argue that he is trying to make sense of the dual vision which characterizes our experience of the world. On the one hand, reality seems to consist of relations of externality and contingency, and we feel ourselves to be caught up in that contingency. On the other hand, there are moments in which we catch glimpses of a prelapsarian state. Aesthetic experience can offer such moments. The twentieth-century phenomenologist Maurice Merleau-Ponty, for example, frequently evokes a world reminiscent of Schelling's primordial world, in seeking to describe the achievement of certain visual artists:

> Anyone who thinks about the matter finds it astonishing that very often a good painter can also make good drawings or good sculpture. Since neither the means of expression nor the creative gestures are comparable, this fact . . . is proof that there is a system of equivalences, a logos of lines, of lighting, of colors, of reliefs, of masses—a conceptless presentation of universal being.[7]

Similarly, in the field of literature, as Paul Ricoeur has argued, the resources of poetic metaphor have a capacity to evoke a fluid, pre-objective, pre-categorial world, in which we feel our existence to be deeply rooted.[8] It is a world which can often seem truer than the world of everyday life.

Of course, one cannot deny that for Schelling the transition to the fragmented world of privatized experience has a theological dimension. It is important for his overall conception of positive philosophy that the emergence a world of isolated, individual subjects and rigidly distinct objects was not dialectically compelled to occur, and that *hubris* drove the human aspiration to become separate from and superior to nature. Sometimes he fills out this thought by stating that it was the human desire to gain control of the potentialities, to play the role of God, which led to the Fall. At the same time, Schelling also belongs in the company of thinkers such as Herder, Kant, and Hegel, who transformed the narrative of the third chapter of *Genesis* into a philosophical conjecture concerning the beginnings of human historical existence. After this shift, the Biblical myth no longer plays its traditional, Augustinian role of placing the burden of responsibility for evil in the world onto human beings. Rather, it functions as the inaugural moment of a progressive narrative, evoking the point at which human self-consciousness began to develop historically, as reason was applied to expand human capacities, although with many conflicts and adversities along the way.[9] It is indicative of this secularizing shift, that late Schelling employs the terms "*Katastrophe*" and "*Umsturz*" (both meaning an overthrow or overturning) far more frequently than the term "*Sündenfall*" (the theological "Fall"). Along with this change of emphasis goes the implication that the catastrophe was in some sense inevitable. Thus, in his 1837 lectures on the philosophy of mythology, Schelling states:

> It is impossible that human beings should have remained in this substantial condition. Human beings must step out of this relation in order to transform it into a free one. In that relation they are nothing; in order to become something, they must step out of that pure, essential relation to God. (PM "Athen"/Eberz: 86)

It should be noted that the "impossible" and the "must" in this statement seem to have a moral connotation, rather than applying to a strictly necessary process. If Schelling states that "primordial consciousness" is only a "moment" of the historical process, this need not entail that human beings were in some way caused to become self-aware: indeed, this notion would be incompatible with the spontaneity which, for the post-Kantian Idealists, is essential to self-consciousness. The most that can be said is that the equilibrium of the potentialities in primordial consciousness was inherently precarious—divine or infinite freedom re-emerging in a finite being—and liable to be disrupted. Because what is at issue here is the emergence of rational self-awareness as such, attributions of responsibility, as is the case with small children, are bound to be problematic.

As we have noted, the use of the myth of the Fall to explore philosophically the moral, cultural, and historical consequences of the emergence of human self-consciousness was well established in Schelling's time. But Schelling gives this trope an original and distinctive twist which is fundamental for his positive philosophy, and which has no parallel in other thinkers. In his account, the unity of being which is disrupted as the world falls apart into rigidly particularized entities cannot be lost entirely because an apprehension of this unity defines human consciousness. However, it is restored as the overbearing *dominance* of the first potentiality—or of what he frequently terms, in his philosophy of mythology, the "real principle"—occupying a field which is intermediate between subjectivity and objectivity:

> As soon as human beings have given way and moved out of the middle point, the periphery becomes confused for them and that divine unity is dislocated, for no longer are they divinely *above* things, but have themselves sunk down to the same level as them. But because they want to retain their central position and the vision connected with it, despite now being in a different place, a middle world arises. This world, which springs from the striving and struggling to hold onto the original divine unity in what is already destroyed and dispersed, we call a world of gods. It is like the dream of a higher mode of being, which human beings continue to dream for a time, after they have sunk down out of it; and this world of gods emerges for them in an involuntary manner, as a result of a necessity imposed on them by their original relationship. (HCI: 143–144/SW, II/1: 206)

We have already considered the similarities between Schelling's description of primordial consciousness and the mode of awareness of a small infant. That comparison might lead one to anticipate psychoanalytical parallels to Schelling's account of the disruption of the original sense of unity. Numerous post-Freudian thinkers have explored the phantasies which arise in the mind of the child in its struggle to compensate for the loss of the bliss of symbiotic unity with the primary carer-giver, traditionally the mother; Schelling's "intermediate world," the "world of the gods"—the world of mythology— displays many similarities with the realm of phantasy and dream explored these theorists. The British analyst Donald Winnicott, for example, is well known for his argument that a transitional domain between the subjective and the objective (a "middle world") emerges by way of compensation of the breaking of the original state of fusion with the mother (a similar conception could be seen as implicit in Freud's view that the ultimate source of dreams in lies in archaic Oedipal desires). Winnicott writes:

> It is assumed here that the task of reality acceptance is never completed, that no human being is free from the strain of relating inner and outer reality, and that relief from this strain is provided by an intermediate area of experience which is not challenged (arts, religion, etc.). This intermediate area is in direct continuity with the play area of the small child who is "lost" in play.[10]

As these psychoanalytic echoes suggest, it is central to Schelling's theory of the development of human self-awareness that the exit from an initial lack of differentiation between self and world is experienced as a distressing loss—as a *Katastrophe* or *Umsturz*—and therefore calls forth compensatory reactions. If we bear this in mind, we may sympathize more with his struggles to evoke such an absence of distinction between subject and object, a non-self-conscious consciousness. Philosophers who feel no need to posit any such form of awareness prior to the emergence of an explicit subject-object polarity—which they often insist arrives only with the acquisition of language—have, in many respects, an easier task. But, at the same time, they lack the resources available to Schelling to think the *compulsive* character of the intermediate domain which, on his account, emerges in an attempt to repair the loss occasioned by the break. Schelling's stroke of genius, in fact, was to perceive the patterns of mythological consciousness as an involuntary repetition, in the human mind, of the dialectic of the potentialities, as this had already played itself out in nature. Human subjectivity is held captive in a trance-like state; it becomes the stage for the playing out of an obscure drama which it neither wills, nor consciously directs or comprehends. This process begins with the objectification of the *Daß* as the unitary power which holds the universe together. In other words, Schelling proposes that a form of monotheism, which he terms "relative monotheism," functions as the *precondition* for the emergence of mythological consciousness. It is only as a *reaction* against this psychically coercive unity, he suggests, that the familiar multiple deities of polytheism begin to emerge:

Thus, with that first determination consciousness is also subjected to the necessary sequence of representations through which actual polytheism arises. Once the first affecting of consciousness is posited, its movement through these forms, one after another, is a process in which thinking and willing, understanding and freedom no longer play any part. Consciousness gets caught up in this movement unintentionally, in a manner which it can no longer comprehend. It relates to it as a *fate*, a *doom* against which there is nothing to be done. It is a *real* power that confronts consciousness, one no longer under its control, which has come to dominate it. (HCI: 134/SW, II/1: 192)

The Mythological Process as Successive Polytheism

The domination of human consciousness by the real principle ("B," in Schelling's notation), or—to put this in religious terms—the exclusive adoration of one all-encompassing god, is the point of departure for what Schelling terms the "mythological process." He describes this mode of consciousness as "relative monotheism" because, in contrast to "supra-historical," God-positing consciousness, it does not *exclude* the possibility of polytheism. On the contrary, it is the starting point for the emergence of a sequence of mythological deities, who will eventually—in some historical cultures—come to form a stable pantheon.[11] Monotheism in this context, however, does not imply a more or less reflective belief in the existence of a unique, all-powerful deity. Rather, it is a situation in which the subject of consciousness is passive, ecstatic, overwhelmed. As Schelling puts it, in this condition:

> humanity is afflicted and struck by a god, and in this sense early humanity found itself in a time of unfreedom, *stupefacta quasi et attonita*, taken over by an alien power, and beside itself. (PM Chováts: 153)

It would be a mistake, therefore, to think of relative monotheism as arising from a sense of the power of nature, as experienced by early, vulnerable human beings in their encounters with the world around them. The gods which dominate consciousness in relative monotheism, and in the forms of polytheism which emerge from it, are the powers of the psyche itself operating in a compulsive, objectified form. This conception underpins Schelling's hard-hitting critique of a range of explanations of mythology proposed by his contemporaries, which occupies the opening chapters of the *Historical-Critical Introduction to the Philosophy of Mythology*. The first of these theories to draw his fire proposes that mythology is simply a product of the poetic imagination—what Schelling calls "*Poesie*" (a word with stronger overtones of fantasy than the alternative German word "*Dichtung*"). Considering the arguments for this view, in particular when applied to the earliest Greek poets, Schelling's points out that what he calls the mythological "system"—i.e., the familial network of gods ruled over by Zeus—was clearly already in place and could be assumed as part of the cosmological background, when Homer wrote his epic poems. And, in the case of Hesiod's *Theogony*, he suggests that Hesiod is *already* beginning to think in philosophical rather than mythological terms; for example, at the very beginning of things he places not an anthropomorphic figure but "Chaos," which in ancient Greek suggests a "chasm." This indicates, Schelling contends, that Hesiod is looking back, depicting an established system of gods, not first inventing it, and already advancing toward more abstract forms of thought. In Schelling's view, Hesiod's poem has the further significance that it recounts the *narrative* of how the system of gods *came into being*. For it should be emphasized that, according to Schelling's conception, the chronology of the emergence of the gods is *not itself fictional* but is rather the record of an actual historical sequence in human consciousness. This theory of "successive polytheism" will be central to his overall philosophy of mythology.

In the *Historical-Critical Introduction*, Schelling then moves on to a critique of what he terms "natural-scientific" explanations of mythology. Here the idea is that concepts of natural powers developed by ancient protoscientific thinkers were *subsequently* personified. One of the most sophisticated of these theorists, the distinguished philologist Gottfried Hermann (1772–1848), proposed that concepts of natural powers were treated as persons by early scientific thinkers, as a kind of theoretical shorthand, and that these figures were then taken literally by the far less educated general population. In his opposition to this kind of explanation, and indeed of all explanations—still popular today—of the "allegorizing" type (which treat myths as the figurative or symbolic representation of natural processes), Schelling stresses their complete misunderstanding of the quality of primitive consciousness. The notion that mythological beliefs can be regarded as a layer of imagery superimposed on a sober, objective relationship to nature is—in his view—utterly anachronistic. As he writes:

In its first movement consciousness was infected by the necessity of the mythological process and . . . in falling victim to the mythological process, human beings did not lapse back into nature, as one likes to imagine, but rather—dislocated from and transferred outside of nature by a genuine enchantment—were transported into that pre-material—that still spiritual—prius of all nature (the pure, not yet subjugated B), which abolished nature for them. (PM, SW, II/2: 184)

However, despite its initial dominance, B is vulnerable because it has *also* been decentered from its proper role as the "ground, in other words the deepest, the innermost, the subject = the primordial status of consciousness" (PM, SW, II/2: 170). In consequence, the unity embodied in B is exclusionary, based on the suppression rather than the grounding and holding together of difference. At this stage, as Schelling puts it, B is the "adversary of everything concrete" (*Widersacher alles Konkreten*) (PO41/42: 214). But this means that B is *internally* conflictual: it both strives to return to its central, quiescent but foundational position, and strives away from it, because a return would involve subordination to A^2, the principle of differentiation. For Schelling, as we know, "materialization" does not mean becoming physical, but rather becoming the basis for the actualization of a higher potentiality. Seen in this perspective, B is torn between its spiritual and its material vectors. As Schelling states, "displaced from its original position, it can only continue to be subject in the sense of being subordinated to what is higher, it is no longer the primordial condition [*Urstand*], but the support [*Unterstand*], basis, material for the realization of the higher" (PM, SW, II/2: 171n).

In terms of the history of religion, Schelling finds the corresponding form of consciousness in what he terms "Zabism," a term which he derives from the Hebrew and Arabic words for "host" (in the sense of "multitude") (PM, SW, II/2, 180), and which he takes as referring to the stars—the "heavenly host"—while also connecting it with the "Sabians," a pre-Islamic monotheistic group who are mentioned several times in the *Qu'ran* (2:62, 5:69, 22:17). His theory is that, as a result of its internal conflict, B splits apart into the multiplicity of heavenly bodies, which are both spiritual—pure light—and incipiently material. Again, Schelling stresses that we should not imagine Zabism, any more than any other religious conception, as arising from an elevation of natural phenomena to divine status. The astral religion "did not so much regard the stars as gods, but rather on the contrary the gods as stars" (PM, SW, II/2: 174). As he states: "it should be evident from my whole deductive procedure that I do not regard so-called star worship as arising from outside, through an empirical view of the actual stars, which are moreover thought to be physical, and their subsequent deification" (PM, SW, II/2: 174). The deep internal conflict of B—here featuring as the overarching astral power (*das Astrale*)—is manifested in stellar motion, which is unceasing and yet circular, combining restlessness and stasis. The incessant movement of the stars, Schelling also suggests, mirrors the nomadic existence of early humanity. However, at this stage, there are no religiously significant differences between the various heavenly bodies. We are confronted with a form of what Schelling calls "simultaneous polytheism," which is still an "*unhistorical* religion" (PO41/42: 216), and which is "always in a certain sense monotheism," as it involves only "the One = B extraverted or reversed into multiplicity" (PM, SW, II/2: 172). Genuine polytheism, on Schelling's account, first appears only with what he terms "successive polytheism": the historical process, full of psychic tension and struggle, through which the gods embodying all three potentialities establish themselves step-by-step in human consciousness: "the principle in accordance with which mythology advances is the principle of a successive emergence of the potentialities, which had been united in primordial consciousness, and which are only successively reunited" (PO, SW, II/3: 395–396).

Schelling's evocation of the ambiguous, conflict-laden character of Zabism already discloses what endows his philosophy of mythology with much of its depth and power: its sensitivity, foreshadowing psychoanalysis, of the ambivalent and often self-contradictory dynamics of the elemental forces within the human mind. In Schelling's interpretation of mythology, one fundamental way in which this ambivalence is expressed is through the transmutation of male into female mythological figures. Thus, when B, in the form of the exclusive power of the heavens, expressed in ancient Greek religion through the god Uranus, begins to become susceptible to the second potentiality, Uranus takes on a feminine form as Urania. This shift of gender signals the transition from the first epoch (which Schelling labels "A") to the second epoch ("B") in his periodization of successive mythology; he describes it the first "*katabole*," or "foundation-laying," for the completed mythological system. (Schelling's use of letters to identify the *stages* of mythological consciousness should not be confused with his abbreviations for the potentialities. For clarity, a schema of the entire mythological process is set out in Figure 2.)

EPOCH A   ONTOLOGY: exclusive dominance of the real principle (B)

         RELIGIOUS CONSCIOUSNESS: "relative monotheism" of the sky-god (URANUS); ecstatic extraversion of consciousness, tension between motion and cyclical stasis

---

FIRST *KATABOLE* (FOUNDATION LAYING): FEMINIZATION OF THE SKY-GOD AS URANIA

EPOCH B   ONTOLOGY: emergence of the second, ideal principle (A^2), principle of form, differentiation

         RELIGIOUS CONSCIOUSNESS: URANIA = awareness of (and receptivity to) the coming liberating semi-divine figure (generic name: DIONYSUS)

EPOCH C   ONTOLOGY: "reaction formation" of harsher version of principle B, struggling to dominate (A^2), which is now actual

         RELIGIOUS CONSCIOUSNESS: CHRONUS = violent repression and exclusion of HERCULES (liberating semi-divine figure as suffering hero)

SECOND *KATABOLE* (FOUNDATION LAYING): FEMINIZATION OF CHRONUS AS CYBELE

EPOCH D   ONTOLOGY: emergence of complete system of A^1, A^2 and A^3 (principle of integration)

         RELIGIOUS CONSCIOUSNESS: CYBELE (maternal sky-goddess) = awareness of (and receptivity to) the coming polytheistic cosmos

---

COMPLETED MYTHOLOGICAL SYSTEM

         ZEUS (A^3)

                 DIONYSUS (A^2)

         HADES (B) (CHRONUS returned to original function as ground)

ELEUSINIAN MYSTERIES

         ONTOLOGY: convergence of A^1, A^2 and A^3: orientation towards future liberation

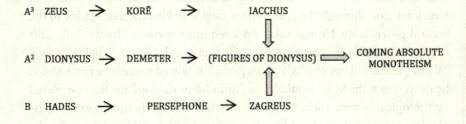

Figure 2   Schelling's Theory of the Mythological Process as Exemplified by Greek Mythology

Epoch B, then, sees the emergence of figures embodying A^2, the ontological principle of form, and hence of the differentiation of entities, as opposed to B, the "real" principle. Schelling's most general term for the mythological embodiment of this second principle is "Dionysus." However, it first appears as figures—such as Melkart in Phoenician mythology, or Hercules in Greek mythology—who are intermediate between the human and divine, and who work in the guise of a servant, performing services for humanity. Their in-between status expresses the fact that A^2 is still subordinate and cannot become fully part of the divine life process until B is subjugated. During the epoch which Schelling labels "B"—not to be confused, as was just stressed, with the *potentiality* B—the first two vectors of being co-exist with varying degrees of tension and friction, but there is no out-and-out struggle.

The transition from this phase to the epoch Schelling terms "C" introduces a further proto-psychoanalytic feature of Schelling's philosophy of mythology. In response to the softening of "B" under the influence of the second principle, there occurs a "reaction-formation," in which B takes on a more violent and aggressive form. Hence, in the successive mythology of the Greeks, Uranus/Urania is overthrown by Chronus, who struggles savagely to block any further advance, even to the point of devouring his own children (in contrast to the familiar interpretation, Schelling sees Chronus not as an embodiment of time, but as the god who seeks to *suppress* time, who refuses to be consigned to the past, thereby preventing the emergence of genuine temporality in the form of the interrelated dimensions of past, present, and future [see PM, SW, II/2: 291–292]). However, this rearguard action cannot be sustained indefinitely, and Chronus finally mutates into the new female figure of Cybele. As opposed to Urania, who expresses the *susceptibility* of B to A^2, Cybele indicates the imminent *actual submission* of B to A^2, which Schelling describes as the second "*katabole*." This is anticipated in "D," the final epoch of "successive polytheism." The system is finally consolidated when Chronus is castrated and deposed by Zeus. At this point, the real principle is forced back into its proper foundational role in the form of "Hades," the god of the underworld, while Zeus functions as A^3, the reconciling principle, ruling over the family of gods from the heights of Olympus. As Schelling states, "Zeus first becomes known to consciousness when the whole multiplicity of gods is known" (PO41/42: 232).

Schelling is well-aware of the fact that, in historical terms, the gradual transformation of the primordial religion (*Urreligion*) of relative monotheism into a stabilized polytheistic system corresponds to the socio-cultural transition, which must have been fraught with intrapsychic conflict, from pre-historic, nomadic hunter-gatherer societies to the neolithic age of fixed settlements, agriculture, and the domestication of animals. Highlighting the ambivalence, he remarks that, although the minds of members of primeval nomadic societies were "ruled by a blind force" (PM, SW, II/2: 183), this need not have resulted in a feeling of total unfreedom. As he puts it, in a characterization of Epoch A:

> Only one who is ruled by two principles, and is uncertain which to follow, feels unfree. Everything decisive appears as free. In human beings there rules only B, which by nature is limitless, universal. Far from feeling unfree in their present condition, they follow the pull of this force, which sets them outside themselves, with a freedom far more complete than is later granted to them, when that universal starts to become inwardly limited for them, and the feeling of individual freedom arises . . . which divides them from themselves and from the world. (PM, SW, II/2: 183)

At the same time, human beings could not have failed to be attracted by the advantages of settlement, a measure of control over nature, and a rule-governed social order. Schelling's philosophy of mythology, then, seeks to elucidate the immense psychological struggles which must have accompanied this epochal transformation in human existence. As Edward Beach has written, "the mythological mind found itself caught in the pincers of a seemingly irresoluble double-bind between the forces of the conscious and the unconscious. On the one hand it was unbearable to think of forgoing the promise offered by the vast new world of culture and civilization; on the other hand, it was agonizing to contemplate forsaking the undifferentiated unity of being to which the mind's very sense of self-identity had previously always been attached."[12] In Schelling's own words, "The lament for the lost god pervades the whole of mythology, longing pursues him and calls him back, he who has gone far away, to the ends of the earth, as it is put in Hesiod's *Works and Days*" (PM, SW, II/2: 273).

The Plurality of Mythological Systems

So far, we have tracked the emergence of one complete mythological system: that of the ancient Greeks. However, Schelling acknowledges the existence of three such mythological systems—the Egyptian, the Indian, and the Greek, along with various partial or incomplete systems. The three complete examples differ according to the roles and interrelations of the potentialities. In ancient Egyptian mythology, the focus is on the conflict between the god Schelling refers to as "Typhon," the Hellenized equivalent of Seth—a wild and violent version of B—and Osiris, the second, emancipatory principle, the god of death and resurrection. Correspondingly, Horus, who embodies the third principle, plays only a background role, as the model of the ideal ruler, promising a reconciliation which is yet to come. In Indian mythology, by contrast, the role of the real principle (Brahma) has been almost entirely erased: "Brahma does not enjoy any kind of reverence in Indian popular belief, it is as if he had disappeared from consciousness, a god who merely *has been*, standing outside any relation to the present" (PO, SW, II/3: 404). This retreat of B allows the destructively differentiating or disintegrating aspect of the second principle, Shiva, to dominate the scene. There also exist, Schelling concedes, elite worshippers of Vishnu, the third reconciling principle, but this principle is insufficiently prominent to establish the unity of the entire system of mythology:

> Because in Indian consciousness Vishnu has lost his true precondition (Brahma and Shiva) or has excluded it rather than taking it up into himself, Indian consciousness could not maintain itself at the height of this spiritual potentiality and is rechannelled from there towards mere fables. There arise the legends of the incarnation of Vishnu, which actually no longer belong to mythology and are more or less inventions. (PO, SW, II/3, 404)

In consequence, "in Indian consciousness the whole of mythology passes over into a kind of decomposition" (PO, SW, II/3, 405)—a claim, as noted in chapter 3, which is echoed in contemporary arguments that it makes no sense to regard "Hinduism" as a unitary "religion." By contrast, in the Greek mythological system we find a harmonious integration of the three potentialities, in which B has been restored to its role as basis:

> The Greek gods arise from a consciousness which gently and systematically releases itself from the power of the real principle, in certain kinds of blissful vistas or visions in which the latter—the real principle—does indeed disappear, but in its disappearing and dissolution continues to cooperate in imparting the determinacy that makes the Greek gods representatives

of necessary, eternal, and enduring—not merely transitory—moments (concepts). Greek mythology is the gentle death, the true euthanasia of the real principle, which in its departure and decline leaves behind in its place a world of beautiful and enchanting appearances. (PO, SW, II/3: 406)

Greek mythological consciousness has not escaped from natural compulsion, as the fact that even the gods remain subject to fate indicates. Nonetheless, the overarching reconciliation of the battling cosmic-psychic vectors in the Greek mythical system, and the easing of coercion in form of the "enchanting world" of the humanized gods, sets the stage for the transcendence of mythological consciousness as such. This Schelling finds enacted in the Eleusinian Mysteries.

The Eleusinian Mysteries and the Crisis of Mythological Consciousness

In the Mysteries the mythological process becomes reflexive, thematizes itself: the entire dialectical development is summarized, recapitulated, and transcended. As Schelling puts it, "The Mysteries are nothing other than the higher comprehending consciousness of mythology itself, and their content is therefore the potentialities" (PO41/42: 237). In this context it is important to recall Schelling's argument that, because female deities express the susceptibility of a principle to the developing power of its successor, they can be understood as expressing the consciousness not only of the currently dominant principle (subjective genitive) but also of the emerging principle (objective genitive). For this reason, Schelling argues, Demeter, a version of Cybele, appears as a central figure of the Mysteries, for Demeter can be seen as "*the consciousness that stands in the middle between the real and the liberating god*" (PO41/42: 226). The emancipatory god in his most general form, as we noted earlier, is Dionysus. But the deep aspiration of the Mysteries is fully to overcome the constraint of mythological consciousness as such, by experiencing the complete identity of the mythical powers. Schelling argues that "the principal content of the Greek Mysteries ... is already *the reconciliation of the consciousness that was wounded by its separation from the real god*" (PO41/42: 230), and this entails that "in order for consciousness to be completely placated with regard to the god who has disappeared, it must come to the conviction that [Dionysus] is—from a spiritual viewpoint—the same as that material One" (PO41/42: 237).

In Schelling's interpretation, then, the Mysteries were a "representation of the sufferings, the struggle and the crisis of mythological consciousness" (PO41/42: 236). This crisis takes the form of an incipient collapse of polytheism, a realization that the gods do not exist in an "indissoluble concatenation" but are "one God or successive personalities" (PO41/42: 237). This identification of the potentialities is achieved through an experience of the fusion of three embodiments of Dionysus, along with that of three corresponding female deities, who express the consciousness of these embodiments: Persephone, Demeter, and Korē. The most popular association of Dionysus is, of course, with wine, revelry, and drunkenness, with the exultation of release from the oppressive, constraining power of the real principle. However, this version of Dionysus—the exoteric version—does not directly appear in the Mysteries (PO41/42: 234). Rather, the first potentiality becomes one with Dionysus in the personification known as "Zagreus," who is associated with the Hades and underworld. This opens the way for the appearance of Dionysus in a third guise specifically associated with the Mysteries—namely, as "Iacchus." At work here is a complex transaction, in which the final abandonment of attachment to B, the real or material principle, is compensated for by its restoration in a higher, spiritual form. As Schelling puts it, "In an already dialectical movement, the third member takes up the first again, the third concept is the potentiality which remains as potentiality. Thus Iacchus is the restored Zagreus" (PO41/42: 241). With this identification achieved, the tension between the principles or cosmic-psychic powers, which had driven forward the entire immense mythological process, is released: "Thus everything is Dionysus; the potentialities only became different in their tension" (PO41/42: 237). Dionysus, in the form of Iacchus, is the outpouring of joy at the final reconciliation of the potentialities, his name derived from the cry of the celebrants—"Iacché!"—as they processed from Athens toward Eleusis. We can therefore regard Iacchus—whose statue was also carried in the procession—as the self-expression of a subjectivity finally emancipated from mythical compulsion. "Iacchus," Schelling suggests, conveys first of all the jubilation, which is only subsequently objectified as a god. The Mysteries, then, were not primarily a set of esoteric doctrines, but a ritualized emancipatory experience, pointing toward a monotheism yet to come: "*The main content of the Mysteries was the one God, spiritualized in all his potentialities after the overcoming of the tension*" (PO41/42, 243). In

Schelling's summary: "The story of the gods became the history of God in the Mysteries, the fable became truth in the history of God" (PO41/42: 244).

An essential feature of Schelling's interpretation of the Mysteries is his explanation of their esoteric character, and of the strict prohibition—ostensibly on pain of death—against disclosure of their secrets. He argues that the enforcement of secrecy suggests an attempt to suppress a germinating awareness that the entire polytheistic structuring of human experience was advancing toward its doom. As the mythologically expressed consciousness of the end of mythology, the Mysteries posed a profound danger to Greek culture. However, the point is not just that the Mysteries anticipated a future in which polytheism would give way to a new, free, and reflective relation to a transcendent—rather than pantheistic—oneness of the divine. After all, Plato's thought displays monotheistic traits, and Aristotle avoided any use of myth as a philosophical resource, placing a unique God at the summit of his metaphysics. For Schelling, the deepest threat to ancient Greek culture consisted in the emergence, in the Mysteries, of a new form of time-consciousness, oriented toward the future—indeed toward the temporal horizon of a humanity united in a common religion. As he states, "It was the futural [*das Zukünftige*]"—that is to say, an existential openness toward the *dimension of the future*, as opposed to awareness of the obvious fact that events would continue to occur, even after the foreseeable decline of the polis—"which closed the mouths of the initiates" (PO41/42: 245).

Against this interpretation it might be objected that Schelling himself portrays the danger sensed by the Athenians as a future, post-mythological religion, which would threaten the distinctive identities of peoples and cultures, rather than a reorientation of the sense of temporality as such. For example, he states:

> *Genuine polytheism could only seize a place in humanity amidst violent battles, and the pain caused by the lost oneness could only be reconciled, when polytheism was recognized as a mere transition, so that a future religion would restore the lost unity.* The future religion should be a universal one, gathering together the whole human race, now entirely divided by polytheism. The religion beyond mythology is in itself the universal religion. (PO41/42: 248)

However, there is no need to draw a strict distinction between the doctrinal content of a future, post-mythological religion, on the one hand, and a new mode of time consciousness on the other. This is because, for Schelling, as we shall soon discover in more detail, the impending religion of revelation will itself bring about a future-directed and universalizing form of consciousness: an orientation toward the breaking down of the barriers dividing humanity into isolated and incommensurable socio-cultural worlds.

Notes

1. Jean-Paul Sartre, *The Transcendence of the Ego* (Routledge Classics: London, 2011), 30; *La transcendence de l'ego. Esquisse d'une description phénoménologique* (Paris: J. Vrin, 1966), 58.
2. See Wayne Martin, *Theories of Judgment: Psychology, Logic, Phenomenology* (Cambridge: CUP, 2005), especially chapter 2, to which I am indebted for the following discussion.
3. See *Theories of Judgment*, 135.
4. Lotze, *Grundzüge der Logik und Enzykopädie der Philosophie* (Leipzig: Verlag von S Hirzel, 1885), 23 (§24).
5. *Grundzüge der Logik*, 23.
6. See John Perry, "The Problem of the Essential Indexical," in *Noûs*, vol. 13 (1979); the longer quotation occurs on page 20.
7. Maurice Merleau-Ponty, "Eye and Mind," in *The Primacy of Perception* (Evanston, IL: Northwestern University Press, 1964), 182.
8. See Paul Ricoeur, *The Rule of Metaphor* (London: Routledge and Kegan Paul, 1986), 303–313.
9. See Friedrich Hermanni, *Die letzte Entlastung: Vollendung und Scheitern des abendländischen Theodizeeprojektes in Schellings Philosophie* (Vienna: Passagen Verlag, 1994), 160–180.
10. Donald Winnicott, "Transitional Objects and Transitional Phenomena," in *Playing and Reality* (London: Routledge, 2005), 18. Winnicott differs here from Schelling in not insisting on the compulsive or involuntary character of what emerges in the intermediate domain, but of course there are many phenomena theorized by psychoanalysis which fit Schelling's description.
11. It should be noted that not all the gods within a mythological system play a role within the "mythological process," which would be highly implausible. Schelling interprets the numerous minor deities within a pantheon, whom he terms "material" as opposed to "formal" deities, as the fragmented remnants of "B"—the primal pantheistic nature god—which emerge once B has been overcome in the course of the process. See PM, SW, II/2: 456–458.
12. Edward Allen Beach, *The Potencies of God(s)* (Albany, NY: SUNY Press 1994), 203. For an exploration of the complex economic and socio-political interactions between nomadic pastoralism, various forms of semi-sedentarism, and the emergence of the first city-states, which confirms Schelling's sense of the deep

psychic ambivalence of the civilizing process, see James C. Scott, *Against the Grain: A Deep History of the Earliest City States* (New Haven, CT: Yale University Press, 2018). Scott is keen to emphasize the frequently disastrous drawbacks of city-dwelling, plague and environmental degradation among them, and the advantages of non-sedentary lifestyles, in a struggle which—in certain respects—still continues today.

8
Reason and Revelation

The *Philosophy of Revelation*: Questions of Method

Schelling interprets the Eleusinian Mysteries as having both an implicit monotheistic core and an anticipatory dimension. The Mysteries point toward the coming of Christianity, with its universalistic gospel, as suggested by the fact that participation was not limited to males, to one social stratum, or even to Athenians: women, slaves, and foreigners could also become initiates.[1] Schelling's treatment of the Mysteries therefore paves the way for the next stage of the positive philosophy, which he calls the "Philosophy of Revelation." An adequate understanding of what Schelling means by the term "revelation" can only be gained by examining his interpretation of Christianity in detail. But an initial orientation is provided by his claim: "*Revelation must contain something which transcends reason*, but something which, without reason, one does not yet possess" (PO41/42: 98).

Clearly, with this declaration, Schelling is staking out a position in the debates concerning the relation between reason and religion, and between the letter and the spirit of religion itself, which had been central to the German Enlightenment, and which continued into the post-Kantian era. These discussions were connected with an important philosophical shift, in which the concept of God lost the foundational position it had occupied in rationalist metaphysics, largely thanks to Kant's deconstruction of the traditional proofs of the existence of God in the "Dialectic" of the *Critique of Pure Reason*. No longer the absolute basis for theories concerning the deep structure of reality, the concept "God" became increasingly problematic. The possible meanings of the concept, along with a whole range of moral and metaphysical issues raised by it, now became the focus of investigation, in a new branch of inquiry called the "philosophy of religion." Kant's own *Religion within the Boundaries of Mere Reason* (1793) can be seen as an important marker of this change. But Schleiermacher's treatise of 1799, *On Religion: Speeches to its Cultured Despisers*, is also to a large extent an exercise in the new sub-discipline, rather than in theology as such.[2] Hegel, of course, entitled the great cycle of lectures which he gave in Berlin 1821, 1824, 1827, and again in 1831, the year of his death, "Lectures on the Philosophy of Religion."

In this context, Schelling's phrase "philosophy of revelation"—and the implicit battle over priority between its two components—captures quite precisely the tension at the heart of the German Idealist approach to religion in general. The Idealists rejected the Enlightenment project of extracting a common deistic core from the positive religions of human history. But Schelling, Hegel, and Fichte (at least, in his post-Jena period) were equally opposed to the Kantian strategy of locating the core of religion in a set of "postulates of practical reason"—in a bridge of "rational faith" (*Vernunftglaube*) connecting hope for the ultimate subordination of nature to morality with hope for an ultimate distribution of happiness in alignment with virtue. In opposition to this minimalist approach, the Idealists regarded Christianity as a vehicle of metaphysical truth and source of existential orientation which could not simply be discarded in the post-Enlightenment context. At the same time, these truths could only be re-activated if their figurative mode of expression proved capable of surviving the scrutiny of philosophical reason. Yet this conception immediately raises the question: does revelation have any intrinsic authority, or is it philosophy, in the last instance, which not only validates the doctrinal content of religion, but in fact speculatively determines it?

Schelling, of course, is acutely aware of this issue, and addresses it explicitly at the beginning of his 1841/42 lectures on the *Philosophy of Revelation*:

> When I gave this lecture course the title: *Philosophy of Revelation, this is for the moment only a verbal announcement*; its meaning must be disclosed through the pursuit of the issue itself. I simply *warn you against taking it to mean that a philosophy owing its existence to the authority of revelation is intended*. There is not anything that may be assigned to one side or to the other. (PO41/42: 97–98)

But how is it possible to strike such a balance between reason and revelation? If the deliverances of revelation must pass the test of reason, then revelation has no independent status as a source of truth; while, if some revealed truths stand above rational scrutiny, then the authority of reason to determine its own scope is restricted, and reason itself is thereby undermined. When the narrative of Schelling's positive philosophy has advanced to the historical turning-point of the emergence of Christianity, he attempts further to clarify his approach to this problem:

> *Christianity* is first and foremost *a fact*; only after a critical sifting-through, without excluding any pointers but taking everything together, can one arrive at the true system, which underlies the scriptures themselves *as their presupposition. It is not a matter of proving Christianity, rather it concerns us as a fact, as an occurrence, which I aim to explain as far as possible in terms of its own premises.* (PO41/42: 259)

The focus of Schelling's philosophy of revelation, then, is the historical fact of Christianity: "the philosophy of revelation cannot be dogmatic, but rather simply explanatory, just as it must set to work in general in a more investigative than assertoric manner" (UPO: 427). Schelling does not aim to produce a "speculative dogmatics"—he no doubt has Hegel in mind here—and denies any interest in whether his results agree or not with "other presentations of the content of revelation, which are in general dogmatic" (PO, SW, II/4: 30). However, one still might object to Schelling's description of his procedure as finding the system that lies at the basis of Scripture, and which—presumably—renders it intelligible. For why attribute any special status to Scripture, and specifically, the writings of the New Testament, at all? This feature of Schelling's approach becomes more comprehensible, however, if his aim is indeed to understand the "fact" of Christianity, in the sense of the impact on human consciousness, and so on world history, of the historical individual Jesus of Nazareth. For almost all the evidence we have of the life and person of Christ, and of the way in which these were experienced and made sense of by his disciples and first followers, is contained in the New Testament. Some of the Pauline epistles, written within a few decades of Jesus' death, are the first documentation we possess, followed by the synoptic Gospels, which date from the last third of the first century CE, while the Gospel of St John was written at most few decades later. Modern scholarship is generally agreed that no other early Christian texts outside of the synoptic Gospels have comparable authority as records of at least some of what Jesus actually said and did, while Paul's letters and St John's Gospel provide evidence of the earliest explicitly theologically reflective responses to his life and death.[3] Naturally, Schelling is aware that the New Testament contains many arbitrary and unreliable passages, and that the texts are inevitably shot through with mythological elements, given that they were written in the midst of critical transition in the development of human consciousness. As he puts it in the *Urfassung* of the *Philosophy of Revelation*:

> The apostles are on the borderline of cosmic religion, and hence this hidden region must have appeared quite different to them than it does to us. Their ideas are written out of the midst of the crisis they lived through: the apostles were witnesses of this crisis. In this respect many expressions of the New Testament can certainly be viewed as analogous to mythological representations, but not in the sense that they should be regarded as phantasies. Rather they must be accepted as true experiences in so far as the apostles came into contact with and saw the force of these powers. (UPO: 668)

Similarly, the Evangelists, as Schelling says elsewhere, "behave in part like mythological consciousness" (PO41/42: 294); in other words, they wrote under a compulsion, with only partial insight into the structure and significance of what they set down. Nonetheless, Schelling believes that he can read the New Testament as the seismographic record of a spiritual earthquake whose after-effects, in a relatively short period of time, historically speaking, toppled the edifice of the mythological powers. By the end of the third century CE, for example, half of the population had converted to Christianity in many parts of the Roman Empire.[4]

But even if the rationale for Schelling's use of the New Testament is accepted, one might still object that his procedure is circular because it is his critical reading of Scripture that is supposed to point toward the "system," which he then takes to underlie the texts and give them their profound meaning. In one sense, of course, this is simply an example of the hermeneutic circle. And one could perhaps defend Schelling's procedure on the basis of its unavoidability in any process of interpretation, if his intention were simply to maximize the coherence and intelligibility of the New Testament texts on which he focuses, much as one might do in the case of a work of imaginative literature. However, his aim is *more* than this because he is trying to access the truth-content of the central events around which the Gospels revolve, and to which the Epistles refer, events constituting a "crisis" which resulted in a transformation of human consciousness and a corresponding ontological realignment, so to speak. This crisis cannot be reduced to the written traces left in its wake, and hence there might be a mismatch between the process and the New Testament record, which a purely internal examination of the texts could not reveal. Even if one assumed that a maximally coherent interpretation of the texts *would* point toward the truth of the process lying behind them, there is no reason to suppose, given their ambiguous, contradictory, and symbol-laden character, that a consensus could even be established on the criteria for coherence, and hence on what maximal coherence would look like.

However, Schelling's hermeneutics is not simply internal. When he refers to the "premises" of Christianity, he is not referring to basic assumptions which could only be gleaned from the New Testament itself. In fact, he states explicitly: "the reality of the principles by means of which revelation is grasped has already been made certain for us, independently of revelation, through the major historical event which was mythology" (PO, SW, II/3: 530). These premises or principles consist in the theory of potentialities which guides Schelling's interpretation of mythology, and indeed structures his whole account of both the process of nature and the evolution of human consciousness. Schelling evidently takes what he regards as his uniquely comprehensive and theoretically coherent interpretation of mythological consciousness to have validated the objectivity of his principles, as a hermeneutic framework. Hence, at the start of his 1841/42 lectures on the *Philosophy of Revelation*, he states: "if revelation is a reality, it must stand in a historical context, and thus one requires, in order to comprehend it, a higher-level historical context, which goes beyond revelation itself. Without this, revelation cannot be comprehended" (PO41/42: 98). At this point, however, one might begin to wonder whether "revelation" still has any standing as an independent source of knowledge or insight at all. For Schelling seems to be claiming that revelation is a "reality" which can only be grasped through its incorporation into his overall theory of the history of consciousness. It is true that Schelling also suggests that Christianity can best be understood with the resources Christianity itself provides. For example, he states: "*We* have merely explained Christianity out of itself, like every significant occurrence, it holds the *key* to its own comprehension. This *lies in the relation of succession of the highest causes*" (PO41/42: 311). But this quotation might lead one to think that Christianity can be explained "out of itself" for Schelling only because he finds in it an adumbration of the potentialities (the "highest causes") and their interrelations which coincides with dynamic ontology of his own late philosophy. If this is the case, we might well suspect that Schelling is only taking out of the Christian revelation what he has read into it. His claim to have established an equilibrium in which both reason and revelation receive their due still looks problematic.

We can perhaps make more headway with this question if we note that, for Schelling, revelation is not a matter of acquiring knowledge by supposedly supernatural means at all—but is rather what he calls a "happening" (*Erscheinung*) or a "thing of concern" (*eine Sache*). It is a question of a shift in the structure of consciousness, rather than a disclosure of content unattainable by reasoning alone. This means that the *Philosophy of Revelation* is not the endeavor of reformulating a cannon of revealed truths and their corollaries in terms of a self-standing philosophical theory. Furthermore, Schelling strongly suggests that any religious dogma will be inadequate as an attempt to determine the character of the revelatory event because it will be shaped by contingencies of time and place. Therefore, his enterprise has no interest in either confirming or refuting doctrinal claims. The *Philosophy of Revelation*, as he states, "has no wish to be a doctrine, and therefore does *not* aim to be *the antithesis of any dogma*. The subject matter, revelation, is older than every dogma, and it is only with this subject matter than we are concerned, not with subjective determinations" (PO41/42: 258; see also 196). As regards the nature of the happening or matter of concern, Schelling states explicitly that "*In a philosophy of revelation it is solely a matter of explaining the person of Christ. He is not a teacher, not a founder, but the content of Christianity*" (PO41/42: 260). What the philosopher should seek to understand, then, is what occurred in and through the life and death of the historical person, Jesus Christ—and specifically why the appearance of this particular individual on the world stage marked a major break in the history of human consciousness.

Liberation from the Mythological Process

For Schelling, the life and death of Christ were the process in which the struggle between B and A^2 was *definitively* superseded. In pre-Christian religions, a temporary reconciliation of B and A^2 could be achieved through the practice of sacrifice. But sacrificial rituals had to be constantly repeated because B—the "primordial principle" (*Urprinzip*)—had not been undermined from within, but only placated or temporarily pacified. To put this in another way, sacrifice remained a matter of *self-interest*—albeit masked by gestures of submission and obeisance—and therefore could not avoid confirming the power of B, the principle of exclusionary selfhood. This cyclical process could only be brought to a definitive end by a self-sacrifice of oppositional identity as such. Only a complete renunciation of any claim to superiority or sovereignty on the part of A^2 *as a cosmic power* could deprive B of the antagonist it dialectically required to sustain its own identity. As Schelling states, in the 1841/42 *Philosophy of Revelation*:

> Since the mediating potentiality offers itself as a sacrifice, it has rendered all further exclusion impossible for the other principle. However, that contrary principle consists only in the exclusion of the mediating potentiality. If the exclusion is made impossible for it, then its own force is broken. +A and –A (for example as opposed electricities) only have reality in their mutual exclusion. If one gives up its selfhood, then the other cannot be what it is. (PO41/42: 302–303)

This complete surrender of selfhood is enacted by Christ in his acceptance of arrest, torture and execution on the cross; only by voluntarily going to his death could he fully disarm B, and thereby bring about the reconciliation of the potentialities, whose tension (*Spannung*), in their guise as cosmic-psychic powers, obscurely dominated mythological consciousness.

For Schelling, then, the truth-content of the Christian revelation is confirmed by the precipitous decline of mythological religion in the regions to which Christianity spread. In the previous chapter we noted some of the proto-psychoanalytic insights implicit in Schelling's theory of mythology; viewed from this angle, mythological consciousness can be compared to dream consciousness, as understood by Freud and his successors—a state in which the mind is estranged from itself and unaware of being confronted with its own productions. Such consciousness cannot engage—at least not fully—in "reality-testing," to use a Freudian term, just as the dreaming subject is unable to take a critical, reflective distance from the objects of her oneiric awareness. For Schelling, this "ecstatic" character of mythological consciousness has the important consequence that it could not be brought to an end by a further event *within* such consciousness, or by any mythological figure. The emancipatory event could only irrupt from outside, in the form of the life and death of an actual historical person, who was able to enact the cosmic process of reconciliation. Through the impact of this event human beings were freed to comprehend their own freedom. They found themselves awakening to a world which they were now able to understand as shaped by their own agency. At the risk of pleonasm, it might be termed a "mundane world"—one in which human beings have their feet fully planted on the ground. As discussed at the end of chapter 3, Schelling here anticipates an important element of the theory of the "Axial Age" put forward a century later by Karl Jaspers: it is only when human beings grasp the notion of a fully *transcendent* God—definitively disclosed, in Schelling's view, through Christ's humanly finite yet unconstrained freedom—that the historical world appears in its contingency, contestability, and transformability. As he puts it:

> When the things themselves arrive, their mere shadows disappear. Confronted with such an *objective* fact, which occurred before the eyes of the disenchanted world, everything previously believed vanished and *became* a fable, even though at the beginning it was not mere poetic invention, but most certainly grounded in a certain subjective necessity. It is well known that history has taken on a quite different meaning since the appearance of Christ than it had before it. (PO, SW, I/4: 175)

Hegel on Christianity as the Turning-Point and on the Concept of Religion

Hegel shares with Schelling the view that the coming of Christianity marks a major turning point in human history. In his *Lectures on the Philosophy of World History*, he asserts that God is recognized as spirit only when also apprehended as triune, and that this new principle is "the axis on which the history of the world turns" (LPH: 319/W20, 12: 386). Trinitarian theology—in which the becoming human of the divine is an essential moment of the divine life itself—expresses a realization that "the human being is himself contained in the concept of God" (LPH: 324/W20, 12, 392). As Hegel puts it, the "higher spirit" revealed by Christianity, erupting into a Roman world devoid of any genuine sense of the divine, brought about:

> the reconciliation and liberation of spirit, since human beings receive the consciousness of spirit in its universality and infinity. The absolute object, the truth, is spirit, and since the human being is himself spirit, he is present to himself in this object and thus has found the essence and his essence in his absolute object. But in order for the objectivity of the essence to be overcome and for spirit to be at home with itself, the naturalness of spirit,

in which the human being is something particular and empirical must be negated, so that what is alien is cancelled and the reconciliation of spirit is brought about. (LPH: 319/W20, 12: 386)

This elevation above the natural in turn brings about a new consciousness of freedom, which Hegel depicted in striking terms in his lectures on the philosophy of religion:

> Subjectivity has given up all external distinctions in this infinite value, distinctions of mastery, power, position, even of sex and wealth. Before God all human beings are equal. This comes to consciousness for the first time here and now, in the speculative and negative [elements] of the infinite anguish of love; herein lies the possibility and the root of truly universal justice and of the actualization of freedom. (LPR3: 138/VPR3: 74)

Despite Hegel's and Schelling's shared sense of the coming of Christianity as a profound emancipatory moment in the history of human consciousness, there are obvious differences of emphasis between the two accounts. Hegel stresses the demand for freedom and justice that arises from the realization that the self-consciousness of human beings, regardless of their natural characteristics or social position, is itself "as simple self-relation the universal, the self-identical," that "finite spirit is thus itself posited as a moment of God" (LPH: 324/W20, 12: 392). Schelling, however, emphasizes the manner in which reality becomes "disenchanted," is experienced as contingent and alterable, once a fatalistic sense of the world as the playground of cosmic-mythological forces (the "principalities and powers" of *Ephesians* 6:12) is replaced by a conception of the divine as "spirit," since spirit is "that which ought-to-be ... the potentiality of the future" (*das Sein-sollende ... die Potenz der Zukunft*) (PO41/42: 269). This difference of perspective flows from divergent conceptions of the very nature of religion as a pervasive feature of human society and culture. Hegel argues that religion arises from the human capacity for thought:

> Religion has its seat and soil in the activity of thinking. The heart and feeling that directly sense the truth of religion are not the heart and feeling of an animal but of a thinking human being; they are a thinking heart and a thinking feeling, and whatever [measure] of religion is in this heart and feeling is a thought of this heart and feeling. (LPR3: 257/VPR3: 184)

In this respect, Hegel remains remarkably Kantian, since Kant also argues that of the concept of God is generated by the immanent drive of reason toward the unconditioned. The difference between Kant and Hegel becomes clear, however, if we consider the latter's suggestion of what follows from the most basic definition of God as the "One" or the "universal":

> If we now ask ourselves what we call this aspect of our consciousness for which the universal on the whole is, whether it be determined abstractly or concretely within itself, then the answer is *thought*. For thought is alone the soil for this content, is the activity of the universal—the universal in its activity and efficacy. (LPR1: 120/VPR1: 372–271)

Thought, then, does not simply grasp the universal, it *is* the universal itself at work in human consciousness. Correspondingly, Hegel does not regard God as an *object* of thought, in the manner which even Kant's conception of the Ideal of pure reason still suggests. This is made clear by his account of God *as* the concept, in his distinctive sense:

> As far as the concept is concerned, it is immediately this universal that determines and particularizes itself—it is this activity of dividing, of particularizing and determining itself, of positing a finitude, negating this its own finitude and being identical with itself through the negation of this finitude. This is the concept as such, the concept of God, the absolute concept; this is just what God is. (LPR1: 436–437/VPR1: 325)

Because it makes no sense to suppose that there could be two qualitatively distinct forms of conceptuality, Hegel's theory implies that—in the last instance—the human thinking of God is identical with God's return to himself in thought, his negation of his own necessary self-externalization in the realm of finitude. It is not surprising, then, that in his lectures on the philosophy of religion, Hegel scolds contemporary theologians for failing to rise to this speculative height, and quotes approvingly from Meister Eckhart: "The eye with which God sees me is the eye with which I see him; my eye and his eye are one. In justice I am cradled in God, and He in me. If God were not, I would not be; if I were not, He would not be" (LPR1: 347–348/VPR1: 248; also W20, 16: 209).

Given this Hegelian conception of the relation between the human and the divine, Schelling is clearly on the wrong track in suggesting that his own philosophy implies a "real relation" (*reales Verhältnis*) of human consciousness to God, whereas, in Hegel's case, the relation is merely conceptual or "ideal." Hegel, of course, would not concede the legitimacy of the distinction. Indeed, perhaps the most basic opposition in Hegel's philosophy of religion is that between a form of consciousness which *does* relate to God as something objectified, separate from and standing *over against* human subjectivity—a form described by Hegel as "*Vorstellung*" ("representation")—and a mode of thinking which has overcome this limitation, and which he identifies with his own speculative philosophy. The difference between Hegel and Schelling, then, lies elsewhere. We might say more accurately that, from Schelling's perspective, the problem with Hegel's conception of religion is not so much that it fails to allow for a *real* relation between the human and the divine, but rather that it fails to allow for a real *relation*—for a genuine encounter with the transcendent. Here, then, there *is* a basic dispute about the source of religious experience. For Hegel, it is to be found in the human capacity for thinking, for reasoning. For Schelling, the source is rather the transcendental field of consciousness as such. As we noted at the start of chapter 7, Schelling argues that because agents can perceive and act unselfconsciously—and in his view, before the beginning of the mythological process, generally did so—experience must already be a unified field prior to the emergence, through an act of reflection, of an ego or subject of consciousness. This entails that the source of unity can only be the being of the world as such—the transcendent point of synthesis, the *Daß*. The underlying issue, then, is whether the self-relating structure of reason is sufficient to account for self-consciousness, as Hegel assumes, or whether it rather presupposes it. In Dieter Henrich's view, Hegel's approach is one-sided—one of two possible paths out of Kant, the other being taken by Fichte. Hegel's central questions in this domain, he contends, concern how self-consciousness could be *both* singular *and* universal, and Hegel therefore concentrates—in itself, a legitimate focus—on the development of logical structures able to accommodate such an apparently contradictory unity.[5] However, as Henrich has stressed on numerous occasions, while self-relatedness may be a necessary, it is not a sufficient condition for self-consciousness: "no study of any self-relations in the world, not even those which (seen from a third-person perspective) are my own," can bring about the original disclosure of my conscious existence.[6] Schelling, similarly, considers consciousness (which—after the *Umsturz*—always harbors the possibility of self-consciousness) to be more basic than thought because even transcendental thinking is something experienced ("*Das*

Denken ist also auch Erfahrung" [DRP, SW, II/1: 326]). Such experience could not itself be explained by a further act of thinking without producing an infinite regress.

This divergence is reflected in the fact that, for Hegel, the developmental sequence of pre-Christian religions is driven by the quest of human thought for an adequate representation of the absolute. However, there is no sense, as in Schelling, that consciousness has fallen victim to an immanent compulsion, from which it must be liberated by a shock. Rather, in Hegel's narrative both ancient Judaism and Greek religion, have—in their contrary ways—already risen above nature and begun to grasp the spirituality of the divine. In Greek religion, which Hegel terms the "religion of beauty," the gods are given an aesthetically achieved representation in human form—the form most adequate to express outwardly the actuality of spirit. However, in Greek myth, the abstract power of fate continues to dominate even the gods, who are subjected to contingencies of nature. In Jewish religion, the "religion of sublimity" as Hegel calls it, the divine is understood for the first time as wholly wise and beneficent, and as a "spiritually subjective unity"— in a manner which the subsequent religious traditions of the West will consider worthy of the name "God" (see LPR2: 669/VPR2: 561). However, in the ensuing Roman religion, the "religion of expediency," we find a debased form of consciousness that in many respects recapitulates the primitive proto-religious stage of magic: the gods are reduced to instrumental status, to a "machinery devoid of sense" (LPR2: 693/VPR2: 585). They become mere intermediaries for the promotion of practical human purposes, while the only "universal" purpose has no genuinely religious dimension, being simply the expansionist drive of the Roman *imperium* itself. In this spiritually inhospitable environment, many conscientious individuals retreat into the cultivation of private virtue, finding solace in the doctrines of Stoicism or Skepticism (see LPR3: 308/VPR3: 231–232). But, just as magic indicates a pre-religious state of consciousness, so—for Hegel—Roman religion can be seen as a *Götterdämmerung*; it triggers a crisis expressed in a profound spiritual longing, thereby paving the way for the new dawn of Christianity.

The Christologies of Hegel and Schelling

Hegel's interpretation of Christianity should be of interest not simply to those concerned with the philosophy of religion, nineteenth-century theology, or the overall structure of Hegel's system. For in the decade or so following Hegel's death, the question of the relation between Hegelian philosophy and the Christian religion became the crucial issue which fractured the Hegelian school, with consequences for the development of European philosophy with which we are still living today. While "Right Hegelians" asserted the full compatibility of Hegel's thought and Lutheran Christianity, the increasingly radical "Left Hegelians" concluded that the consequences of Hegel's philosophy were fundamentally atheistic, and that Hegelianism pointed the way toward the supersession of both religion and metaphysics, as these had developed in the West. This post-Hegelian turmoil raises an obvious question: how was it possible for Hegel's treatment of Christianity to be so profoundly ambivalent that it could give rise to such incompatible responses?

The answer to this question lies in Hegel's theory of the dialectical development of human consciousness, combined with his claim, already touched on, that religious thought occurs in the medium of "representation"—of narrative, image, and symbol. Hegel argues that religious consciousness was logically required to enter a stage in which the unity of the human and the divine—understood as a philosophical insight concerning the locus of the self-consciousness of absolute spirit—would be experienced by human beings as the unique divinity of a specific human being. This argument follows from Hegel's conception of human consciousness as advancing historically from "certainty" to "truth," and from the immediacy of the sensory and empirical to rationally transparent conceptualization. Thus, when Hegel comes to discuss the doctrine of the Incarnation, he states:

> Furthermore, the consciousness of the absolute idea that we have in philosophy in the form of thinking is to be brought forth not for the standpoint of philosophical speculation or speculative thinking but in the form of certainty. The necessity [that the divine-human unity shall appear] is not first apprehended by means of thinking; rather it is a certainty for humanity. In other words, this content—the unity of divine and human nature—achieves certainty, obtaining the form of immediate sensible intuition and external existence for humankind, so that it appears as something that has been seen in the world, something that has been experienced. It is essential to this form of non-speculative consciousness that it must be before us; it must essentially be before me—it must become a certainty for humanity. (LPR3: 312–313/VPR3: 237–238)

As this passage illustrates, Hegel's theory of the Incarnation encourages conflicting interpretations (it should be borne in mind that the German term *Menschwerdung*— "becoming human"—has very different connotations to its English counterpart). Is Hegel claiming that the Idea (the conceptual unity of thought and being, the infinite and the finite) really did become available to "immediate sensuous perception" by externalizing itself in a particular human being—that this process is part of what is means for it to be the Idea? Or is he asserting that human beings, at a certain point in history, are determined by the dialectic of religious consciousness to *experience* a certain human being—we might add: who happened to be Jesus of Nazareth—*as if he were* the incarnation of the Idea? Some distinguished commentators, Michael Theunissen for example, have defended the view that Hegel really is committed to a "theology of kenosis," to a conception of divine "alienation in love" which merges with the "logic of alienation" of the Idea.[7] However, it is hard to overlook that, in the quotation just given, Hegel speaks of what is essential to a "form of consciousness," of how the idea "must appear." In his treatment of the coming of Christianity in his *Lectures on the Philosophy of World History*, where one might surmise that he felt less need to compromise with theological convention, Hegel clearly explains the "ultimate need of spirit" to be that human beings should "receive the speculative concept of spirit in representation." He then goes on to draw a particularly sharp version of the distinction, familiar from the history of modern Protestant theology, between the "Christ of faith" and the "Jesus of history": "Make of Christ what you will, exegetically, critically, historically speaking ... the question is only what the truth is in and for itself" (LPH: 325–326/W20, 12: 394).

These interpretive issues, which were so explosive for the destiny of the Hegelian school in the 1830s and 1840s, continue to provoke debate. What is hard to contest, however, is that, in his philosophy of religion, and of Christianity in particular, Hegel is not concerned to use the evidence of religious experience or conceptions based in religious revelation to *establish* or *support* philosophical truths. As he states unambiguously, "Philosophy is only explicating *itself* when it explicates religion, and when it explicates itself it is explicating religion" (LPR1: 152–153/VPR1: 63). Hegel's aim, rather, is to *validate philosophically* the essential doctrinal content of Christianity and defend it from what he regards as the corrosively subjectivist tendencies of the theology of his own day. Thus, the doctrine of the Incarnation, and the narrative of Christ's crucifixion and resurrection, can be rendered intelligible as the representational version of Hegel's theory of the activity of spirit, as a process of externalization or self-manifestation, and of return-to-self out of the singularity and finitude of this manifestation. The full extremity of this entry into finitude for the sake of its suspension is expressed in the narrative of God's execution as a criminal. As Hegel puts it, "The death of Christ is however the death of this death itself, the negation of the negation" (LPR3: 324n/VPR3: 247n). The Cross and the Resurrection, in other words, are the pictorial version of a logical operation: the story of the Passion and its aftermath presents the "*absolute history of the divine Idea*, what—in itself—has occurred and which occurs eternally" (LPR3: 127/VPR3: 62). For Hegel, this entails that "finitude, humanity and humiliation are posited as something alien to Christ, to him who is simply God" (LPR3: 324n/VPR3: 247n). Furthermore, it is in the religious community's shared worship that God's self-consciousness, his return-to-self from finitude is fully achieved, and Hegel therefore tends to merge the Resurrection and the coming of the Holy Spirit at Pentecost. In this perspective, the Resurrection can be construed as Christ's continued existence in the shared life and spirit of the community of believers. Correspondingly, Christianity is entitled to be called the "consummate" or the "revealed" religion, because—in a reflexive turn not achieved by any previous faith—its representational content is the demise of the oppositional structure of representation, and hence a pictorialized expression of the essence of religion as such: the unity-in-difference of the human and the divine.

The emphasis of Schelling's account of Christ's death and resurrection seems, at first sight, strikingly different to that of Hegel. His interpretation finds compressed form in the statement: "Christ's resurrection is the most decisive proof of the irrevocability of his incarnation, and of the fact that he retained nothing of his divinity except his divine frame of mind" (UPO: 598–599). A few pages later, in the *Urfassung* of the *Philosophy of Revelation*, Schelling states of Christ:

> He did not cease to be a human being after death; he did not retreat back into divinity, but remained a human being, as his resurrection demonstrates. For this is the immense significance of the resurrection, that this subject did not cease to be a human being, even in his transfiguration. It is precisely in his humanity that his being outside God—*praeter Deum*—consists, his being self-standing in the most inward unity with God. (UPO: 604)

There is an unmistakeable contrast between these formulations and Hegel's view that Christ's death and resurrection are "the mediation whereby the human is stripped away and . . . what subsists-in-itself returns to itself, first coming to be spirit thereby" (LPR3: 327/VPR3: 250). However, the precise meaning of Schelling's statement will depend on how we understand what it means to be "self-standing in the most inward unity with God," and more generally on how we interpret his key concept of Christ's "divine frame of mind" (*göttliche Gesinning*) (e.g., PO41/42: 296–297). One way in which to approach this question is to return to the dilemma of finite freedom, as explored by Sartre in *Being and Nothingness*.

In the short concluding section of the book, called "Moral Perspectives," Sartre asks again what would be involved in accepting the groundlessness of one's own freedom, rather than incessantly seeking to ground it by fusing the in-itself and the for-itself, in a simulacrum of the divine *causa sui*. Such a move, Sartre says, would consist in giving up the striving to realize determinate values, which, in bad faith, we fail to recognize as *posited* by our freedom, and in taking freedom itself as the sole value. However, he then asks, would that very move not ultimately be driven—from behind, as it were—by the attempt to become *causa sui*? Is there any escape at all from this self-defeating quest? After all, if there were, the result would be *paradoxical*: "A freedom which wants itself as freedom is in fact a being-which-is-not-what-it-is and which-is-what-it-is-not, which chooses, as its ideal of being, being-what-it-is-not and not-being-what-it-is" (BN: 627/EN: 691). In other words, to coincide with ourselves *as* freedom we would have to cease striving to achieve freedom by coinciding with ourselves. As Sartre puts it, a free being "chooses not to *recover* itself but to flee itself, not to coincide with itself, but to be always at a distance from itself" (BN: 627/EN: 691). Hence the very process through which we seek to escape bad faith and achieve what could be termed "authenticity"—although Sartre himself is reluctant to use this word, which he associates with Heidegger—involves self-relinquishment, an acceptance that our freedom is not ours to command. On this interpretation, Christ's "divine frame of mind" could only show up, was only possible *because* he was human—and because he played the historically transformative role of A^2 *divesting itself* of its standing and power as a cosmic deity. The consequence is that Christ was divine only and precisely in his *abandonment* of divinity. In this way Schelling seeks to resolve the age-old theological problem of Christ's two natures (see, e.g., PO41/42: 288–289). In line with this account, the narrative of Christ's appearance in *human* yet *transfigured* form after his crucifixion—Schelling does not defend the notion of a literal rising from the dead—becomes a proclamation of the supreme value of an earthly existence lived in a fully authentic manner (this value cannot be rendered null by death), and a confirmation of the enduring possibility of such finite freedom.[8] It is to this that the central character in Sally Rooney's novel *Beautiful World, Where Are You* seems to respond, in an email to her closest friend:

> I find it hard to separate the Jesus who appears after the resurrection from the man who appears before; they seem to me to be all of one being. I suppose what I mean to say is that in his resurrected form, he goes on saying the kind of things that "only he" could say, that I can't imagine emanating from any other consciousness. But that's as close as I get to thinking about his divinity.[9]

For Schelling, then, the essence of the Christian *revelation*—that is, a disclosure of truth which could not have been anticipated by autonomous reason—consists in the fact that liberated freedom, freedom paradoxically liberated from itself, has been disclosed as *possible* because it was *actual*. As a result of the conviction, spreading among Christ's disciples and followers, of the reality of this liberation, mythological consciousness begins to disintegrate. As Schelling puts it:

> With this event *ecstatic* history transitions into actual history. The ecstatic condition, which was also an inner history of consciousness, could only be brought to an end by a more transcendent, objective fact ... It is with Christ that real, external history first begins. (PO41/42: 293)

It is tempting to emphasize the contrast between Schelling's focus, in his interpretation of the Gospel narrative, on the experience of finite freedom, and Hegel's view of the same narrative as the expression—at the level of representation—of a timeless process in which finite human existence features only as a moment. Hegel himself offers plenty of material for such a counterposing. He argues, for example, that St Paul's claim that Christ has died for all (2 *Cor.* 5: 14–15) refers not to "a single act but to the eternal divine history: it is a moment in the nature of God himself; it has taken place in God himself" (LPR3: 328/VPR3: 251). But even though such formulations appear to dissolve the finitely human into the divine, reading them that way would not do justice to the complexity of the process which Hegel calls "*Aufhebung*." As might be expected, he makes considerable efforts to counter an excessively neoplatonic view of his interpretation of Christian faith, stating, for example:

> "God himself is dead," it says in a Lutheran hymn, expressing an awareness that the human, the finite, the fragile, the weak, the negative are themselves a moment of the divine, that they are within God himself, that finitude, negativity, otherness are not outside of God and do not, as otherness, hinder unity with God. (LPR3: 326/VPR3: 249–250)

If there remain significant differences between Schelling's and Hegel's interpretations of Christianity, the notion of an endorsement of the infinite value of finite human existence is not sufficient on its own to pick them out.

Hegel's Critique of Religious Subjectivism

We can make more headway with this question by considering two central aspects of Hegel's theory of religion: firstly, that religious faith is in fact a form of *knowledge*; secondly, that the process which Christianity discloses in the form of religious representation is an eternal process. This entails that, for Hegel, Christianity discloses the inherent rationality of the course of the world, and thereby allows us to feel at home in the role—infinitesimal and yet endowed with the dignity of reason—which each of us is destined to play in it. In this way, Christianity brings about our reconciliation with reality—as does speculative philosophy, by establishing in definitive conceptual form the truth content of Christianity. Indeed, Hegel can go so far as to say that "philosophy is itself the service of God, it *is* religion" (LPR1: 152n/ VPR1: 63n). Unlike philosophy, however, religion as doctrine and ritual practice expresses this content in a form which is accessible in principle to all, and which appeals not only to the head, but to the heart and the senses. For this reason, Hegel argues in the *Philosophy of Right* that religion is essential to the stability of the state, for it confirms the meaningfulness of—the divine reason implicit in—the political and ethical orders in which human beings live out their lives. Hegel develops this argument in the long and complex §270 of the *Philosophy of Right*, on the relations between the political state and religion:

> The content of religion is absolute truth, and it is therefore associated with a disposition of the most exalted kind. As intuition, feeling, and representational cognition, whose concern is with God as the unlimited foundation

and cause on which everything depends, it contains the requirement that everything else should be seen in relation to this and should receive confirmation, justification, and the assurance of certainty from this source. It is within this relationship that the state, laws, and duties all receive their highest endorsement, as far as consciousness is concerned, and become supremely binding upon it. (EPR: §270/W20, 7: 417)

Of course, this can only be true to the extent that "[t]he state is the divine will as present spirit, *unfolding* as the actual shape and *organization of a world*" (EPR: §270/W20, 7: 417–418). But this is precisely what Hegel sets out to demonstrate. However, not all versions of religion, and especially not certain forms of Protestant Christianity, perform the required socially integrative role. In the same paragraph of the *Philosophy of Right*, Hegel polemicizes against the religion of feeling, which simply drives forward the social disintegration fostered by modern individualism, and may even consider itself entitled to take up a critical stance toward the state:

Those who "seek the Lord" and assure themselves, in their uneducated opinion, that they possess everything immediately instead of undertaking the work of raising their subjectivity to cognition of the truth and knowledge of objective right and duty, can produce nothing but folly, outrage, and the destruction of all ethical relations. (EPR: §270/W20, 7: 419)

Hegel has a difficult balancing act to carry out. He believes that religion is necessary for social integration and the commitment of individuals to the state, but he does not wish religion *also* to provide a vantage point from which to challenge the socio-political order. To solve this problem, he argues that it is the *state* which must have the last word because it is the outward and practical—rather than merely inward—actualization of spirit.

It is noteworthy that here Hegel reverses the superiority of absolute over objective spirit, as dictated by his system. However, setting this inconsistency aside, it is clear that religion can only buttress the state if it is not simply a matter of feeling, with all its instability, but has cognitive content, implicitly grasps the state's rationality. Accordingly, Hegel's interpretation of Christianity, places great importance on doctrine. Indeed, the prefatory material to the second and third editions of the *Encyclopaedia* is given over, to a considerable extent, to the question of the relation between philosophy, on the one hand, and Christianity as doctrinal system on the other. In these texts Hegel does far more than insist on the compatibility between his own philosophy and religion. He goes forcefully on the offensive. He attacks the forms of Protestant religiosity, prevalent in his time, which insisted on the primacy of faith and feeling, which were his hostile to his philosophical enterprise, and in many cases to philosophy in general. He portrays such a stance as in fact complicit with the attacks on religion of what he describes as the "*Verstandesaufklärung*"—an Enlightenment based on the understanding, in his semi-technical sense, or on what he also terms "finite categories and one-sided abstractions" (Enc.1: 11/W20, 8: 24). What both these positions, the pious and the shallowly rationalistic, undermine is the substance and the content of the Christian religion—the words "*Gehalt*" and "*Inhalt*" occur repeatedly throughout these pages. As Hegel says of his religious opponents:

> they stand by the name of the Lord Christ in a completely barren fashion as far as the basic import and intellectual content of the faith itself is concerned; and they deliberately and scornfully disdain the elaboration of doctrine, which is the foundation of the faith of the Christian church. For the spiritual, fully thought-out, and scientific expansion [of the doctrine] would upset, and even forbid or wipe out, the self-conceit of their subjective boasting which relies on the spiritless and fruitless assurance—rich only in evil fruits—that they are in possession of Christianity, and have it exclusively for their very own. (Enc.1: 20/W20, 8: 35)

The Fate of Christianity

A striking feature of this approach to Christianity is Hegel's seeming lack of awareness of the danger that his own conception of the relation between philosophy and religion could pose to the survival of religion. By insisting that faith should be understood as a form of implicit knowledge, by providing a "scientific" elaboration of doctrinal content, and by asserting the ultimate superiority of philosophy as far as speculative cognition is concerned, Hegel paved the way for the argument that philosophy could replace religion, as a now superseded shape of consciousness. The end of the preface to the 1827 edition of the *Encyclopaedia* is especially forthright in this regard:

> Science understands feeling and faith, but science itself can only be assessed through the concept, as that on which it rests; and since science is the self-development of the concept, an assessment of science through the concept is not so much a judgment upon it as an advancing together with it. (Enc.1: 17/W20, 8: 31)

Apparently, Hegel does not anticipate that such declarations will provoke a wave of post-religious, anti-religious, and atheistic thinking, as occurred from the later 1830s onwards in Left Hegelian milieu, and in the various radical traditions which emerged from it. In other words, Hegel's attempt to save the Christian religion, and what he sees as its vital socially integrative role, was too ambivalent to succeed. He interpreted religious consciousness as "representational knowledge," thereby erasing the distinction between knowledge and the existential dimension of faith, whose origins date back to Luther, and which Kant helped to consolidate as central to modern philosophy and theology. But this had—to a large extent—the opposite effect to the one intended. Hence Marx, on the one hand, and Kierkegaard, on the other, stand for two paradigmatic responses to Hegel's enterprise, both profoundly critical of it, despite being imbued with Hegelian motifs, in a clear indication of their dialectical lineage.

In Schelling, we find a very different philosophical sensibility. Indeed, Schelling and Hegel exemplify, at the highest level of sophistication and erudition, two contrasting philosophical models applied to the question of religion. Hegel's approach tracks developmental processes, the results of which emerge as the fully unfolded and differentiated truth of what was merely implicit in the beginning—which means, in effect, that the result is the summation of the process of its own emergence. We can be assured of this because we are able track the implicit logical pattern of the unfolding temporal process, which concludes in a differentiated return to the origin. Schelling's approach is not *diametrically* opposed to this procedure. His thinking could not really be placed within the orbit German Idealism at all if there were *no* developmental dimension in his conception of truth; if he were committed, for example, to retrieving a primordial experience from which we can only become further and further removed by the passage of time. However, for Schelling development can be ambiguous—it can distort and cover over as well as disclose. Therefore, in order to evaluate theological developments, to determine what constitutes an enlargement of truth and what represents a regressive occlusion or distortion of it, there is a need to shuttle back and forth between an orientation toward the moment of origin and a focus on the current endpoint, in a process of reflective equilibrium. Of course, this entails that there cannot be a definitive terminus, which could validate itself as the truth fully unfolded.

What does this imply for the relation of philosophy to Christianity—of reason to revelation—in Schelling's account? First, at the center of his view of Christianity stands a liberation from the opaque power of mythological consciousness, through the disclosure of a new, non-self-cancelling freedom, lived out by the historical individual Jesus Christ. An existential encounter with the person who exemplified this freedom, an encounter mediated by the New Testament but not codified as a system of quasi-epistemic claims, stands at the center of Christian faith. Schelling—in contrast to Hegel—sees doctrine as a shifting series of attempts to articulate a core experience. However, this does not mean that he regards the theological elaboration of doctrine as exempt from requirements of rational consistency and intelligibility. On the contrary, he considers the theology of central Christian doctrines such as the Incarnation to be, for the most part, hopelessly deficient, and believes that his own interpretation, structured by the theory of the potentialities, offers a more coherent and rationally transparent alternative. But this approach highlights another major divergence between Hegel and Schelling. The former aims to provide a conceptual rendering of the implicit cognitive content of the Christian faith; in other words, to translate the meaning of the religion into a non-religious vocabulary. He believed, albeit mistakenly, that in this way he could rescue Christianity from the corrosive effects of a subjectivistic focus on religious feeling, and also respond to the challenge of shallow post-Enlightenment conceptions of rationality. Schelling, however, repeatedly states that his aim is to "explain" Christianity—by which he means account for its internal dynamic as a major turning-point in the history of humanity. In doing so, he locates Christianity within a broader historical narrative. But that narrative cannot be purely conceptual. As we have seen, it is grounded in the hypothesis of an originary "absolute event"—the decompression of blind being-ness—which invites interpretation in theological— although not necessarily Christian—terms (indeed, the notion that God is in some sense *dependent* on his own contingently necessary being is clearly deviant, unorthodox). In short, whereas Hegel provides a philosophical interpretation of Christianity which—against his own intentions—directly paved the way for an assault on religion by major figures in later nineteenth-century thought, beginning with Left Hegelians such as Ludwig Feuerbach and Bruno Bauer, Schelling could be said to elaborate not a Christian theology, but rather a theology *of* Christianity, as one determinate form of religion—as one historical manifestation of the intrinsically "God-positing" consciousness of human beings.

The distinction between Christian theology and a theology of Christianity is not an easy one to draw. And this helps to account for many of the ambivalences and confusions that characterize Schelling's treatment of the Christian faith in his late philosophy, where his conception of it becomes so expansive that it often seems to imply dissolution. There can be little doubt that Schelling himself was struggling to understand where he stood. However, in contrast to Hegel's deeply ambiguous defence of Christianity, there is one clear sign that Schelling *is* indeed looking beyond the Christian religion. This is the invocation of what he terms "philosophical religion," which—as he repeatedly makes clear— "does not yet exist." Schelling describes philosophical religion as "the *free* religion, the religion of spirit, which can only be fully actualized as philosophical, since its nature is only to be sought and only to be found with freedom" (DRP, SW, II/1: 255). Such a religion would contain the same principles as mythological and revealed religion:

> Its difference from these could consist only in the *manner* in which it contains them, and furthermore this difference could only be that the principles, which are effective but uncomprehended in those [forms of religion], would be comprehended and understood in this one. (HCI: 173–174/SW, II/1: 250)

In other words, the lucidity characterizing philosophical religion, which cannot be based on authority but must be worked out freely, would be supplied by a clarifying hermeneutics of the history of the religious experience of humankind, of the sort which Schelling believes he has achieved in his positive philosophy. Humanity is moving, albeit over the long term, out of the epoch of "revelation," with the tutelage of reason which this implies. Just as revelation once shattered the grip of mythological religion over human consciousness, so the beginnings of the emancipation of modern consciousness from revelation, achieved in the thought of Descartes and his successors, is the precondition for free religion (see DRP, SW, II/1: 260–269). However, unlike modern proponents of the "secularization thesis," Schelling does not foresee an ultimately religion-less world. Rather his *anticipation* of philosophical religion implies that we have reached a stage in which a reflexive distance has opened up between forms of religious experience, on the one hand, and the symbols and rituals in which such experience is articulated and expressed, on the other.

This rift had long been a preoccupation of Schelling's. In his influential 1803 lectures on the architectonic of university disciplines he argued, as we noted in chapter 3, that Christianity involves an awareness of the inadequacy of religious representations to their content; Christian symbols are "subjective"; in other words, they are experienced as pointing beyond themselves; they do not achieve a life independent of their meaning (see OUS: 90–91/H-K, I/ 14: 125). And at the end of the *Urfassung* of *The Philosophy of Revelation* he refers to an "outer process" and an "inner process." There can be no viable religion without an outer process—a tradition of doctrine, ritual, and festival— but this should not be confused with the inner process which it nourishes and sustains. Schelling emphasizes that "[t]he inner process is of course for each person the main thing" (UPO: 709). It is interesting to compare this diagnosis with Hegel's heroic—and, one must conclude, regressive—effort to clamp doctrine, ritual, and the subjectivity of religious experience back together by philosophical means, especially in the light of the development of theology and religious consciousness in the West over the last two hundred years. Overall, the downgrading of doctrine in favor of the experiential, which Hegel deplored, accompanied by an opening toward other world religions, has continued unabated. One need think only of leading twentieth-century Protestant theologians such as Dietrich Bonhoeffer, with his sense that "religion"—the whole inherited apparatus of dogma and ritual—is no more than the outdated "garment of Christianity," in a time when humanity has "come of age" and feels no need of God as a stopgap;[10] or Paul Tillich, with his demand to transcend the "God of theological theism" and his engagement with the Judaism of Martin Buber and, late in life, with Japanese Buddhism.[11] As regards Catholicism, the Second Vatican Council of the early 1960s was marked by abandonment of the doctrine "*extra Ecclesiam nulla salus*," and led to a multiplicity of initiatives in interfaith dialogue.[12] Furthermore, although the secularization thesis may be on the defensive at the current historical moment, its central claim that—even for the religiously musical—modern individualism results in the erosion of institutionalized religion, and encourages the dilution of dogma, and its selective, personalized appropriation, seems hard to contest.[13] As the matter is sometimes put, it is religion that nowadays brings certain people to a church, rather than the other way round. Overall, given the probative importance of an ultimate correspondence between the historical and the logical in Hegel's philosophy, the failure of his attempt to shift the emphasis back from the experiential to a metaphysically shored up version of doctrine must surely raise doubts, formulable in Hegelian terms, regarding his approach to religious faith. His philosophy of religion can be seen as a valiant but doomed attempt to revalidate, in the context of the modern world, a Christianity for "dwellers" rather than "seekers," to use the terminology popularized by Charles Taylor.[14] Schelling was more prescient in this respect. In his late work, he regards philosophy as *mediating* between modern consciousness and determinate traditions of doctrine and practice, by drawing on the complexity of the religious history of humanity, in a spirit which anticipates the slogan of the distinguished historical sociologist of religion Robert Bellah: "Nothing is ever lost."[15] It is not quite correct to suggest, however, as does Christian Danz, that this process of mediation is precisely what Schelling means by "philosophical religion."[16] Rather, philosophical religion can be understood as the virtual terminus of the process—the endpoint at which the lack of transparency to reason of doctrine and symbol, along with the dangers of obscurantism and domination, and the damage to human communication, which that opaqueness brings with it, would be fully overcome. If, as Schelling declares in the first sentence of his *Darstellung der reinrationalen Philosophie*, "philosophical religion, as we demand it, *does not exist*" (DRP, SW, II/1: 255), this is because it will *always* be to come.

Notes

1. See Walter Burkert, *Greek Religion* (Cambridge, MA: Harvard University Press, 1985), 285–290.
2. See Friedrich Schleiermacher, *On Religion: Speeches to its Cultured Despisers* (Cambridge: CUP, 1996).
3. For details see Graham Stanton, *The Gospels and Jesus* (Oxford: OUP, 2002).
4. Jürgen Habermas, *Auch ein Geschichte der Philosophie. Band 1. Die okzidentale Konstellation von Glauben und Wissen* (Frankfurt: Suhrkamp, 2019), 516.
5. See Dieter Henrich, "Fichtes ursprüngliche Einsicht," in *Dies Ich, das viel besagt. Fichtes Einsicht nachdenken* (Frankfurt: Vittorio Klostermann, 2019), 45.
6. Dieter Henrich, *Fluchtlinien. Philosophische Essays* (Frankfurt: Suhrkamp, 1982), 148.
7. See Michael Theunissen, *Hegels Lehre vom absoluten Geist as theologisch-politischer Traktat* (Berlin: de Gruyter, 1970), 280: "Hegel's theology is certainly based on a logic of externalization, but conversely his logic is based on a theology of *kenosis* which, in love, converges with externalization. When, in the middle of a theoretical analysis, a statement concerning the 'universal,' that it 'descends' to immediate singularity, jumps out, then theology and logic flow together in an indifference which prohibits a derivation of one from the other."
8. The argument that at the core of Schelling's Christology stands an encounter with the successful living out (*Vollzug*) of finite freedom is the central thesis of Christian Danz's outstanding book *Die philosophische Christologie F. W. J. Schellings* (Stuttgart-Bad

Canstatt: frommann-holzboog, 1996). I am much indebted to Danz's work but should make clear that the use of Sartre to illustrate the paradoxical structure of finite freedom is not part of his approach.

9. Sally Rooney, *Beautiful World, Where Are You* (London: Faber & Faber, 2021), 185–186.
10. Dietrich Bonhoeffer, *Letters and Papers from Prison* (London: Fontana, 1968), 91.
11. See Paul Tillich, *The Courage to Be* (New Haven and London: Yale University Press, 2014), 167–175. For Tillich's engagement with Zen and Pure Land Buddhism, see Marc Boss, "Tillich in Dialogue with Japanese Buddhism," in *The Cambridge Companion to Tillich*, ed. Russell Re Manning (Cambridge: CUP, 2009); for his response to Judaism, and Buber especially, see his "Jewish Influences on Contemporary Christianity," *Crosscurrents* 2, no. 3 (1952).
12. For documentation, see Thomas Albert Howard, *The Faiths of Others: A History of Interreligious Dialogue* (New Haven and London: Yale University Press, 2021), ch. 4.
13. See Steve Bruce, *Secularization: In Defence of an Unfashionable Theory* (Oxford: OUP, 2011).
14. See Charles Taylor, "The Church Speaks—to Whom?" in *Church and People: Disjunctions in a Secular Age*, ed. Charles Taylor, Jose Casanova, and George F. McLean (Washington, DC: The Council for Research and Values in Philosophy, 2012).
15. Robert Bellah, "What is Axial about the Axial Age?," *Archives Européennes de Sociologie* 46, no. 1: (2005): 72.
16. See Christian Danz, "Philosophie der Offenbarung," in *F. W. J. Schelling*, ed. Hans Jürg Sandkühler (Stuttgart/Weimar: Metzler Verlag, 1998), 171–173.

9
History as Liberation

Kant and the Paradox of Autonomy

Despite Hegel's far-reaching criticisms of Kant's philosophy, in his Berlin lectures on the history of philosophy he endorses the revolutionary tenor of the Kantian conception of freedom in the most enthusiastic terms. He declares that it is Kant who established that:

> there is no other end for the will than the one created out of the will itself, the goal of its own freedom. The establishment of this principle was a great advance; human freedom is the ultimate pivot upon which humanity turns, the ultimate and absolutely firm pinnacle that is not open to influence, such that we do not grant validity to anything, to any authority of whatever form, if it goes against human freedom. This grand principle has won widespread diffusion and sympathy for the Kantian philosophy, in the respect that humanity finds within itself something utterly firm and unwavering. There is a firm center point, the principle of freedom; everything else that does not rest firmly upon this point is precarious, with the result that nothing is obligatory in which this freedom is not respected. This is the principle.
> (LHP 1825–1826/3: 244–245/VGP 1825–1826/3: 168)

It would be hard to contest that human freedom is one of the central concerns of German Idealism, as this encomium makes clear. However, a problem arises as soon as we try to take freedom as our fundamental principle, as "something utterly firm and unwavering," as Hegel puts it here. For whatever our full account of human freedom may turn out to be, the modern understanding of freedom surely involves—at least as one component—a capacity to detach oneself from prevailing assumptions, to question their validity, and—if necessary—to strike out in new directions, whether in thought or in action. But this suggests not simply that we are under no obligation to accept any authority which goes against our freedom, as Hegel affirms. It implies that the acceptance of the foundational status *any* determinate principle which we might use to construct our philosophical system is incompatible with freedom. If a basic principle has its status *only because* we have freely decided to endorse it, then it is not really a basic principle. To put this in another way, the notion of freedom can easily appear incompatible with the notion of a final philosophical grounding because the foundation must be absolute, unquestionable. A central impulse of the German Idealists is to respond to this dilemma by making freedom itself the basis of their systematic constructions. But to make freedom itself the ultimate foundation seems to be self-defeating because it lacks the fixity and stability which would enable it to function in this role.

In recent philosophical discussion, the manner in which this difficulty surfaces in Kant's own philosophy has come to be known as the "paradox of autonomy." Debate around this issue has a far longer history, however, and can be traced back to the objection raised—notably by Reinhold—to Kant's claim in the *Groundwork of the Metaphysics of Morals*, that "a free will and a will under moral laws are one and the same" (GMM: 57/AA, 4: 447). As noted in chapter 2, Reinhold argued that the equation of moral agency with the effectivity of practical reason, and of the latter with freedom, made responsibility for immoral actions problematic. In response, Kant introduced in later writings an explicit distinction between two dimensions of the will: *Wille* and *Willkür*, or rational will and power of choice. He distinguished the individual's spontaneous choosing of an action—referred to by some commentators as the "executive" aspect of the will—from the "legislative" aspect, the rational construction of the moral law. But he was then confronted with the question: why should we experience the categorical imperative as having overriding normative force, given that any action we chose will presuppose *some* rationale, as a condition of being an action at all? In his *Commentaries on the Idealism of the Wissenschaftslehre*, and in the *System of Transcendental Idealism*, Schelling proposed his own solution to the difficulties generated both by Kant's theory and Reinhold's response to it. He argued that the "power of choice" should be seen as the manner in which the unconditioned status of the rational will manifests itself under finite conditions. However, the vista of practical chaos which this argument opened up forced him to advance to a socio-historical level, and to argue, in effect, that the rational will also operates objectively to shape historical development, over the very long-term, in the direction of a just international order. The rational will, then, operates in two different modes in the *System of Transcendental Idealism*. And, from our present perspective, we can regard the conception of the aesthetic unity of conscious and unconscious activity with which the *System* concludes as a response to the paradox under consideration. However, this solution—reliance on the objective validity of the metaphysical content of aesthetic experience—depended on contentious claims regarding the status of art and was not one with which Schelling could remain satisfied. And this dissatisfaction was to have a decisive impact on the later development of his thinking.

Hegel's Theory of Freedom

At first glance, Hegel's portrayal, in his *Philosophy of Right*, of "the *state* as freedom, which is equally universal and objective in the free self-sufficiency of the particular will" (EPR: §3/W20, 7: 88) seems remote from Kant's conception of freedom as based on *individual* self-legislation. Nonetheless, many recent commentators have argued that Hegel, in his political philosophy, tries to work out how a modern society—a society with a market economy, which enshrines formal equality before the law, acknowledges the right of individuals to a sphere of preference in such matters as religion, trade or profession, and choice of marriage partner, and offers some form of political representation to its populace—can sustain the autonomy of its members in something like the Kantian sense. Hegel's unreserved praise for the break-through character of his predecessor's conception of freedom undoubtedly lends this approach plausibility. Naturally, there is no denying that participation in social life, and the conscientious fulfillment of the obligations which flow from our roles, both chosen and naturally and socially determined, place constraints on our freedom to do what we will. But, for Hegel, obligation or duty in this sense is liberation. It is a liberation *both* from exposure to the arbitrariness of our contingent and shifting natural desires, *and* from the indeterminacy of a reflective subjectivity which is unable to generate principles of action purely from within itself, and which may even revel in its lack of commitment, despite the ineffectuality which goes along with it. As he states:

> A binding duty can appear as a limitation only in relation to indeterminate subjectivity or abstract freedom, and to the drives of the natural will or of the moral will which arbitrarily determines its own indeterminate good. The individual, however, finds his liberation in duty. On the one hand, he is liberated from his dependence on mere natural drives, and from the burden

he labors under as a particular subject in his moral reflections on obligation and desire; and on the other hand, he is liberated from that indeterminate subjectivity which does not attain existence [*Dasein*] or the objective determinacy of action, but remains within itself and has no actuality. In duty, the individual liberates himself so as to attain substantial freedom (EPR: §149/ W20, 7: 297–298).

Clearly, such formulations can be seen as attempts to resolve the paradox of autonomy, by locating the source of normativity in established social practice—in what Hegel famously theorizes as "*Sittlichkeit*"—rather than in the rational legislative capacity of the person. However, this solution can only work if one is able to show that, in general, there need be no conflict or tension between our modern commitment to the subjective freedom of the individual and the authority of the practical norms embedded the existing socio-political order. And it is here that Hegel's conception shows signs of strain. He expresses the view that no real conflict need arise in upbeat statements such as the following:

> The principle of modern states has this enormous strength and depth of allowing the principle of subjectivity to attain fulfilment in the self-sufficient extreme of personal particularity, while at the same time bringing it back to substantial unity and so preserving this unity in the principle of subjectivity itself. (EPR: §260/W20, 7: 407)

From a contemporary perspective, however, Hegel's concept of the state as the "substantial spirit" in which "personal individuality" pursues its "*ultimate end*" (EPR: §260/W20, 7: 406–407) fails fully to comprehend the connection between the modern conception of the fundamental rights of individuals and the limitation of state sovereignty. One clear illustration of this is the fact that Hegel allows no constraint of the legislature on the right of the monarch to declare war, and thus to require citizens to sacrifice their lives, liberty, and property. Indeed, notoriously, Hegel argues that war may be beneficial for the health and cohesion of the socio-political order, by encouraging individuals to will their own "evanescence" (EPR: §324/ W20, 7: 492) relative to the "substance, as the state's absolute power over everything individual and particular" (EPR: §323/W20, 7: 491). More generally, Hegel's conception of basic rights does not accord them a constitutional status which would allow individuals to *appeal against* legislation which may entail injustice, or the against actions of the government.[1] These features of his political thought are connected with his downright opposition to the modern tradition which founds political authority on the consent of the governed. But, absent this basis, his only recourse is to make a premodern appeal to a religious foundation of political authority: "The Idea, within [the context of] religion, is spirit internalized in emotion, but it is this same Idea which gives itself secular expression in the state and secures an existence and actuality for itself in knowledge and volition" (EPR: §270/ W20, 7: 430). There is room to doubt, then, that Hegel's attempt to resolve the paradox of autonomy through a shift from Kantian moral individualism to a socio-political register is successful, rather than simply perpetuating, in an externalized form, the compulsive features of practical reason, which emerge when its legislative activity is no longer something we can *choose* to endorse.

The universal to which individuals are raised by their participation in socio-political community organized as a nation state is what Hegel terms a "concrete universal." It cannot be reduced to a system of laws or social rules, but it is better understood by analogy with the life sustained and expressed through the inter-animation of the parts of an organism. This means that, for Hegel, there is a limit to the degree of universality which a particular socio-political form of life can achieve. It will go through the equivalent of a lifecycle, in which it develops and flourishes—providing an existence full of meaning and purpose for its members—but eventually begin to decay and disintegrate. As this occurs—Hegel believes—a new, more comprehensive universal will start its ascent in the form of another people organizing itself as a state. It is for these reasons the *Philosophy of Right* concludes by considering the problem of interstate relations, and then moves on to a sketch of Hegel's philosophy of history. In his view, the world spirit, in its ultimate universality, can only be expressed through a temporal sequence of states. As He puts it:

> The principles of the spirits of nations are in general of a limited nature because of that particularity in which they have their objective actuality and self-consciousness as existent individuals, and their deeds and destinies in their mutual relations are the actually occurring dialectic of the finitude of these spirits. It is through this dialectic that the universal spirit, the spirit of the world, produces itself in its freedom from all limits, and it is this spirit which exercises its right—which is the highest right of all—over finite

spirits in world history, as the world's court of judgement. (EPR: §340/W20, 7: 503)

It is clear from this statement that the unrestricted universality of spirit can be comprehended by the philosopher of history, but that no individual nation state can exemplify it in practice.

A problem arises, however, when Hegel refers to the "right" enjoyed by spirit in world history, as at the beginning of §30 of the *Philosophy of Right*, where he states: "Right is something utterly sacred, for the simple reason that it is the existence of the absolute concept, of self-conscious freedom." The difficulty is that for Hegel there exists no form of *self-conscious* freedom—no form of *practical* consciousness—which corresponds to the right of world history. In other words, he specifies no *duties* with respect to the practical field of the evolving history of humankind as a whole. In this respect, Hegel is inconsistent because in §155 of the *Philosophy of Right* he argues that "right" and "duty" are strictly correlative concepts: "Hence *duty and right* coincide in this identity of the universal and the particular will." In contravention of this principle, the so-called "right" of world history is immunized against ethical assessment in terms of any corresponding duties, making the very use of the term cosmetic.[2] This is made clear when Hegel declares that:

> Justice and virtue, wrongdoing, violence, and vice, talents and their [expression in] deeds, the small passions and the great, guilt and innocence, the splendor of individual and national life, the independence, fortune, and misfortune of states and individuals—all of these have their determinate significance and value in the sphere of conscious actuality, in which judgement and justice—albeit imperfect justice—are meted out to them. World history falls outside these points of view. (EPR, §345/W20, 7: 505)

It is this tension between the ultimate universality of the course of history and the domain of "conscious actuality" (*bewußte Wirklichkeit*—the practical life of a particular state) which leads Christoph Menke to propose that it is "historicity" which reveals the paradox of autonomy that Hegel has in fact failed to master.[3] The processes through which social formations come into being, within which individuals can be raised up and trained to participate in the self-replicating patterns of social life, are not themselves expressions of autonomous agency.

It might be objected that Hegel does have a conception of the form of practical agency which delivers the transition from one determinate actualization of the world spirit to another—namely the activity of what he terms "world historical individuals." However, he stresses that such individuals are entirely driven by a dominating passion, and not by any awareness of the new principle of social life whose emergence they push forward: "Since these individuals are the living expressions of the substantial deed of the world spirit and are thus immediately identical with it, they cannot themselves perceive it and it is not their object and end" (EPR: §348/W20, 7: 506). In other words, there is no place in Hegel's scheme of things for projects for the enhancement of freedom which are simultaneously actualizations of freedom. In this respect he is entirely consistent because—for him—to be free means to act in accord with the immanent rationality of an existing system of practices. Accordingly, he is unable to acknowledge the critical assessment and transformation of collective ways of thinking and acting as a valid aspect modern political life; he has no place for social movements, which is striking given that he lived in the age of Abolitionism, arguably the first international social movement in the modern sense.

The Illusion of the Practical Standpoint in Hegel

A related difficulty in Hegel's thought is that, although the "progress of the consciousness of freedom" is presented as the guiding thread of his theory of history (LPH: 54/VPG, W20, 12: 32), this developing sense of freedom does not stand in any feedback relation to modes of historical agency. Hegel makes this abundantly clear when he states:

> Since history is the process whereby the spirit assumes the shape of events and of immediate natural actuality, the stages of its development are presented as *immediate natural principles;* and since these are natural, they constitute a plurality of separate entities such that *one of them* is allotted to *each nation* in its *geographical* and *anthropological* existence. (EPR: § 346/ W20, 7: 505)

One might have expected, however, that as the consciousness of freedom develops in the course of history, the principles organizing the stages of its development would cease to be immediately natural, as Hegel puts it, and would themselves come to be shaped, at least to some extent, by conscious human purposes. In line with this thought, commentators sympathetic to Hegel, such as Allen Wood, have suggested that his theory *does* allow for "rational action to actualize the existing social order, reforming it by correcting (as far as we are able) its (inevitable) contingent flaws and bringing it as fully as possible into harmony with its rational idea."[4] A similar suggestion occurs in the work of the Axel Honneth, whose conception of social change is deeply influenced by Hegel. Honneth speaks of a "normative surplus of the principles of recognition with respect to their social interpretation" which can be realized by moral-political action.[5] But attractive as such proposals might be, they are incompatible with Hegel's own conception of philosophical understanding and its relation (or lack of relation) to practice, according to which the principles governing a socio-political world—its "rational idea," as Wood puts it—can *only* be comprehended retrospectively, when that world is already in decline and destined for replacement.

Hegel presents the basis for his view, in its most demandingly abstract form, toward the end of the *Logic*, where he discusses the "Idea of the Good" and its relation to the absolute Idea. It will be recalled that, in the final part of the *Logic*, the "Idea" first emerges in the shape of life, that is: the *immediate* unity of being and the concept. In the antithetical moment, life then splits apart into the Idea of the True and the Idea of the Good. In the former, the objectively rational structure of reality is acknowledged—but only in a passive manner. The dimension of active subjectivity integral to actuality is still missing. However, in the complementary Idea of the Good this activity is not fully *self*-realizing—rather it is the drive or striving to transform the world into what the human agent believes it *ought* to be. Hegel detects a fundamental contradiction in this form of consciousness. On the one hand, what appears to be of paramount importance is commitment to a subjective conception of the good that is yet to be realized. On the other hand, the very struggle to *realize* this conception indicates that what is of supreme importance is not the willing of the good, but the rationality embodied in objective existence. This inconsistency, Hegel contends, is only resolved when we grasp that the good has *always already* been realized in the world process. Thus, he writes in the *Zusatz* to §234 of the *Encyclopaedia Logic*:

> But we must not, then, come to a stop with this finitude [of the striving will], of course, and it is through the process of willing itself that this finitude is suspended, together with the contradiction that it contains. The

> reconciliation consists in the fact that the will returns, in its result, to the presupposition of knowing, and thus consists in the unity of the theoretical and practical Idea. The will knows the purpose as what is its own, and intelligence grasps the world as the concept in its actuality. This is the true standpoint of rational knowing.... Unsatisfied striving vanishes when we recognize that the final purpose of the world is just as much accomplished as it is eternally accomplishing itself. (Enc.1: §234/W20, 8: 387)

It is important to note Hegel's claim that it is the "process of willing" itself which overcomes the contradiction. As he states a little later in the same passage, "the agreement of being and the ought" (*Sein und Sollen*) is not something "rigid and devoid of process" (*erstarrt und prozesslos*). If the will accomplishes the unity of the theoretical and practical Idea as its result, this is because, for Hegel, in the very that fact that human beings constantly strive to *realize* the good, the good is already realized. As he puts it in the *Science of Logic*, "this activity is in truth just as much the positing of the *implicit* [*an sich seiend*] identity of the objective concept and immediate actuality" (SL: 733/W20, 6: 547).

Hegel's statement that "one cannot come to a stop with this finitude of the will" (*bei dieser Endlichkeit des Willens ist nicht stehenzubleiben*) is revealing. From the standpoint of the finite agent, the good always remains something to be realized, and Hegel reinforces this point, when he states, in the remark to §212 of the *Encyclopaedia Logic* that, "In the finite we cannot experience or see that the goal has truly been attained" (*Im Endlichen können wir es nicht erleben oder sehen, daß der Zweck wahrhaft erreicht ist*). The problem is that this statement opens a gap between the standpoint of the finite acting individual and the standpoint of the speculative philosopher, for whom the "identity of the objective concept and immediate actuality" has become *explicit*. But not only this. What is remarkable about the content of this remark is the admission that the speculative standpoint of the *Logic* is *demotivating*, since it dissipates the notion that the good is something not yet realized, which we must strive to bring into existence. As Hegel puts it:

> The carrying out of the infinite purpose consists simply in suspending the illusion that it has not yet been carried out. The good, the absolutely good, is eternally accomplishing itself in the world, and the result is that it is already accomplished in and for itself, and does not need first to wait for us. This is the illusion in which we live, and it is this alone which activates

us, and on which our interest in the world is based. The Idea in its process produces this illusion for itself, posits another over against itself, and its activity consists in suspending this illusion. Only out of this error does truth emerge, and it is in this that reconciliation with error and finitude lies. (Enc.1: §212/W20, 8: 367)

The final words of this passage make clear that Hegel aims to defuse any awkwardness produced by the suggestion that the motivation of our activity as finite individuals depends on an "illusion" (*Täuschung*—also translatable as "deception"), by assimilating the overcoming of this illusion to the process, familiar throughout his system, in which a mode of thinking or shape of consciousness is superseded by a higher and more adequate form. Usually, such processes can be described in terms of a transition from a state of being "in-itself" to one of being "for-itself," or—in the experiential language of the *Phenomenology of Spirit*—from "certainty" to "truth." In such transitions a mistaken perspective is overcome, when the inner structure of the object is revealed as a reified version of the implicit relation between subject *and* object, thereby shifting the standpoint of the subject to a new meta-level.

However, the "illusion" which, in the passage just quoted, Hegel describes as generated by "the Idea in its process" does not fit into this model. This is because the conviction of the finite, practical agent that the "good" is something for whose realization one must strive is not disclosed as the objectification of a subject-object structure. Rather, this conviction is annulled altogether. As Hegel puts it, the *absolute* good has always already been realized, and "does not need to wait for us." This gap in Hegel's dialectic is indicated by the fact that the subject of the illusion switches from "we" (presumably: we finite human beings) to the Idea, which is said to produce the illusion "for itself" (*macht sich selbst jene Täuschung*) by positing the other which is suspended. But, of course, there can be no "illusion" for the Idea—the embodiment of the absolute view—when what is at issue is simply its own overall process: it "knows" from the outset that apparent otherness has always already been overcome. Hence the inconspicuous shift of subject serves to conceal the fact that it is the entire practical standpoint, and not just misleading objectifications generated from within it, which is cancelled by the transition to the level of the absolute Idea.

A comparable section of the *Science of Logic* states, as noted earlier, that "what still *limits* the objective concept is its own *view* of itself, which vanishes through reflection on what its actualization is *in itself*; through this view it is only standing in its own way, and thus needs to turn, not against an outer actuality, but against itself" (SL: 733/W20, 6: 547). To reinforce the point: in other cases of dialectical transition, the Hegelian philosopher can continue operating with categories belonging to a lower level, while being aware of their restricted validity. For example, she can continue thinking—for everyday purposes—in terms of cause and effect, or of essence and appearance, while being aware that our ultimate conception of the world cannot be couched in these terms. But this is not the case with the practical illusion concerning the still-to-be-realized status of the good. This illusion is comprehensive. As Hegel says, we "live" in it. The basic purpose of constructing a system, in the work of the German Idealists, is to integrate the divergent ways in which human beings experience themselves and their world—ways which often seem incommensurable, if not downright incompatible—into a coherent overall conception of reality. It seems clear, however, that Hegel is unable to accommodate our future-oriented practical perspective within his system. In short, to reduce this perspective to a "moment" is to eliminate it entirely. Understanding this point is one way of grasping the motivation for the distinctive dualism of Schelling's late system.[6]

Hegel's Theory of the Will

Hegel's own awareness of the depth of the problem raised by the concept of autonomy emerges clearly from the transcript of his 1824/25 lectures on the philosophy of right. He points out that there are:

> two moments which belong to the will as such. The first is the negation of all that is particular, the second the negation of all indeterminacy; the first is the transition to indeterminacy, the second the transition to particularity; the first [is] to free myself from all determination, the second [is] to posit all determination. Every human being will find these two determinations in his self-consciousness: this is freedom. The human being appears now as a being full of contradictions; he is contradiction itself and only through this [contradiction] comes to consciousness. It is the power of spirit which can endure this contradiction within itself; no other natural being can exist with it. Spirit, however, is not merely the existence of this contradiction, but is just as much its resolution, and this is the concept of the will.[7]

As the conclusion of this quotation makes clear, while he is conscious of the extreme difficulty, Hegel is also convinced that his theory of the will overcomes it. As he states in the published version of the *Philosophy of Right*:

> The will is the unity of both these moments—*particularity* reflected into itself and thereby restored to *universality*. It is *individuality* [*Einzelheit*], the *self-determination* of the "I," in that it posits itself as the negative of itself, that is, as *determinate* and *limited*, and at the same time remains with itself [*bei sich*], that is, in its *identity with itself* and universality; and in this determination, it joins together with itself alone.—I determines itself in so far as it is the self-relation of negativity. As this *relation to itself*, it is likewise indifferent to this determinacy; it knows the latter as its own and as *ideal*, as its mere *possibility* by which it is not restricted, but in which it finds itself only because it posits itself in it. (EPR: §7/W20, 7: 54)

Clearly, Hegel is aiming for a synthesis: "freedom thus consists neither in indeterminacy nor in determinacy, rather it is both" (EPR: §7, *Zusatz*/W20, 6: 57). But is a synthesis possible here? Is the process of negation between determinacy and indeterminacy fully reciprocal, or is it rather asymmetric? Although a freedom which was never realized in *any* specific actions would clearly be nugatory, freedom does not have to be actualized in *any particular action* or set of actions. This is implied by Hegel's own description of determinacy as a "mere *possibility* by which the [the I] is not restricted." In other words, while the capacity for reflection negates or suspends particular determinations *as necessities* by transforming them into *possibilities*, determinations of the will do not negate or suspend reflection *as a permanent possibility* by transforming it into a process with a *necessary outcome*. Rather, the possibility of further reflection always remains. Hegel in effect concedes this when he points out that the subject, in its self-relatedness, does not specifically negate, but is "indifferent" toward its determinations; this indifference does not apply the other way around because socially institutionalized determinations of agency cannot be indifferent to the fashion in which subjects choose to behave, given that this may be in a manner that brings about institutional collapse. It seems, then, that Hegel cannot hold determinacy and indeterminacy together in a coherent structure—which is equivalent to saying that he is defeated by the paradox of autonomy.

We find this defeat illustrated concretely at the point in the "Introduction" to the lectures on the philosophy of history where Hegel confronts the following problem: "The will of the individual is free if he can determine his volitions absolutely, abstractly, in and for himself. How, then, is it possible for the universal or the rational to determine anything whatsoever in history?" (ILHP: 71/ VPG[H]: 83) In response to this difficulty Hegel reaches for an analogy: that of house-building. The elements employed in producing the materials to construct a house are eventually limited and controlled by the resulting edifice itself:

> The final result is that the air which helped to build the house is shut out by the house itself, as are the torrents of rain and ravages of fire (in so far as the house is fireproof). The stones and beams obey the law of gravity and press downwards making it possible for high walls to be built. Thus the elements are utilised as their respective measures allow, and they act together to create a product that restricts their own activity. (ILPH: 71-2/VPG[H]: 84)

The problem with this analogy, of course, is that elements such as fire and water do not possess free will. Hence the comparison is lame; it is really an *illustration* of Hegel's theory, in which "the Idea... expresses itself through the medium of the human will or of human freedom" (ILPH: 71/VPG[H], 83), rather than providing any philosophical support for it. It does not render any less problematic Hegel's statement that:

> In individual instances, men pursue their particular ends in defiance of universal justice, and behave as free agents. But this does not destroy the common ground, the underlying substance, the system of right. And the same applies to world order in general. (ILPH: 72/VPG[H]: 84)

In short, facing a problem which Schelling found himself confronting in the final part of the *System of Transcendental Idealism*, one which he concedes to be a "paradox" (ILPH: 71/VPG[H]: 83), Hegel fails to provide a purely conceptual solution demonstrably superior to other strategies—such as Schelling's appeal, in that work, to aesthetic experience, as the lived, but not theoretically comprehended, unity of conscious and unconscious activity.

Schelling's Theory of the Double Structure of Spirit

In chapter 6 we began to examine what could be termed Schelling's theory of the "double structure" of absolute spirit. As we saw, Schelling portrays spirit as determined by the necessary dialectic of the potentialities of being and yet, simultaneously, as *das Überseyende*, as *exceeding* its own necessity. At the time, Schelling may have appeared to be lost in abstruse metaphysical speculations, devoid of concrete or practical relevance. But we are now able to appreciate their bearing on the question of freedom and its historical realization. German Idealism takes seriously the need to build a conception of freedom into the foundations of the systematic enterprise. Freedom cannot be injected at some subsequent point into a system whose construction is already underway because the explanatory integration required by the system leaves no space to introduce the indeterminate moment of freedom. If freedom is the "firm centre point," as Hegel puts it in his paean to Kant, then it must stand at the very beginning. Accordingly, the most fundamental concepts in the systems of both Hegel and the late Schelling must articulate their basal view of freedom, which is then specifically actualized in human existence. We can see this quite clearly in the case of Hegel. In his lectures on the philosophy of religion, Hegel defines God or spirit (*Geist*) as "immediately self-relating negativity" (*die sich unmittelbar auf sich selbst beziehende Negativität*) (LPR3: 83/VPR3: 21). As Dieter Henrich has persuasively argued, it is in this looping back on itself of pure negativity that Hegel's foundational philosophical move (his "*Grundoperation*") consists.[8] Self-relating negativity negates itself, resulting in the positive and determinate. But because the positive has the status of a *result*, its positivity turns out to be what might be termed a "pseudo-positivity," which negates itself in turn (in religious terms the world is "created"—it is "free and independent," yet is "ideal," does not possess "genuine actuality" [LPR3: 292–293/VPR3: 217]). To put this in another way: "self-relating negativity" splits into two moments— negated negation and negating negation—which constitute the relation between the positive and the negative, or between determinacy and indeterminacy. As we have just observed, this process is replicated exactly in Hegel's theory of the human will. From his standpoint, human beings are not free because they enjoy some libertarian exemption from the rational necessity of the world-process. Rather they are free when the structure of their agency becomes a microcosmic version of that process. This is why Hegel states that the will which is "free for itself" is "the Idea in its truth" (EPR: §21/W20, 7: 72).

Like Hegel, Schelling employs the term "spirit" as an ultimate category. But clearly, his theory of spirit—and of the freedom of spirit—differs fundamentally from that of Hegel. In Hegel's philosophy it is of course possible for human beings to act in ways which are not congruent with reason. But such actions will simply fall prey to an arbitrariness which contradicts the intrinsic rationality of the will. In Hegel, the duality of the rational and the contingent is exhaustive. "The sole aim of philosophical enquiry is to **eliminate the contingent**" and—in the historiographical field—to disclose history as "the image and enactment of reason", a "copy of the archetype" (*Abbild des Urbildes*) in a particular element, in the nations. (ILPH: 28/VPG[H]: 29, 30). By contrast, late Schelling's theory of history centers on the notion of a striving for "liberation" (*Befreiung*). It narrates a series of emancipatory breaks from existing forms of determination—where "determination" does not imply simply particularization, but also a mode of compulsion, which nonetheless remains a genuine stage in the advance of reason. In other words, between the logically necessary and the contingent Schelling introduces a distinct concept of freedom. In his account, freedom is realized in the emancipatory impulse which strives to transcend a form of rationality become coercive. Rather than attempting to "solve" the paradox of autonomy Schelling builds the paradox into his basic conception of the historical process.

In accord with the principle enunciated above, Schelling must—of course—also integrate his conception of freedom into the foundations of his system. And here he faces the problem of explaining how rational determination and the element of indeterminacy or openness in choice can be in *conflict* with one another, without endorsing a metaphysically problematic dualism. But this is precisely what the theory of potentialities seeks to achieve. Schelling generates the dialectic of the potentialities, which constitute the "organism of objectively posited reason," *immanently* from the *potentia potentiae* (the potentiality for potentiality), or "decompressed" un-pre-thinkable being. But, at the same time, the structure of modalities of being generated from the un-pre-thinkable provides it with the platform for "existing out beyond" itself, for becoming *das Hinausexistierende* (PO41/42: 171). The result is a structure in which freedom transcends even its own necessary self-determination *as* freedom. As Schelling puts it:

> Absolute spirit goes beyond all forms. It is the spirit which is free from its own being-spirit—for it, being-spirit is only a form of being . . . Thus perfected spirit would not be perfected, if it were only the third figure [i.e., the third potentiality]. Perfected spirit is beyond all modes of being; it is in this that its absolute transcendence consists. (UPO: 78–79)

For Schelling, then, freedom in the ultimate sense must include the capacity to take a distance from oneself, from one's own—nonetheless rational—nature. And it is this freedom to which human beings aspire, and of which they long for the world to be the "moving image," to borrow from Plato. Further, it is here that we find the wellspring of the religious dimension of existence:

> This freedom from oneself first gives [to spirit] the extravagant freedom which, one might say, so fills up and extends all the vessels of our thinking and knowing, that we feel that we have reached the highest—we feel that we have reached that above which nothing higher can be. *Freedom* is our highest and the highest of divinity. This is what we want as the ultimate cause of all things. (UPO: 78–79)

Evidently, one casualty of this conception is the ontological argument, which is still endorsed by Hegel in his own distinctive version:

> If there is a rational or freely posited being, it must be this spirit. But this formulation makes it clear that we have not conceptualized spirit as absolute necessity, but hypothetically . . . Reason is there only because this spirit exists, and spirit does not exist so that there should be rational being. (UPO: 69)

We can also understand Schelling's definition of spirit, and the contrast between his conception and that of Hegel, in terms of a key element in the theory of freedom. For thinkers inclined toward incompatibilism, freedom is to be understood as what Helen Steward has termed a "*two-way* power." As she writes:

> Actions (including decisions) must be things . . . whose occurrence is always non-necessary relative to the totality of their antecedents. What this implies is that they must be exercises of a power that *need not* have been exercised at the moment or in the precise way that it was in fact exercised. The power to act, as many philosophers have remarked, is a *two-way* power: to act or refrain from acting. That is what makes it special. (MF: 155)

This two-way character is essential to Schelling's conception of pure potentiality, and the manner in which it generates the framing dialectic of both the negative and the positive philosophy. Pure potentiality must actualize itself entirely *as* potentiality; but it would not be *potentiality* if it did not *also not* actualize itself—in other words, remain as what Schelling terms "*das rein Seiende*"—pure being-ness (PO41/42: 105). It is this contradiction which sets off the movement of pure thinking, culminating in the concept of spirit, which both *does* and *does not* actualize itself in the dialectic of potentialities. Human beings represent the return of spirit within nature because their existence embodies this same tension. In line with the tradition Steward evokes, for Schelling refrainings or forbearances are genuine actions; and because one can only *deliberately not do* what one genuinely *could have* done, this conception disqualifies determinism. In this domain it is not easy to interpret Hegel's position. At the beginning of the *Philosophy of Right* he presents the capacity to rise above every determination, the negative dimension of freedom, as something which human beings can readily access through introspection: "Anyone can discover in himself an ability to abstract from anything whatsoever, and likewise to determine himself, to posit any content in himself by his own agency" (EPR: §4/W20, 7: 49). However, Hegel also argues that the capacity of the I to posit itself as something determinate is the complementary dimension of freedom, without which negative freedom remains "abstract." The question is whether refraining can be described as positing oneself as something determinate. If refraining is characterized correctly, as "doing not-A" (for example, stopping oneself from eating the plums in the icebox), as opposed to "not doing A," then it appears to consist in positing oneself as *not determinate* in a specific way, rather than as determinate. Hegel, however, in Spinozist fashion, identifies the will and the understanding. As he puts it, we should not imagine that the human being "has thought in one pocket and volition in the other" (EPR: §4/W20, 7: 46). But this means that he is unable to accommodate genuine forbearances, as volition must be distinct from thought, if capable of responding to the content of a thought in a positive *or* a negative manner.

Schelling's Hermeneutics of the History of Human Consciousness

By far the larger part of Schelling's "positive philosophy" consists in a hermeneutics of world mythologies and of Christianity, which interprets the history of human consciousness in the light of his initial "hypothesis" concerning the decompression of blind existing-ness and its consequences. As we found in chapter 6, Schelling argues that consciousness in its primordial form must be "God-positing consciousness" because otherwise it would not be possible to account for the alienated or "ecstatic" character of the mythological world, which in turn is the precondition for the emancipatory breakthrough of revelation. As a result of the *Katastrophe*, subjectivity lost its non-self-centered openness to the world and was plunged into the twilight of mythic compulsion. Here the distinction between subjective and the objective is blurred, and human beings are unable to detach themselves reflectively and critically from their experience—to raise incisively the question of its truth or untruth. In this respect, mythological consciousness is comparable to dream consciousness, in which the dreamer is unable to recognize the dramatization of her own thoughts and feelings, as Schelling himself suggests (see HCI: 144/SW, II/1: 206). After the catastrophe, the split between subject and object generates a "middle world" of lost unity, in the form of an oppressive, all-encompassing nature god. Gradually, however, an impulse germinates to break out of the stabilizing but stifling oneness—toward plurality and differentiation. The profound psychic conflict which ensues during the transition to the neolithic age is eventually resolved by the emergence of a unifying principle which, in ancient Greek mythology, features as Zeus, the ruler of the gods of Olympus.

It is a defining feature of Schelling's thinking, which first emerged during the period of *The Ages of the World*, that even the third, supposedly reconciling principle (A^3 in his shorthand) has an inherent tendency to revive the compulsion of A^1 in a new mode. In effect, it *is* the restoration of A^1, the principle of unity, initially in a more flexible, reconciling form, but ever liable to slide back into coercion. Because of this, the entire structure of mythological consciousness *as such* starts to be experienced as constraining, initiating the process which Schelling finds occurring in the Eleusinian Mysteries. The new reflexive distancing focuses on A^2, the Dionysian, differentiating principle, but also apprehends the unity of the divine obscurely implicit in polytheism, thus anticipating the trinitarian Christian revelation. In Schelling's interpretation, Christ overcomes the conflict of A^1 and A^2 by enacting the total submission of A^2, thereby liberating A^1 to emerge as A^3, and opening the way to a new experience of God *as* self-transcending freedom. In consequence, mythological consciousness begins to decline and disintegrate, and human beings start to acquire a sense of themselves as agents participating in the future-oriented movement history. Continuing the dream metaphor, Schelling writes of:

The final awakening . . . in which [human beings], having attained self-knowledge, commit themselves to this world beyond the divine, overjoyed to have been released from the immediate relation they were unable to maintain, and all the more determined to put a mediating relation, which at the same time leaves them free, in its place. (HCI:144 /SW, II/1: 206)

However, after the coming of Christ, the submission of consciousness to an objectified power begins again. With the establishment of the Catholic Church, revelation congeals into opaque, dogmatic authority, in accord with Schelling's view that emancipatory breakthroughs tend to lapse back into forms of repression. Eventually this new constraint provokes the response of the Reformation—a liberation of subjectivity, of pure faith and religious insight from heteronomous constraint. In Schelling's narrative the Reformation has two fundamental consequences. From the perspective of philosophical ecclesiology, it points forward to a church of the future, which he associates with the theology of St John the Evangelist—a church which could reconcile ecumenical unity with the free, personal dimension of faith. However, the Reformation's liberation of subjectivity also prepares the ground for radical a new departure in philosophy: by handing ultimate authority to the reflecting self, Descartes launches the secularizing, emancipatory drive of modern thought. Yet, in accord with Schelling's fundamental schema, this development is *also* vulnerable to a lapse into objectification, a process whose supreme expression is found in Spinoza's monistic ontology of substance. Schelling does not deny the grandeur of Spinoza's thought or its enduring significance as the model for a certain shape of human consciousness, any more than he denies the astral splendor of the god of pre-mythological monotheism: Spinoza "counts among the great phenomena of the world" (SdW: 29). However, comprehensive rationalism, of which Leibniz's philosophy offers a variation, inevitably produces an empiricist backlash, in which the standpoint of the experiencing subject and the pluralism—and resistance to rationalization—of the experienced world are defended. Finally, in Kant and in post-Kantian idealism, a strenuous attempt is made to ground the *objective* world in the *basic structure of subjectivity itself.* Schelling credits Fichte with being the first to attempt to develop such an account in a purely *a priori* manner. In this sense, Fichte is to be honored as the inventor of what Schelling terms "pure rational science" (*reine Vernunftwissenschaft*), which arises from the realization that the essence of substance itself is "I-hood" (see SdW: 45). A schema of Schelling's history of consciousness, which culminates

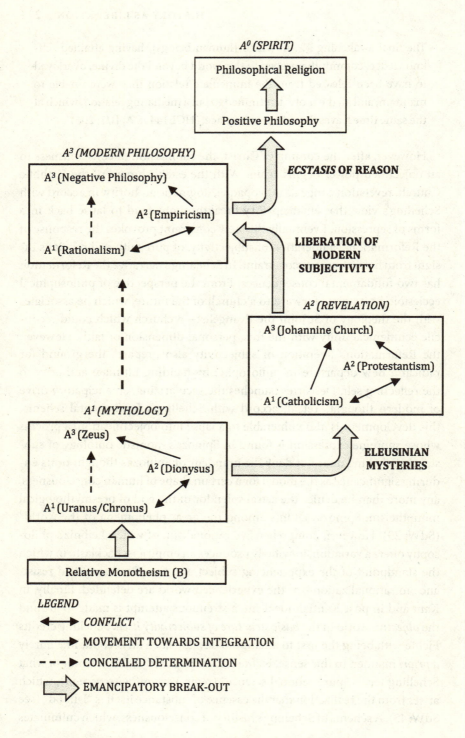

Figure 3 Schelling's Theory of the History of Consciousness

in the process through which this history itself comes to consciousness, is presented in Figure 3.

The diagram may help to throw light on certain ambiguities which repeatedly cause confusion in debates over the interpretation of Schelling's late philosophy. In a sense, all these controversies revolve around the role which Schelling allots to Christianity—the obscurity of which is on full display in Schelling's very first lecture in Berlin. Here he acknowledges the "great longing" of the time for a new beginning and registers an undeniable sense that the old order cannot be restored as it was. But he also insists that the impending transformation does not require the abandonment of Christianity. He then asks:

> *Have you, then, already got to know Christianity? How would it be, if a philosophy for the first time opened up its depths?* Christianity cannot be anything *set beside* something else. This other, such as philosophy for example, has attained far too wide a compass for Christianity to subsist *beside* it. *Christianity can only continue in existence by dint of being everything.* (PO41/42: 97)

This is hardly a strong defense of Christianity. Firstly, Schelling admits that pressure on the Christian faith has been mounting because of the increasing scope of philosophy, behind which lies the momentum of the modern secular world (the "other"—presumably—which Christianity cannot simply stand alongside). And, secondly, he suggests that Christianity will reveal its full depth and significance only through a philosophical interpretation of it. Finally, to propose that Christianity can only survive by becoming "everything" is, in effect, to say that it can—paradoxically—only endure by losing its distinct identity *as* Christianity. A few lines later Schelling confirms the direction of his argument when he stresses that the "philosophy of revelation"—the notional topic of the lecture course, which in fact surveys his late system as a whole—does not depend on the "authority of revelation" (PO41/42: 98). A similar ambiguity appears at the end of the same series of lectures, where Schelling lays out his interpretation of the history of the Christian Church, which he divides into three phases, Petrine, Pauline, and Johannine. The church of St Peter is the Catholic Church, which secures the foundation and the institutional continuity of Christianity but only at the cost of imposing a "blind unity" (PO41/42: 322) on its members. The church of St Paul is the church of the Reformation, which brings liberation from this coercive unity, promoting a "free and mobile life" to such an extent that it can even tolerate the loss of the appellation "church" (PO41/42: 321). Schelling emphasizes, however, that Protestantism is only a "transitional" form. Like all avatars of A^2, it has a destructive as well as an emancipatory aspect. A vital question, then, concerns what is supposed to emerge in this case as the principle of integration of A^1 and A^2.

The dilemma Schelling faces here stems once again from his deep awareness of the tendency for the moment of reconciliation to congeal into a new form of oppression disguised as an integrating unity—a unity which then requires breaking apart in turn. We observed this occurring in the case of mythological consciousness, where the supreme deity (in Greek mythology, Zeus) consolidates the power of the mythological system as a whole, calling forth the religious response of the Eleusinian Mysteries, with their opening toward the forbidden dimension of the future—ἔλευσις (*eleusis*) means "coming," "arrival." However, we now perceive this danger emerging again, in Schelling's own argument that the institutional rigidity of Catholicism and the inner principle of faith animating Protestantism require integration in a third future form of Christianity, which Schelling associates with St John, and hence with a theology of the word, of the *Logos*. In his very sketchy envisioning of it, the Johannine Church would bring the "external process" into balance with the "inner process," so that neither is subordinated to the other (UPO: 709). There are least two difficulties with this conception, however. The first is that, once a reflective distance between inner and outer process has opened up in this way, is hard to see how they could ever be fused seamlessly back together again. As we noted in the previous chapter, Schelling sometimes suggests that it is philosophy that must now mediate between inner and outer, and that this process points not toward a new form of Christianity, but rather toward what he calls "philosophical religion," which would comprehend and supersede the historical conflict between revelation and the forms of mythological consciousness. The second difficulty is that the very concept of a "church" ("*ecclesia*" refers etymologically to those who are "called forth" or called away from the world) indicates a certain limitation or exclusivity, as Schelling himself emphasizes (PO41/42: 321). He finds himself struggling with this implication of the term church, when he states:

> My standpoint is Christianity in the totality of its historical developments; my goal, to build up that first truly universal church (if church is still

the right word here) simply in the spirit, and *only in a complete fusion of Christianity with universal science and knowledge*. (PO41/42: 320–321)

It is not difficult to see that, once again, this "goal" points beyond Christianity in any recognizable form.

These problems with Schelling's conception of the future of religion stem from the double role that the Reformation plays in his historical schema. On the one hand, it is the turning point *within* the history of Christianity, but one whose concentration on the "inner process" demands its own corrective, a counterbalancing tradition of doctrine, festival, and ritual in a future church which Schelling refers to as the Johannine Church. On the other hand, the Reformation is also the *turning point within the turning point*—the A^2 of A^2. Its emancipation of subjectivity opens the way for the autonomous development of philosophical reason, beginning with Descartes. It is at this point that Schelling develops his distinctive critique of metaphysics. Revelation, after breaking the power of mythology, develops, in Catholicism, into what could be called a re-mythologized form of consciousness, but— in accordance with this same dynamic—modern reason follows a similar course. Post-Cartesian emancipated reason, which Schelling refers to as "natural reason" (e.g., DRP, SW, II/1: 260), initiates a further repetition of the dialectical process, which tends toward unfreedom. The identity of thought and being, understood by Fichte in a transcendental mode, and perfected in Hegel's absolute idealism, results in a rationalism that perpetuates what is, at its root, the compulsion of blind being-ness. And Schelling has no doubt that these philosophical systems reflect a general reification of modern consciousness. As he writes:

> Our inner life obeys the general principles which determine us in our judgments, for example the law of cause and effect, in almost the same way as a body obeys the law of gravity, and we judge in accordance with it not because we wish to, or as a result of genuine insight, but because we cannot do otherwise. In just the same way the laws of logical inference exercise a completely blind power over us, before and without us being aware of them. (DRP, SW, II/1: 263–264)

Thus, the Reformation functions, in Schelling's positive philosophy, *both* as an emancipation *within the sphere of revelation* from a revelation become oppressive dogma, *and* as the basis for a development that transcends revelation entirely and initiates a new sphere, but which also leads from liberated subjectivity to the dominance of "natural reason." It was easy, then, for the difference to become blurred in his own mind between a *religious* corrective for the anomic "private Christianity" (*Privatchristentum*) (UPO: 709) whose possibility was opened up by the Reformation, namely his imagined Johannine Church, and an overcoming of the reification, and suppression of historical consciousness, induced by the secular or natural reason which the Reformation also originally set loose. At times, however, Schelling does spell out the implication of his overall schema: namely, that societies shaped by Christianity have now passed beyond the sphere of revelation, and that the second, more advanced goal can only be achieved in the form of a positive philosophy—through an anamnetic disclosure of human history as a dialectic of constraint and liberation, ultimately driven by a deep ontological impulse toward a future of universal emancipation.

Hegel, Schelling, and the Question of Religious Pluralism

From Schelling's standpoint, we can perceive the coercive fusion of logic and being characteristic of natural reason in Hegel's theory of the state. The Hegelian formula of the "concrete universal" offers a false solution to the paradox of autonomy, by absorbing the transcending moment of potentiality, of the power to be or not to be. Schelling, of course, cannot compete as a socio-political thinker with Hegel, whose work offers so many penetrating insights into the problems of modern society and politics. What Schelling does achieve, however, is the holding open of a dimension of universality which Hegel closes off. He looks beyond the limits of the state, which—unlike Hegel—he is far from inclined to exalt. Already in the *Stuttgart Private Seminars*, delivered a year after the publication of the *Freiheitsschrift*, he declared:

> We all know of efforts that have been made, especially since the advent of the French revolution and the Kantian concepts, to demonstrate how unity could possibly be reconciled with the existence of free beings; that is, the possibility of a state that would, properly speaking, be the condition for the highest possible freedom of individuals. Quite simply, such a state is an impossibility.[9]

Hegel's socio-political answer to the paradox of autonomy, then, is unviable in Schelling's view. The *Philosophy of Right* concludes with the acceptance of a "state of nature" which is not projected back to the founding moment of the individual state, as in social contract theory, but rather seen as the inevitable condition of relations between sovereign states, to whom Hegel reserves the right to tear up treaties (for Hegel, *pacta* non *sunt servanda*) and to declare war in circumstances of their choosing. In §550 of the 1830 *Encyclopaedia*, one of his last published writings, Hegel gives carte blanche to the polity embodying the currently highest stage of *Geist* to behave as it sees fit on the international stage. He is an unabashed theorist of unipolarity: "Against this absolute will, the will of the other particular spirits of peoples is without rights, that people is the one who rules the world" (Enc.3: §550/W20, 10: 352–353). By contrast, Schelling looks forward to a universal human solidarity, which might at least mitigate the power of the individual sovereign state, which he regards as a necessary evil. Such solidarity could not be motivated simply by the abstract universalism of practical reason, however. In Schelling's thought, as in Hegel's, religion functions in a quasi-Durkheimian manner, as the supreme expression of the implicit worldview shaping a specific socio-cultural form of life. In fact, Schelling quite explicitly rejects any pseudo-biological explanation of ethnicity, stating, in the context of his theory of mythology, that "the communality of consciousness makes the people" (*die Gemeinschaft des Bewußtseyns macht das Volk*) (PM Chováts: 126). Our ethical impulses, in Schelling's view, are nourished, no matter how remotely, by such religiously shaped consciousness. Of course, he differs from Hegel in not being resigned to the self-enclosed character of the cultures of nation states, presumed simply to succeed each other in historical dominance. But he then faces the question, which Hegel does not address, of how a plurality of religiously shaped cultures and worldviews can be brought into dialogue.

This is not to deny, however, that the thought of *both* Hegel and Schelling contains resources relevant to the issues raised by the variety of world religions. Since the second half of the twentieth century, in fact, questions of religious pluralism and the possibility of inter-faith dialogue have advanced to a prominent position on the philosophical and theological agenda, reflecting the phenomena of mass migration, the rise of multi-cultural societies, and the vertiginous expansion of global markets and communications.[10] From our current vantage point, in the midst of this ferment, the philosophies of religion of Schelling and Hegel appear, in different ways, as strikingly prescient, but also as remarkably double-sided. Both thinkers have a strong and—it must be admitted—unconscionably Eurocentric commitment to the superiority of Christianity over other world religions. For Hegel, Christianity is the "revealed" or "consummate" religion, in the sense that it discloses in representational form the ultimate truth implied by the phenomenon of religion as such. For Schelling, it is the religion which definitively breaks the grip of mythological consciousness and releases human beings from cyclical, mythical temporality into a genuinely historical and future-oriented world. But, at the same time, both philosophers were deeply engaged with the explosion of knowledge concerning non-European religions and cultures which occurred in the early nineteenth century, and both interpret other religions as profound and genuine—if incomplete or one-sided—repositories of truth. In terms of the current standard classification of basic positions in the theology of religion, neither thinker could be characterized as a Christian "exclusivist." But neither are their views completely relativistic, in the manner categorized as "pluralist." Rather, they are "inclusivists," who treat pre-Christian and non-Christian religious traditions as partial disclosures of the truth which is fully revealed in Christianity.[11]

At the same time, Hegel quite clearly seeks to establish Christianity as the religious correlate of his own unsurpassable metaphysics, and to present it in effect as the required existential foundation of the modern constitutional state: Religion is "the representation of the spirit of the state in absolute universality;" it should be seen as "necessarily inseparable from the political constitution, from secular government and from secular life" (ILPH: 107, 109/VPG[H]: 127, 130). This whole conception cannot help but appear anachronistic in the contemporary context, and it is arguable that Schelling's philosophy of religion offers more points of connection with the current philosophical and theological discussions concerning the pluralism of world religions, inter-religious dialogue, and the nature of religious truth. After all, he is quite clear that the stabilizing relation between religion and political authority envisaged by Hegel is no longer possible in the more fluid, free-thinking modern world. As he puts it:

> Out of fear of destroying a comfortable situation, we avoid getting to the bottom of things, or saying out loud that the moral and spiritual powers by which the world was held together, even if only through force of habit, have long since been undermined by the advance of scientific knowledge. (PO, SW, II/3: 9)

Furthermore, as we have seen, in his late work Schelling envisages the supersession of Christianity in the direction of what he terms "philosophical religion." Because philosophical religion is portrayed, quite explicitly, as involving a retrieval of the complexity and richness of the religious history of humankind, a task for which Schelling's global survey of mythologies can be seen as paving the way, it is not implausible to regard this notion as an encouragement to inter-religious dialogue. Such dialogue can draw sustenance from a recognition, absent in Hegel, that other major world religions—no less than Christianity—are also the result of an axial turn, a transcendence of the cultural provinciality of mythological consciousness toward one or another form of ethical universalism.

As we saw at the end of chapter 3, Schelling himself pioneered the notion that such breakthroughs occurred in close chronological proximity on a global scale, during the first millennium BCE. In this respect there is much to build on in his thinking, even though Occidental chauvinism allowed him to identify a fully completed axial turn only in the case of the Christian revelation. However, the pursuit of dialogue also presupposes the ability of each religion gradually to achieve a reflexively "broken" relation to its own history and traditions, without abandoning commitment to them. Such a process, many forms of which are underway despite the high global visibility of various fundamentalisms, can be seen as a further application of the universalism of the axial turn to the religious traditions within which differing versions of ethical universalism were first incubated.[12] Viewed in this context, Schelling's concept of "philosophical religion," which gestures toward a utopian end point of the process, can also be regarded as the forward-looking practical correlate of the history of consciousness schematized in his positive philosophy. There is one *a priori* element in Schelling's theory of this history, namely blind existing-ness itself. But otherwise, the theory is abductive: as we discovered in chapter 6, the positive philosophy rests on a "hypothesis", one that may be viewed as resulting from an inference to the best explanation. Schelling therefore describes the hybrid method of his positive philosophy as "metaphysical empiricism" (PO41/42: 145). This implies that the account of history is intrinsically open to revision; new considerations–not least, the future course of events–may require modification of the hypothesis. Hence we can say that philosophical religion is the point at which consciousness, in a final break-out, transcends the primarily passive stance of provisional, retrospective reconstruction and becomes a confidence or faith in the meaning of history sufficient to motivate action.

Notes

1. For an informative discussion of these problems with Hegel's political theory, see Rolf-Peter Horstmann, "How Modern is the Hegelian State?," in *Hegel's Elements of the Philosophy of Right. A Critical Guide*, ed. David James (Cambridge: CUP, 2017).
2. For this point, and a penetrating assessment of Hegel's philosophy of history as a whole, see Emil Angehrn, "Vernunft in der Geschichte? Zum Problem der Hegelschen Geschichtsphilosophie," *Zeitschrift für philosophische Forschung* 35, no. 3/4 (1981).
3. See Christoph Menke, *Autonomie und Befreiung: Studien zu Hegel* (Frankfurt am Main: Suhrkamp, 2018), 27.
4. Allen W. Wood, *Hegel's Ethical Thought* (Cambridge: CUP, 1990), 232.
5. See Nancy Fraser and Axel Honneth, *Umverteilung oder Anerkennung? Eine politisch-philosophische Kontroverse* (Frankfurt: Suhrkamp, 2003), 220 and 159–224 *passim*.
6. In his *Studies in the Hegelian Dialectic*, McTaggart makes a similar critical point, also with reference to the passage on "*Täuschung*" in the *Encyclopaedia Logic*: ". . . if the universe appears to us to be only imperfectly rational, we must be either right or wrong. If we are right, the world is not perfectly rational. But if we are wrong, then it is difficult to see how *we* can be perfectly rational. And we are part of the world. Thus it would seem that the very opinion that the world is imperfect must, in some way or other, prove its own truth." John McTaggart, *Studies in the Hegelian Dialectic* (Cambridge: University Press, 1922), 172–173. See also McTaggart, *A Commentary on Hegel's Logic* (Cambridge: University Press, 1910), 302n.
7. Hegel, "Philosophie des Rechts 1824/25, nach der Vorlesungsnachschrift K. G. V. Griesheims," in *Vorlesungen über die Philosophie des Rechts 1818–1831*, vol. 4 (Stuttgart-Bad Canstatt: frommann-holzboog, 1974), 118.
8. See Dieter Henrich, "Hegels Logik der Reflexion," in *Hegel im Kontext* (Frankfurt: Suhrkamp, 1971).
9. Schelling, "Stuttgart Seminars," in *Idealism and the Endgame of Theory*, trans. and ed. Thomas Pfau (Albany, NY: SUNY Press, 1994), 227 (*Stuttgarter Privatvorlesungen*, SW, I/7: 462).
10. See, for example, Christian Danz and Friedrich Hermanni, eds, *Wahrheitsansprüche der Weltreligionen. Konturen gegenwärtiger Religionstheologie* (Göttingen: Vandenhoeck and Ruprecht, 2006).
11. For further discussion of these distinctions, see Gavin D'Costa, "Theology of Religions," in *The Modern Theologians*, ed. David F. Ford and Rachel Muers (Oxford: Blackwell, 2005); also Andrés Torres Queiruga, *Diálogo de las religiones y autocomprensión cristiana* (Santander: Sal Terrae, 2005), 9–29. The footnotes to Queiruga's work provide comprehensive documentation of the theological debate around inter-religious dialogue in several European languages.
12. A model of what may be achieved in this respect is the 1948 Universal Declaration of Human Rights, which was painstakingly forged out of debate and discussion between representatives of different world religions, as well as secular politicians, lawyers, and thinkers. For details see Hans Joas, *Die Sacralität der Person. Eine neue Genealogie der Menschenrechte* (Frankfurt: Suhrkamp, 2015), ch. 6. See also Joas, *Sind die Menschenrechte westlich?* (Munich: Kösel Verlag, 2015), ch. 5.

Conclusion
Schelling's Affirmative Genealogy

Reason, Freedom and the Ethic of Suspicion

It is characteristic of the history of philosophy that a new discovery or insight can rapidly lead to polarization—to a conflict of extremes which subsequent thinkers feel obliged to attenuate through a search for mediating elements. Such was certainly the course of philosophy in the wake of Kant's first *Critique*. One basic feature of the *Critique of Pure Reason* which provoked much consternation amongst Kant's immediate successors was the tension between the foundational role of self-consciousness in forging our experience of a unified objective world, and the recognition that our attempts to conceptualize such self-consciousness result in a fathomless circularity—that, as Dieter Henrich has put it, "'I' can never step out of the role of being a prefix."[1] In broad terms, Kant's successors can be said to have responded to this difficulty by transforming the circularity into a positive advantage. As Fichte stated in his early "*Aenesidemus* Review," "The Critical Philosophy . . . points out to us that circle from which we cannot escape. Within this circle, on the other hand, it furnishes us with the greatest coherence in all of our knowledge."[2]

Two aspects of this general response were of paramount importance for what followed. Firstly, there was the claim, pioneered by Reinhold in his *Versuch einer neuen Theorie des menschlichen Vorstellungsvermögens*, that the self's awareness of itself expresses the basic, all-embracing structure of reason. Self-consciousness, Reinhold argued, is not awareness of a special object, one which coincides with the subject of consciousness, but rather awareness of an activity, of the very activity in which conscious experience itself consists. Self-consciousness therefore, regarded as what Reinhold terms the "absolute subject," embodies and completes the quest of reason for the unconditioned—a quest which for Kant could not reach a theoretical conclusion.[3] Secondly, there was Fichte's insistence that self-consciousness simply cannot be understood in terms of the kinds of explanation which are valid for the whole domain of nature, but belongs to a qualitatively different dimension: "Intellect and thing are thus exact opposites: they inhabit two worlds between which there is no bridge" (IWL1: 17/GA, I/4, 196).

These developments also indicate how the post-Kantians sought to remedy what they considered another deeply flawed aspect of Kant's philosophy: the split between theoretical and practical reason. Radical self-determination becomes, for them, the essence of both forms of reason. For Fichte, this entails that there can be no compromise between a thoroughgoing transcendental philosophy—or "idealism," as he terms it—and "dogmatism": the basing of philosophy on a principle supposedly external to the experiencing self. In his view, any concession to what we would now call "naturalism" must annihilate freedom as rational autonomy (e.g., IWL1: 13–15 GA, I/4, 192–193). Of course, while the younger German Idealists were as convinced as Fichte of the unique character of self-consciousness, and also took for granted that the "self-reverting activity" of consciousness defines the essential structure of reason-as-freedom, they were hostile to the Fichtean dualism of intellect and thing—of "I" and "not-I"—which wrenched human beings out of their embeddedness in nature. It is against this background that Hegel concluded that only an ambitious philosophical project which showed reason, the relation of pure self-grounding whose paradigm is self-consciousness, to be the inner scaffolding of both the subjective *and* the objective world, and indeed as systematically uniting them, could conserve the central, irreversible emphasis on freedom of the post-1789 world, while also acknowledging the legitimate force of what Fichte had dismissed as "dogmatism." His work stands, of course, as the supreme example of such an attempt at all-embracing vindication of reason. As Hegel states in the 1830 "Introduction" to the *Lectures on the Philosophy of World History*, reason is:

> infinite *power*, for reason is sufficiently powerful to be able to create something more than just an ideal . . . and it is the infinite *content*, the essence and truth of everything, itself constituting the material on which it operates through its own activity. (ILWH: 27/VPG[H]: 28)

For philosophers today one problem with such a comprehensive rationalism is its seeming incompatibility with another vital strand in the outlook of modernity, one which can be traced back to the Hegelian aftermath. This current enjoins epistemological wariness—the need to be on the lookout for, and to uncover, hidden determinants of human thought and action, of the kind whose very possibility Fichte's early work had sought to exorcize. In a well-known passage, Paul Ricoeur coined the phrase "masters of suspicions" to refer to the founders of the three most influential intellectual traditions exemplifying this approach—Marx, Nietzsche, and Freud. For these authors, the forces shaping human thinking and experience foster misperception and illusion; they make the form of consciousness itself into a shackle that holds human subjects in a condition of unfreedom. As Ricoeur wrote:

> If we go back to the intention they had in common, we find it in the decision to look upon the whole of consciousness primarily as "false" consciousness. They thereby take up again, each in a different manner, the problem of Cartesian doubt, in order to carry it to the very heart of the Cartesian stronghold.[4]

Defenders of Hegel are often inclined to present his philosophy as so comprehensive as to incorporate even what is valid in the viewpoint of the masters of suspicion. After all, the *Phenomenology of Spirit* portrays successive "shapes of consciousness" as far from lucid concerning themselves. Their internal structural conflicts, and the logic of the transitions between them, can be traced retrospectively by the philosopher, but they operate "behind the back" of the human subjects whose forms of experience are in question. Hegel, so the claim would go, is far from being a paladin of transparency. In the Hegelian view, however, a shape of consciousness cannot systematically *block* progress to a new, freer, and more comprehensive level of awareness by exerting a restricting force or retrogressive pull, even though it may take time for the inner logic to work itself out. In other words, shapes of consciousness—the evolving forms of the subject-object or subject-subject interrelation—cannot, in Hegel, function in an *oppressive* or *constraining* manner because they always adequately express the stage of self-development and self-knowledge which spirit has attained; consequently, they are exemplified, at the level of individual subjectivity, in a way which is appropriate to that stage. Hegel makes this approach clear in the *Science of Logic*, where he states:

> But if a subject matter, say the state, did not *at all* conform to its idea, that is to say, if it were rather not at all the idea of the state; if its reality, which is that of the self-conscious individuals, did not correspond at all to the concept, its soul and body would have come apart; the soul would have taken refuge in the secluded regions of thought, the body been dispersed into singular

individualities. But because the concept of the state is essential to the nature of these individualities, it is present in them as such a powerful impulse that they are driven to translate it into reality, be it only in the form of external purposiveness, or to put up with it as it is, or else they needs must perish. The worst state, one whose reality corresponds least to the concept, in so far as it continues in existence, is still Idea; the individuals still obey a concept which has power. (SL: 672–673/W20, 6: 465–466)

In this scenario, socialized individuals are only ever obeying the "power" of a concept, which is "essential to [their] nature." Despite appearances, there can be no generation by social structures of forms of consciousness which involve misrepresentation or miscategorization, and which are therefore detrimental to human interests. It is a tribute to Hegel's integrity, however, that he comes close to undermining his own argument. In a capitalist society, for instance, the majority of workers, since they have no independent means of supporting themselves, must "put up with" (*sich gefallen lassen*) selling their labor-power—and, according to Marx, be deprived of its full fruits, submit to exploitation—or else they "needs must perish." This can scarcely be dismissed as posing no challenge to the view that a society based on the private ownership of the means of production is rational. In the light of such examples, it is far from obvious that, as Hegel contends, for a state—the conscious political organization of a human collective—merely to be actual is *de facto* for it to conform to the Idea (that is, embody reason) to a sufficient extent.

Hegel's and Schelling's Definitions of Freedom

The core element of Hegel's thinking which sustains this view is his claim that the ultimate motive force of things is autonomous or self-related negation—the process which Dieter Henrich has identified as Hegel's "basic operation" (*Grundoperation*).[5] This identification has powerful textual support; for example, in the statement that God himself is "infinitely self-relating negativity" (LPR III: 83/VPR III: 21). The *Grundoperation* lies behind Hegel's argument that the world of particular institutions and social practices, which often seems to negate the negativity—in the sense of the openness or indeterminacy—of freedom, turns out to be that very freedom making itself concrete: the positive is the autonomous negation of the negative. It also informs Hegel's well-known core definition of freedom as being at home—or remaining with oneself—in the other: "denn die Freiheit ist eben dies, in seinem Anderen bei sich selbst zu sein" (Enc.1: §24, *Zusatz*/W20, 8: 84). For Hegel, the reality of freedom in this sense is guaranteed once we view the world aright—in terms of the logic of self-relating negation.

There is perhaps no clearer way of highlighting the opposition between Hegel and Schelling than by comparing the Hegelian definition of freedom with Schelling's encapsulation of what it would mean to think spirit as freedom:

> Whatever in being is potentiality, and does not cease to be potentiality, and conversely, whatever is potentiality that can pass over into being without losing any of its power (over being), thus whatever can be and also not be, that is *the completely free* [*Was im Sein Potenz ist und nicht aufhört Potenz zu sein, und umgekehrt, was Potenz ist, die ins Sein übergehen kann, ohne von ihrer Macht (über das Sein) zu verlieren, was also sein und nicht sein kann, das ist* das vollkommen Freie]. (PO41/42: 106)

As this statement makes clear, Schelling's definition incorporates Hegel's key idea—but also goes beyond it. Potentiality actualizing itself in being without ceasing to be potentiality is Schelling's equivalent for the subjectivity which find itself at home with itself in its other. But in his definition, potentiality must not thereby *lose its power* over being—must not be forced to be free, as a Rousseauian would put it. In short, for Schelling freedom should certainly not be equated with a mere power of detachment from or negation of the given, but rather involves the experience of fully realizing oneself *in* the concreteness of world. But if this is to be genuine freedom it must include the freedom *not to find oneself* in the world—not to be determined by what the world has made you, not even when this determination could be characterized as rational, as an expression of the "power" which is "essential" to your nature. This is an insight of enduring value. Hence, at the end of the "Freedom" chapter of *Negative Dialectics*, Theodor Adorno offers a twentieth-century version of a similar conception in the language of "identity" and "non-identity":

> Subjects are free . . . in so far as they are conscious of and identical with themselves; and then again, in such identity they are unfree in so far as they stand under and perpetuate its compulsion. They are unfree as non-identical, as diffuse nature; and yet, as that nature they are free because in the

impulses which overpower them—the subject's non-identity with itself is precisely this—they are released from the compulsive character of identity.[6]

Schelling's *Grundoperation*

It accords with the method of Schelling's positive philosophy that we should move from an experience of freedom to the basic operation which he invokes to account for it. As we have noted several times, a philosophical system of the German Idealist type cannot insert its conception of freedom at any point subsequent to the founding moment. In Schelling's case, the definition of what it would mean to be truly free must also imply the possibility of unfreedom: namely, an actualization of potentiality in which potentiality falls under the dominance of being. He therefore needs to specify a *Grundoperation* which can allow for both outcomes. In theological language, this operation is expressed in the claim that "*we must . . . start from a primal being of God which precedes God himself*" (Vielmehr müssen wir von einem Ursein Gottes ausgehen, das ihm selbst zuvorkommt) (PO41/42: 166), or—even more succinctly—that God is "alienated in an un-pre-thinkable way" (*entäussert ist er unvordenklicher Weise*) (PO41/2: 177). In ontological terms, it can be said that the essence (that is, the original noetic template of the potentialities of being) "is not at all posited *as* essence, but *posited outside itself, totally ecstatically*, precisely as being-ness. The essence has not alienated itself, but alienated before it thinks itself. There is in it *the antipodes of every Idea*, but in this opposition it is itself Idea, because of this total reversal" (PO41/42: 167).

Admittedly, at first sight this rather baroque construction may well appear less intelligible, as an ultimate foundation, than Hegel's seemingly more pellucid operation of self-relating negation. To grasp its motivation, we need to bear in mind the following considerations. Firstly, once one accepts the legitimacy of reason's quest for an absolute foundation, as do the German Idealists, it becomes apparent that the only thing this foundation could be is *freedom as such*. Freedom—absolute spirit—cannot be "caused" or "produced" by a process or sustained by anything other than itself; it alone can function as the true *causa sui* (Hegel and Schelling agree on this—they simply differ profoundly in their definitions of freedom). However, the structure of freedom as Schelling understands it, total self-determination and the iterative transcendence of that determination, cannot explain the existence of that structure as such, any more than reflective self-consciousness can account for its own existence simply by reflecting on itself one more time. He therefore draws the conclusion that the distinctive mode of being of freedom as self-exceeding possibility, namely non-being or the *néant*, can only be understood as the potentialization—the *néantisation*—of un-pre-thinkable being. The *Daß* precedes freedom—but only for the instant required for it to become freedom's own being. As Schelling puts it aphoristically: "being-ness is being-able-to-be—only not in advance!" (*das Seyende ist das Seynkönnende, —nur nicht voraus!*) (PO41/42: 165). This demanding thought is required to overcome the problem which Kant considered insurmountable for any attempt to think an absolute ground: namely, that whatever is fixed upon will be "too large for the understanding" yet "too small for reason" (A422/B450). In Schelling's account *reason pushes the understanding* to frame a hypothesis concerning the founding event of the potentialization of blind being-ness, a theory whose legitimacy stems from its ability to account for our experience of a world pervaded by *traces* of freedom, but far from embodying its adequate realization. At the same time, *the understanding obliges reason* to acknowledge an untranscendable limit to its demand for explanation because reason—the capacity for grounding which presupposes self-grounding—only *comes into being* through the hypothesized process.

The avowedly conjectural status of Schelling's *Grundoperation* reminds us that his positive philosophy seeks to establish a reflective equilibrium between our experience of freedom and what we must presuppose about fundamental ontological processes to account for it (as he puts it, positive philosophy "*konkresziert mit der Erfahrung*"—knits together with experience [PO41/42: 147]). That experience is deeply ambivalent: a dialectic of freedom and unfreedom. On the one hand, the double structure of the absolute *prius*, as Schelling portrays it, puts the process of liberation at the heart of his system: freedom as the *original suspension* or *overcoming* of blind being. This entails that—in principle—freedom cannot be definitively obliterated by the resurgence of an avatar of blind being: for example, by generating a logical process into which it becomes entirely absorbed. As Schelling puts it, "Precisely because potentiality did not precede un-pre-thinkable being, it could not be overcome by the *actus* of this un-pre-thinkable existingness" (AD, SW, II/3: 338). But on the other hand, the original asymmetry of the relation between being and freedom can never be entirely cancelled by their interdependence. In Manfred Frank's formulation, "being proves itself to be what is non-sublatable precisely through its negation."[7] This entails that freedom is haunted, as it were, by the blind being from which it is the very process of emancipation; freedom in its finite form, in a world where the potentialities are in an unstable tension, can very readily succumb to necessity—although never hopelessly or irreversibly, as nothing can abolish the implicit oneness of the potentialities, which exerts a reconciling, emancipatory pressure even at the deepest levels of compulsion. In this way, Schelling's *Grundoperation* not only enables him to incorporate the genealogical perspective—taking "genealogy" as the general term for a hermeneutics of concealed distortion—in a manner ruled out by Hegel's central concept of self-negating negativity. It also allows him to avoid the opposite problem to that posed by Hegel's "fundamentalism of reason":[8] the *impasse* toward which a totalizing genealogy inevitably leads. If our seemingly rational beliefs and our acts of self-determination are only ever epiphenomena, shaped by hidden underlying forces, how could there ever come to be the freedom for the sake of which—presumably—the inquiry into covert determinants was undertaken in the first place?

An Affirmative Genealogy

Schelling's basic operation, the hypothesis which inaugurates his positive philosophy, establishes the framework for his hermeneutics of the history of consciousness. The positive philosophy has the conceptual means to track the relapses into compulsion to which human existence shows itself to be vulnerable. To begin with, the merging of potentiality and being in primordial human awareness is lost when human beings reflectively distance themselves from and objectify nature, thereby also objectifying their own subjectivity in an egological structure. The mythological figures and narratives which subsequently emerge to dominate consciousness are—in Schelling's well-known term—"tautegorical" (HCI: 136/SW, II/1: 196). In other words, they are self-referential expressions of the activity of cosmic-psychic powers, not representations referring to something other than themselves, and therefore candidates for belief or disbelief. As Schelling puts it:

> Mythological ideas are neither invented not voluntarily accepted . . . Peoples as well as individuals are only tools of this process, of which they have no overview, and which they serve without comprehending it . . . [the representations] *are* in them, without them being aware of how; for they

emerge from the interiority of consciousness itself, to which they present themselves with a necessity which permits no doubt as to their truth. (HCI: 135/SW, II/1: 194)

Mythological consciousness operates in a compulsive manner. It can provoke fear and dread, enforce painful sacrifices, and propel communities into practices—for example, ritual prostitution (see PM, SW, II/2, 237–248)—which they would normally regard as morally repugnant. In a passage anticipating Freud's portrayal of religious ritual as closely analogous to the forms of obsessional neurosis, Schelling writes:

> Precisely because those mythological representations were not free, but blind products of consciousness, they became immediately *practical*. Consciousness was driven to deeds and actions by them and was *forced* to express itself through deeds and actions, just as it is a general psychological observation that human beings express in deeds and action representations which arise involuntarily in them, and which they cannot get mental control of, cannot mentally objectify. (PM, SW, II/2: 241)

In short, human beings are far from being "at home" in their mythological experience of the world, but are rather outside themselves, alienated, or "ecstatic," to use Schelling's term. As we have seen, his narrative of the development of human comprehension of the world, and of the place of human freedom within it, analyzes repeated lapses into analogues of mythological consciousness. The false identification of freedom and the logical unfolding of self-relating—we might even say "tautegorical"—negation in Hegel's system is, for him, the most momentous and damaging recent example of such a relapse. In effect, this identification can be understood as a resurgence of the enduring philosophical peril of transcendental illusion—the confusion of pure thinking and knowing.

At the same time, Schelling does not deny that such compulsive forms of consciousness are in some sense true, or that their emergence and development can constitute a stage in an emancipatory process. Thus, mythology is an "original and natural religion which springs from an essential and hence natural relation to God" (PM "Athen"/Eberz: 99). It is neither a matter of arbitrary poetic invention nor a coded representation of a reality external to it, whether historical, natural, or even religious. Rather, it consists in the playing out of the genuine drama which is inaugurated by the setting-in-tension of the potentialities. This is why Schelling can declare that, "in mythology we already have the Idea which exists in everything, the Idea of the process and the Idea of the oneness which nothing can cancel" (PM "Athen"/Eberz: 106). As the final part of this statement suggests, the mythological process can be considered as true in the sense that it expresses, through conflict and its resolution, a striving toward the ultimate unity of the potentialities, which must be assumed always to exert a latent pressure, else there would be no tension. However, the process reaches a limit in the sense that it can only express that unity in an ecstatic or alienated form. Mythologically constricted subjectivity is unable to comprehend the unity as its *own* freedom, and therefore implicitly longs to escape from itself.

Mutatis mutandis, something similar can be said of Hegel's philosophy, from Schelling's perspective. Hegel's *Logic* takes the form of a quest for the reconciled unity of the Idea, which proceeds through the repeated resolution of contradictions. However, the Idea—as Hegel presents it—unfolds with rational necessity: it allows no space for the other dimension of freedom: the possibility to be or not to be. This would not pose a problem if Hegelian logic were able to acknowledge its own limit, *as* negative philosophy—but this it is constitutively unable to do because it takes itself to have fully articulated, in the Idea, the structure of the immediate "being" with which it began, but which, from Schelling's viewpoint, is already an occlusion of being-ness as possibility (it is $A^1 \to B$). At the same time, Schelling concedes—at least, he does so at one generous and upright moment in his first Berlin lectures (PO41/42: 129–130)—that it was Hegel's pushing of negative philosophy to its limit which brought him to understand that his own identity philosophy was in fact a version of negative philosophy. It was a matter of realizing that, if pure rational science, as Hegel himself emphasizes, needs to make a transition into "*another sphere and science*" (SL: 752/W20, 6: 573), the Idea, in its very rational transparency and completion, must entail an exclusion of what demands that transition. The totalizing claim points toward what has been left out of account. As Schelling puts it: "What is incomplete and unconscious necessarily moves of itself, but *the Idea is subject-object, as ideal-real, and has no need to become anything further*" (PO41/42: 130). Hegel's philosophy, in other words, represents an advance toward a truth which it cannot itself articulate because it insists that the "original division" between "is" and "ought"—between *Sein* and *Sollen*—has always already returned into unity; that, from an absolute standpoint, there remains no unfulfilled drive, no practical surplus (see SL: 586/W20, 6, 349–350).

Schelling's genealogy, then, can be termed an "affirmative genealogy," because it does not hollow out the meaningfulness of striving for freedom in the very process of elucidating the compulsions which inhibit its realization.[9] Deceptive, reified forms of consciousness can also embody emancipatory advances, which can be grasped if they are read against the grain, and through this reversal released from the constraints which they unknowingly impose upon themselves. The task, as Schelling puts it in his *Darstellung der reinrationalen Philosophie*, is "to bring reason back *to itself* out of the self-alienation of merely natural, that is to say unfree knowing" (DRP, SW, II/1: 282). By pushing the modern conception of rational necessity to its limit, a project which Kant initiated but did not follow through to the end, such forms of consciousness can be made to reveal what lies beyond them. The ensuing transition from negative to positive philosophy then *enacts* the process of liberation which stands at the heart of Schelling's late thinking. As he explains, in a declaration we have already noted:

> In positive philosophy negative philosophy triumphs; for negative philosophy is the science in which thinking sets itself free from all necessary content; therefore in its truth it is itself positive, since it sets the positive outside itself and strives towards it. (PO41/42: 153)

Philosophy's Orientation to the Future

As we have already seen, this self-transcendence of negative philosophy results in an aporetic conception of freedom: potentiality must fully actualize itself, and yet survive as potentiality; identity must remain non-identical with itself. However, if Schelling is right in his conviction that both aspects, although seemingly inconsistent with one another, are fundamental to our overall understanding of freedom, the most plausible philosophical move is to make the resulting notion of freedom an object of practical aspiration, rather than of theoretical explanation: a goal toward which we can advance without ever realizing it fully. But because this solution appears so close to Kant's response to the dialectic of pure practical reason, a response which Hegel subjected to a powerful critique, it is worth underlining the ways in which Schelling's account of the practical dimension of his late philosophy differs from the manner in which Kant handles our orientation to the supreme good. The fundamental point is that what Schelling terms "spirit" is not simply a remote, normatively generated goal, whose status is sustained by faith, in the form of the postulates of practical reason. Rather, spirit is the third basic ontological potentiality—but is also the potentiality of the future (*die Potenz der Zukunft*). As "that-which-ought-to-be," *das Seynsollende*, it is always already at work in the world, striving to reconcile the possible and the necessary, the particular and the universal, the materially contingent and the ideal. But it can only be at work insofar as it constantly supersedes itself, anticipating its own more adequate realization, in a proleptic structure that Schelling encapsulates in his phrase: "*das seyn Sollende ist auch schon ein Seyn*" (that which ought to be is also already a mode of being) (PO, SW, II/4: 146).

Schelling's positive philosophy, then, has an irreducible future-oriented dimension. As he states in his first Berlin lecture course:

> Positive philosophy is nothing other than the constantly advancing, constantly growing demonstration; just as reality is never closed, so neither is the demonstration. This entire philosophy (*philosophia*, since it is a striving for wisdom) is a knowing which is only ever advancing, and only a demonstration for those with the will to keep thinking [*die Fortdenkenwollenden*]. There belongs to it not merely a thinking, but also a willing. Only the foolish say: there is no God. The demonstration is not closed at any point, and even the present is no barrier for it; a future opens up for the positive philosophy which is itself nothing other than an ongoing demonstration. (PO41/42: 147)

We may wonder why Schelling suddenly interpolates an allusion to *Psalm 53*—the assertion that only the foolish flatly reject the existence of God. His point is not that the existence of God has been proven, as this whole passage emphasizes, but rather than there is no basis for *denying a priori* that the cosmos *may* be animated by a "will not to be blind being"—the minimal definition of God put forward in *System der Weltalter* (SdW: 117). But we should not overlook the complementary aspect of this philosophical stance: its remoteness from any triumphalism of reason, or from any suggestion that "rational faith" can provide in a non-cognitive—and hence empirically unshakeable—mode what speculation is unable to supply. Schelling's late philosophy reveals how modern reason falls prey repeatedly to self-incurred paralysis, how meaning teeters on the brink of unmeaning, and how the realization of the universal scope of human freedom has the status of a hypothesis, a hope—which success in overcoming opacity and constraint can reinforce, but not validate—that the world will turn out to have been driven by something other than blind being. Viewed in the light of this future anterior, from which the continuing path of humanity hangs suspended, Schelling's late philosophy as a whole takes on the shape of a question—a patient, intricate, and searching question—rather than an answer.

Notes

1. Dieter Henrich, "The Origins of the Theory of the Subject," in *Philosophical Interventions in the Unfinished Project of Enlightenment*, ed. Axel Honneth, Thomas McCarthy, Claus Offe, and Albrecht Wellmer (Cambridge, MA: MIT Press, 1992), 52.
2. Fichte, "Review of *Aenesidemus*" in *Early Philosophical Writings*, trans. and ed. Daniel Breazeale (Ithaca and London: Cornell University Press, 1988), 69 (GA, I/2: 55).
3. See Carl Leonhard Reinhold, *Versuch einer neuen Theorie des menschlichen Vorstellungsvermögens* (Prague and Jena: C. J. Widtmann and I. M. Mauke, 1795 [first edition, 1789]), 526–541. As Reinhold writes: "Through the idea of the absolute subject what underlies the appearances of external sense *objectively* and of inner sense *subjectively* becomes nothing other than *thing in itself*, but represented in the form determined by the nature of reason" (541–542).
4. Paul Ricoeur, *Freud and Philosophy. An Essay on Interpretation* (New Haven and London: Yale University Press, 1970), 33.
5. See Dieter Henrich, "Hegels Grundoperation," in *Der Idealismus und seine Gegenwart*, ed. Ute Guzzoni, Bernhard Rang, and Ludwig Siep (Hamburg: Felix Meiner Verlag, 1976).
6. Theodor Adorno, *Negative Dialektik* (Frankfurt: Suhrkamp, 1975), 294. For further discussion of connections between Adorno and Schelling, see Peter Dews, "Dialectics and the Transcendence of Dialectics: Adorno's Relation to Schelling," *British Journal for the History of Philosophy* 22, no. 6 (2014).
7. Manfred Frank, *Der unendliche Mangel an Sein: Schellings Hegelkritik und die Anfänge der Marxschen Dialektik* (Frankfurt: Suhrkamp, 1975), 153.
8. Christian Iber uses the expression "*Vernunftfundamentalismus*" in connection with Hegel in *Subjektivität, Vernunft und ihre Kritik. Prager Vorlesungen über den Deutschen Idealismus* (Frankfurt: Suhrkamp, 1999), 233.
9. I owe the term "affirmative genealogy" to Hans Joas, who applies it to the methodology of the theologian, historian and sociologist Ernst Troeltsch, in chapter 4 of *Die Sakralität der Person* (Berlin: Suhrkamp, 2015). Joas employs the phrase to characterize an approach which seeks to illuminate the socio-historical context of the emergence of structures of value, without thereby cancelling any claim of the values at issue on the present—without the consequence that genesis entirely undermines validity. For Joas, Troeltsch's procedure is *genealogical* in the sense that it analyzes the historically contingent emergence of ethical and cultural ideals; but at the same time, it is

affirmative, since his ultimate aim in investigating conditions of genesis is not to debunk, but to clarify—and reanimate the relevance of—such ideals, as transformed in the light of what concerns us now. Schelling's investigation of historical forms of consciousness—primarily of religious and philosophical consciousness—clearly has an intention similar to that of Troeltsch, suggesting the aptness of the term "affirmative genealogy" for his method. However, I would argue that Schelling's approach is *more adequately genealogical*, without thereby ceasing to be affirmative. This is because Schelling, unlike Troeltsch, has a theory of basic ontological processes, which produce effects of distortion, repression and alienating *ecstasis* comparable to those theorized by psychoanalysis, without ceasing to be an expression of the "ought," the *Sollen*, which—as Joas puts it—"being itself contains" (186). By contrast, a purely reductive genealogy misrepresents the metaphysical state of affairs, in its commitment to the epiphenomenal status of meaning and purpose, and furthermore rebounds to undermine the validity of the genealogical enterprise itself. The equilibrium of Schelling's affirmative genealogy is elegantly captured by Edward Allen Beach: "While pursuing a hard-headed and critical hermeneutics, Schelling simultaneously retains a transcendent reference point." (*The Potencies of God(s)* [Albany, NY: SUNY Press, 1994], 249.) The relevance of this formula to more recent philosophical enterprises with an emancipatory intent, such as the Critical Theory of the Frankfurt School, should be evident.

Bibliography

Collected Editions

FICHTE

Johann Gottlieb Fichte, *Gesamtausgabe der Bayerischen Akademie der Wissenschaften*, edited by Erich Fuchs, Hans Gliwitzky, Reinhard Lauth, and Peter K. Schneider. Stuttgart-Bad Canstatt: frommann-holzboog, 1962–2012.

KANT

Immanuel Kant, *Akademie-Ausgabe* (*Gesammelte Schriften* initiated by the *Königlich-Preußiche Akademie der Wissenschaften*). Berlin and Leipzig: de Gruyter, 1922–.

HEGEL

Georg Wilhelm Friedrich Hegel, *Werke in zwanzig Bänden*, edited by Eva Moldenhauer and Karl Markus Michel. Frankfurt: Suhrkamp Verlag, 1986.

SCHELLING

Friedrich Wilhelm Joseph Schelling, *Historisch-kritische Ausgabe*. Stuttgart-Bad Canstatt: frommann-holzboog: 1976–.

Friedrich Wilhelm Joseph Schelling, *Sämmtliche Werke*, edited by K. F. A. Schelling. Stuttgart: J. G. Cotta, 1856–1861.

Individual Works

Note: "CUP" denotes Cambridge University Press; "OUP" denotes Oxford University Press; "Frankfurt" always denotes Frankfurt am Main. Dates following details of texts from Fichte, *Gesamtausgabe*, and Schelling, *Historisch-kritische Ausgabe*, refer to the date of publication of the individual volume concerned.

Adorno, Theodor. *Negative Dialektik*. Frankfurt: Suhrkamp, 1966.
Adorno, Theodor. *Vorlesung über Negative Dialektik*. Frankfurt: Suhrkamp, 2007.
Alderwick, Charlotte. *Schelling's Ontology of Powers*. Edinburgh: Edinburgh University Press, 2021.
Allison, Henry. *Kant's Transcendental Idealism: An Interpretation and Defense*. London: Yale University Press, 1983.
Angehrn, Emil. "Vernunft in der Geschichte? Zum Problem der Hegelschen Geschichtsphilosophie." *Zeitschrift für philosophische Forschung* 35, no. 3/4 (1981).
Beach, Edward Allen. *The Potencies of God(s)*. Albany, NY: SUNY Press, 1994.
Beiser, Frederick. "Normativity in Neo-Kantianism: Its Rise and Fall." *International Journal of Philosophical Studies* 17, no. 1 (2009).

Beiser, Frederick. *The Fate of Reason: German Philosophy from Kant to Fichte*. Cambridge, MA: Harvard University Press, 1987.
Bell, David. "Transcendental Arguments and Non-Naturalistic Anti-Realism." In *Transcendental Arguments: Problems and Prospects*, edited by Robert Stern. Oxford: Clarendon Press, 1998.
Bellah, Robert N. *Religion in Human Evolution: From the Paleolithic to the Axial Age*. Cambridge, MA: Belknap Press, 2011.
Bellah, Robert N. "What is Axial about the Axial Age?" *Archives Européennes de Sociologie* 46, no. 1 (2005).
Boehm, Omri. *Kant's Critique of Spinoza*. New York: OUP, 2018.
Bonhoeffer, Dietrich. *Letters and Papers from Prison*. London: Fontana, 1968.
Boss, Marc. "Tillich in Dialogue with Japanese Buddhism." In *The Cambridge Companion to Tillich*, edited by Russell Re Manning. Cambridge: CUP, 2009.
Bowie, Andrew. *Schelling and Modern European Philosophy: An Introduction*. London: Routledge, 1993.
Breazeale, Daniel. "The Standpoint of Life and the Standpoint of Philosophy." In *Thinking Through the Wissenschaftslehre: Themes from Fichte's Early Philosophy*. Oxford: OUP, 2013.
Bruce, Steve. *Secularization: In Defence of an Unfashionable Theory*. Oxford: OUP, 2011.
Burkert, Walter. *Greek Religion*. Cambridge, MA: Harvard University Press, 1985.
Danz, Christian. *Die philosophische Christologie F. W. J. Schellings*. Stuttgart-Bad Canstatt: frommann-holzboog, 1996.
Danz, Christian. "Philosophie der Offenbarung." In *F. W. J. Schelling*, edited by Hans Jürg Sandkühler. Stuttgart/Weimar: Metzler Verlag, 1998.
Danz, Christian, and Friedrich Hermanni (eds). *Wahrheitsansprüche der Weltreligionen. Konturen gegenwärtiger Religionstheologie*. Göttingen: Vandenhoeck and Ruprecht, 2006.
D'Costa, Gavin. "Theology of Religions." In *The Modern Theologians*, edited by David F. Ford and Rachel Muers. Oxford: Blackwell, 2005.
Della Rocca, Michael. "A Rationalist Manifesto: Spinoza and the Principle of Sufficient Reason." *Philosophical Topics* 31, no. 1/2 (Spring and Fall 2003).
Dews, Peter. "Dialectics and the Transcendence of Dialectics: Adorno's Relation to Schelling." *British Journal for the History of Philosophy* 22, no. 6 (2014).
Dews, Peter. "Theory Construction and Existential Description in Schelling's Treatise on Freedom." *British Journal for the History of Philosophy* 25, no. 1 (2017).
Düsing, Klaus. "Spekulation und Reflexion: Zur Zusammenarbeit Schellings und Hegels in Jena." *Hegel-Studien* 5 (1969).
Fichte, J. G. "A Crystal Clear Report to the General Public Concerning the Actual Essence of the Newest Philosophy." In *Philosophy of German Idealism*, edited by Ernst Behler. New York: Continuum, 1987.
Fichte, J. G. "Concerning the Difference between the Spirit and the Letter in Philosophy." In *Early Philosophical Writings*, translated and edited by Daniel Breazeale. Ithaca, NY: Cornell University Press, 1988.
Fichte, J. G. "Die Bestimmung des Menschen." In *Gesamtausgabe*, I/6 (1981).
Fichte, J. G. "Erste Einleitung in die Wissenschaftslehre." In *Gesamtausgabe*, I/4 (1970).
Fichte, J. G. "First Introduction to the Science of Knowledge." In *The Science of Knowledge*, translated and edited by Peter Heath and John Lachs. Cambridge: CUP, 1982.

Fichte, J. G. *Foundations of Natural Right*, edited by Fred Neuhouser. Cambridge: CUP, 2000.
Fichte, J. G. *Foundations of Transcendental Philosophy (Wissenschaftslehre nova methodo 1796/99)*, translated and edited by Daniel Brezeale. Ithaca/London: Cornell University Press, 1992.
Fichte, J. G. "Grundlage des gesammten Wissenschaftslehre." In *Gesamtausgabe*, I/2 (1965).
Fichte, J. G. "Grundlage des Naturrechts nach der Prinzipien der Wissenschaftslehre." In *Gesamtausgabe*, I/3 (1966) (part one); I/4 (1970) (part two).
Fichte, J. G. "On the Ground of Our Belief in a Divine World-Governance." In *J. G. Fichte and the Atheism Dispute (1798–1800)*, edited by Curtis Bowman and Yolanda Estes. London: Routledge, 2010.
Fichte, J. G. "Review of *Anesidemus*." In *Early Philosophical Writings*, translated and edited by Daniel Breazeale. Ithaca: Cornell University Press, 1988.
Fichte, J. G. "Second Introduction to the Science of Knowledge." In *The Science of Knowledge*, translated and edited by Peter Heath and John Lachs. Cambridge: CUP, 1982.
Fichte, J. G. "Sonnenklarer Bericht an das größere Publikum, über das eigentliche Wesen der neuesten Philosophie." In *Gesamtausgabe*, I/7 (1988).
Fichte, J. G. *The Science of Knowledge*, translated and edited by Peter Heath and John Lachs. Cambridge: CUP, 1982.
Fichte, J. G. *The Vocation of Man*, translated by Peter Preuss. Indianapolis, IN: Hackett, 1987.
Fichte, J. G. "Über den Grund unseres Glaubens an eine göttliche Weltregierung." In *Gesamtausgabe*, I/5 (1977).
Fichte, J. G. "Über Geist, und Buchstabe in der Philosophie." In *Gesamtausgabe*, II/3 (1971).
Fichte, J. G. "Zweite Einleitung in die Wissenschaftslehre." In *Gesamtausgabe*, I/4 (1970).
Fincham, Richard. "Refuting Fichte with 'Common Sense': Friedrich Immanuel Niethammer's Reception of the Wissenschaftslehre 1794/5." *Journal of the History of Philosophy* 43, no. 3 (2005).
Förster, Eckhart. *The Twenty-Five Years of Philosophy: A Systematic Reconstruction*, translated by Brady Bowman. Cambridge, MA: Harvard University Press, 2012.
Frank, Manfred. *Der unendliche Mangel an Sein: Schellings Hegelkritik und die Anfänge der Marxschen Dialektik*. Frankfurt: Suhrkamp, 1975.
Frank, Manfred. "Einleitung des Herausgebers." In *Philosophie der Offenbarung 1841/42*, by F. W. J. Schelling, edited by Manfred Frank. Frankfurt: Suhrkamp, 1977.
Fraser, Nancy, and Axel Honneth. *Umverteilung oder Anerkennung? Eine politisch-philosophische Kontroverse*. Frankfurt: Suhrkamp, 2003.
Frege, Gottlob. "Über Begriff und Gegenstand." *Vierteljahrsschrift für wissenschaftliche Philosophie*, 16, no. 2 (1892).
Frege, Gottlob. "Über Sinn und Bedeutung." *Zeitschrift für Philosophie und philosophische Kritik*, NF 100 (1892).
Gardner, Sebastian. "Sartre, Schelling and Onto-Theology." *Religious Studies* 42, no. 3 (2006).
Gardner, Sebastian. "The Metaphysics of Human Freedom: From Kant's Transcendental Idealism to Schelling's *Freiheitsschrift*." *British Journal for the History of Philosophy* 25, no. 1 (2017).

Gardner, Sebastian. "The Status of the *Wissenschaftslehre*: Transcendental and Ontological Grounds in Fichte." *Internationales Jahrbuch des Deutschen Idealismus/International Yearbook of German Idealism*, 7 (2009).

Gardner, Sebastian. "Transcendental Philosophy and the Possibility of the Given." In *Mind, Reason and Being-in-the-World. The McDowell-Dreyfus Debate*, edited by Joseph K. Schear. London: Routledge, 2013.

Gilson, Étienne. *Being and Some Philosophers*. The Hague: Europe Printing, 1961.

Groos, Karl. *Die reine Vernunftwissenschaft: systematische Darstellung von Schellings rationaler oder negativer Philosophie*. Heidelberg: Georg Weiß, 1889.

Guéroult, Martial. *L'évolution et la structure de la doctrine de la science chez Fichte* (2 vols). Paris: Les Belles Lettres, 1930.

Guyer, Paul, and Allen Wood. "Introduction to the *Critique of Pure Reason*." In *Critique of Pure Reason*, by Immanuel Kant. Cambridge: CUP, 1998.

Habermas, Jürgen. *Auch eine Geschichte der Philosophie* (2 vols). Frankfurt: Suhrkamp, 2019.

Habermas, Jürgen. "Dialektischer Idealismus im Übergang zum Materialismus. Geschichtsphilosophische Folgerungen aus Schellings Idee einer Contraction Gottes." In *Theorie und Praxis*. Frankfurt: Suhrkamp, 1971.

Habermas, Jürgen. *The Philosophical Discourse of Modernity*. Cambridge, MA: MIT Press, 1987.

Hare, John E. *The Moral Gap: Kantian Ethics, Human Limits and God's Assistance*. Oxford: Clarendon, 1996.

Hartmann, Klaus. "Hegel: A Non-Metaphysical View." In *Hegel: A Collection of Critical Essays*, edited by Alasdair MacIntyre. Notre Dame and London: University of Notre Dame Press, 1972.

Hartmann, Nicolai. *Die Philosophie des deutschen Idealismus. Teil 1: Fichte, Schelling und die Romantik*. Berlin: de Gruyter, 1960.

Hegel, G. W. F. "Die Differenz des Fichteschen und des Schellingschen Systems der Philosophie." In *Werke in zwanzig Bänden*, vol. 2 (1986).

Hegel, G. W. F. *Die Vernunft in der Geschichte. Einleitung in die Philosophie der Weltgeschichte*, edited by Georg Lasson. Leipzig: Meiner, 1930.

Hegel, G. W. F. *Elements of the Philosophy of Right*, translated by H. B. Nisbet and edited by Allen W. Wood. Cambridge: CUP, 1991.

Hegel, G. W. F. *Encyclopaedia of the Philosophical Sciences (1830). Part 3. Hegel's Philosophy of Mind*, translated by A. V. Miller. Oxford: Clarendon Press, 1971.

Hegel, G. W. F. "Enzyklopädie 1830. Dritter Teil. Die Philosophie der Geistes." In *Werke zwanzig Bänden*, vol. 10 (1986).

Hegel, G. W. F. "Enzyklopädie 1830. Erster Teil. Die Wissenschaft der Logik." In *Werke in zwanzig Bänden*, vol. 8 (1986).

Hegel, G. W. F. "Grundlinien der Philosophie des Rechts." In *Werke zwanzig Bänden*, vol. 7 (1986).

Hegel, G. W. F. *Lectures on the History of Philosophy. The Lectures of 1825–6. Volume III: Medieval and Modern Philosophy*, translated by Robert F. Brown and J. M. Stewart, with H. S. Harris, edited by Robert F. Brown. Oxford: Clarendon Press, 2009.

Hegel, G. W. F. *Lectures on the History of Philosophy. Volume 3: Medieval and Modern Philosophy*, translated by E. S. Haldane and Frances H. Simpson. Lincoln, NE: University of Nebraska Press, 1995.

Hegel, G. W. F. *Lectures on the Philosophy of History. Introduction: Reason in History*, translated by H. B. Nisbet. Cambridge: CUP, 1975.

Hegel, G. W. F. *Lectures on the Philosophy of Religion. Volume I: Introduction and the Concept off Religion*. Translated by R. F. Brown, P. C. Hodgson, and R. M. Stewart, with the assistance of H. S. Harris, edited by P. C. Hodgson. Berkeley and Los Angeles: University of California Press, 1988.
Hegel, G. W. F. *Lectures on the Philosophy of Religion. Volume II: Determinate Religion*. Translated by R. F. Brown, P. C. Hodgson, and R. M. Stewart, with the assistance of H. S. Harris, edited by P. C. Hodgson. Berkeley and Los Angeles: University of California Press, 1998.
Hegel, G. W. F. *Lectures on the Philosophy of Religion. Volume III: The Consummate Religion*, translated by R. F. Brown, P. C. Hodgson, and R. M. Stewart, with the assistance of H. S. Harris, edited by P. C. Hodgson. Berkeley and Los Angeles: University of California Press, 1998.
Hegel, G. W. F. *Lectures on the Philosophy of World History*. Introduction, translated by H. B. Nisbet and introduced by Duncan Forbes. Cambridge: CUP, 1975.
Hegel, G. W. F. "Phänomenologie des Geistes." In *Werke zwanzig Bänden*, vol. 3 (1986).
Hegel, G. W. F. *Phenomenology of Spirit*, translated by Terry Pinkard. Cambridge: CUP, 2018.
Hegel, G. W. F. "Philosophie des Rechts 1824/25, nach der Vorlesungsnachschrift K. G. V. Griesheims." In *Vorlesungen über die Philosophie des Rechts 1818-1831*, vol. 4. Stuttgart-Bad Canstatt: frommann-holzboog, 1974.
Hegel, G. W. F. *The Philosophy of History*, translated by J. Sibree and introduced by C. J. Friedrich. New York: Dover Publications, 1956.
Hegel, G. W. F. *The Encyclopaedia Logic with the Zusätze*, translated with introduction and notes by T. F. Geraets, W. A. Suchting, and H. S. Harris. Indianapolis, IN: Hackett, 1991.
Hegel, G. W. F. *The Science of Logic*, translated by George di Giovanni. Cambridge: CUP, 2010.
Hegel, G. W. F. "Vorlesungen über die Geschichte der Philosophie." In *Werke zwanzig Bänden*, vols 18–20 (1986).
Hegel, G. W. F. *Vorlesungen über die Geschichte der Philosophie. Teil 4. Philosophie des Mittelalters und der neueren Zeit*, edited by Pierre Garniron and Walter Jaeschke. Hamburg: Felix Meiner, 1986.
Hegel, G. W. F. "Vorlesungen über die Philosophie der Geschichte." In *Werke zwanzig Bänden*, vol. 12 (1986).
Hegel, G. W. F. "Vorlesungen über die Philosophie der Religion." In *Werke zwanzig Bänden*, vols 16 and 17 (1986).
Hegel, G. W. F. *Vorlesungen über die Philosophie der Religion. Teil 1. Einleitung. Der Begriff der Religion*, edited by Walter Jaeschke. Hamburg: Felix Meiner, 1993.
Hegel, G. W. F. *Vorlesungen über die Philosophie der Religion. Teil 2. Die bestimmte Religion*, edited by Walter Jaeschke. Hamburg: Felix Meiner, 1994.
Hegel, G. W. F. *Vorlesungen über die Philosophie der Religion. Teil 3. Die vollendete Religion*, edited by Walter Jaeschke. Hamburg: Felix Meiner, 1995.
Hegel, G. W. F. *Vorlesungen über die Philosophie der Weltgeschichte. Band 1: Die Vernunft in der Geschichte*, edited by Johannes Hoffmeister. Hamburg: Felix Meiner, 1994.
Heidegger, Martin. *Schellings Abhandlung über das Wesen der menschlichen Freiheit*. Tübingen: Max Niemeyer, 1971.
Henrich, Dieter. "Andersheit und Absolutheit des Geistes. Sieben Schritte auf dem Wege von Schelling zu Hegel." In *Selbstverhältnisse*. Stuttgart: Reclam, 1982.
Henrich, Dieter. *Between Kant and Hegel: Lectures on German Idealism*, edited by David S. Pacini. Cambridge, MA/London: Harvard University Press, 2003.

Henrich, Dieter. "Die Identität des Subjekts in der transzendentalen Deduktion." In *Kant. Analyse-Probleme-Kritik*, edited by H. Oberer and G. Seel. Würzburg: Konigshausen & Neumann, 1988.
Henrich, Dieter. *Der ontologische Gottesbeweis*. Tübingen: Max Niemeyer, 1960.
Henrich, Dieter. "Fichtes ursprüngliche Einsicht." In *Dies Ich, das viel besagt. Fichtes Einsicht nachdenken*. Frankfurt: Vittorio Klostermann, 2019.
Henrich, Dieter. *Fluchtlinien. Philosophische Essays*. Frankfurt: Suhrkamp, 1982.
Henrich, Dieter. "Hegels Grundoperation." In *Der Idealismus und seine Gegenwart*, edited by Ute Guzzoni, Bernhard Rang, and Ludwig Siep. Hamburg: Felix Meiner Verlag, 1976.
Henrich, Dieter. "The Origins of the Theory of the Subject." In *Philosophical Interventions in the Unfinished Project of Enlightenment*, edited by Axel Honneth, Thomas McCarthy, Claus Offe, and Albrecht Wellmer. Cambridge, MA: MIT Press, 1992.
Hogrebe, Wolfram. *Prädikation und Genesis. Metaphysik als Fundamentalheuristik im Ausgang von Schellings "Die Weltalter"*. Frankfurt: Suhrkamp, 1989.
Horstmann, Rolf-Peter. *Die Grenzen der Vernunft. Untersuchungen zu Motiven und Zielen des deutschen Idealismus*. Frankfurt: Vittorio Klostermann, 2004.
Hösle, Vittorio. *Hegels System: Der Idealismus der Subjektivität und das Problem der Intersubjektivität* (2 vols). Hamburg: Felix Meiner, 1987.
Houlgate, Stephen. *An Introduction to Hegel: Freedom, Truth and History*. Oxford: Blackwell, 2005.
Houlgate, Stephen. "Schelling's Critique of Hegel's 'Science of Logic'". *The Review of Metaphysics* 53, no. 1 (1999).
Houlgate, Stephen. *The Opening of Hegel's Logic: From Being to Infinity*. West Lafayette, IN: Purdue University Press, 2006.
Howard, Thomas Albert. *The Faiths of Others. A History of Interreligious Dialogue*. New Haven and London: Yale University Press, 2021.
Hutter, Axel. *Geschichtliche Vernunft. Die Weiterführung der Kantischen Vernunftkritik in der Spätphilosophie Schellings*. Frankfurt: Suhrkamp, 1996.
Iber, Christian. *Subjektivitat, Vernunft und ihre Kritik. Prager Vorlesungen über den Deutschen Idealismus*. Frankfurt: Suhrkamp, 1999.
Jacobi, Friedrich Heinrich. "David Hume on Faith, or Idealism and Realism, A Dialogue." In *The Main Philosophical Writings and the Novel Allwill*, translated and edited by George di Giovanni. Montreal and Kingston: McGill-Queen's University Press, 1994.
Jaspers, Karl. *On the Origin and Goal of History*, translated by Michael Bullock. New Haven: Yale University Press, 1953.
James, David. *Fichte's Social and Political Philosophy: Property and Virtue*. Cambridge: CUP, 2011.
Joas, Hans. *Die Sacralität der Person. Eine neue Genealogie der Menschenrechte*. Frankfurt: Suhrkamp, 2015.
Joas, Hans. *Sind die Menschenrechte westlich?* Munich: Kösel Verlag, 2015.
Joas, Hans, and Robert N. Bellah (eds). *The Axial Age and its Consequences*. Cambridge, MA: Belknap Press, 2012.
Kant, Immanuel. "Conjectural Beginning of Human History." In *Toward Perpetual Peace and Other Writings on Politics, Peace and History*, edited by Pauline Kleingeld. New Haven: Yale University Press, 2006.
Kant, Immanuel. *Critique of Judgment*, translated by James Meredith, revised, edited, and introduced by Nicholas Walker. Oxford: OUP, 2007.

Kant, Immanuel. *Die Metaphysik der Sitten*. In *Akademie-Ausgabe*, vol. VI (1922–).
Kant, Immanuel. *Die Religion innerhalb der Grenzen der bloßen Vernunft*. In *Akademie-Ausgabe*, vol. VI (1922–).
Kant, Immanuel. "Idea for a Universal History from a Cosmopolitan Perspective." In *Toward Perpetual Peace and other Writings on Politics, Peace and History*, edited by Pauline Kleingeld. New Haven and London: Yale University Press, 2006.
Kant, Immanuel. "Ideen zu einer allgemeinen Geschichte in weltbürgerlicher Absicht." In *Akademie-Ausgabe*, vol. VIII (1922–).
Kant, Immanuel. "Kritik der Urteilskraft." In *Akademie-Ausgabe*, vol. V (1922–).
Kant, Immanuel. *Metaphysics of Morals*, translated by Mary Gregor. Cambridge: CUP, 1991.
Kant, Immanuel. "Mutmaßlicher Anfang der Menschengeschichte." In *Akademie-Ausgabe*, vol. VIII (1922–).
Kant, Immanuel. *Religion within the Boundaries of Mere Reason*, translated and edited by Allen Wood and George di Giovanni. Cambridge: CUP, 2018.
Kaplan, Grant. "Did Schelling Live on in Catholic Theology? An Examination of his Influence on Catholic Tübingen." *International Journal of Philosophy and Theology* 80, no. 1–2 (2019).
Kemp Smith, Norman. *A Commentary to Kant's Critique of Pure Reason*, with a new introduction by Sebastian Gardner. Basingstoke: Palgrave MacMillan, 2003.
Kierkegaard, Søren. *Concluding Unscientific Postscript*, trans D. F. Swenson and W. Lowrie. Princeton, NJ: Princeton University Press, 1968.
Korsch, Dietrich. *Der Grund der Freiheit. Untersuching zur Problemgeschichte der positive Philosophie und zur Systemfunktion des Christentums im Spätwerk F.W.J. Schellings*. Munich: Kaiser, 1980.
Korsgaard, Christine. "Morality as Freedom." In *Creating the Kingdom of Ends*. Cambridge: CUP, 1996.
Kosch, Michelle. *Fichte's Ethics*. Oxford: OUP, 2018.
Kreines, James. "Aristotelian Priority, Metaphysical Definitions of God and Hegel on Pure Thought as Absolute." *Hegel Bulletin* 40, no. 1 (2020).
Kreines, James. "Fundamentality without Metaphysical Monism: Response to Critics of *Reason in the World*." *Hegel Bulletin* 39, no. 1 (Spring/Summer 2018).
Kreines, James. "Hegel's Metaphysics: Changing the Debate." *Philosophy Compass* 1, no. 5 (2006).
Kreines, James. *Reason in the World: Hegel's Metaphysics and its Philosophical Appeal*. Oxford: OUP, 2015.
Krings, Hermann. *Die Entfremdung zwischen Schelling und Hegel (1801–1807)*. Munich: Verlag der Bayerischen Akademie der Wissenschaften, 1977.
Leibniz, G. W. *Die philosophischen Schriften*, edited by C. I. Gerhardt. Berlin: Weidmann, 1875–1890, vol. IV.
Lin, Martin. "Rationalism and Necessitarianism." *Noûs* 46, no. 3 (2012).
Lotze, Hermann. *Grundzüge der Logik und Enzyklopädie der Philosophie*. Leipzig: Verlag von S. Hirzel, 1885.
Lumsden, John. *At the Limit of the Concept: Logic and History in Hegel, Schelling and Adorno*. PhD thesis, University of Essex, 2016.
Marquet, Jean-François. "L'articulation sujet-objet dans la dernière philosophie de Schelling." In *Restitutions: Études d'histoire de la philosophie allemande*. Paris: Vrin, 2001.

Marquet, Jean-François. "La philosophie de Schelling." In *Chapitres*. Paris: Les Belles Lettres, 2017.
Marquet, Jean-François. *Liberté et existence. Étude sur la formation de la philosophie de Schelling*. Paris: Éditions Gallimard, 1973.
Martin, Wayne. *Idealism and Objectivity: Understanding Fichte's Jena Project* (Stanford CA: Stanford University Press, 1997)
Martin, Wayne. *Theories of Judgment: Psychology, Logic, Phenomenology*. Cambridge: CUP, 2005.
McDowell, John. *Mind and World*. Cambridge, MA/London: Harvard University Press, 1994.
McTaggart, J. M. E. *A Commentary on Hegel's Logic*. London: Routledge/Thoemmes, 1999.
McTaggart, J. M. E. *Studies in the Hegelian Dialectic*. Cambridge: University Press, 1922.
Menke, Christoph. *Autonomie und Befreiung. Studien zu Hegel*. Frankfurt: Suhrkamp 2018.
Merleau-Ponty, Maurice. "Eye and Mind." In *The Primacy of Perception*, edited by James M. Edie. Evanston, IL: Northwestern University Press, 1964.
Moore, Adrian. *The Evolution of Modern Metaphysics: Making Sense of Things*. Cambridge: CUP, 2014.
Morgan, Michael L. "Plato and Greek Religion." In *The Cambridge Companion to Plato*, edited by Richard Kraut. Cambridge: CUP, 1992.
Murray, Penelope. "What is a Muthos for Plato?" In *From Myth to Reason. Studies in the Development of Greek Thought*, edited by Richard Buxton. Oxford: OUP, 2002.
Neuhouser, Frederick. *Fichte's Theory of Subjectivity*. Cambridge: CUP, 1990.
Nagel, Thomas. *Mind and Cosmos*. Oxford: OUP, 2012.
Niethammer, F. I. "Von den Ansprüchen des gemeinen Verstandes an die Philosophie." *Philosophisches Journal einer Gesellschaft Teutscher Gelehrten*. Hildesheim: Georg Olms Verlagsbuchhandlung, 1969.
Pinkard, Terry. *Hegel's Dialectic: The Explanation of Possibility*. Philadelphia, PA: Temple University Press, 1988.
Pinkard, Terry. "Klaus Hartmann: A Philosophical Appreciation." *Zeitschrift für Philosophische Forschung*, 46, no. 4 (1992).
Pippin, Robert. *Hegel's Idealism: The Satisfactions of Self-Consciousness*. Cambridge: CUP, 1989.
Queiruga, Andrés Torres. *Diálogo de las religiones y autocomprensión cristiana*. Santander: Sal Terrae, 2005.
Quinn, Philip L. "Kant's Philosophical Ecclesiology." *Faith and Philosophy* 17, no. 4 (2000).
Redding, Paul. "Robert Pippin's Hegel as an *Analytically Approachable* Philosopher." *Australasian Philosophical Review* 2, no. 4 (2018).
Reinhold, Karl Leonhard. "Einige Bermerkungen über die in der Einleitung zu den "Metaphysischen Anfangsgründen der Rechtslehre" von I. Kant aufgestellten Begriffe von der Freiheit des Willens." In *Materialien zu Kant's "Kritik der praktischen Vernunft"*, edited by Rüdiger Bittner und Konrad Cramer. Frankfurt: Suhrkamp, 1975.
Reinhold, Karl Leonhard. *Versuch einer neuen Theorie des menschlichen Vorstellungsvermögens*. Prague and Jena: C. J. Widtmann and I. M. Mauke, 1795 (first edition 1789).
Rickert, Heinrich. "Fichtes Atheismusstreit und die Kantische Philosophie: Eine Sekulärbetrachtung." *Kant-Studien*, vol. 4 (1900).

Ricoeur, Paul. *Freud and Philosophy. An Essay on Interpretation*. New Haven and London: Yale University Press, 1970.
Ricoeur, Paul. *The Rule of Metaphor*. London: Routledge and Kegan Paul, 1986.
Rooney, Sally. *Beautiful World, Where Are You*. London: Faber & Faber, 2021.
Roux, Alexandra. *Schelling—l'avenir de la raison. Rationalisme et empirisme dans sa dernière philosophie*. Paris: Éditions du Félin, 2016.
Rush, Fred. "Schelling's Critique of Hegel", in *Interpreting Schelling: Critical Essays*. Cambridge: CUP, 2014.
Rowe, Christopher. "Myth, History and Dialectic in Plato's *Republic* and *Timaeus-Critias*." In *From Myth to Reason. Studies in the Development of Greek Thought*, edited by Richard Buxton. Oxford: OUP, 2002.
Sartre, Jean-Paul. *Being and Nothingness. An Essay on Phenomenological Ontology*, translated by Hazel E. Barnes, introduced by Mary Warnock. London: Routledge, 1991.
Sartre, Jean-Paul. *La transcendence de l'ego. Esquisse d'une description phénoménologique*. Paris: J. Vrin, 1966.
Sartre, Jean-Paul. *L'être et le néant. Essai d'ontologie phénoménologique*. Paris: Gallimard, "Collection TEL," 1980.
Sartre, Jean-Paul. *Nausea*. London: Penguin Classics, 2000.
Sartre, Jean-Paul. *The Transcendence of the Ego*. London: Routledge Classics, 2011.
Schelling, F. W. J. "Abhandlung über die Quelle der ewigen Wahrheiten." In *Sämmtliche Werke*, II/1 (1856–1861).
Schelling, F. W. J. "Abhandlungen zur Erläuterung des Idealismus der Wissenschaftslehre." In *Historisch-kritische Ausgabe*, I/4 (1988).
Schelling, F. W. J. "Andere Deduktion der Prinzipien der positive Philosophie." In *Sämmtliche Werke*, II/4 (1856–1861).
Schelling, F. W. J. "Bruno, oder über das göttliche und das natürliche Prinzip der Dinge." In *Historisch-kritische Ausgabe*, I/11 (2016): 2.
Schelling, F. W. J. *Bruno, or On the Natural and the Divine Principle of Things*, edited, translated and introduced by Michael G. Vater. Albany, NY: SUNY Press, 1984.
Schelling, F. W. J. "Commentaries Explicatory of the Idealism in the Science of Knowledge." In *Idealism and the End of Theory: Three Essays by Schelling*, translated and edited by Thomas Pfau. Albany, NY: SUNY Press 1994.
Schelling, F. W. J. "Darlegung des wahren Verhältnisses der Naturphilosophie zur verbesserten Fichteschen Lehre." In *Sämmtliche Werke*, I/7 (1856–1861).
Schelling, F. W. J. "Darstellung des Naturprocesses." In *Sämmtliche Werke*, I/10 (1856–1861).
Schelling, F. W. J. "Darstellung des philosophischen Empirismus." In *Sämmtliche Werke*, 1/10 (1856–1861).
Schelling, F. W. J. "Darstellung meines Systems der Philosophy." In *Historisch-kritische Ausgabe*, I/10 (2009).
Schelling, F. W. J. "Die Weltalter Druck 1." In *Die Weltalter. Fragmente*, edited by Manfred Schröter. Munich: C. H. Beck, 1979.
Schelling, F. W. J. "Die Weltalter." In *Sämmtliche Werke*, I/8 (1856–1861).
Schelling, F. W. J. "Einleitung in die Philosophie der Offenbarung oder Begründung der positiven Philosophie." In *Sämmtliche Werke*, II/3 (1856–1861).
Schelling, F. W. J. "Einleitung zu seinem Entwurf eines Systems der Naturphilosophie." In *Historisch-kritische Ausgabe*, I/8 (2004).

Schelling, F. W. J. *First Outline of a System of the Philosophy of Nature*, translated by Keith Peterson. Albany, NY: SUNY Press, 2004.

Schelling, F. W. J. *Ideas for a Philosophy of Nature*, translated by Errol Harris and Peter Heath. Cambridge: CUP, 1988.

Schelling, F. W. J. *Initia Philosophiae Universae* ("Grundzüge der gesammten Philosophie"). In *Historisch-kritische Ausgabe*, II/10, 2 (2020).

Schelling, F. W. J. *Of Human Freedom*, translated by James Gutman. Chicago: Open Court Publishing Co., 1936.

Schelling, F. W. J. *Of the I as Principle of Philosophy*. In *The Unconditional in Human Knowledge: Four Early Essays* (1974–1976), translated by Fritz Marti. Cranbury, NJ: Associated University Presses, 1980.

Schelling, F. W. J. *On the History of Modern Philosophy*, translated by Andrew Bowie. Cambridge: CUP, 1994.

Schelling, F. W. J. *On the Method of Academic Studies*, translated by E. S. Morgan, edited with an introduction by Norbert Guterman. Athens, OH: Ohio University Press, 1966.

Schelling, F. W. J. "On the Nature of Philosophy as Science." In *German Idealist Philosophy*, edited and introduced by Rüdiger Bubner. London: Penguin 1997.

Schelling, F. W. J. "On the Source of the Eternal Truths," translated by Edward Allen Beach. *The Owl of Minerva* 22, no. 1 (1990).

Schelling, F. W. J. *Philosophical Inquiries into the Nature of Human Freedom*, translated by James Gutman. La Salle: Open Court Press, 1992.

Schelling, F. W. J. "Philosophical Letters on Dogmatism and Criticism." In *The Unconditional in Human Knowledge: Four Early Essays (1794–1796)*, translated by Fritz Marti. Cranbury, NJ: Associated University Presses, 1980.

Schelling, F. W. J. *Philosophie der Mythologie* (Mitschrift Chováts). In *Philosophie der Mythologie in drei Vorlesungsnachschriften 1837/1842*, edited by Klaus Vieweg and Christian Danz. Munich: Wilhelm Fink, 1996.

Schelling, F. W. J. *Philosophie der Mythologie* (Nachschriften "Athen" und Eberz). In *Philosophie der Mythologie in drei Vorlesungsnachschriften 1837/1842*, edited by Klaus Vieweg and Christian Danz. Munich: Wilhelm Fink, 1996.

Schelling, F. W. J. "Philosophie der Mythologie." In *Sämmtliche Werke*, II/2 (1856–1861).

Schelling, F. W. J. *Philosophie der Offenbarung 1841/42*, edited by Manfred Frank. Frankfurt: Suhrkamp, 1977.

Schelling, F. W. J. "Philosophie der Offenbarung." In *Sämmtliche Werke*, II/3–4 (1856–1861).

Schelling, F. W. J. "Philosophie und Religion." In *Historisch-kritische Ausgabe*, I/14 (2021).

Schelling, F. W. J. "Philosophische Briefe über Dogmatismus und Kriticismus." In *Historisch-kritische Ausgabe*, I/3 (1982).

Schelling, F. W. J. "Philosophische Einleitung in die Philosophie der Mythologie, oder Darstellung der reinrationalen Philosophie." In *Sämmtliche Werke*, II/1 (1856–1861).

Schelling, F. W. J. "Philosophische Untersuchungen über das Wesen der menschlichen Freiheit." In *Historisch-kritische Ausgabe*, I/17 (2018).

Schelling, F. W. J. *Statement on the True Relationship of the Philosophy of Nature to the Revised Fichtean Doctrine*, translated by Dale E. Snow. Albany: SUNY Press, 2018.

Schelling, F. W. J. "Stuttgart Seminars." In *Idealism and the Endgame of Theory*, translated and introduced by Thomas Pfau. Albany, NY: SUNY Press, 1994.

Schelling, F. W. J. "Stuttgarter Privatvorlesungen." In *Sämmtliche Werke*, I/7 (1856–1861).

Schelling, F. W. J. "System der gesammten Philosophie und der Naturphilosophie insbesondere." *Historisch-Kritische Ausgabe*, II/7, 1–2 (2021).

Schelling, F. W. J. *System der Weltalter* (Münchner Vorlesung 1827/28), edited by Siegbert Peetz. Frankfurt: Klostermann, 1990.

Schelling, F. W. J. *System of Transcendental Idealism*, translated by Peter Heath. Charlottesville, VA: University Press of Virginia, 1978.

Schelling, F. W. J. *The Ages of the World*, translated and introduced by Frederick de Wolfe Bolman. New York: Columbia University Press, 1942.

Schelling, F. W. J. *The Grounding of Positive Philosophy. The Berlin Lectures*, translated and introduced by Bruce Matthews. Albany, NY: SUNY Press, 2007.

Schelling, F. W. J. *The Philosophical Rupture between Fichte and Schelling. Selected Texts and Correspondence 1800–1802*, translated and edited by Michael Vater and David Wood. Albany, NY: SUNY Press, 2013.

Schelling, F. W. J. "Über den wahren Begriff der Naturphilosophie und die richtige Art ihre Probleme aufzulösen." In *Historisch-kritische Ausgabe*, I/10 (2009).

Schelling, F. W. J. "Über die Natur der Philosophie als Wissenschaft." In *Historisch-kritische Ausgabe*, II/10, 2 (2020).

Schelling, F. W. J. *Über die Quelle der ewigen Wahrheiten*. In *Sämmtliche Werke*, II/1 (1856–1861).

Schelling, F. W. J. *Urfassung der Philosophie der Offenbarung*, edited by Walter. E. Ehrhardt. Hamburg: Felix Meiner, 1992.

Schelling, F. W. J. "Vom Ich als Prinzip der Philosophie überhaupt, oder über das Unbedingte im menschlichen *Wissen*." In *Historisch-kritische Ausgabe* I/2 (1980).

Schelling, F. W. J. "Von der Weltseele." In *Historisch-kritische Ausgabe*, I/6 (2000).

Schelling, F. W. J. "Vorlesungen über die Methode des akademischen Studiums." In *Historisch-kritische Ausgabe*, I/14 (2021).

Schelling, F. W. J. "Zur Geschichte der modernen Philosophie." In *Sämmtliche Werke*, I/10 (1856–1861).

Schelling, F. W. J., and J. G. Fichte. "Philosophical correspondence." In *Historisch-kritische Ausgabe* III/2, 1 (2010).

Schleiermacher, Friedrich. *On Religion: Speeches to its Cultured Despisers*. Cambridge: CUP, 1996.

Schopenhauer, Arthur. *The World as Will and Representation*. Cambridge: CUP, 2020 (2 vols).

Scott, James C. *Against the Grain: A Deep History of the Earliest City States*. New Haven, CT: Yale University Press, 2018.

Sellars, Wilfred. *Empiricism and the Philosophy of Mind*. Cambridge, MA: Harvard University Press, 1997.

Sellars, Wilfrid. "Philosophy and the Scientific Image of Man." In *In the Space of Reasons: Selected Essays of Wilfred Sellars*, edited by Kevin Scharp and Robert B. Brandom. Cambridge, MA: Harvard University Press, 2007.

Seymour, Robert. "Negative and Positive Philosophy in the Late Work of Fichte and Schelling." PhD Thesis, University of Essex, 2019.

Shanahan, Timothy. *The Evolution of Darwinism: Selection, Adaptation and Progress in Evolutionary Biology*. Cambridge: CUP, 2004.

Spinoza, Benedict de. *Ethics*, edited and translated by Edwin Curley, with an introduction by Stewart Hampshire. London: Penguin, 1996.

Stietencron, Heinrich von. "Der Hinduismus", in *Säkularisierung und Weltreligionen*, edited by Hans Joas and Klaus Wiegandt. Frankfurt: Fisher Taschenbuch Verlag, 2007.

Steward, Helen. *A Metaphysics for Freedom*. Oxford: OUP, 2012.
Strawson, Galen. "Panpsychism? Reply to Commentators, with a Celebration of Descartes." In *Consciousness and its Place in Nature*, edited by Anthony Freeman. Exeter: Imprint Academic, 2006.
Taylor, Charles. *Hegel*. Cambridge: CUP, 1975.
Taylor, Charles. *Hegel and Modern Society*. Cambridge: CUP, 1979.
Taylor, Charles. "The Church Speaks—to Whom?" In *Church and People: Disjunctions in a Secular Age*, edited by Charles Taylor, Jose Casanova, and George F. McLean. Washington, DC: The Council for Research and Values in Philosophy, 2012.
Theunissen, Michael. "Die Aufhebung des Idealismus in der Spätphilosophie Schellings." *Philosophiches Jahrbuch* 83 (1976).
Theunissen, Michael. *Hegels Lehre vom absoluten Geist as theologisch-politischer Traktat*. Berlin: de Gruyter, 1970.
Tillich, Paul. "Jewish Influences on Contemporary Christian Theology." *Crosscurrents* 2, no. 3 (1952).
Tillich, Paul. *The Courage to Be*. New Haven and London: Yale University Press, 2014.
White, Alan. *Absolute Knowledge: Hegel and the Problem of Metaphysics*. Athens OH: Ohio University Press, 1983.
Winnicott, Donald. "Transitional Objects and Transitional Phenomena." In *Playing and Reality*. London: Routledge, 2005.
Witt, Charlotte. *Substance and Essence in Aristotle: An Interpretation of* Metaphysics *VII–IX*. Ithaca and London: Cornell University Press, 1989.
Witt, Charlotte. *Ways of Being: Potentiality and Actuality in Aristotle's Metaphysics*. Ithaca, NY: Cornell University Press, 2003.
Wittgenstein, Ludwig. *Tractatus logico-philosophicus*, translated by D. F. Pears and B. F. McGuiness, with an introduction by Bertrand Russell. Oxford and New York: Routledge (Routledge Classics), 2001.
Wood, Allen W. "Editor's Introduction." In Hegel, *Elements of the Philosophy of Right*. Cambridge: CUP, 1991.
Wood, Allen W. *Fichte's Ethical Thought*. Oxford: OUP, 2016.
Wood, Allen W. *Hegel's Ethical Thought*. Cambridge: CUP, 1990.

Index

abduction
  as method of the positive philosophy, 178, 279
Adorno, Theodor
  on the aporetic structure of freedom, 285–286
  his critique of Hegel on being, 129
affirmative genealogy
  Hans Joas' conception of, 293–294n9
  Schelling's version of, 288–291
Aristotle
  on contrary and contradictory negation, 128
  his *Metaphysics* as precedent for the theory of potentialities, 134
  his monotheism, 224
  as negative philosopher, 118–120
  potentialities and casual powers, 136
  Schelling's critique of his theory of matter, 202
Axial Age
  Schelling as theorist of, 111–115, 234
  See also Jaspers

Bellah, Robert, 251
Boehme, Jakob, 121
Bonhoeffer, Dietrich, 250
Buddhism, 114, 250

Catholic Church/Catholicism, 112, 120, 271, 273–275
  and religious pluralism, 250
Chinese religion, 114
Christianity
  ambivalence of Schelling's treatment of, 247–250, 273
  comparison of Hegel and Schelling on, 234–238
  as culmination of the axial turn, 111–112
  explosive impact of Hegel's interpretation of, 246–247
  failure of Hegel's philosophical rescue of, 278–279
  relation of German Idealism to, 228
  and religious pluralism, 276–279
  Schelling's philosophical interpretation of, 229–234
  Schelling's theory of the evolution of, 273–276
Christology
  of Hegel, 238–241
  of Schelling, 241–244
consciousness
  as God-positing, 206–209
  Schelling's history of, 269–276
Creation, 193, 196

Darwin, Charles, 202–203
Descartes
  as emancipator of modern reason, 249, 271, 275
  on the eternal truths, 168
  Schelling's interpretation of his ontological argument, 189–190
  and Schelling on the *cogito*, 34

ecstasis
  as the character of mythological consciousness, 214, 233, 243, 270, 289–290
  as a form of alienation, 294n9
  as successor to intellectual intuition, 110
  in the transition to positive philosophy, 148, 154–155
Egyptian Mythology, 221
Eleusinian Mysteries, 222–225, 227
  and the futural (*das Zukünftige*), 224–225

the Fall
  Fichte's transcendentalism as inadvertent theory of, 84–85

308　INDEX

the Fall (*cont.*)
　as the *Katastrophe*, 209, 211
　philosophical interpretation of,
　　209–212
Fichte
　his conception of the absolute, 56–57
　conflict of life and speculation in, 27–32
　correspondence with Schelling, 49–57
freedom
　its emergence in nature, 197–204
　Hegel's theory of, 255–259, 284–285
　Schelling's definition of, 285–286
　as liberation 105–106
　as a "two-way" power (Helen Steward),
　　268
Frege, Gottlob 101–103
Freud, Sigmund, 143, 213, 233, 283, 289
the future
　philosophy's orientation to, 291–293
　das Seynsollende as the potentiality of,
　　292
　see also Eleusinian Mysteries

God
　as absolute freedom in Schelling,
　　192–193
　Aristotle's conception of, 119–120
　Boehme's conception of, 121
　his dependence on un-pre-thinkable
　　being, 184, 192
　the finite world as not-being-in-God,
　　80–81
　as having a distinct ground of his
　　existence, 90
　Hegel's conception of, 163
　as radical transcendence, 112–113
　as source of the eternal truths, 168–169
　Schelling on God as the Ideal of pure
　　reason in Kant, 142–146
　Schelling on Spinoza on, 125–126, 190
　Schelling's critique of Hegel's theory of
　　the concept as, 162–163
　as universal, 112, 114
　See also Creation; God-positing
　　consciousness; ontological
　　argument
God-positing consciousness, 206–209
Grundoperation (foundational
　philosophical move)

　of Hegel, 266, 284–5
　of Schelling, 286–288

Habermas, Jürgen
　on modernity, 10–11
Hartmann, Klaus, 4–5, 161, 164
Hartmann, Nicolai, 76–78
Hegel
　his logic, 156–160
　Pippin's interpretation of, 3–4
　practical standpoint in, 259–263
　Taylor's interpretation of, 2–3
　his theory of the will, 263–265
　see also Adorno; Christianity;
　　Christology; freedom; God;
　　Grundoperation; Hartmann (Klaus);
　　Horstmann; Hösle; the Idea;
　　liberation; McTaggart; ontological
　　argument; Pippin; Protestant
　　theology; religion; Schelling;
　　suspicion; Theunissen
Heidegger, Martin, 242
　on the *Freiheitsschrift*, 88, 185–186
Henrich, Dieter, 27, 35, 186
　on Hegel's *Grundoperation*, 266, 284
　on Kant's transcendental deduction, 22
　compares the metaphysics of Schelling
　　and Hegel, 77–78
　on self-consciousness, 237, 281
Hesiod, 215, 220
Hinduism, 114–115, 221
Honneth, Axel, 260
Horstmann, Rolf-Peter
　on the relation of Hegel's *Logic* to
　　nature, 156, 164–165
Hösle, Vittorio
　on problems of correlating Hegel's *Logic*
　　and *Realphilosophie*, 157–160

the Idea
　Hegel's theory of, 150–155
　in Schelling and as a Kant's Ideal of pure
　　reason, 142–146
　transition to nature from, 155–156,
　　194–196
impasse of *The Ages of the World*,
　106–107
　its avoidance in the *Spätphilosophie*,
　　191–192

indexicality, 80, 209–210
intellectual intuition, 23, 49
   art as objective version of, 70
   in Fichte, 26–27
   misrecognized by Kant, 23, 33
   in Schelling's *Ichschrift*, 34–36
   supplanted by *ecstasis*, 110
Islam, 113–114

Jacobi, Friedrich, 1, 10, 20, 29, 121
Jaspers, Karl, 112–113, 234
Joas, Hans, 293–294n9
Judaism, 113, 114, 238, 250

Kant
   and the Ideal of pure reason, 142–146
   and the paradox of autonomy, 253–255
   Schelling's critique of his treatment of the antinomies, 121–123
   on self-consciousness in, 19–23
   on the subject-object nexus, 19–23
   his theory of evil, 89–90
Kreines, James
   his interpretation of thought as absolute criticized, 164–170
   on "that-dependency" and "what-dependency," 164–167

Leibniz, 75, 156, 271
   on the eternal truths, 168
liberation
   from blind being-ness, 192
   from indeterminacy of morality in Hegel, 255–256
   of materiality, 201
   from the mythological process, 232–234, 247–248
   as the transition from negative to positive philosophy, 149, 291
Lotze, Hermann, 208–209

Marx, Karl, 247, 283, 284
McTaggart, John
   his critique of Hegel's theory of the rationality of the universe, 280n6
   his interpretation of Hegel on being, 129

Menke, Christoph, 258
Merleau-Ponty, Maurice, 137, 210
metaphysical empiricism, 279
Moore, Adrian
   his critique of Frege, 102
mythological consciousness, 206–225
   Gospels shot through with, 229–230
   liberation from, 232–234
   plurality of mythological systems, 220–222
   proto-psychoanalytic aspects of Schelling's theory of, 212–213, 217–219, 289

Nagel, Thomas, 10, 203
negative philosophy
   dialectic of, 132–138
   in the history of philosophy, 117–121
   internal development of, 140–142
   the starting point of, 123–126
New Testament, 229–231
Nietzsche, Friedrich, 243, 283

ontological argument
   Hegel on, 185–189
   Schelling on, 189–193

Pantheism Dispute, 1
paradox of autonomy
   Hegel's response to, 253–265
   Schelling's response to, 265–269
Perry, John, 209–210
philosophical religion, 249–252, 272, 274, 279
Pinkard, 4–5, 17n8, 164
Pippin, Robert
   and the "normative" reading of Hegel, 3–6
Plato, 114, 205n13, 224
   positive and negative philosophy in, 118–120
polytheism, 114
   evolution of, 214–220
positive philosophy
   in the history of philosophy, 117–121
   transition to, 146–150
   See also abduction; mythology; revelation

potentialities, 16, 117–118, 134, 147, 151, 160, 185, 267–269, 288, 290
  dialectic of, 132–138, 192–193, 196
  repeated in mythological consciousness, 213–214, 217
  their emergence through the decompression un-pre-thinkable being, 181–183, 197
  in the Eleusinian Mysteries, 222–224
  in Fichte, 31
  in the negative philosophy, 139–142
  noetic unity of, 194, 201, 286
  in Schelling's interpretation of Christianity, 231–233
  in Schelling's late philosophy of nature, 197–204
Protestantism, 240, 245
  Schelling's historical interpretation of, 274
Protestant theology, 240
  Hegel's critique of, 245–247
  twentieth-century developments in, 250

the Qu'ran, 216

Realphilosophie, 150–151
  problem of correlation with Hegel's *Logic*, 156–160
Reformation, 120
  as the liberation of subjectivity, 271
  its role in Schelling's positive philosophy, 273–276
Reinhold, Karl Leonhard, 59–62, 254–255, 281
religion
  problem of pluralism of, 276–279
  and the state in Hegel, 244–246
revelation, 112, 231–232, 243
  axial turn achieved by the Christian version of, 113, 279
  modern emancipation from, 275–276
  philosophy of revelation not dependent on, 273
  and reason in Schelling, 227–229
Ricoeur, Paul
  on the masters of suspicion, 283
  on the pre-predicative world, 210

Sartre, Jean-Paul
  on consciousness as *causa sui*, 184
  on the *en-soi* (in-itself), 173–174
  metaphysics, his conception of, 175–179
  the paradox of freedom in, 242
  on the ego as a transcendent structure, 207
Schelling
  Abfall (fall from the absolute), 84–85
  his conception of freedom in the identity philosophy, 78–81
  his direct critique of Hegel, 160–163
  his critique of Kant's moral theory, 61–62
  his critique of Kant's theory of the organism, 41–43
  his critique of Reinhold's moral theory, 61–63
  his early philosophy of history, 67–71
  and Hegel on being, nothing and non-being, 126–132
  his conception of freedom as liberation, 105–107
  matter, his concept of, 201–202
  on the metaphysical status of art, 70–71
  his philosophy of identity, 74–85
  Pippin's delegitimation of, 6–8
  on the relation between *Naturphilosophie* and transcendental philosophy in, 71–74
  on the "un-ground" (*Ungrund*), 94–95
Schopenhauer, Arthur, 85
Sellars, Wilfrid, 5–6
Socrates, 118
Spinoza
  his concept of substance as "imprisoning thought," 147
  criticized by Schelling in the *Freiheitsschrift*, 94
  critique of his theory of perception, 81–84
  his lure as supreme theorist of blind being, 125–126
  his monism, 20
  his ontological argument, 190
  and the principle of sufficient reason, 10
  Schelling on his grandeur, 271

spirit
　Schelling's theory of the double structure of, 265–269
Steward, Helen, 116n14, 198–205
　her theory of freedom compared with Schelling, 197–204
suspicion
　ethics of, 282–283
　Hegel's relation to ethics of, 283-4

Taylor, Charles, 2–3, 11–12, 251
Theunissen, Michael
　on Hegel's "theology of kenosis," 240, 251n7
　on the powerlessness intrinsic to the power of reason, 147–148
Tillich, Paul, 250
Troeltsch, Ernst, 293–294n9

un-pre-thinkable being, 115, 148, 155, 170, 172–192, 194, 197, 267
　"decompression" of, 179–185

Winnicott, Donald, 213, 225n10
Wittgenstein, Ludwig, 198, 208

Zabism, 216–217
Zoroastrianism, 112